FRIENDLY SPIES

FRIENDLY SPIES

*How America's Allies
Are Using Economic Espionage
to Steal Our Secrets*

Peter Schweizer

THE ATLANTIC MONTHLY PRESS
NEW YORK

Published simultaneously in Canada
Printed in the United States of America

Library of Congress Cataloging-in-Publication Data

Schweizer, Peter, 1964–
    Friendly spies: how America's allies are using economic espionage to steal our secrets / Peter Schweizer.
    Includes bibliographical references.
    ISBN 0-87113-497-7
    1. Business intelligence—United States.   2. Espionage—United States.   I. Title.
HD38.7.S39   1993   364.1′68—dc20   92-34924

Design by Laura Hough

The Atlantic Monthly Press
19 Union Square West
New York, NY 10003

First printing

For Rochelle

Contents

Acknowledgments

Many people made this book possible in a variety of ways. I would like to thank those who took the time to talk with me: former CIA Directors Richard Helms, Stansfield Turner, and William Colby; former NSA Directors William Odom and Bob Inman; former directors of French intelligence Pierre Marion and Pierre Lacoste; former CIA officials John Quinn, Ray Cline, Cord Meyer, Russell Bowen, and Herb Meyer; former FBI assistant director Raymond Wannall; Ambassadors Richard Walker and Michael Smith; former Justice Department Director of Internal Security John Davitt; Professors Robert Angel and Chalmers Johnson; former staff member of the House Select Committee on Intelligence Herb Romerstein; former NSA official Noel Matchett; and industry consultants and officials Henry Clements, Robert Courtney, and James Lamont. I am also grateful to the many other intelligence officials from a variety of countries who insisted on anonymity. They alone know what they did for me.

A writer is only as good as the material he has to work with, and I was fortunate enough to be blessed with several outstanding research assistants. Brad Lovelace, John Dutton, John Duncan, and Charles Reyes were very helpful. Chuck Howard, especially, went beyond the call of duty.

I have also been blessed with a number of mentors, who have guided me during and since my college days. I wish to thank in particular Dr. Ronald R. Nelson, Dr. Fritz G. A. Kraemer, and my Oxford supervisor, James Sherr. The friendship, encouragement, and support of Ron Robinson, Herman Pirchner, and Jed Snyder were also greatly appreciated.

My agent, Joe Vallely, has been most helpful in all aspects of this book, and Morgan Entrekin at Atlantic Monthly Press has been a pleasure to work with. I thank you both for this adventure.

Finally, I wish to thank my patient family. My parents, Erwin and Kerstin Schweizer, have always been there and mean the world to me. My brother-in-law and sister, Joe and Maria Duffus, are always encouraging and supportive. My brother-in-law and my mother-in-law, Richard and Evelyn Rueb, through their kindness and friendship, have given me strength. But most of all, I wish to thank my patient and lovely wife for all her hard work on this project and others. Rochelle, thanks for putting up with me.

The author alone is responsible for the contents.

FRIENDLY SPIES

1

A Matter Between Friends

If you don't think we're being exploited by friends *and enemies, Buster,*
you're crazy.

—the late Walter Deeley, deputy director
of the U.S. National Security Agency

When most Americans think about spies and espionage, the image
that comes to mind is a hostile and devious enemy with designs on this
country's secrets, sending ruthless agents abroad to get them. Usually
these images take the form of Nazis during the Second World War or,
more recently, Soviet-bloc agents. These agents will stop at nothing—not
blackmail, deception, bribery, or perhaps even murder—to accomplish
their mission. Usually they seek military plans or perhaps even the designs
for a new, powerful weapon.

Rarely if ever do Americans conjure up images of U.S. allies spying
on us. Far from it—Americans see our allies as partners in the fight against
hostile enemy services, working courageously to protect Western secrets.
Yet although this country's allies have indeed oftentimes been gallant in
their efforts to counter Soviet intelligence activities and espionage perpetrated against the West, they have all too often engaged in the same
activities with the United States as their victim. And they have been
enormously successful. Which U.S. allies engage in economic espionage

3

against the United States? "Practically all of them," says a candid Pierre Marion, a former director of French intelligence. "It's a fact of life."

In a private speech in New York City on October 25, 1990, William Sessions, director of the Federal Bureau of Investigation, laid the groundwork for a dramatic change in U.S. counterintelligence policy. Sessions began by speaking about the 1980s and how Soviet espionage had been widespread in the United States and how the bureau had fought it during that decade. He spoke, too, about how the superpower competition would change in the 1990s but how the East-West shadow war would continue. All this is pretty regular stuff by FBI standards. Sessions's bombshell came in only one sentence (as significant shifts in intelligence policy often do), and it was therefore largely overlooked by the media and, consequently, by the public. The FBI director revealed that his bureau would begin devoting a greater share of its assets to combating "the intelligence activities against U.S. interests by so-called 'friendly' intelligence services."

That the FBI was beginning to focus its attention on the intelligence and espionage activities of traditional U.S. allies was confirmed by Patrick Watson, the bureau's deputy assistant director, in a speech five months later in Washington, D.C. It was not so much that what he said was different as it was that how he said what he said was so significant. Like Sessions, he warned of the growing general intelligence and espionage threat to the United States and the need for greater counterintelligence capabilities to cope with it. He made clear the need to remember that the threat to U.S. security interests posed by the Soviet Union still existed and that Soviet espionage in the West was continuing to grow. At first glance, nothing very extraordinary here. But the real message was in the subtleties. What was different from bureau speeches of the past was the shift in terminology. For more than two decades, the bureau had always spoken of "a hostile intelligence threat" that America was facing. The phrase was regularly used to refer to hostile nations, like the Soviet Union, Cuba, Libya, and the former Soviet satellites in Eastern Europe. But Watson didn't use that phrase this time. Rather, for the first time in recent memory, he used a broader term, "foreign intelligence services," in describing the espionage threat to the United States. The idea was that the threat was now coming from a number of places. *Foreign intelligence services* was used to include U.S. friends and allies in the espionage threat facing this country.

In the world of spies and espionage, secrets are a currency more valuable than money. Stealing and protecting secrets are the focus of all spycraft. It is a delicate topic that is rarely discussed openly. Subtle changes in public pronouncements often signal deep shifts in policy. Sessions and Watson were pointing to a new U.S. attentiveness to an espionage problem that has faced America for more than twenty years but has only recently received official attention. Unlike the endeavors of the Soviet Union's State Security Committee (the KGB) and other "hostile intelligence services," which are commonly understood by most Americans, the espionage threat posed by our allies is known by only a select few. These operations have rarely been talked about publicly; agents carrying them out in the United States and against U.S. interests overseas have been largely uninhibited. The FBI and the Central Intelligence Agency have almost exclusively focused their attentions elsewhere, most importantly on the KGB. U.S. corporations, common targets of friendly spies, have in many cases been unaware that these operations were taking place or have assumed that they were the work of "free-lancers" trying to make a quick buck.

But most economic espionage directed against U.S. industry is not the work of free-lancers. Ambassador Michael B. Smith has spent more than thirty years dealing with international trade issues and has served as the U.S. deputy trade representative in both the Carter and the Reagan administrations. "There is no question friendly countries and companies have been over here raiding the store," Smith says. "Both Europe and Japan have blanketed this country to acquire technology information." In many instances, friendly spies work for intelligence services that were developed, organized, trained, and outfitted with the help of the U.S. government. The intelligence services of Germany, Japan, South Korea, and France, for example, were all developed with the assistance of the U.S. intelligence community. Their methods, even their eavesdropping equipment, came from the United States. Many of these assets are now being used against the United States in the name of economic competitiveness.

These friendly spies and their operations are the dirty little secret of the spy business. Why have they remained so secret for so many years? The fact is that over the years the United States has come to rely on many of these countries for intelligence support in tracking events in the Soviet

Union. Electronic eavesdropping facilities in Germany, South Korea, and Japan, among other places, were critical in following Soviet internal developments during the Cold War. The U.S. intelligence community and the Department of Defense feared they would lose such cooperation if complaints of friendly spying were brought up. For obvious reasons, U.S. allies have been unwilling to acknowledge the existence of these activities to begin with.

Sessions's speech was confirmation from the highest levels of the U.S. intelligence establishment that friendly spying is a serious threat indeed. But still Americans have heard of only a few instances of such spying. This has largely been by government design. According to Herb Meyer, a former vice chairman of the National Intelligence Council at the CIA, there has been a consensus in the agency for quite some time that allied spying is "reprehensible and indefensible." But, he says, the U.S. intelligence community often "turned a blind eye to it" in order to accomplish the more immediate task of countering the most important intelligence threat: the Soviet Union and its cohorts around the world. Allied intelligence cooperation in the name of winning the Cold War was considered a much more important intelligence objective, one that overrode all other considerations.

"Friendly countries engaging in industrial espionage were obscured from attention by the Cold War," says Admiral Bob Inman, a former director of the National Security Agency and an ex–deputy director of the CIA. Says Meyer, "Industrial espionage only received attention when the Soviets were involved. In those instances where the activity of friendly intelligence services have been particularly abhorrent, Washington has handled the matter quietly rather than by going public and raising a huge international stink that would fracture relations with our Cold War allies."

Raymond Wannall, a cautious former FBI assistant director for intelligence, tells a similar story. "Not much publicity has been given to it by design," he explains. "Our State Department tended to downplay it. Espionage is always a sticky business. When you mix in that a friendly country is involved, you have what at State they call 'a complex diplomatic situation.' And they like to avoid those."

This attitude stands in sharp contrast to the intensity with which some allies have engaged in espionage against the United States. Some have devoted the majority of their intelligence resources to the task. For example, a 1987 classified CIA survey entitled *Japan: Foreign Intelligence and Security Services* estimates that 80 percent of Japan's intelligence assets are directed toward gathering intelligence on the United States and, to a lesser degree, on Western Europe. Friendly intelligence agents have bugged and tracked American business executives and trade negotiators overseas. Friendly spies have stolen vital trade and technology secrets from U.S. companies at home and abroad.

But the U.S. intelligence community is not alone in maintaining silence on this delicate subject. Industry has also been reluctant to go public with instances of friendly spying. Few business leaders like to talk about it, for fear of public embarrassment; admitting to being a victim of industrial espionage is saying that a company can't keep its secrets. "Anytime anybody's talked about this, they've gotten badly burned," says Meyer. Victimized companies that have gone public have seen their stock prices drop, company morale plummet, and corporate partners pull out of projects for fear of losing their secrets. When companies have blamed U.S. allies by name, they have been known to lose large contracts in those countries. And when foreign companies from allied countries have been caught engaging in espionage, the legal penalties have often been so slight as to make prosecution no remedy at all.

When corporations have aggressively sought out the perpetrators, the cost in time and money has often been extremely high. The experiences of Rohm and Haas, a Philadelphia chemical manufacturer, is a case in point. The company spent more than five years tracking down the theft of a secret formula for making latex paints. The search led to Australia, where Rohm and Haas found a firm that was duplicating its product "molecule for molecule," according to company officials. The spy who got the formula to Australia was eventually caught, but only after a high-speed, wrong-way car chase on a Manhattan parkway.

In the handful of friendly spy cases made public, the reaction in the United States has usually been a mix of surprise and disbelief. When Jonathan Jay Pollard, a thirty-one-year-old analyst in the Naval Investigative Service, was arrested by FBI officers in November of 1985 as an Israeli spy, official Washington was shocked. The thought that a close friend might try to pry secrets from us struck American officials as incredible.

7

Said State Department spokesman Charles Redman, "We are shocked and saddened at the notion that something like this might occur."

But as we shall see, friendly foreign intelligence operations against the United States have been routine and widespread. Wannall believes it makes sense that the United States has been "target number one" of a lot of intelligence services, "even friendly ones." He says, "There has always been an effort by our friends to steal economic and technological secrets from the U.S. After all, this is where most of the best ones are." Pollard is only a tiny blip on the radar screen. He was in some ways one of the least important and least effective of the friendly spies.

Economic espionage by American friends is an often-overlooked component of the spy business. According to Maynard Anderson, assistant deputy undersecretary of defense for counterintelligence and security, it has been common "because the risk of exposure and severe penalties to the foreign intelligence service representatives are much lower than for conventional espionage." It is also a high priority target for U.S. friends who happen to be economic competitors. Says Richard Helms, a clever and bookish former director of the CIA, "The national intelligence agencies of many friendly countries have industrial and commercial targets that are of greater significance to them than military and political targets. And they are safer targets, too."

Intelligence services are tools that nation-states use to advance particular ends. The Soviet Union, for example, through both the KGB and the Soviet military intelligence (the GRU), tended to concentrate on gathering military and political intelligence or engaged in espionage to acquire military secrets. The Soviet Union's interest in secrets of economics and technology was most apparent when those secrets had military applications. U.S. allies, like Japan, in contrast, have tended to use their intelligence services mostly to target secrets of science and technology. These secrets—not military ones—are of most interest to Japanese intelligence. Whereas friendly intelligence services routinely follow foreign political and military trends in ways similar to those of the U.S. intelligence community, these services have also seen espionage as an effective way to advance their interests in the economy and technology. Consequently, friendly intelligence services have sought from the United States not only political and military information but also scientific and technological information. Oftentimes this information is passed on to native corporations.

There has been a great difference between U.S. intelligence activities and those of our allies during the past four decades. As Herb Meyer put it in an interview,

> For the last forty years, the primary national effort in the United States has been to prevent the Soviets from winning the Cold War. I think history will show when we look back on it that we poured not only an incredible amount of money into this but an incredible part of our national attention and our national energies. The British did the same thing pretty much, but nobody else did. Our allies were doing two things simultaneously: one, helping us because it was in their interest to do it, but also, competing economically. They put a lot of their energy into, if you will, taking advantage of us while our attention was somewhere else.

Pierre Marion defends economic espionage operations being conducted against the U.S. He says,

> I think you have to separate very clearly what are the fields which are covered by an alliance and the fields which are not covered by an alliance. It's clear that when you are allies, you have certain sectors. I'm speaking of the armaments. I'm thinking of diplomatic matters where normally you should not try to gather intelligence. But in all of the other fields, being allied does not prevent the states from being competitors. Even during the Cold War, the economic competition existed. Now the competition between the states is moving from the political-military level to the economic and technological level. In economics, we are competitors, not allies. I think that even during the Cold War getting intelligence on economic, technological, and industrial matters from a country with which you are allies is not incompatible with the fact that you are allies.

Allied industrial espionage has plagued American corporations and business executives in such foreign locales as Paris, Tokyo, Seoul, Frankfurt, and Rome. In the United States, friendly spies have reached almost every corner of the country. Big cities like New York and Los Angeles have been the backdrop of dozens of intelligence operations, as has small-town America. Places like Battle Creek, Michigan; Northborough, Massachusetts; and Greer, South Carolina, have all been the stage for friendly spy operations. According to Dr. Ray Cline, a former deputy director of the CIA, countries like Japan and France regularly attempt to "penetrate corporations in America to steal their secrets."

And what has been true in the past will be even more so now that the Cold War is over. Herb Meyer explains that "foreign intelligence services are rapidly swinging to a greater focus on helping their companies to compete globally. They are basically going at it by continuing what they've been doing for the last forty years, but more so, which is primarily using espionage and espionage-type activities to assist companies." Other officials share the same belief. Ambassador Richard Walker, a member of the CIA's Senior Review Panel and a consultant to CIA Director Robert Gates, also holds the view that friendly spying will only get worse: "Increasingly the attitude in other economically advanced countries who also happen to be allies is 'We need to be on top of all developments in science and technology.' And, of course, to do that, you need to engage in espionage." Oklahoma Senator David Boren, chairman of the Senate Select Committee on Intelligence, concurs in a speech: "As we go into the next century, and as international relations become much more a matter of economic competition than military competition, it's going to increase."

Some intelligence operations perpetrated against this country by U.S. allies rival those of the Soviet KGB in complexity and sophistication. No less than three close allies—South Korea, the former West Germany, and France—have placed, or attempted to place, "agents of influence"— moles—among the White House senior staff. Foreign agents from friendly services have infiltrated major U.S. corporations, including IBM, to steal industry secrets, and U.S. businesspeople traveling overseas have been tailed by agents and had their hotel rooms searched. In some friendly countries, such as South Korea and Japan, intelligence agents and businesspeople regularly orchestrate attempted seductions of American business executives visiting their countries. Admiral Inman remarks that in both countries American business executives are "provided entertainment in the hopes of ferreting out information, and I'm not only talking about dinner entertainment but for the rest of the evening, if you know what I mean."

Friendly foreign agents have the luxury of traveling uninhibited in the United States. As former FBI Director William Webster has admitted, the United States has focused almost exclusively on the activities and movement of Soviet-bloc spies in this country. This has not been by choice but by necessity. The FBI maintains a "criteria country list," which determines which intelligence threats the bureau deems necessary to watch. Yet throughout the past two decades, several friendly intelligence services have appeared on that list, including France, South Korea, Japan, West Germany, and Israel. But the FBI has been unable to track their agents because it has lacked counterintelligence resources. "In the past, the bureau has veered away from economic espionage, instead concentrating on the Soviets and their proxies. But now they are going to have to deal with it. They are going to have to shift assets and get more resources and manpower to counter this economic and technological spy threat," says Raymond Wannall.

Foreign multinational corporations have also conducted acts of industrial espionage in the United States, or they have targeted the overseas offices of U.S. multinationals. Often aided by intelligence assets larger and more sophisticated than those of many small countries, corporate spying has been enormously profitable.

Only recently have U.S. officials begun to talk about friendly spies. The end of the Cold War and the collapse of the Soviet Union has led to a breaking of the silence. In 1990, Oliver Revell, the FBI associate executive director for investigations, admitted in an interview that "a number of nations friendly to the U.S. have engaged in industrial espionage, collecting information with their intelligence services to support private industry." Revell's admission is still the most straightforward public confirmation by a senior counterintelligence official. Privately FBI and CIA officials are even more frank. Says Raymond Rocca, a former CIA deputy director for counterintelligence, "They're robbing us blind." One former CIA director is just fed up. "This sort of thing has gone far enough. It's got to stop."

One of those who has been the most vocal about this problem is Senator David Boren. As he made clear on April 3, 1990, American friends and allies sought an economic advantage through spying: "An increasing share of the espionage directed against the United States comes from spying by foreign governments against private American companies aimed at stealing commercial secrets to gain a national economic advantage." Writing in the *New York Times,* Boren went even further: "The fastest growing area of espionage activities by foreign governments against the U.S. is not the theft of military secrets, but the theft of commercial secrets from private American companies to further national economic interests."

With the collapse of the Soviet Union and with allied harmony now less essential than it was during the height of the Cold War, former intelligence officials are beginning to go on record regarding their knowledge of friendly spy activity. Admiral Stansfield Turner, director of the CIA under President Carter, admits that during his tenure he saw "a number of instances" of friendly foreign intelligence agencies spying on U.S. firms for industry secrets. "And I think that's increasing as it's rapidly becoming one big international market out there." Two other former directors of the CIA, Richard Helms and William Colby, express concerns about this problem as well. Helms believes that the problem will only get worse: "I think that with three economic blocs in the world—Europe, the U.S., and Japan—and with a race to win the technological competition, economic and technological espionage between these blocs will dramatically increase, because it's so useful. That is particularly the case now that the Cold War is over."

With the Cold War thaw has come an increase in the number of press reports on the activities of friendly spies. "Foreign intelligence operatives from Japan and Western Europe routinely bug hotel rooms of U.S. business executives. They also snatch corporate trade secrets from facsimile messages and phone calls," reported Tom Squitieri of *USA Today.* In 1990, John Hillkirk of *USA Today* noted, "For more than a decade, allies such as France, West Germany, Belgium and Japan have been using their spy networks to eavesdrop on U.S. firms." A front-page article by William Carley in the *Wall Street Journal* noted that "some U.S. companies increasingly suspect that foreign intelligence agencies, working for nations traditionally friendly as well as those often unfriendly, are seeking to scoop up sensitive, potentially valuable information."

Friendly foreign intelligence officials are understandably sensitive about suggestions that they spy on the United States. They are probably slightly embarrassed by the subject, given that the activity occurs behind a veil of allied cooperation, solidarity, and honesty.

In part, too, this is how the intelligence game is played. "You just get used to the fact that while you're cooperating, they might be knifing you in the back," says a senior FBI official. Deceit is at the heart of espionage. Like the magician who seeks to mystify his audience, espionage agents use misdirection, disguise, and denial in their campaign. And just because the intelligence officials in question are friends doesn't mean they don't practice industrial and economic espionage.

The cold, hard reality is that industrial espionage perpetrated against the United States has been enormously profitable for this country's allies. One of the few foreign spy masters willing to go on record publicly is the flamboyant Count Henri de Marenches, a French aristocrat with charm and a knack for spying. After serving Charles de Gaulle in an intelligence capacity during the Second World War, de Marenches served from 1970 to 1981 as the director of the French secret service, then known as the Service de Documentation Extérieure et de Contre-Espionnage (SDECE). In this post, de Marenches oversaw all French foreign intelligence operations, his position akin to that of the director of the CIA. He served as the head of the French secret service longer than any other French official in modern times. In *Dans les secrets des princes,* his 1986 memoir that was a best-seller in France, de Marenches admitted that engaging in industrial espionage against friends was "very profitable." He writes:

> Spying in the proper sense is becoming increasingly focused on business and the economy, science and industry—and very profitable it is. It enables the Intelligence Services to discover a process used in another country, which might have taken years and possibly millions of francs to invent or perfect. This form of espionage prevails not only with the enemy but to some extent among friends, it has to be said. . . . In any Intelligence Service worthy of the name you would easily come across cases where the whole year's budget has been paid for in full by a single operation. Naturally, Intelligence does not receive actual payment, but the country's industry profits.

13

France as well as other U.S. allies have profited by the billions through industrial espionage against this country. Noel Matchett, a former area director of data network security at the National Security Agency, believes some sectors of the U.S. economy are losing "billions every year" as a result of this activity. Chemical formulas and compounds, valuable research and development data, sales information, and strategic corporate plans—all have been systematically sought, and all have been stolen at one time or another. Ambassador Michael Smith says that this country's allies "wouldn't be doing it and taking the risk if it weren't very profitable."

Political spying has also occurred. U.S. allies have gone after top-secret CIA documents, bugged rooms in which senior American officials, including a U.S. president, were in private conversation, and planted spies in the White House and on Capitol Hill. American trade negotiators traveling overseas have also been targets of espionage. Information obtained from senior officials can be critical in securing an advantage at the trade-negotiations table.

It would be more than a bit disingenuous for the United States to accuse its allies of spying and then claim to be innocent of having carried out similar activities. No senior U.S. intelligence official will do so because it is a matter of record that the United States has from time to time spied on our friends and allies. Richard Helms was once asked by an overseas magazine whether the United States spied on its friends. Helms gave the honest answer, "I hope so."

Over the years, CIA operations have been uncovered in many parts of the world. Close U.S. allies have not been immune from American snooping. In 1985, for example, American diplomats were kicked out of Spain, the Spanish Ministry of Defense having accused them of spying. In 1979, the U.S. defense attaché and two aides were thrown out of South Africa (a friend of sorts) for photographing military installations. South African officials had discovered sensitive cameras on the attaché's plane, which had been flown all over southern Africa. During the height of the so-called Koreagate scandal, in which it was revealed that numerous U.S. congressmen had been bribed by members of the Korean Central Intelligence Agency, our CIA was widely believed to have collected some of its best evidence on the case by bugging the Blue House, the South Korean presidential mansion. During the 1956 Suez crisis, the U.S. military was deciphering coded messages passing among Great Britain, France, and Israel. Other cases will no doubt be uncovered in the future.

U.S. intelligence targets in allied countries have almost always been of a political or military nature. The operations almost always hinge on a need or desire to know more about the internal military and political developments in friendly countries or on a need or desire to influence events overseas. It is an aim of this book to demonstrate that the U.S. effort has never been as extensive as that of our allies. This has been due in part to our near total commitment to winning the spy war against the Soviet bloc. But more important, U.S. intelligence operations carried out against our allies have been much less comprehensive than those our allies have carried out against us because American efforts completely lack an industrial espionage component.

For the United States to carry out industrial espionage against our allies would be simply impossible given our social and cultural traditions. Says Leo Cherne, for forty years a member of the President's Foreign Intelligence Advisory Board, "The U.S. is truly handicapped by its culture, laws, the nature of our society and our belief in the market economy in our dealings with foreign countries to whom all this is quite alien." Furthermore, if the CIA were to stumble across an industrial formula worth hundreds of millions of dollars, U.S. law would prohibit the agency from handing it over to a U.S. company. Yet most foreign countries have no such limitations on the activities of their secret service organizations. The National Security Agency, our most secret intelligence agency, with responsibility for electronic eavesdropping worldwide, regularly intercepts the communications of foreign corporations. But the information never leaves the NSA. Says the current NSA director, Vice Admiral William O. Studeman, "This country does not have, if you will, the business ethic and the arrangements that some of the other Western countries have that do engage in economic intelligence collection." Some, both inside and outside the intelligence community, hope this will change. They believe America's unwillingness to engage in economic espionage seriously handicaps the United States vis-à-vis our major economic competitors, who willingly engage in such espionage.

Many governments in Western Europe and Asia have given their intelligence agencies full legal authority to carry out industrial espionage against the United States. Many of these countries have in their spy agencies regular branches whose responsibilities include spying on the United States. Most friendly spy operations are well planned, professional, and well executed. They almost always have the complete backing of their country's cabinet officials.

In France, the Direction Générale de la Sécurité Extérieure is responsible for all foreign intelligence operations. The DGSE is divided into a number of departments. One of them, Service 7, is responsible for conducting espionage within and outside France. High on its list of priorities are soft targets—U.S. and other Western businessmen.

Service 7 operates in a number of ways. It regularly monitors Western businessmen in France and at times targets them for eavesdropping or bag operations. At other times it seeks out specific business executives overseas in order to purloin their secrets. At several prominent hotels in Paris, the DGSE has hotel clerks and bellhops who turn a blind eye when a room needs to be entered and sensitive materials gone through. According to a former member of Service 7, the branch has conducted hundreds of operations against U.S. businessmen in Western Europe and America. They have also been known to use prostitutes and bribes to obtain information from traveling businessmen.

From time to time, the DGSE has also conducted an active campaign to infiltrate U.S. corporations in the hope of planting agents and sources, or moles. Both IBM and Texas Instruments have been the target of such operations. The DGSE has also blackmailed Swiss bankers in the hope of gaining access to financial information about wealthy Americans and the foreign accounts of American corporations.

The staff of the French consulate in the United States has occasionally had a hand in conducting foreign espionage. Consulate officials have set up small, temporary listening posts in Silicon Valley and Seattle to eavesdrop on microwave communications, and they have also been caught rummaging through the household trash of prominent American business leaders in the hope of finding valuable business information.

The French national telephone company is notorious among U.S. corporate security officials for regularly eavesdropping on the telephone, fax, and telex communications of U.S. corporations based in France and of U.S. business executives visiting there. Air France and other French companies have actively cooperated with the DGSE.

The German intelligence service, the Bundesnachrichtendienst (BND), has also conducted intelligence operations against the United States. Although not as concerted or large-scale as the DGSE effort, the BND's effort involves a significant portion of the organization's resources and operations. According to a former employee, the BND controlled an "agent of influence" in the Nixon White House to promote the "German point of view" on international and trade issues. There was also a serious attempt—one that included two White House officials—at establishing a spy network in the White House. The BND regularly eavesdrops on transatlantic business communications, with the full cooperation of the German national telephone company. And there are reports that outside of Frankfurt the BND is training technicians in the art of illegally entering the corporate data bases of foreign corporations, an attempt to apply computer hacking to the collection of intelligence. Division II of the BND gathers information technically and electronically on a number of countries, and it also conducts "clandestine technical operations" against the United States.

Israel in a number of instances has carried out industrial espionage against the United States, largely through a little-known organ known as LAKAM, which is the Hebrew acronym for Scientific Affairs Liaison Bureau. Once a small department in the Israeli Defense Ministry, it was thought to be shut down after the notorious Pollard affair. But rumors of its demise have been greatly exaggerated. LAKAM survives, today as a reconfigured division in the Israeli air force. Over the years, its primary mission has been to gather scientific and technological information overseas, by legal and illicit means. LAKAM is responsible for several instances of theft and bribery in high-tech U.S. firms. Jonathan Pollard, Israel's most famous American spy, was recruited by a LAKAM agent—this was not an operation of Israel's famed Mossad. But Israel's intelligence operations within the United States did not stop with Pollard. In the 1980s, LAKAM had contact with, and recruited, Pentagon officials more senior than Jonathan Pollard.

South Korea's intelligence agencies have been particularly active in conducting operations against the U.S. government and U.S. industry. The National Security Planning Agency, known until 1980 as the Korean Central Intelligence Agency, is one of the largest intelligence services in the world, despite South Korea's relatively small population of forty-five million. The NSP is active widely overseas and has a close relationship with the enormous conglomerates that dominate the Korean economy. According to a defector, in 1975 the KCIA sought the "implantation of an intelligence network" in the Ford White House. Korean intelligence has also actively targeted U.S. corporations, particularly those doing business in Asia. The NSP has run scores of bag operations against U.S. businesses in Tokyo, using agents posing as janitors and office cleaners to glean valuable business information. Visitors to Korea and Japan have also experienced NSP bugging, as well as the use of prostitutes to lure business-men away from their hotel rooms. U.S. bankers have been a favorite target, one defector claiming to have been involved in bugging and purloining information from the rooms of David Rockefeller, who visited South Korea in 1980 to discuss new loans to that country. Other targets have included U.S. trade negotiators visiting Seoul, as well as President Reagan. The NSP has not been above using Japan's *yakuza* (organized-crime gangs) to carry out their campaign against Japanese and American corporations in Tokyo, Kyōto, Ōsaka, and Kōbe.

The Japanese intelligence system is perhaps the most comprehensive and complex of the friendly spy networks being used against the United States. The Japanese secret service is small, as are the Japanese military intelligence services. But much of the intelligence and espionage network is run through other institutions, and these have considerable resources. A large part of the intelligence network is made up of Japanese multina-tional corporations, such as Mitsubishi, Hitachi, and Matsushita. These corporations possess substantial intelligence resources—according to Herb Meyer, Matsushita's intelligence operation takes up two floors of a Manhattan skyscraper. The quasi-official Japanese External Trade Organi-zation has also been used as an intelligence asset, gathering information and even supporting espionage. But it is the Japanese Ministry for Interna-tional Trade and Industry that serves as the hub of this network. A small division of the Naicho, the prime minister's Cabinet Research Office, is also involved in overseeing the network's operations.

The Japanese effort has included planting moles in U.S. corporations (particularly in Silicon Valley), using bribery to purchase valuable blue-prints and plans, using Japanese graduate students in the United States to gather intelligence on scientific research being conducted at leading

American universities, and collecting intelligence on senior U.S. government officials. Japanese corporations gained access on a regular basis to highly classified CIA documents and purchased top-secret technological information on the Strategic Defense Initiative (Star Wars) program. Japanese companies have also engaged in what Senator Orrin Hatch called "legal industrial espionage" through the widespread use of the Freedom of Information Act. The Japanese national telephone company, Nippon Telephone and Telegraph, regularly monitors, and eavesdrops on, U.S. corporate telephone and fax communications. In addition, the Annex Chamber, Second Section of the Investigation Division of the Ground Self-defense Forces (known as Chobetsu) within the Japanese Defense Agency, which is responsible for military communications intelligence, eavesdrops on corporate communications.

U.S. intelligence officials insist that even Canada (which few probably even know has an intelligence service) engages in intelligence operations against her neighbor to the south. The Canadian Security and Intelligence Service, created in 1982, conducts operations against the United States. The CSIS has the authority to spy on U.S. businesses by virtue of Section 16 of the CSIS Act, which set up the service. Economic intelligence collection and dissemination is quietly carried out by the Intelligence Coordinating Unit, under the deputy director general of CSIS for general operations. In 1984, concerned about growing pressures for protectionist measures in the United States, the CSIS set up a loose collaborative arrangement with the Canadian Manufacturers Association, a private organization of Canadian businesses. This was part of an effort to gather more intelligence on U.S. industry and the U.S. government. The Communications Security Establishment, an agency responsible for communications intelligence and eavesdropping, has from time to time turned its efforts southward, listening in on U.S. commercial, corporate, and, when possible, government communications.

Almost all of the intelligence services of this country's chief economic competitors have a legal mandate to spy for economic advantage. But more than these mandates drive friendly spy services to spy on U.S. industry and the U.S. government. More important, perhaps, is the fact that our allies are not "much encumbered by scruples," says Herb Meyer. They don't have any ethical qualms about spying on the U.S. government or profiting from industry and technology secrets they have stolen. What would be regarded by most Americans as unfair or unethical behavior is acceptable in much of the rest of the world. In 1989, Noel Matchett warned his clients that "many American business people naively assume a professional ethic that is nonexistent, particularly overseas. . . . In Europe and Asia, a long tradition of industrial espionage is recognized, and travelers from these areas correctly assume that hotel rooms, conference rooms, and offices are usually bugged by independent agents, competing businesses, and/or the host government."

In most foreign countries, government and industry view espionage as part of doing business. As one security consultant to the U.S. government has put it, "They don't know not doing this." Ambassador Richard Walker says that friendly intelligence services would shiver at the use of the term *espionage* to describe these activities. "They, from their perspective, regard it as 'unconventional means of getting information.' " He notes that in many countries, "there is a different attitude toward what we as a legalized society would call espionage." Both Japan and Switzerland, for example, have industrial espionage schools, to train businessmen in the art of spying. The Institute for Industrial Protection, as the Japanese school is called, was started in part with government funds. Japanese and European laws on eavesdropping and buying information from disloyal employees are much more lax than corresponding American laws. There is, consequently, intelligence gathering and sometimes overt acts of espionage among domestic companies in Europe and Asia.

In the United States, industrial espionage among U.S. companies is not unheard of, but it is pretty minor by comparison. According to Robert Courtney, a cagey, seasoned veteran in the security field who served as IBM's director of data security and privacy between 1967 and 1981, it is difficult to find instances of U.S. companies spying on each other: "Domestically, there's not a major problem; there just isn't one. The exchange of employees between companies is such that it becomes a principal source of information transfer between major American corporations." Former CIA director William Colby, now a consultant to businesses, draws the same conclusion. He says that American businessmen are just "less willing to cut corners" than many foreign companies are when it comes to gaining access to information.

When domestic companies have been approached by disgruntled employees from competing companies and offered trade secrets for a price, they almost always go to the police. The potential costs, legally and in terms of public relations, are just too high to allow most American corporations to ponder engaging in industrial espionage. In the summer of 1979, for example, a disgruntled manager at QYX named Orion Briel resigned from his post and sent a letter to IBM. A new and highly successful division of Exxon, QYX at that time had captured between 20 and 25 percent of the market in computerized typewriters, a market once dominated by IBM. Briel wrote to Daniel McGlaughlin, vice president of IBM's Office Products Division, offering to steal some top-secret Exxon documents, including plans for new products, research and development plans, and marketing strategies. "They were the family jewels," admitted an Exxon official, who valued the documents at a half-billion dollars. Briel's asking price was a hundred thousand dollars. As tempting as it might be, IBM said no to the offer. The corporation promptly reported the incident to Exxon and the FBI—without even looking at the stolen secrets.

The public record bears out how different the standards of many foreign corporations are. In 1982, for example, an FBI sting operation in Silicon Valley caught a number of senior officials from Hitachi and Mitsubishi trying to buy illegally top-secret information on the latest IBM microchip. Japanese business and industry responded to the event with outrage. Their anger was not directed toward Hitachi, however, but toward the FBI and IBM. Japanese government and business leaders actually accused Washington of playing "unfair," by carrying out the sting operation. The home of the president of IBM-Japan, outside Tokyo, was the site of loud demonstrations and protests.

Perhaps even worse has been the experience that American companies and the FBI have had with France. Between 1987 and 1989, the French secret service, the DGSE, recruited spies in the European branches of IBM, Texas Instruments, and other U.S. electronics companies. The moles collected company secrets, and the DGSE then passed them along to Compagnie des Machines Bull, the computer manufacturer owned by the French government. Through diligence and hard work, the FBI and the CIA uncovered the operation in a joint effort, and Washington sent a diplomatic protest to Paris. Not only did the French government not apologize, but nine months later it announced that Bull had plans to purchase Honeywell Federal Systems, Incorporated, just down the street from CIA headquarters in Langley, Virginia. By the way, this Honeywell unit provides systems integration, computer products, and technical services to the U.S. government, including the two agencies that uncovered the plot in the first place: the CIA and the FBI.

Dr. Lynn Fischer, chief of the Security Awareness Division at the Department of Defense Security Institute, wrote in the department's limited-circulation publication for industry, "We are, in terms of technology targeting, being threatened both by potential adversaries and *also* nations we have come to consider as allies. At the interpersonal level, most of us expect open and honest behavior by friends, and covert, deceitful behavior by enemies. Many people are surprised when it doesn't work out that way at the international scene." Fischer argues that Americans must begin to see "the world in less simplistic terms. When it comes to protecting critical information, it's no longer a case of the Soviet Bloc against the Free World or, friends vs. enemies—it never was that simple." Some cynics have suggested that this changing view of the threat reflects the intelligence community's attempt to justify itself in a changing world. By creating a new threat, the community creates a need for its own services. This might make sense were a real threat absent, but the evidence overwhelmingly indicates that U.S. allies have significant portions of their intelligence networks aimed at the United States.

The collapse of the Soviet Union has for the first time given the U.S. intelligence community the opportunity and the luxury to take a close look at the intelligence activities of its economic competitors. With the ex-Soviet states unlikely to pose a predatory threat anytime soon, attentions are beginning to shift to the espionage threat facing us in general, particularly that posed by allies. According to Maynard Anderson, "Our first task is to re-orient the intelligence and security community away from the narrow concept of the 'hostile intelligence threat' posed by specific intelligence services of adversary countries." Anderson predicts that despite the declining fortunes of America's adversaries in the next decade, "the cost of espionage committed against the United States in the new decade will increase in both absolute and relative terms."

Economic competition has become a point of contention between the United States and our major allies. Espionage will increasingly be used to gain an advantage, and there are changes in attitude afoot throughout the U.S. intelligence community. According to Greg Gwash, Defense Investigative Service director for industrial security, Pacific region, "We need to stop directing our audience's attention to just 'hostile intelligence' activities as THE THREAT. The threat is broader than that."

This change in attitude has brought a shift in U.S. counterintelligence policy, which determines how foreign spies are caught. In the summer of 1991, the FBI began to change its counterintelligence mission, focusing more on the espionage threat posed by "friendly countries." In October, a senior official quietly announced that the bureau's traditional Country Criteria List, which listed hostile intelligence services that needed watching, would gradually be phased out. Taking its place, according to FBI Deputy Assistant Director for Intelligence Harry Brandon, would be a National Security Threat List. In a speech to the private International Security Systems Symposium outside of Washington, D.C., Brandon announced that U.S. friends and allies now deemed watching. "Our thrust is going to be very different than in the past," he said. The National Security Threat List, according to Brandon, gives the FBI the flexibility to watch *any* foreign intelligence agency that poses a threat to U.S. security interests, which includes the theft of "proprietary technological information" by economic competitors. Whether this new mandate will translate into more resources being used against economic spies remains to be seen. Some argue that the espionage threat is now, or soon will be, pervasive and that any foreign government—foe, neutral, or friend—will see the potential benefit of engaging in efforts to counteract it. "The threat is still very much with us," says James Lamont, a specialist in security training who is a consultant to the U.S. government and private industry. "It's just that rather than springing from a single country or even a bloc of countries, it is now generic."

Espionage, whether coming from friendly or hostile sources, is expected to expand and become pervasive largely because the competition between friendly countries is relegated to economics and technological prowess. Industrial espionage among friends is a form of economic competition. It is this post–Cold War reality that will "change the character of the intelligence world," according to Dr. Ray Cline. When justifying economic espionage against the United States, Pierre Marion said, "In economic competition we are all competitors." As technological competition heats up among the United States, Japan, and the European Communities, friendly spying activities carried out against this country will grow dramatically. Former CIA director William Webster has warned that "as countries focus more on economic competitiveness, what will be sought is sensitive information that will give a country a competitive edge."

In 1990, the staff of the Senate Intelligence Committee, under the direction of its chairman, David Boren, undertook a study of the future of espionage. It came to largely the same conclusion. Senator Boren saw espionage becoming increasingly a function of economic competition between the United States and its allies. He said in an interview with Tom Squitieri of USA Today, "More and more the aim of espionage is to steal private commercial secrets for the sake of national economic purposes, rather than to steal military secrets for building military strengths in the spying countries. It's against private commercial targets in the U.S., carried out not by foreign companies but by foreign governments." The committee itself noted that with the declining fortunes of what was then the Soviet Union, defense secrets would matter less: "As defense secrets become less important, economic and technological data will become the focus of espionage."

In fact, friendly spies have been enormously damaging to the U.S. economy. Espionage by America's competitors, says Herb Meyer, "is costing American business a lot of money." How much? A private estimate developed by the White House Office on Science and Technology puts the cost at one hundred billion dollars annually. Noel Matchett estimates that eavesdropping on U.S. corporate communications alone costs American companies "billions and billions a year—no question about it."

International industrial espionage is a game of high stakes, and the return can be enormous for the perpetrator and devastating for the victim. As business writer Harlow Unger puts it, "Industrial espionage takes place on an international level as well as between competitors in local industries. But it's on the international level that such espionage can cause enormous disruptions in trade and can often cost thousands of workers their jobs." For many Western intelligence services, as de Marenches points out, spying is "very profitable." Effective spying means gaining access to information that can be enormously helpful to possess. Michelle Van Cleave, deputy director of the White House Office of Science and Technology Policy, pointed out in 1991 that "access to the U.S. research and technology base has been of great value to our foreign competition."

Friendly industrial espionage also has a long-term corrosive effect on a nation's science and technology base. Such espionage is essentially a parasitic act, relying on others to make costly investments of time and money in technological research. The foreign spy seeks to bypass such work simply by stealing the relevant information. And when the espionage becomes skillful and common, the cost to the innovator becomes high. Suddenly there is little return on investment, because the competition has the same technological information you have but has obtained it at a fraction of the cost. Businesses begin to wonder whether the investment is worthwhile. After all, why pay millions for research if you can steal the results from someone else?

In the pharmaceutical industry, for example, it takes more than two hundred million dollars to research, develop, test, and bring to market a new drug. If a foreign competitor can get the drug for nothing through espionage, the competitive advantage is lost. Indeed, the thief is suddenly the chief beneficiary of the research, by having the information and not paying for it. As Frank Cary, chairman of IBM's Executive Committee, put it in 1983, shortly after Hitachi and Mitsubishi attempted to steal secrets concerning IBM's new computer chips, "To destroy the rewards of investment is to destroy the incentive to innovate." The effects of successful economic espionage are not easy to gauge. U.S. Attorney Joseph P. Russoniello, the prosecutor in the IBM case, went even further when he said, "If we are unable to protect research and development, we have lost our advantage." Security consultant Irwin Ross sums up the problem: "Industrial espionage is a serious crime, for it subverts progress. If companies cannot protect their discoveries—whether these are processes or products—then they will ultimately lose the motivation to invest in development."

Some argue that friendly spies pose a serious threat not only to individual companies but also to the country's national technological prowess. Research and cutting-edge-technology companies in the United States are seriously damaged by industrial espionage. Furthermore, continual espionage operations have a cumulative effect on the U.S. technology sector. Losses mount, and the competitive race becomes increasingly difficult to run. As ex-CIA chief Richard Helms put it in a speech before corporate security officials, "In the end the compelling reason for protecting American business secrets against espionage is to ensure the survival of our economic system." One security official writes, "We have already suffered crippling blows to our economy from unfair foreign competition based on espionage. . . . While we may still be number one in high technology, if industrial espionage continues to suck us dry, we will lose this superiority as well."

The problem of friendly spies is only likely to get worse, due to a number of important changes in world political events, technology, and the nature of the international economy. Futurist Alvin Toffler has gone so far as to predict "info-wars" in the not too distant future: "There is going to be far more espionage, but it's going to be economic, financial espionage. Knowledge is strategic intelligence. Corporations are going to be hotbeds of spies. They will be reporting back to governments, and the fusion of private intelligence and public is inevitable."

The competition in the discovery, design, and manufacture of high technology is not only important in today's economy but is also part of the sweepstakes for determining technological dominance and prowess tomorrow. It is a race not only to lead but also to avoid obsolescence. For individual companies, the stakes and pressures can be enormous if they fall behind. Each company must offer up-to-date products and develop cutting-edge technologies to stay in the race. But creative abilities are unequal: some will forge ahead, and others will desperately try to close the gap. As one overseas security consultant says, "General technology is advancing so quickly that industrial espionage will become a necessary part of industry."

Intelligence agencies in many countries are talking about shifting a greater share of their intelligence assets to friendly countries in the hope of gaining a competitive advantage. "What this means to American companies," says Richard Helms, "is that the adversary, in the campaign to protect information vital to survival is, as often as not, a nation, a country, a national intelligence enterprise, and not simply one or more industrial or commercial competitors." James Lamont says, "If I were a European intelligence official right now, I'd be licking my chops. This is a golden opportunity to step up intelligence operations against neighbors, friends, and allies, particularly the United States."

Ex-CIA official Herb Meyer believes that most intelligence services in the West are at a point of transition. With traditional threats and challenges declining, many services are focusing even more on economic competition. He says firmly, "Western intelligence agencies are shifting their resources to spy more on American industry." Professor Hayden Peake of the Defense Intelligence College and a former intelligence official, shares that view. He says U.S. allies will "collect intelligence to make a profit. And if it hurts the U.S., their attitude is 'so what.'"

Adjusting to this new reality will not be easy. Lamont fears that Americans, being idealistic about the world around them, may be unable to recognize this threat, having entered a comfortable "post–Cold War mentality." "We have been so conditioned with the red menace," he says, "now nothing has taken its place. You had this huge bear outside the door, but one day he is gone. Trouble is, we never noticed the wolves behind him."

Some of the changes in the post–Cold War era will create the potential for new institutional opportunities to spy on friends as well. Industry security concerns involving chemical-arms control and the chemical industry are an example of this problem. Since 1980, the Conference on Disarmament in Geneva has been drafting a proposed convention on chemical weapons. Currently the text calls for the creation of a new international organization to conduct systematic on-site inspections of industrial facilities producing or using supertoxic chemicals and substances that could be precursors to chemical-weapons agents. The inspectors visiting industrial facilities worldwide would be of different nationalities. Although such on-site verification makes good sense for controlling or banning the production of chemical weapons, some fear it has the potential to create a perfect vehicle for industrial spying, as nations use "inspections" to learn critical secrets about other nations' chemical industries. According to Kyle Olsen of the Chemical Manufacturers Association, as many as fifty thousand industrial sights in the United States might be subject to systematic international inspection and monitoring. That worries Burrus Carnahan, a former U.S. military lawyer and a senior analyst with the Science Applications International Corporation. He writes,

> This prospect has raised justified concerns for the protection of trade secrets and other forms of intellectual property. In the chemical industry, even having access to the layout of a plant can provide valuable information to competitors. American competitiveness in international trade is becoming an increasingly troublesome issue, and it is natural to question the wisdom of revealing confidential industrial plans and processes to foreign national inspectors, even in the context of a world-wide ban on chemical weapons.

Carnahan believes that the United States ought to insist on "measures that might prevent or deter industrial espionage" when it comes to on-site inspections to enforce arms-control agreements. A chemical-industry official looks at the dilemmas posed by the post–Cold War era this way: "What are you going to do if, say, a German inspector comes for an inspection and you know he's passing the information to Hoechst [Germany's largest chemical manufacturer]? You can't exclude him, we're bound by a treaty and the feds would force us to admit him. This sort of [on-site] verification is the most perfect sort of cover for intelligence gathering you could want."

Changes in global technology are also adding incentives for greater friendly spy activity to be carried out against the United States. Increasingly governments and industries around the world, including in the United States, have come to rely on computers and electronic communications to hold, process, and transmit information. These activities are handled by enormous networks on a massive scale. There is virtually no place on earth that is not electronically linked to someplace else. Telecommunications has connected the continents to one another and created an international information revolution. Government and corporate data bases in the United States contain enormous amounts of information, the sort that used to be relegated to the file cabinet. And as computer files replace paper ones, espionage becomes much easier. The computer has inaugurated an era in which the United States "has become increasingly vulnerable to espionage carried out by foreign intelligence services or even business competitors," said Michelle Van Cleave in 1990. While file cabinets full of valuable information can be protected with locks and guards, information stored by computer can (with enough patience and expertise) be accessed from remote sites, including foreign soil. Security passwords are "easily broken down, and often very predictable," says James Lamont. High school computer hackers have managed to enter many corporate and government computer data bases. A group of teenage hackers in Germany even managed to access top-secret military files in the United States and were caught only after they had caused significant damage.

The skillful computer thief doesn't leave a mark. That is, of course, if he or she doesn't want to. Some fear that friendly spy activities will not be limited to stealing data and information. Says Professor George Roukis of Hofstra University in Hempstead, New York, "Planting false information or willfully subverting a competitor's data base is possible under these circumstances." Computer sabotage or terrorism, the flip side of accessing information, may become more common in the future as well.

The development of espionage technology is also likely to favor an expansion of spying among economic competitors. Today's espionage equipment is much more sophisticated than ever before: difficult to detect, powerful, efficient, and inexpensive. Gone are the days, for example, of the crude bug or the on-line wiretap, with its recognizable clicking. If you want to eavesdrop today, advanced technologies allow you to avoid detection almost entirely. The sound waves generated by a conversation cause the glass in a nearby window to vibrate slightly, and if a laser beam is bounced off the window, its reflection will be modulated by the vibration. All the eavesdropper needs in order to hear what is being said is a demodulating device that extracts the audio from the reflected laser beam. Infinity bugs, attached to phone lines, can be triggered from hundreds of miles away. Noninvasive bugs don't need to be attached to the phone line at all: the bugger simply places the device next to a telephone wire, and the electric impulses that constitute a telephone conversation can be translated into the conversation and recorded on tape. Other bugs that are being developed store conversations for days, transmitting them to home bases in a single burst. There is also technology now that allows secrets to be stolen from a computer after they've been erased from the computer's memory. Thus, even documents that have been removed from a computer's files for security reasons can still be stolen. The effectiveness of the new spy technologies and the ease with which a spy can escape detection will make espionage too tempting for some to avoid.

Espionage between friends is likely to continue to grow as long as economics is seen as an aspect of national security because technology is becoming the new determinant of national power. A country's ability to develop and produce technologies determines its power and influence in the world. For that reason, thwarting economic spies from competing countries is critical, said Richard Helms in a 1991 speech. "Industrial, commercial, financial, business operations of all kinds—and, particularly those which are competing in the international arena—require the same kinds of protection which are afforded to military operations or political gambits."

According to Maynard Anderson, the Defense Science Board at the Department of Defense believes that there is a "new reality," in which the advancement and application of technology has become globalized, effectively replacing territory as the new determinant of world power. Success at exploiting new technologies for economic and military purposes, concludes the board, will determine the relative power of the competing states. The relative standing of the ex–Soviet Union and Japan in the world-power equation is particularly instructive in this regard. In the end, territorial expansion did not offer the Soviet Union staying power. Its economy was in utter shambles. In contrast, Japan is an economic powerhouse with limited military power. And increasingly Japan has a larger say in international affairs by virtue of its economic power, despite the fact that the Soviet Union possessed a population and a land mass many times the size of Japan's and an enormous nuclear arsenal.

Economic strength is increasingly seen by U.S. officials as a critical measure of national power and an important determinant of national security. As Michelle Van Cleave put it in a 1991 speech before the National Security Institute, "The nation's economic strength is just as essential to our security as our military capability." Economic standing is becoming something as firmly protected as military standing. Joshua Bolter, the general counsel in the Office of the U.S. Trade Representative, explains, "The business of trade negotiations is as central to U.S. national-security interests now as arms control negotiations were during the last forty years." For many of America's best trading partners, that has always been the view. Many allied countries have used espionage to understand better the U.S. position on trade issues. As we shall see, American trade negotiators have been hired away, spied on, and even had their ranks infiltrated by moles.

In the past, the United States has always shied away from viewing espionage as an economic tool, whereas many of our allies have embraced this view for quite some time. Our beliefs that economics and politics are totally divorced from each other, that trade is almost exclusively a harmonious, mutually beneficial process, and that all forms of government action to assist industries should be rejected out of hand are unique. Many of our allies have a distinctly different view of the economic world, seeing economics as immersed in politics and economic security indistinguishable from national security. This explains Japan's and continental Europe's (not to mention the rest of the world's) embrace of trade policies that we might find unacceptable. It also explains why many countries, according to Herb Meyer, "have always been more willing than the U.S. to deploy their national intelligence services to help selected industries and even selected companies."

31

2

Spies Like Us

As ironic as it may sound, after the Cold War, counterintelligence will be more important than before.
—Ambassador Richard Walker, member of the CIA's Senior Review Panel

That the United States has become the target of choice for friendly spies should not be in doubt. This country still has the world's most advanced technology base and many of the greatest scientific research facilities in the world. It is also the single power with the most influence in international political and economic affairs. But perhaps more important is the relative openness of American society, which makes friendly spy operations easy to conduct. Most scientific research is fairly accessible. Unlike other countries, where much research is done in private company laboratories that have little turnover in staff, in the United States much research is done at universities or national laboratories, and these have greater turnover and are much more open. American laboratories tend to be much more accessible and less well protected than those elsewhere in the world. Says Professor Hayden Peake, a former intelligence official now with the U.S. Defense Intelligence College, "The advantage that foreigners have here is that they don't stick out. There are indigenous people from around the world here—German, French, Korean, Japanese. More and more hiring for U.S. firms is taking place overseas, where there is little institutional loyalty built up." Ambassador Richard Walker envisions "new nationalisms" in many countries now that the Cold War has ended. He believes that heightened nationalism will emerge in many parts of the world, based largely on economic interests. And, he says, "I think the concomitant part of the new nationalisms will make our counterintelligence more important, because we are a hyphenated society." The fact that the intelligence threat will now come from friendly countries with emigrants here makes counterintelligence, "more sensitive but also more important," according to Walker.

Dealing with friendly spies will prove a more difficult counterintelligence task than any other we have ever faced. When he was director of internal security at the Justice Department, John Davitt reviewed FBI espionage investigations. Recently he said, "The Soviet Union for forty or fifty years was perceived as the enemy; it made education about espionage easier. You simply instructed people, 'If you are approached by a Soviet, report it immediately.' That was the technique. With this problem, you cast too big a net to ask someone to report contact and approaches by a foreign national from a friendly country. It's simply impossible."

The organization of the U.S. government also makes intelligence collection here easy. The U.S. political system is more open than many others, and government workers in a variety of sensitive positions come and go frequently. For example, U.S. trade officials regularly leave government service to work for foreign governments or corporations, often taking critical trade or technology secrets with them. Few industrial spies are ever prosecuted, and fewer still face retribution for gathering intelligence to be used against the U.S. government. It has just not been perceived as a problem.

The U.S. work force is relatively fluid, making information mobile and accessible. Americans tend to be open people and are oftentimes too willing to share information. "We are much more talkative and open than other people," says John Davitt. "We are too naive and too open for our own good."

These wonderful qualities of American life make us a soft target for friendly spies. Legal, social, and other constraints on spying in other countries do not apply in the United States. Says Professor Peake, "If they

33

are willing to spend the time and money, it is easy to recruit employees at U.S. firms, particularly nondefense ones."

For these reasons, friendly spies have been enormously successful in the United States. They have gathered important political intelligence within the U.S. government, influenced U.S. foreign policy to serve their countries' political objectives, and dramatically helped their countries compete economically against the United States. At critical times, industrial espionage carried out by friendly countries has severely damaged U.S. competitiveness. Foreign countries have targeted American cutting-edge technologies and conducted well-orchestrated campaigns to gather intelligence and carry out espionage activities to gain a substantial national advantage.

Perhaps nowhere else has this been more true than in the computer industry. An industry that many consider crucial in determining the economic prowess of nations for decades to come, the computer industry in particular has been targeted by friendly foreign intelligence services and corporations for espionage operations. Friendly spies in Silicon Valley during the early 1980s had a devastating effect on the U.S. computer industry. IBM alone, according to internal company documents, was targeted twenty-five known times by foreign entities between 1975 and 1984. In 1983, then-IBM Chairman John Opel found it necessary to distribute a handbook to his employees warning that "IBM increasingly is a target for people interested in illicitly acquiring significant business secrets. Over the years, there have been a number of actual thefts." Japan espionage in Silicon Valley nearly devastated the U.S. computer industry. As Harlow Unger put it in the newsmagazine *Canadian Business,* "The economic future of the American electronic firms is now being threatened by the activities of Japanese industrial spies prowling California's famed 'Silicon Valley.' " The political costs to the countries associated with these operations were minor, primarily relegated to behind-the-scenes tussles with U.S. intelligence and security officials; few paid any commercial or financial price for their activities. Given this reality, there should be little surprise that friendly spying—especially in its industrial-espionage form—is perceived as a low-risk, high-gain activity.

What motivates Americans with access to valuable information to sell it to a foreign intelligence service? Usually it is money. While Julius and Ethel Rosenberg's political sympathies motivated them to pass atomic-bomb secrets to the Soviets, ideology in recent years has rarely played a role in motivating Americans to become spies. "It used to be ideology," says William Baker, a former assistant director of the FBI, "particularly the world Communist movement. But that began to taper off after the Soviet invasion of Hungary in 1956."

A look at the most notorious spies for the Soviets or other countries in the past two decades bears out that money is what has increasingly motivated U.S. spies. John Walker, head of the notorious Walker spy ring, which sold submarine technology to the Soviets, received $1 million over a seventeen-year period for his efforts. Ronald Pelton, an employee of the National Security Agency who sold communications and encryption information to the KGB, received $35,000. Thomas Cavanaugh, an engineer for the Northrop Corporation, in 1984 offered to sell drawings of the Stealth aircraft to FBI agents posing as Soviet agents; he too had a price, albeit a small one: $25,000. Larry Wu-Tai Chin, a CIA analyst who passed information to agents from the People's Republic of China, received $180,000 in gold deposits from Beijing for thirty-two years of spying. Richard Miller, an FBI agent who sold counterintelligence secrets to the KGB, first asked $2 million for his services—he got only small gifts and promises. Jonathan Jay Pollard, the Navy employee who passed classified information to Israel, was supposed to receive $300,000 over a ten-year period. (He ended up seeing only $45,000 of it, being caught after serving as a spy for only eighteen months.) Jerry Whitworth, a Navy code clerk and a member of the Walker spy ring, received $332,000 for his efforts.

In the last two decades financial difficulty or dreams of riches have led these individuals to betray their country. Larry Wu-Tai Chin had $96,700 in Las Vegas gambling debts and was being hounded by debtors. Ronald Pelton had $64,000 in personal debts at one time, forcing him to declare personal bankruptcy in 1979. Jerry Whitworth was simply tired of living on a tight budget and decided to spy to achieve an "enhanced life-style for himself and his wife."

All of these spies were captured, convicted, and found guilty of betraying their country. Jonathan Pollard, Ronald Pelton, Jerry Whitworth, John Walker, Thomas Cavanaugh, and Richard Miller are all serving life terms or more in prison (Larry Wu-Tai Chin committed suicide before his trial). Whitworth has the dubious distinction of receiving a 365-year prison sentence. In all, a heavy price to pay, especially in light of the fact that the money wasn't all that good. Despite all their hopes for riches, many of these spies discovered that the Soviets simply couldn't afford to pay much. "The Soviets are notorious for being poor payers," says Phillip Knightly, a British expert on Soviet espionage. Cash poor, the KGB often relied on the sheer desperation of an individual to drive him to spy for next to nothing.

Spying for friendly countries, on the other hand, can be enormously profitable. Unlike the Soviet Union, these countries can afford to pay more for information. Consider the case of Ronald Hoffman: he received more than $600,000 from four Japanese companies between 1986 and 1991 in exchange for technology secrets on the Strategic Defense Initiative. Or Chien Ming Sung, an employee of General Electric: he received $1 million per year from South Korean agents to pass secrets about GE's synthetic-diamond formula to a South Korean company—that is what John Walker got in seventeen years of spying for the Soviets. Harold Farrar, the plant manager at the Celanese plant in Greer, South Carolina, received $130,000 from Japan's Mitsubishi Corporation to pass along secrets about Celanese's specialized film used in satellites, rockets, computers, and X-ray devices. He received almost as much as Wu-Tai Chin did for thirty-two years of spying for China.

In fact, no spying is more profitable than spying for U.S. friends and allies. Enormous amounts of money may be at stake when it comes to economic espionage. Individual companies can gain or lose hundreds of millions, even billions of dollars because of it. The GE formula that Sung sold to the South Koreans has been estimated by some to be worth five hundred million dollars annually in future sales. The one million dollars paid to him per annum was a relatively cheap price in comparison. Most U.S. friends can afford to pay the kind of money that may attract more spying. And that worries U.S. intelligence officials. "Think of the number of people who sold out for the meager pay-offs coming from the Soviets. Can you imagine the problem we might have when real big money is offered?" asks one senior U.S. intelligence official.

The risks of spying for U.S. allies are relatively low. Consider Harold Farrar, the Celanese plant manager who sold secret company documents to Mitsubishi. He received a sentence of only four years for selling what the judge in the case admitted was "a monumental sell-out" of the company's technology secrets. Because economic secrets have not been considered as important as military or political secrets, the penalties have been much lighter. And because the culprit is a U.S. friend, the Americans involved are seen as less sinister than those who sold out to the Soviet Union.

Some U.S. intelligence officials worry that friendly spying may blossom as a result of this attitude. Spying for an enemy like the former Soviet Union is morally repugnant to the vast majority of Americans. But spying for an ally may be less black-and-white, especially if a person is in a desperate situation. After all, lives are most likely not at stake, nor is national security. "A person in desperate straits who would never have dreamed of selling their country down the river by selling secrets to the KGB, just might convince himself that selling the same to an ally really isn't so bad," warns one FBI official. The few Americans caught engaging in friendly spying often seem shocked when legal charges are brought against them.

The openness, mobility, and independence of most Americans are characteristics that lend themselves to friendly industrial espionage in a number of ways. Americans often willingly share secrets of their employers' that they shouldn't share. Oftentimes friendly spies are able to gather important intelligence legally simply by discussing matters openly with their employers, neighbors, and friends. No doubt, the use of such legal methods and techniques is preferred, but friendly foreign intelligence services and corporations have not been above engaging in illicit activities as well to gather intelligence on the United States.

One surprisingly common form of espionage used by friendly spies is compromising employees of an American company or the U.S. government. American workers, government employees, and employees of American companies overseas have all been hired by allied intelligence services to spy. With shifting post–Cold War sands, the environment is right for even more recruitment in the future. Almost every company or government agency—whether large or small—has an employee who is disgruntled, in financial or other difficulty, or unhappy with his or her lot in life. The scope of potential recruits is enormous. Says one security consultant, "The entire range of employees from top executives down to the mail carrier or the cleaning staff are potential spies given the right price."

In the United States there is not a firmly developed sense of corporate loyalty. Particularly if an employee faces financial difficulty, he or she can often be convinced that passing information to an American "friend or ally" is nothing more than an awkward business transaction. The same can be said for U.S. government employees. While selling military secrets to the Soviets is extremely distasteful, selling political or economic ones to allies is not so bad by comparison. "A common defense is that the information is not a classified military secret, and therefore it was not illegal to share it," says John Davitt. If a person is unwilling to be recruited by an agent, he or she may be moved to participate in "false-flag" operations, which appeal to an ulterior motive for betraying a loyalty. Such operations will be easier to carry out with the lowering of Cold War barriers.

What friendly intelligence agents want in an industrial spy is a person with access to inside expert knowledge, someone who can provide the necessary information and make sense of it. Such access to a wide variety of information by a knowledgeable employee is often easier to come by than it might seem. In the computer age, diskettes can hold hundreds or even thousands of pages of information, and they can be easily concealed or slipped into a pocket. James Lamont describes how he would conduct an operation: "If I want information on, say, a new computer chip, I would find out what person or team developed it. I would just find out who the players are. I would then go after anybody and everybody who worked on it. I would try to hire them away, try to penetrate the team and find out their weaknesses. I would then try to recruit or compromise them."

An operation run against the high-tech firm of Fairchild Semiconductors is a textbook case of this sort of arrangement. From 1977 to 1986, Japanese agents operating out of the Japanese consulate in San Francisco had a middle-level researcher at Fairchild stealing secrets on computer developments and corporate plans. The employee passed enormous amounts of information along to the Japanese consulate officials and to consultants to Japanese firms—by some estimates, 160,000 pages of confidential research results and corporate plans. Despite the damage he was causing Fairchild, he was never caught. He apparently left the company before he could be identified. And despite one episode in which he nearly was caught, he eluded corporate security so effectively that by internal company estimates, it would have been at least another half year before he would have been tracked down. According to a former intelligence official knowledgeable about the case, the American mole spoke perfect Japanese and had access to a wide array of research and management information. For the first two years of the operation, every two weeks he would bring computer disks to consulate officials, who met him in the lobby of the local Holiday Inn. He was paid so much money, company officials believe, that he could eventually quit working for good.

The information critically affected Fairchild's ability to maintain its technological edge against its Japanese competitors. On October 23, 1986, Japan's largest computer maker, Fujitsu, announced its plans to buy 80 percent of Fairchild Semiconductors. The deal failed to go through, largely due to opposition expressed by Secretary of Defense Caspar Weinberger and Secretary of Commerce Malcolm Baldridge. Some Fairchild officials allege that Fujitsu made its bid based on some of the information purloined earlier by the mole.

Whereas the Fairchild case was ideal from the spy's standpoint, situations providing less immediate access can be helpful to other agents. From time to time, cleaning people at American companies have been used either to grant access to U.S. manufacturing facilities overseas or to collect information directly. While cleaning personnel may have little knowledge of the work being done at the company they are cleaning, they have the sort of access to facilities that are perfect for espionage activities. They usually work at night or during off-hours and with little or no supervision. And they are usually contract workers, who have little if any loyalty or allegiance to the company whose facility they happen to be cleaning. In one instance, according to a security consultant, one janitor's value was recognized by two foreign competitors. While supervising the cleaning of the corporate offices of a major U.S. chemical company, he was getting payoffs from both German corporate representatives and South Korean agents for allowing them access to computer data bases. Having agents run through computer files is perhaps difficult, but it is not always necessary. Valuable information can come at a critical time in strange forms. As one security consultant has put it: "If somebody gets hold of your wastebasket, he might as well have your file."

At times, recruiting informants is given a fig leaf of respectability through the creation of consulting arrangements and firms, thus giving the procurement of information a business-as-usual air to it. Japan, Germany, France, and South Korea have all used this technique. Usually a foreign corporation sets up a small consulting firm near a high-tech research and development area such as Silicon Valley, the Route 128 corridor around Boston, or the Research Triangle in North Carolina. Sometimes the firm is established by a dummy company that is actually a front for a foreign intelligence service. The consulting firm then offers fat consulting fees to Americans employed by high-tech companies or the U.S. government. But it is less interested in the individual than in the information he or she can procure. Likely recruits are picked not so much on the basis of their capabilities as on the basis of the company they work for. They are offered consulting arrangements only if they have access to particularly helpful information. Locating possible recruits is not difficult, and the process is often made easier by scanning a company phone directory. Such "consulting" efforts have been so successful that some American companies have been forced to take new security precautions. Both Hewlett-Packard and IBM have gone so far as to "classify" internal company phone directories at some of their facilities. The hope is to limit the access that these so-called consulting firms have to the names and phone numbers of critical employees.

Foreign agents at times go even further to insulate themselves, using free-lancers to conduct their espionage campaign for them. "There are espionage persons who sell their services for specific assignments and espionage gangs who conduct ongoing espionage activities across the spectrum of industry," says security specialist Norman Bottom. "There are also groups of spies who operate in specific areas as specialists." Freelancers are paid enormous amounts of money and are therefore often able to retire after only a handful of jobs. Private detectives are sometimes quite willing to carry out such missions, particularly if the price is right. Some have been known to receive one hundred thousand dollars per week for their services. One Milan-based industrial spy, who masterminded the

1959 theft of pharmaceutical information from the U.S. company American Cyanamid, was able to retire in the lap of luxury after that one theft, finally establishing himself in a beach-front, seven-bedroom home in Nice, in the south of France.

Some U.S. intelligence officials allege that a few foreign governments and businessmen have not been above using organized-crime syndicates in the United States to snatch secrets. Organized crime can be very effective in this capacity, using, in the words of Norman Bottom, "kickbacks, bribes, discounted stolen goods, free contraband, prostitution, and loans to corrupt officials in both the public and private sectors. In these ways, organized crime acquires informants, if not actual agents-in-place or moles." Because these syndicates are often very security conscious and capable of effectively grappling with law-enforcement agencies, they make particularly appealing vehicles for the darker operations that some companies can be tempted to engage in. Their use has been rare, for obvious reasons—the potential for embarrassing revelations about such cooperation is enormous. But according to former intelligence officials in some countries, the *yakuza* in Japan, as well as West Coast and New York crime syndicates, are quite capable of efficiently gathering information. Some security officials, perhaps knowledgeable about these relationships, believe that the growing stakes in technology secrets may lead to a new brutality in the not-too-distant future, in which crime syndicates might figure more prominently.

Some foreign agents and corporations unable to procure the information they want by means of an informant, have planted their own agents in American corporations and have attempted to do so as well in the U.S. government. Job mobility and open-hiring practices when it comes to many foreign nationals mean that a competitor or foreign intelligence service can place an agent in the target company as an employee or a consultant. Credentials and references are easily doctored. "Few companies conduct the requisite background checks to weed out a spy within their ranks," says security specialist and lawyer August Bequai. A former intelligence officer with the Korean CIA has said that once the organization has one mole inside, he acts like a vacuum cleaner, sucking up information. Once he has become an inside, recognized member of the company, he gets access to information that may not be even remotely connected to his ostensible work. Co-workers in other departments are all too willing to chat with a new employee over lunch or in a bar after work about their job and their work. Often such moles work to recruit American employees—whether through offers of money or through blackmail—to procure information.

Planting agents inside U.S. corporations is often a desperate measure, a sign that the intelligence service has been unable to establish a pipeline of information in a more conventional, less elaborate manner. Planting agents, in comparison with recruiting existing employees, is not highly effective. Says Robert Courtney, a former senior official at IBM: "It's a crap shoot. You don't know what you get when you plant a mole. Chances are he'll probably be hired and employed in the wrong division or section and then you're still no closer than when you started."

In addition to planting moles or recruiting American spies, many other methods are used by friendly spies to gather intelligence on U.S. industry and government. Electronic eavesdropping on U.S. corporate communications is perhaps the most common and successful method of stealing American secrets. As a matter of course, the overseas facilities of American companies communicate valuable information to their headquarters in the United States. Intercepting these communications is easy, detection is difficult, and the activity is often enormously profitable. "Every time valuable information is transmitted on unprotected circuits, there is the possibility it is being intercepted by competitors," says Noel Matchett. A tall, thin, lanky man with twenty years' experience as a communications specialist with the National Security Agency, Matchett is now president of Information Security, Incorporated, a consulting firm. "Frequently, transmissions are routed over satellite, microwave, and even cellular phone circuits," he notes, "making theft of information undetectable." A number of U.S. allies routinely intercept, or eavesdrop on, the communications of U.S. companies and then share their findings with their own companies. In other cases, foreign companies have been known to do the eavesdropping themselves, using readily available technologies.

In many instances, U.S. companies operating overseas use the local telephone networks, which may be nationalized or owned by competing companies. The IBM Corporation's internal information network is a case in point. In Europe, it runs on lines controlled by state-owned telephone companies and partially or wholly state-owned computer companies, which are among IBM's European competition. While this network is scrambled, or encrypted, IBM is required to share the keys to the codes with several European governments. Robert Courtney and others believe that these governments regularly eavesdrop on IBM communications. By some estimates, seventy foreign governments regularly eavesdrop on U.S. corporate communications being transmitted on telephone systems overseas.

Other forms of corporate communication are also subject to interception by friendly governments and foreign corporations. Microwave communications and satellite communications are two examples. Microwave communications, although highly directional, are vulnerable to interception anywhere near the transmitter. Major urban centers are a likely interception point, and foreign intelligence services have been known to intercept microwave communications that are reflected by buildings and other structures. In some instances, this interception is carried out by allied governments using advanced signals-intelligence (SIGINT) technologies provided by the U.S. government. It was intended that this technology would be used to eavesdrop on the Soviet Union and other hostile powers. In the case of Japan, as we shall see in Chapter 4, at least two facilities built with the help of U.S. intelligence have been used to eavesdrop on the United States and other friendly countries. In addition, friendly foreign intelligence services have established mobile facilities in the United States to eavesdrop on certain communications.

Satellite communications are particularly vulnerable to this same sort of eavesdropping. Using broadcast satellites to transmit information, which many American companies do, poses a particular problem. "They may be getting your most confidential information by intercepting satellite transmissions, and it's a good bet they won't get caught," says Noel Matchett.

"A signal spreads as it travels," says Brian Hollenstein, former chairman of the American Society of Industrial Security's Committee on Safeguarding Proprietary Information. "When it reaches the ground, the area it covers can be as big as California, and any antenna can pick it up."

With technology advancing so quickly, eavesdropping has become increasingly easy for many corporations to engage in. "Anyone with minimal resources, modest engineering skills, and dedication can intercept and exploit unprotected corporate or government information," says Matchett. And while the activity is illegal in the United States, it is "routine and accepted practice in most parts of the world."

Often friendly spies who listen in on corporate communications are looking for information on pricing, corporate strategic planning, or research and development results. The advantages gained from eavesdropping can be enormous. Notes Herb Meyer, "If an American company is in a foreign capital negotiating a deal, [then] eavesdropping on their dinner conversations in their corporate offices [sic], can be enormously useful to the local company in terms of understanding their negotiating positions on specific things. So that's incredibly valuable if you can get it." In one instance, for example, a foreign contractor twice underbid a U.S. telecommunications company in multimillion-dollar contracts for jobs in Southeast Asia, both times underbidding the American competitor by only several thousand dollars. When communications routes were changed, the firm was no longer underbid.

Not all friendly spy activity directed against the United States is illegal. Indeed, there is a vast array of valuable information available legally to any foreign government or industry official willing to do a little legwork. This legally obtainable information is often not as valuable as that obtained by stealth. But it should still be of concern, says Michelle Van Cleave. Obtaining information legally is in itself "an intelligence type of activity" and poses serious problems for U.S. industry and government.

The use, or perhaps abuse, of the Freedom of Information Act by foreign corporations and some friendly foreign governments is an example of legal intelligence activity. The FOIA was designed to offer a healthy dose of public disclosure of U.S. government operations to those interested in watching government activities. It has ended up being used largely by those with special interests in government work. This includes, in the words of Utah Senator Orrin Hatch, "foreign requesters who use FOIA to get information about our own domestic companies." He classifies some of this activity as a form of "commercial espionage."

Often working through consulting and law firms in the United States, many foreign corporations systematically file FOIA requests to gather information on U.S. corporate secrets and technological information. Mitsubishi Corporation, for example, in 1986 made a decisive plan to enter the space business, designing and building rockets and other equipment. Along with its regular research and development efforts in the laboratory and at the draftsman's table, Mitsubishi embarked on a systematic effort to gather substantial amounts of rocketry and space shuttle data from the National Aeronautics and Space Administration. By some estimates, this included approximately fifteen hundred requests in 1987 alone. Another user of FOIA is foreign drug companies, which regularly receive information on U.S. drug companies based on information originally provided by the Food and Drug Administration.

Similarly, chemical companies have seen their industry secrets fall into foreign hands by virtue of the Environmental Protection Agency's regulation that certain information set forth by the Toxic Substances Control Act be submitted to the government. The act requires that the government then compile a master list of chemical substances produced and used in the United States. In a number of instances, this information has been disclosed to foreign competitors.

Several countries also use graduate students studying at American universities to collect information on advanced research in a number of technologies. "I have no doubt that a lot of graduate students come to our universities and report back to their governments concerning specific research going on at American universities," says Ambassador Walker.

"There are lots of creative ways—both legal and illegal—to get valuable and secret information," said Richard Helms in a recent speech. And because access to secrets offers a competitive edge, there is a powerful incentive for developing methods and recruiting agents to that end. It may be that in the not-too-distant future the intelligence agent, bent on stealing a valuable economic secret, will become a new standard character in popular fiction, a reflection of a new reality.

3

Big Blue's Crown Jewels

Bob, I think one of my clients has gotten your crown jewels.
—Maxwell Paley, Silicon Valley consultant

On November 20, 1980, a quiet, Haitian-born computer scientist named Raymond Cadet resigned from his post at IBM's computer development center in Poughkeepsie, New York. He had been happy at Big Blue but figured it was time to move on, perhaps to a smaller company where he could earn more and be given more responsibility. Like all employees at IBM, before he was hired, Cadet had signed a pledge that he would take no confidential material with him when he left the company. On that cool November day, his last in the office, not too much was made of the agreement. After all, the parting of employee and employer seemed amicable enough. IBM managers simply asked Cadet whether he was taking any information, and Cadet gave them his word that he was not.

Unfortunately for IBM, the clever scientist was lying—and it was a very big lie. Before leaving the quiet offices of IBM, he had smuggled from the building secret documents worth potentially billions of dollars to IBM's competitors. With Big Blue controlling two thirds of the world computer market at the time, eager competitors would have loved to have the secrets Cadet carried out with him. But even the clever Haitian probably never imagined that because of his lie, he would set in motion a series of international events reminiscent of a spy novel, with high stakes for everyone involved. It would include a complex FBI sting operation and a cast of international characters meeting quietly in hotel rooms at late hours to negotiate the purchase of Cadet's papers for hundreds of thousands of dollars. The international drama would include wiretaps and bribes, the involvement of the Japanese government in an attempt to acquire the secrets, an FBI raid, and the arrest of senior Japanese businessmen.

Raymond Cadet resigned from IBM on the promise of employment with a Washington, D.C.–based computer company. He quickly settled into his new job, but the potential value of the information he carried with him stuck firmly in his mind. He had spirited away IBM's "crown jewels" as the company called them, a series of design workbooks called the *Adirondack Workbooks*. The books contained the technology secrets of the new computers IBM was planning and unlocked the mystery of the direction in which the industry leader was moving. The FOR INTERNAL IBM USE ONLY warning prominently printed on each page of every book did not dissuade Cadet. He began shopping the information around and almost immediately had a bite. Barry Saffaie, an elusive Iranian-American computer consultant in California, knew immediately the value of the workbooks. He also knew that whereas American companies would shy away from buying such confidential information illegally, some of his best Japanese clients wouldn't. On June 1, 1981, he convinced Cadet to come work with him at National Advanced Systems, or NAS, in Silicon Valley. Saffaie shortly thereafter made copies of the workbooks and began thinking about how to market them.

During the summer of 1981, Barry Saffaie shuttled across the Pacific to brief Hitachi experts on computer developments in the United States. While in Tokyo, he shared with senior company officials the fact that he had the coveted *Adirondack Workbooks*. By August, he cut a deal with Hitachi managers and delivered copies of the ten workbooks to Hitachi's computer specialists. Hitachi engineers were duly impressed. They recognized that possession of the workbooks would substantially aid Hitachi's efforts to capture large segments of the world computer market from IBM. The workbooks would cut the cost of research and development by more than half for some Hitachi products.

At about the same time that Cadet left IBM, the FBI made several inquiries at computer companies in Silicon Valley about criminal activities and espionage operations being run against the American computer industry. The activity of the Soviet KGB was of particular concern to FBI officials, who recognized that legal and illegal technology transfers to Moscow were substantially helping the Soviet military in its efforts to modernize the armed forces. The response to these FBI inquiries was truly shocking to the bureau. "We couldn't believe some of the stories we heard," says one bureau special agent who was involved in the preliminary dealings in the valley. "This sort of stuff—spying, espionage, and theft—was more widespread than anyone had assumed." Motivated by a new-found concern, on November 21, 1980, the bureau moved to launch a formal program to investigate a series of major thefts in the electronics industry. The semilegal "gray market" for technology became a new epicenter of FBI activity to counter the operations of foreign intelligence agents. The Soviets were presumed to be the biggest player in the espionage game. But losses for U.S. computer companies were also mounting, a result of spying by foreign Western computer makers. The ever-increasing theft of integrated circuits and high technology in northern California was causing distress in technology circles, where it was seen as a threat to profitability and competitiveness. Some feared that losses would mount, and some producers might be forced to close as a result.

What had also developed in the valley was an extensive black market, which included a sophisticated distribution network for stolen computer components. Stolen chips were often pedaled to computer manufacturers and users around the world at a fraction of the price a customer would pay if the goods were purchased directly from the manufacturer. In addition, Soviet intelligence agents were roaming the valley, hoping to arrange the shipment of advanced technologies back to Moscow. And a number of economic competitors from around the world were showing a growing interest in computer chips and designs. German and Japanese companies, for example, were dabbling on the Silicon Valley black market.

The incoming Reagan administration pledged to increase the amount of U.S. counterintelligence and law-enforcement resources committed to countering the activities of the KGB. But there was one major flaw in the new administration's plan: it assumed that only hostile countries were stealing American computer secrets.

The FBI decided to act. Special Agent Ken Thompson was assigned by FBI regional offices in San Francisco to survey the problem and to propose an effective plan to plug the technology leak. Thompson quickly recognized the insidious nature of these operations and realized that overt law-enforcement operations would not be very successful in thwarting them. So he recommended an undercover investigation of all aspects of the underground network in the valley: chip fraud, the illegal export of high technology to foreign countries, especially the Soviet Union, and the theft of technology secrets. His proposal was forwarded to Assistant U.S. Attorney Gregory Ward, who approved his aggressive plan to the letter.

Thompson wanted a campaign to infiltrate the underworld of Silicon Valley. He recognized that muscling in or infiltrating current illegal operations would pose problems. Results might be long in coming. So he asked, Why not just set up shop and offer our "services" to those interested in them?

William Neuman, the special agent in charge of the San Francisco FBI office, was so impressed by Thompson's plan that he almost immediately forwarded it to FBI headquarters in Washington, D.C. Then-FBI Director William Webster, getting heat from some in the Carter administration about challenges to the U.S. computer industry, immediately approved the operation. The director also ordered that the bureau cooperate with U.S. computer manufacturers in Silicon Valley to develop extensive campaigns to stress security consciousness among their employees.

IBM, as the largest computer company in the world, was the bureau's logical first choice to offer "technical support" as a prototype for cooperation that other companies might follow. Big Blue worked with the bureau and organized training seminars, which were directed by Gerald Holcom, security manager of IBM's San Jose division, to help identify any efforts to obtain IBM's computer secrets illicitly. By May 1981, the seminars had begun. Employees were trained in identifying possible information leaks and in dealing with an "approach" by a foreign spy. In every instance, the prototype spy was a Soviet-bloc agent. So strong was the assumption that the perpetrator would be from a hostile country that employees were taught to identify key warning signs, like Slavic accents and certain ethnic features.

On July 21, 1981, IBM agreed to serve as a cover for FBI agents, which meant the company would play a vital role in training and setting up fronts for the agents. That role included providing them with employee identities. The agents were given complete employment histories, special training so they could speak in great detail about IBM technological matters, and residential homes nearby in order to enhance their cover.

The "new identity" program was carried out under the direction of an IBM special consultant named Richard Callahan. A marine captain during the Korean War, Callahan flew American and Marine Corps flags at his home in Pebble Beach, California. An FBI special-agent veteran of seven years, he had joined the bureau in his early twenties and was of the old school, trained and employed under the legendary FBI director J. Edgar Hoover. As a fed, he'd had an outstanding career, with foreign intelligence investigations his primary responsibility at the bureau. In 1973, he had become a senior consultant to the Office of Legal Counsel at IBM and was responsible for "special security projects."

IBM-FBI cooperation was sealed in August 1981, when Callahan met with FBI agents Alan J. Garretson and Ken Thompson in a Palo Alto hotel lobby to discuss the program. A legal cooperation agreement was signed, and it was given final approval by senior FBI officials two days later. Code-named Operation PENGEM (an acronym for "penetrating grey markets"), the plan was about to commence. The pieces were all in place. Now it was only a matter of waiting for an approach.

By design and intent, PENGEM had been directed mainly at Soviet espionage activity. Through a labyrinth of "consulting firms," Soviet agents had been working feverishly to export technology to Moscow. But no one figured on what would happen next. "We had always assumed that we would be busting foreigners with Russian accents," says one FBI official who was involved in the planning of PENGEM. "That is where we assumed the spy threat was coming from. I guess we never figured that we would be busting Japanese businessmen who were working through the Japanese consulate in San Francisco."

On a hot California July day in 1980, a foreign visitor in Maxwell Paley's San Jose office promised to make him rich. An intense man of great ability in science and engineering, Paley had formed his own company in San Jose in 1970, after more than twenty years at IBM. Palyn Associates, Incorporated, was a consulting firm that primarily evaluated technological and business developments in a variety of companies in the computer industry. His firm was an industry watcher. Two able assistants helped Paley in his work. Robert Domenico was a former IBM engineer, and Dr. George Rossman, a specialist in computer architecture. There were quite a few firms that paid Paley good money to keep them current on what their competitors were doing and the success they were having with certain technologies. One of his cardinal rules was to operate within the boundaries of the law. He never cut corners, he was paid extremely well, and he lived a comfortable life. Then one day a mysterious visitor walked through his door.

The bookish, diminutive visitor explained that his company wanted to obtain specifications on the latest IBM had to offer: the new powerful disk drive dubbed the 3380. He emphasized how important the information might be to his company and how much gratitude it might be willing to show Palyn. He talked in a cool, businesslike, and calculating way to underscore the seriousness of his proposition. He then pulled out his business card and handed it to Paley. The visitor was Zkenji Hayashi, a senior engineer for the computer planning department of the Hitachi Corporation.

At first, Paley, Rossman, and Domenico didn't know what to make of Hayashi's request. They simply explained that the specifications would not be available until 1981, when IBM made its first 3380 customer shipment.

"What do you want the 3380 for?" asked Rossman. "Are you interested in reverse engineering?"

Hayashi explained that no, they were not interested in taking it apart to understand how it worked. Rather, his company wanted its new products to be compatible with IBM's product at a subsystem level—Hitachi wanted to ensure that its computer peripherals would be compatible with the new 3380. "We already have a compatible product," Hayashi said; it was just a matter of confirming the technical specifications of the 3380.

Trouble was, Hayashi was lying. Hitachi knew only a little about the 3380. But to admit the truth, Hayashi would have been revealing what he really wanted Paley to do: steal the specifications so Hitachi could be ready when the 3380 came on the market.

Several weeks after this first puzzling meeting with Hayashi, Paley and Domenico received invitations to meet with Hitachi officials in October at Hitachi's facility in Odawara, Japan. They accepted the invitation, as much out of curiosity as anything else. This was Hitachi's cutting-edge facility, where the company designed and manufactured disk drives and other computer peripherals. The Odawara meeting started where the first meeting with Hayashi had left off. Senior Hitachi officials expressed their interest in the specifications of the IBM 3380. This time the request came from Katsuhiko Kato, the manager responsible for disk-storage engineering at Hitachi. He assured Domenico that Hitachi had already developed an equivalent project. All they wanted was the IBM specifications. The meeting ended as the first one had, with Paley puzzled by what exactly Hitachi was asking him to do.

It was on an unusually muggy California day, August 19, 1981, that Hayashi made another pitch to Paley. This time he met Paley and his associates in the Palyn offices in Santa Clara and brought with him Katsumi Takeda, an engineer in the San Jose offices of the Computer Sales and Service Division of Hitachi America. Takeda was brought along to underscore Hayashi's line on the first visit: Hitachi's keen interest in the IBM 3380 specifications. But he also wanted to know what Rossman thought about IBM's new central-processing units with a thirty-one-bit addressing capability. Domenico offered to sell Hitachi a Palyn report on the IBM 3081 and gave Hayashi the index to that report as a prospectus to take back to his superiors so they could think about it.

One week later, on August 26, Hayashi sent a telex to Rossman, indicating that he wanted to acquire the Palyn report on the IBM 3081. Then Hayashi suddenly dropped a bombshell. He explained that the Palyn report would help to supplement information Hitachi had from some of

IBM's top-secret *Adironadack Workbooks*. The series was well-known in industry circles but had been seen by only a select few. Cadet's secret was now out, shared carelessly with Palyn.

Rossman quickly showed the telex to Paley, who knew the immense value of the workbooks. Suddenly it was clear why Hitachi wanted the information on the 3380: they already had the specifications on it, thanks to the workbooks. Hitachi had not developed a similar system; they wanted information to supplement what they had to complete their technical knowledge. Once they had it, they would have a big head start in the race to develop 3380 peripherals, a market worth billions.

After reading the telex, Paley knew what he had to do. He picked up the phone and called his former boss at IBM, B. O. Evans, and explained the situation. "Bob," he sullenly told his old friend, "I think one of my clients has gotten your crown jewels."

He explained a little bit about what he had discovered but did not reveal the name of the company. Evans asked for a fuller briefing and pulled together IBM senior managers and security officials. Paley, Rossman, and Domenico met with IBM officials two weeks later to discuss the matter in detail. A key figure in the meeting was Assistant General Counsel Donato Evangelista, a tall and robust cigar chomper who oversaw the direct efforts to protect IBM's technology secrets. Paley and his associates described to him Hayashi's interest in the 3380 and how the telex clearly indicated the company had access to some of the highly secret and much-coveted *Adirondack Workbooks*.

After the meeting with Evangelista, a new player in the drama was brought in. The mere presence of Richard Callahan, the tall, distinguished-looking, white-haired security consultant, almost immediately raised eyebrows. "If you saw Callahan in the building," says one former executive, "you knew something big was going on or about to come down."

What Callahan brought to the case was a no-nonsense approach to security and a flair for catching even the most sophisticated technology thieves. But he also brought something else—a knowledge of PENGEM. It was through Callahan that the search for the workbooks and Operation PENGEM would converge. No one discussing the *Adirondack Workbooks* at IBM—except Callahan—knew about Operation PENGEM.

After Paley met with Callahan, officials at IBM convinced him to telex

Hitachi on September 14 to string Hayashi along. According to Callahan, "This telex was designed to keep the client's pursuit of IBM confidential information in abeyance until we could pursue the matter further. The telex emphasized the sensitive nature of the information Hitachi was seeking and cautioned against discussing such matters by international telex."

Callahan was convinced that PENGEM would be helpful and would send a powerful message to IBM's rivals who might be tempted to steal the company's secrets. So he approached his friends at the bureau about getting involved. At first, says Assistant U.S. Attorney Greg Ward, "the FBI wasn't sure it wanted to get involved." After all, the PENGEM trap was designed to stop Soviet espionage, not spies from an allied country. But in the end, Callahan convinced the bureau that the crime was indeed serious and that Hitachi's activities posed a real threat to America's technological security.

On September 15, Callahan brought together Palyn Associates and IBM's director of security, Joe Rosetti, to make plans for the next move. With the telex Paley was persuaded to send, Hitachi had been placated and time had been bought. Now it was time to begin building the trap that would snare Hitachi. It was decided that Callahan would travel with Paley and Domenico to Tokyo to brief them before they met with the Hitachi officials. Callahan wanted to be certain that Hitachi's claim of holding the "crown jewels" was not just a bluff. He also hoped to get some idea of where the company had got the *Adirondacks*. Callahan would stay behind the scenes in Tokyo, but he planned to be close by when Paley and Domenico met with Hayashi, in case something went wrong.

On October 2, 1981, Domenico and Paley met with Hayashi at the Imperial Hotel in Tokyo while Callahan lurked in the shadows, out of sight. Domenico was carrying a complete index of the IBM *Adirondack Workbooks,* which had been provided by Callahan for displaying to Hayashi to confirm that these were indeed the books Hitachi had got its hands on. The index was clearly labeled IBM CONFIDENTIAL RESTRICTED and DO NOT COPY, a not-so-subtle reminder to the Hitachi officials that the books were private, confidential IBM information.

Hayashi confirmed that, yes, indeed, Hitachi did have some of the workbooks, but not all of them. He and other Hitachi officials wanted to obtain the others "by any means necessary," however. He then took Domenico's index and placed letters next to each one of the books listed, establishing priorities for getting the other books. A was for top priority, B for intermediate priority, and C for those workbooks Hitachi already had but wanted an updated version of, if they were available.

Hayashi was clearly pleased with the relationship he believed he was forging with Palyn. He was confident enough in the lavish surroundings of the Imperial Hotel to present Paley with a new laundry list of other IBM secrets Hitachi was interested in. It came in the form of handwritten questions entitled "Questions about New MVS."

Paley was amazed at Hayashi's candidness and the extent of the Hitachi wish list. The questions concerned IBM's latest computer system, the MVS/SP Version 2, a confidential project that was known to only a select few at IBM. The company wasn't even planning to mention the project until October 21, with projected availability set for the first three months of 1983. It had become clear to Paley that Hitachi had direct access to IBM's best-kept secrets. He could only wonder how much more information Hitachi had that Hayashi wasn't telling him about.

Paley pressed Hayashi for information about how the workbooks had been obtained in the first place. Much to Paley's surprise, Hayashi was quite open about Hitachi's operations in the United States. He said the workbooks had come from "a source" in the United States, but he also revealed that Takeda, who had visited Palyn earlier and was assigned to Hitachi America, was principally responsible for collecting information, by both overt and covert means. "Takeda has IBM friends," Hayashi told Paley with a large, sheepish grin. He also named Wannabe Inoue as a Hitachi employee engaged in intelligence gathering and espionage operations for the company, explaining that both Takeda and Inoue had "their own budgets" to acquire information "by any means." Nevertheless, Hayashi made clear to Paley, Hitachi was always interested in new "pipelines" that could pass secrets from IBM and other computer companies.

A second meeting was scheduled for October 6, again to take place at the Imperial. In the interim, Callahan debriefed Paley and Domenico. Paley told Callahan that Hitachi wanted "very badly" to obtain volumes 5, 14, 24, and 27 of the *Adirondack,* to complete the set. Callahan told Paley to fish for more information, to discover how extensive Hitachi's efforts were in the valley, and to get any details he could about Hitachi operations against IBM.

At the October 6 meeting, the Hitachi wish list grew. Hayashi brought along three volumes of the *Adirondack Workbooks,* proof that Hitachi did indeed have the confidential, highly valuable IBM materials. Also along for the meeting was Yoshiyuki Hirano, who was connected with Hitachi's central research laboratory and was involved in the company's IBM 3380–Equivalent project, an effort to make Hitachi products compatible with IBM systems almost immediately after the IBM systems were developed.

Hirano said that Hitachi was interested in getting a sneak preview of the IBM 3380, to take photographs and get specifications. He emphasized that Hitachi would pay handsomely for such access. Paley, on the advice of Callahan, agreed to arrange a secret viewing. In a near admission that he understood the deviousness of arranging such a viewing, Hirano made clear to Paley that given the sensitivity of a covert viewing, Hitachi management wanted to finance the operation through dummy or front companies, and they wanted funds and payoffs to flow through indirect channels. That would presumably avoid any embarrassment to Hitachi if the plan went amiss. He proposed going through such intermediaries as Nissei Electronics or establishing a new front company.

Hirano also told Paley that from then on communications regarding the workbooks should be in code. He said that telexes would henceforth go through the secure diplomatic channels of the Japanese consulate in San Francisco. He also proposed setting up code words for discussing the plan, suggesting "H Series Forecast Study" or "Memory Hierarchy Study Phase II."

The meeting was ended, and Paley was given instructions to contact Takeda in San Francisco about "making arrangements."

On October 13, after the Americans returned to California, Domenico called Takeda at the San Francisco offices of Hitachi America. He asked whether Takeda had spoken with Hayashi about the recent meetings in Tokyo. Takeda replied that he had received telex instructions based on the meetings. According to FBI officials, the telex had come through diplomatic cables, through the Japanese consulate, and was given to Takeda by a commercial representative at the consulate. For the first time, it became clear that the Japanese government was involved in the illegal acquisition of IBM secrets, by supporting Hitachi's efforts.

Callahan, upon returning to the United States, contacted his old friends at the FBI about the Tokyo meetings. He felt the groundwork had been laid for PENGEM to swing into full force. He had been truly distressed about Japanese access to IBM information, finding all the sophistication expected from a Soviet operation for stealing high-tech secrets. On October 23, 1981, Ken Thompson of the FBI met with Callahan in San Jose to discuss ways to pursue the matter. Thompson and Callahan agreed to set up a sting operation, using the private viewing of the IBM 3081 as an appetizer. Once Hitachi officials had their appetites whetted, the FBI would snare them when they came for the main dish: the list of technical information Hayashi had presented to Paley in Tokyo.

The FBI would work through a dummy storefront consulting firm it had only recently established in Santa Monica. Glenmar Associates appeared at first glance to be the typical high-tech consulting firm, but it was manned and operated by FBI special agents, who had a wide array of electronic gadgetry that would be useful in counterespionage campaigns. The FBI would direct the operation through Glenmar, recording transactions and conversations with Hitachi officials on hidden video cameras and wireless microphones. It was agreed by both Thompson and Callahan that Glenmar Associates would be offered to Hayashi as the firm arranging the private viewing of the 3380. The price would be ten thousand dollars, a small price for Hitachi to pay for what the company saw as an enormous help in its planning.

On October 27, Assistant U.S. Attorney Greg Ward was brought in from San Jose to discuss the implementation of the program and the sting plan. Ward agreed that the FBI should use undercover agents to meet Hitachi's representatives and that the viewing should be used as the means of setting it up. In the meantime, IBM had transferred a complete set of *Adirondack Workbooks* to the FBI, to be used by Glenmar to establish credibility in the eyes of Hayashi. Paley called Hayashi and told him about Glenmar, which he described as a firm that could be "very helpful" in giving Hitachi what it wanted.

Between October 26 and November 6, arrangements were made for Special Agent Alan Garretson to meet Hayashi in Las Vegas. The FBI now took over. Meanwhile, Hitachi officials, anxious to get their secrets, knew nothing.

As the investigation progressed, the FBI assumed control of all aspects of the operation. Paley and Domenico were gradually replaced by Callahan and the FBI agents, principally Special Agent Alan Garretson. In late November 1981, the transfer of control was completed when Paley introduced Callahan and Garretson to Hayashi as consultants who could acquire the information Hitachi sought. They claimed to work for Glenmar Associates, which they described as a high-tech-information consulting firm.

The early viewing of the 3380, code-named Operation Odawara Study by Hitachi officials, was to be spearheaded by Jun Naruse, a senior engineer at Hitachi. An ambitious and highly intelligent specialist, Naruse was straight business and hard as nails. Callahan and Garretson agreed to set up a viewing at the Pratt and Whitney facility in Hartford, Connecticut, and requested the ten thousand dollars. Naruse emphasized that he wanted to pay in cash and warned Callahan that if the viewing went wrong, there would be "big trouble." Callahan assured Naruse that there was no need to worry.

At 5:00 A.M. on November 15, 1981, a cold New England morning, Garretson met with Naruse in a Hartford hotel lobby. From there, they drove directly to a parking lot near Pratt and Whitney, where they met a man who gave each of them identification badges to gain entrance to the facility. The plan was going like clockwork. Garretson handed the man an envelope and explained to Naruse that it contained money. In fact, it contained nothing of the sort—the man in the parking lot was an FBI special agent.

Garretson, Naruse, and the third man left the parking lot and drove to Pratt and Whitney headquarters, where they produced their identity badges and were readily admitted. They slowly and quietly weaved their way through the facility, avoiding eye contact with individuals they met in the hallway. After a ten-minute walk, they approached a locked door with a sophisticated combination lock. At that point, the man told Garretson and Naruse to hide in a nearby darkened office while he got a guard to unlock the door. Eventually they gained access to the 3380. Everything went smoothly, and Naruse took numerous photos. The third man instructed Naruse not to take any pictures that might expose the background and thereby allow the location of the 3081 to be determined. Naruse agreed, but said he did want a memento. Smug about his triumph, he persuaded Garretson to photograph him hugging the 3380.

On December 2, 1981, Garretson received a letter from Hayashi, thanking him for the courtesy extended to Naruse. But Palyn never received its 15-percent "commission" on the ten-thousand-dollar fee for arranging the viewing, which Hitachi had promised. Since everything had to look like a strict, serious business operation, Callahan complained to Hayashi on Palyn's behalf. At first, the Hitachi representative suggested that Palyn sell the IBM workbooks to other companies in order to make up the money lost on the commission. When Callahan persisted, Hayashi arranged for Palyn to get some money for "miscellaneous consulting."

For the FBI, the ultimate purpose of the sting was to catch Hitachi transporting stolen goods. But for Callahan and IBM, it was critical that they uncover the source inside IBM who had taken the workbooks in the first place. The person who had given the books to someone outside the company had to be caught. Otherwise the flow of valuable information would continue unabated, with or without the indictment of Hayashi. On November 11, 1981, Paley and Domenico held a meeting with Hayashi, and they pressed him for the name of the original source. To their surprise, Hayashi was again very open: he explained that Hitachi had procured the workbooks from Saffaie. He even sent Paley a letter containing a diagram showing how they had been taken by Cadet and how the former-IBM employee and Saffaie had sold them to Hitachi. IBM was very pleased. It was now time to move the operation into its final phase.

Hitachi was still very interested in the MVS/SP Version 2 operating system, and they indicated that they would be willing to pay handsomely for information regarding the system's specifications and design. Garretson told Hayashi in a November meeting that in order to acquire the necessary modules, it would be necessary to steal the source code. Hayashi said he recognized that, and that for his trouble Garretson would get a fee of between fifty thousand and one hundred thousand dollars.

The transfer of funds from Hitachi to Glenmar was a constant source of tension in the relationship. Hayashi, unlike Naruse, said Hitachi was uncomfortable paying cash because such a payment would be "discrete" on the company's books. It was "contrary to the company's image," and he suggested that a "tunnel company" be set up to channel the money. The tunnel company would front for Hitachi and, it was hoped, would prevent a paper trail that would link Hitachi with the payments to Glenmar. Hayashi made clear to Garretson and Paley that he knew the criminal nature of his efforts and that Hitachi needed to be protected at all cost. Callahan, in a later letter, agreed to the arrangement. He wrote that "the fake contract you suggest would be a further protection for Hitachi and Glenmar, and I think it is an excellent suggestion."

In a December 1981 meeting, Michihiro Hirai, a representative of Hitachi's Kanagawa facility, asked Garretson whether he could provide 3081 design documents. He said yes, but for a price. Garretson told Hirai point-blank that his source would be taking a great risk by procuring them and that he could "lose his job and would go to jail if he were caught." The money Hayashi had offered earlier was not adequate, said Garretson. Hirai told Garretson that money was no object.

For the FBI to move in and make arrests, it was necessary to prove that the Hitachi conspirators knew the exact criminal nature of their operation. In December 1981, Callahan wrote an aggressive letter to Hayashi, warning him of the criminal nature of what he was asking Callahan to do.

Beginning in early 1982, the Hitachi conspiracy moved into a new phase. In March, Hitachi officials inquired of Callahan and Paley about the possibility of their procuring "the assistance" of retiring IBM executives, to learn more about the IBM computer program. They made clear that they wanted former executives who could get them the design documents for the IBM 3081 and that they would pay $150,000 to any former executive who provided the documents. In addition, they offered annual "salaries" of $30,000 to $40,000 to retain the services of these former executives for a period of twenty-five to thirty days a year. Spying for the Soviet Union would never have been so profitable.

Callahan, on first hearing the proposal, played his role perfectly. He claimed that such a scheme could work only if more senior Hitachi officials were brought in. He told Hayashi that IBM executives were of a high caliber and only with assurances from the highest level at Hitachi would they consider such an offer. He used the suggestion as leverage to climb the Hitachi corporate ladder, to determine the corporate height from which the Hitachi conspiracy was being directed.

But as the pieces of the sting operation slowly fell into place, a new quarter was exerting pressure on the FBI for a quick move on Hitachi. There was growing concern in IBM that the costs of participating in the sting might be too high. Increasingly, crucial computer information was being given to Hitachi, and although IBM officials attempted to minimize the value of the information by editing, altering, and revising some of the critical data, they could not be assured that the information was unusable, and they feared the damage to the company could be enormous. In January 1982, Hitachi purchased from undercover FBI agents the source microcode for IBM's 3033 Extended Function system and a read/write head for the 3380 for a total of twenty-two thousand dollars. Some at Big Blue thought the information could be extremely valuable to Hitachi and feared what the effect might be if too much more found its way into Hitachi hands.

On May 12, 1982, the final deal of many was arranged. Garretson informed Hayashi and Dr. Ksaburo Nakazawa, general manager of the Kanagawa facility, that the information they had requested had been pro-cured. The Peak Architecture, five volumes of the *Adirondack Workbooks*, a thermal-conduction module board, the complete source code for the MVS/SP Version 2, and source microcodes for the 3380 and 3081 had all been acquired by Glenmar and was ready for purchase. The potential value of this information was enormous. It would give Hitachi the opportunity to draw even technologically with IBM in the development of personal computers, promising potentially hundreds of millions of dollars in new revenue. Garretson recognized the value of the materials and offered it for $700,000, with $30,000 in advance. On May 17, Hayashi called with a counteroffer: $525,000. Garretson agreed. The bait was taken. The trap would now be set.

The two parties agreed to meet on June 21 in Santa Clara to discuss the transfer. Garretson and Callahan met with Hayashi and Ohmishi. The two Americans insisted on confidentiality, telling Hayashi that if it became known that Hitachi had confidential IBM information, a manhunt would ensue. Hayashi gave Callahan his personal assurance that Callahan had nothing to fear. He even instructed Callahan to call Sadao Kawano, the deputy manager at Hitachi's Odawara facility, to get Kawano's personal assurance of confidentiality. Hayashi made it clear that Hitachi had a "special design room" where these sorts of goods were kept, and they hadn't had a leak yet. Only four persons would have access to the room, they assured Callahan. All indications were that this sort of activity was nothing new to Hitachi.

At the meeting, Hayashi closely examined the MVS/SP Version 2 source code, the TCM board, and the 3081 design documents. They were genuine, up-to-date, and exactly what Hitachi had wanted. With pleasure, Hayashi made the final arrangements with Callahan. He and his cohort agreed to pick up the material at the Glenmar offices at nine o'clock the next morning. In the meantime, Hayashi would have employees at NCL Data, a subsidiary, transfer the more-than-half-a-million-dollar payoff to Garretson's bank. Hayashi left the meeting with a large grin on his face. Everything was set—or so he thought.

The next morning at the scheduled time Hayashi and Ohmishi arrived at Glenmar in Yoshida's brown Volkswagen to claim their goods. Yoshida stayed in the car, keeping watch, while Hayashi went into the office. Upon seeing the materials, Hayashi was ecstatic. He picked up an IBM carton, ripping off the IBM CONFIDENTIAL sticker, and promptly put the sticker on his clipboard as a souvenir. He laughed, bragging, "These are the property of Hitachi now!"

Just as the last word trickled out, the doors to the offices flew open, and armed FBI agents flooded the room. "FBI! It's all over. We are FBI agents!"

Hayashi fell into a nearby chair. He held his head in his hands, shaking it in disbelief. Totally ashamed, he began to whimper.

Within minutes of Hayashi's arrest, FBI agents moved into a number of other locations: they arrested Yoshida outside, waiting in his Volkswagen; they picked up Inoue and Shirai in San Francisco. The next day they arrested Saffaie just as he was leaving his office at National Advanced Systems for lunch.

The sting was complete. Business and political leaders on both sides of the Pacific were stunned. FBI Director William Webster called the operation a complete success, an "example of effective bureau enforcement of the law." Reactions in Japan were otherwise. Hitachi refused to apologize. The only mention of the case by the giant's president, Katsu-shige Mita, was in a meeting of company stockholders in Tokyo on June 28. In a businesslike manner, he said, "It is regrettable for us to be a target of suspicion, and I apologize to our stockholders and all the people concerned for all the inconveniences caused to you." He stopped short of admitting any wrongdoing in the case. Taiyu Kobayashi, chairman of the electronics giant Fujitsu called Paley "traitorious" for tipping off IBM and, as a result, the FBI. The Japanese press, while reporting the incident, analyzed the problem as one of image, not illegal behavior. The influential daily *Yomiuri Shimbun* said, "Whatever the truth of the matter, the worst thing is that it may strengthen the American public's view that Japan is a 'sneaky' country." One member of the Japanese cabinet said that Japan had been "slapped in the face" by the FBI.

Hitachi officials at the highest levels were implicated in the espionage operation. Dr. Nakazawa, the Kanagawa general manager, one of Hitachi's more important posts, was implicated as a conspirator. So, too, were other senior executives. The shear volume of money being poured into the operation indicates that this was no rogue plan concocted by Hitachi subordinates. "To be able to deliver six hundred thousand dollars for this sort of thing, boy, you need approval from the very highest levels," says one FBI agent involved in the sting. "A lower-level, overly zealous employee might have misunderstood his mission, and he could have access to twenty-six thousand dollars. But the amount involved with Hitachi is much greater, and it is unlikely that a lower-level employee could raise more than $600,000," says Ulric Weil, an industry analyst at Morgan Stanley and Company.

The FBI had hundreds of hours of video- and audiotape documenting Hitachi's efforts. Questions about the company's intentions and efforts in the case were never in doubt. And yet in the end, the cost to Hitachi was not so great. A California federal court fined the company a paltry ten thousand dollars. As Congressman Doug Walgren of Pennsylvania noted at the time, "The fine is so low that it is just a cost of doing business to a company like Hitachi." The judge overseeing the case ruled against any jail terms for the conspirators. "Confinement," he declared, "would not seem to serve any purpose." The Japanese government did not pressure Hitachi to force the conspirators to stand trial, and few of them appeared in court; in all, twelve Japanese defendants in the case never even came to the United States for the trial. What did hurt Hitachi was an out-of-court settlement of civil damages: reportedly some three hundred million dollars was paid to IBM.

And yet in the larger scheme of things, even with the civil settlement, Hitachi perhaps still came out ahead. In Japan, there was a surge of support for the company and a coolness toward IBM. "Many users of IBM machines have told me they are thinking of switching to Hitachi," wrote Yasou Naito, editor-in-chief of the newsletter *Nikkei Computer*. Hitachi computer sales increased after the sting operation. The U.S. Social Security Administration even went so far as to grant Hitachi a seven-million-dollar contract over IBM only two months after the case.

Hitachi was well ahead of the competition in bringing out computer products very similar to those accompanying the IBM 3081. And in August of 1982, the Japanese firm unveiled its newest computer, which was also very similar to the IBM product. The information Hitachi had obtained through the sting proved enormously helpful to the company. And although in the California court that tried the case it agreed not to use the information it had obtained for the development of its systems, the knowledge was already so firmly integrated into Hitachi's research and design program that the promise proved meaningless.

Hitachi also seemed undeterred by PENGEM and the sting. Burned by what it saw as an IBM trap, the company, with the cooperation of the Japanese government, embarked on an effort to get revenge, of sorts, on IBM. A Japanese consortium made up of Hitachi and other companies, working through surrogates and distributors in Europe, pressured several European companies into supporting the European Economic Community's antitrust suit initially brought against IBM in 1980. Hitachi's hope was that during the trial, or as part of the settlement, IBM would be forced to reveal many of its most valuable trade secrets.

Pressure was most directly applied on two European companies heavily reliant on Hitachi technologies for the production and distribution of their goods. Both Olivetti and BASF were threatened with the withdrawal of millions of dollars in contracts, according to company officials, unless they joined in the suit against IBM. As the predominant supplier of computers to Olivetti and BASF, Hitachi was in a prime position to exert pressure. The European companies had little choice, and they joined in the suit. Fortunately for IBM, the case did not force the company to reveal its secrets, and the Hitachi gambit for revenge failed.

4

Stagehands in the Dark

The Japanese are experts in the matter. . . .
—Count de Marenches, former director of French intelligence

In Japanese playhouses, there are no stage curtains. If the scenery needs to be changed or props moved, the stage is slowly darkened, and stagehands dressed in black move stealthily about the stage, making the necessary changes. If they do their job well, they aren't seen or heard.

In some ways, Japan's industrial spies have performed like stagehands in assisting the country's monumental climb to economic preeminence. Spying has played an enormous role in Japan's ability to manufacture and develop high technologies. The Hitachi campaign against IBM is by no means an isolated case when it comes to the Japanese intelligence effort against the United States. A House Energy and Commerce Committee's oversight and investigations subcommittee reviewing the Hitachi case in July of 1983 concluded that the case was "just the tip of the iceberg." The committee's chairman, Congressman John Dingell of Michigan, was particularly concerned about the committee's findings, saying that "we must not overlook the national security implications of this problem." Admiral Bob Inman, a former director of the National

Security Agency and deputy director of the CIA during the Hitachi-IBM case, shares the opinion of the House Energy and Commerce Committee on the case. "There was and is significantly more going on than just this one case," he says. Adds Herb Meyer, former vice chairman of the National Intelligence Council at the CIA, "The only unusual thing is [Hitachi] got caught."

As director of French intelligence from 1981 to 1982, Pierre Marion found a vast amount of evidence of Japanese industrial espionage. "Well," he says, "it's clear to me that Japan has always engaged in technological and industrial espionage. And there Japan is very much at an advantage over the other countries, because it's clear that the Japanese corporations are very much sealed from the outside. It's very difficult for a foreigner to enter it and to know what's going on in it. On the contrary, the Western corporations are quite open and Japan is taking advantage of that." What methods have Japanese government and company officials used? "They do it by eavesdropping, they do it by taking notes, they do it by putting moles in companies, and they do it by recruiting moles in companies."

In part, say U.S. intelligence officials, these activities reflect a Japanese corporate attitude. Says Dr. Ray Cline, a former deputy director of the CIA, "Japanese corporations feel they have an obligation and a right to discover foreign technology, and that often means stealing it from U.S. companies." Former CIA Director William Colby, who has consulted for Japanese companies, concurs. He notes that when Japanese companies collect information in the United States, they regularly "cut corners." "The Hitachi case didn't surprise me one bit," he adds.

Other Japanese companies have been surprisingly open about their espionage campaigns to steal secrets from IBM. In a remarkable interview in the Japanese monthly *Bungei Shunju*, Taiyu Kobayashi, chairman of the electronics giant Fujitsu, openly admitted to organizing intelligence operations against IBM that were similar to Hitachi's. Kobayashi claimed that Fujitsu's campaign was more subtle than Hitachi's but also more effective.

Fujitsu had to know "exactly what IBM had up its sleeve" so they could produce computers that could run the IBM software programs dominating the world market, Kobayashi said. Hence, Fujitsu needed to arrange to have information "funneled" from IBM covertly. Kobayashi faulted Hitachi, not for its efforts, but for its technique, one that he claimed

Fujitsu had mastered. "It is not a good idea to obtain secret information from IBM directly from IBM," he said. "You are just asking to be done in. But in the United States, individuals have the freedom to move about wherever they wish." He advocated using free-lancers to do the work directly for Fujitsu. His company had done just that in an effort to broaden its market share in computers and computer technology. Unable to compete directly with IBM, either in technology or in design, Fujitsu had embarked on a series of operations aimed at stealing IBM secrets. "Fujitsu was groping around, desperately trying to figure out how to put its hands on, or how to buy, IBM's secret architectural concepts," Kobayashi told *Bungei Shunju.* Fujitsu picked the late 1970s as the moment to move. The time was ripe, according to Kobayashi, because IBM was bogged down in a major U.S. antitrust suit "and was hamstrung. It was in no position to retaliate." The timing was critical, according to Kobayashi. Hitachi got caught, he insisted, because the Reagan administration had freed IBM from the antitrust case.

The Kobayashi interview would have made fascinating reading in the United States, offering a candid, straight-from-the-source confirmation of what had long been suspected in computer circles: that Japanese companies were spying on U.S. companies. In January of 1983, the *Washington Post* had plans to reprint the Kobayashi interview. It secured the rights to do so from *Bungei Shunju,* but Fujitsu got wind of the plans and pressured the monthly to cancel the agreement. "Fujitsu suggested that the complete version not be printed in the *Washington Post,*" said a spokesman for the public relations firm of Ruder and Finn, which represents Fujitsu in this country.

Fujitsu's targets may not have been limited to IBM. According to industry officials, Fujitsu may have helped plant a mole in the high-tech company Fairchild Semiconductors, an industry leader in computer technology that experienced financial difficulties throughout the 1980s. According to security officials, a Japanese mole was in place at Fairchild between 1977 and 1986 and did substantial damage to the company, providing large volumes of information to Fairchild competitors, including, most specifically, Japanese computer manufacturers. The extensiveness of the information Fujitsu was being funneled may have played a big part in its plans to purchase Fairchild in 1986.

As far as security officials at Fairchild are able to surmise, the mole, a middle-level researcher, worked on the production of high-density computer microchips and was deeply involved in researching their further development. As described in Chapter 2, he is believed to have stolen some 160,000 pages of confidential research results and corporate plans, transferring them to consultants in Silicon Valley, who then sold them to the Japanese consulate in San Francisco and Japanese electronics giants, including Fujitsu.

Suspicion hinges on Fujitsu's apparent knowledge of the secret plans Cray Research Corporation was making with Fairchild Semiconductors for closer collaboration in the production of supercomputers. Cray was the world leader in the field, supplying advanced computers to America's intelligence agencies and military services. But when several of the Japanese suppliers Cray relied on for critical semiconductor components made plans to enter the lucrative supercomputer market themselves, Cray found itself vulnerable to companies that would soon be its competitors. No doubt their advantage over Cray would be useful in their efforts to secure part of the market. In one instance, a major Cray supplier in Japan delayed the delivery of certain new components that Cray needed to finish a product, thus giving its own computer group a one-year lead in designing a compatible system for its own machines. Cray's striking an agreement with Fairchild to supply the necessary semiconductors and components would have been a way around the problem. A special joint project between the two companies was begun in an attempt to develop a domestic supplier.

What is curious, according to security officials at Fairchild, was Fujitsu's apparent extensive knowledge of the agreement long before it was announced publicly and before it was known by many in Silicon Valley. "Fujitsu by a number of means acted in ways in an attempt to aggravate the agreement, long before they would have even known about it," says one official. "Based on the other information we have, I don't think that it was just a coincidence."

Fairchild officials began an intensive security campaign in October of 1983 to find the mole and plug the leak. Company officials concentrated their efforts mostly on tracking the movements of both known Japanese agents in the valley and the consulting firms that gathered intelligence for Japanese companies. The hope was that by tracking their movements around the Fairchild Semiconductors research facility, Fairchild might catch someone contacting the source. And while in the end they never caught the mole, they did come close.

According to company officials, they tracked the movements of a Japanese official named Korekiyo Tamaki, a commercial representative at the consulate in San Francisco. It was discovered that Tamaki was a frequent patron of the bar and restaurant at the Holiday Inn near the Fairchild facility. Although there was perhaps nothing unusual about that, what company officials did find interesting were reports from the bar's employees. They claimed that Tamaki met regularly with an American, blond, and well dressed. The American was also fluent in Japanese, and was presumably the Fairchild employee. Conversations between the two were conducted exclusively in Japanese as they sat in the Holiday Inn lounge. The bartenders and waiters were naturally unable to understand the conversations, but on several occasions they did see material being transferred, sometimes paper, but also computer diskettes. These Holiday Inn employees estimated that the meetings took place every two weeks, on early Friday evenings. The two would meet, hold a conversation for approximately twenty minutes, exchange materials, and then depart.

On March 14, 1984, Fairchild officials decided to wait for Tamaki in the restaurant at the Holiday Inn, hoping to witness a meeting and thus identify the possible source. At approximately six-thirty, Tamaki showed up, briefcase in hand. He sat down and ordered a drink, yet he appeared uneasy and slowly got up and left the bar, leaving his briefcase behind. Fairchild officials speculate that perhaps he was making a phone call to his source. The reason for what happened next is unclear. Tamaki returned to his table five minutes later, picked up his briefcase, and left. He didn't bother to taste his drink or to pay for it. The meetings at the Holiday Inn lounge apparently ceased after that date, as Fairchild officials, who continued to keep the place under surveillance, never saw Tamaki there again.

Fujitsu's October 23, 1986, bid to purchase 80 percent of Fairchild came as a surprise to company officials at Cray. The move was well timed, disrupting research that Cray and Fairchild had been conducting on new semiconductor components. Fujitsu appeared to know the full extent of the research program, and company officials at Fairchild speculate that the

Japanese firm may have been a recipient of information that Tamaki had been collecting from his Fairchild source. The mole was also known to be selling information to Silicon Valley consulting firms, which may very well have sold it directly to Fujitsu.

Within the U.S. intelligence community, it has been a firmly held tenet that most Japanese intelligence assets have been directed toward the United States and Western Europe and have not been directed toward the People's Republic of China or the former Soviet Union, viewed historically as the most direct threats to Japan's security. The CIA's 1987 classified report *Japan: Foreign Intelligence and Security Services* claimed that Japanese intelligence priorities were these:

- Intelligence regarding access to foreign sources of raw materials, including oil and food

- Detailed intelligence on technological and scientific developments in the United States and Western Europe

- Intelligence on political decision making in the United States and Europe, most specifically, intelligence relating to trade, monetary, and military policy in Asia and the Pacific region

- Intelligence pertaining to internal political and military developments in the Soviet Union, the People's Republic of China, and North Korea

The report concluded that 80 percent of all Japanese-government intelligence assets were directed toward the United States and Western Europe and concentrated on acquiring secrets about and information on technological developments. According to William Colby, "In general terms, most countries develop intelligence services to meet their needs." In the case of Japan, he says, the needs are mostly economic. The CIA report also noted the critical "intelligence-gathering role" played by semi-official organizations, such as the Japanese External Trade Organization, and Japanese multinational corporations like Hitachi. It noted that in many respects the intelligence operations of Japanese multinational corporations were every bit as sophisticated as the intelligence services of smaller countries.

"Japan does have a very widespread commercial intelligence network," says ex-CIA official John Quinn. He considers Mitsubishi and other massive Japanese multinationals to be vigorous collectors of industrial intelligence. According to Pierre Marion, "All the corporations of Japan are very strongly organized in that direction. There are members of Japanese corporations who travel abroad, and they have responsibility for gathering intelligence, by any means."

The Japanese Ministry for International Trade and Industry and the Japanese External Trade Organization also play an important role, according to Marion. "I think MITI has offices in practically all the countries, including JETRO offices. And their responsibility is clearly an intelligence-gathering function." Admiral Pierre Lacoste, who took over for Marion as head of French intelligence in 1982, believes that the MITI intelligence-gathering apparatus is massive. He says, "They are incredible in what they collect. Something like five hundred thousand messages are sent from MITI and JETRO offices around the world back to Tokyo every day. I understand that these messages are based on information collected both overtly and covertly."

Other observers have drawn similar conclusions about the focus of Japanese intelligence and its central concern with gathering information on the United States and Western Europe. Ambassador Michael B. Smith says, "I never assumed the Japanese devoted much of their intelligence assets to watching the Soviets. They have always been more interested in us and our technology." Robyn Shotwell Metcalfe, a computer-industry consultant and writer, has estimated that "about 85 to 90% of Japan's intelligence-gathering resources are applied toward enhancing its economic and technical status." Others who follow and understand Japanese intelligence put the effort at about the same share.

But Japanese intelligence efforts directed toward the United States not only take a vast share of the espionage pie, but are also highly sophisticated and effective. In 1980, for example, Harlow Unger, a business writer, declared that "the economic future of American electronic firms is now being threatened by the activities of Japanese industrial spies prowling California's famed 'Silicon Valley.' " But perhaps the greatest compliment that spies and intelligence services can get is from a fellow practitioner in another country. Count de Marenches, the flamboyant aristocrat who headed the French intelligence service in the 1970s, says that when it comes to industrial espionage and intelligence, "the Japanese are experts in the matter."

The Japanese intelligence system is in many ways unlike any other intelligence system in the world. After all, how many intelligence services have as their primary mission helping to make their country more prosperous and economically competitive? With the exception of Japan, no other foreign intelligence service concentrates so much of its energy on gathering intelligence that is useful economically.

Japan does devote a significant portion of its intelligence assets to traditional military and security concerns. The country has shown a particular interest in the movement of Soviet naval forces in the seas of East Asia and maintains electronic eavesdropping facilities toward that end. But because Japan's constitution limits its spending for defense to approximately 1 percent of its gross national product, the size of its military forces has been restricted, thereby limiting the need for many orthodox forms of intelligence gathering. Japan's intelligence needs have also been alleviated by the United States, which maintains enormous intelligence-gathering operations in the region. In addition, Japan has been, and in the immediate future will continue to be, a power with truly worldwide interests in economics and commercial affairs but only regional interests in politics and the military.

But Japan's intelligence operations are different as well because they rely less on formal intelligence services than on a wide network of institutions in Japanese society. The largest Japanese corporations have very sophisticated intelligence and espionage capabilities. In ways that might make traditional spy agencies envious, Japanese multinational corporations have gained access to classified CIA national intelligence estimates through the hiring of consultants. Through the direction of the Ministry for International Trade and Industry, which one U.S. senior counterintelligence official calls "the pinnacle of the Japanese intelligence system," these corporations have also engaged in industrial espionage to ferret out extremely valuable American corporate secrets.

† † †

The development of a Japanese intelligence system that worked in cooperation with the government and industry began in the 1950s, when the government began to subsidize the worldwide travel of Japanese businessmen. The purpose of the travel was not only to make trade agreements but also to gather intelligence on foreign technological developments and to bring that information back home. The results of this global probe have been truly phenomenal. By 1956, MITI established a systematic arrangement for sending businessmen overseas, establishing a rule that no fewer than ten thousand persons would be sent abroad per year—principally to the United States—to bring back technology. William H. Forbis, who studied this phenomenon, concluded that it was a profound success: "For a grand total of 2.5 billion dollars, which is only a tenth of what the United States spends every year on research and development, these emissaries bought virtually all the technology of the Western World." Raymond Wannall, a former FBI assistant director for intelligence who spent more than thirty years in the bureau, remembers the clandestine side of the Japanese effort in the United States. He recalls hearing reports from time to time about Japanese intelligence operations on the West Coast, beginning in the early 1950s. "After the end of the war their intelligence apparatus was dismantled. They did have some operations on the West Coast shortly after it, but it was pretty crude. It got more sophisticated as time went on."

One of the many officials involved in this massive intelligence and espionage effort is the current Japanese prime minister, Kiichi Miyazawa. During the 1950s, Miyazawa was an aide in the Japanese Ministry of Finance and a translator-interpreter for senior Japanese officials traveling in the United States. According to a former colleague, on several occasions Miyazawa served as a courier, bringing back to Tokyo intelligence that Japanese agents had obtained from U.S. companies. On at least one occasion in 1961, Miyazawa acted as translator for a member of the Japanese Foreign Ministry who was meeting with several Japanese businessmen in the United States. They had been collecting intelligence on the American steel industry, and they were sharing their results.

Japanese legal intelligence operations have also been widespread and sophisticated. France's de Marenches, who had his share of run-ins with the Japanese, describes this method:

> If the Japanese notice that in this or that high-technology indus-
> try they need a certain machine, they look at the global situation and
> come to the conclusion that, maybe, the French and the Swiss are
> world-leaders in this type of product. They send in an initial delega-
> tion that declares, 'we are customers for some of your products. We
> represent X company in Japan and we want to buy some high-
> precision equipment.' People come rushing along because there is
> talk of big contracts. Factories are thrown open to visitors, who
> generally go in twos or threes with a couple of cameras swinging on
> their stomachs. They ask to see certain machines. If inside one of
> these machines there is a particularly interesting technical innova-
> tion, the matter will be referred to at meetings of the chief delegate's
> party, at which detailed observations as well as photographs from
> successive visits are compared. The jobs are distributed: 'You will get
> so-and-so to talk. You'll take photos,' and so on.
>
> Next day, for the purposes of the visit, the factory is divided
> into segments. In the evening everyone meets in the suite of the
> luxury hotel where the head of the delegation is staying to analyze
> what has been garnered. It is all very well done. And the French
> industrialist, dazzled by the prospect of a fabulous contract, is ready
> to go so far as selling a few specimens of the product, only to come
> across them later on display in his Western market, 'Made in Japan,'
> and at a better price.

It has been called "the most efficient economic intelligence in the world." One reporter in Japan noted that "flocks of technological missions are seen queuing up every day at the Haneda airport departure gates" to be sent on "permanent watching assignments" at critical areas in the United States and Europe. These missions were organized and directed in part by the Japanese industrialist Yoshizane Iwasa. According to U.S. intelligence officials, it was Iwasa who helped determine the targets, orga-nize covers, and recruit agents.

In October of 1962, the campaign to gain access to foreign technol-ogy by use, in part, of espionage was organized even more formally when the Institute for Industrial Protection was established, its financial support coming from MITI, which continued to subsidize the institute for quite some time. In spite of its name, the school was avowedly established to train spies and counterspies for Japanese corporations, most to be sent overseas. Industrial espionage was already a well-established business practice in Japan by that time, with an estimated ten thousand commercial spies roaming foreign industries based in Japan.

The school was headed by a cagey seventy-year-old ex-spy named Tadashi Kurihara, the one-time Japanese ambassador to Turkey. Kurihara was lighthearted about his work, telling one reporter, "We wear trench coats for warmth, not atmosphere." The initial nine-man staff included seasoned operatives from Japan's wartime intelligence services, among them Yuzuru Fukamachi, a one-time navy code specialist with experience working against U.S. forces in the Pacific, and Tatsuo Furuya, the director of wartime intelligence for Japanese forces stationed in Shanghai.

The students at the institute are largely bright young executives in their late twenties. Their companies select them to attend the school and pay their tuition. During the four-month course, they learn how to use dozens of complex espionage devices. For example, they learn techniques to tap a telephone from a distance by beaming a ray from an infrared listening device into the receiver, and they learn to coat documents with a colorless dye that will penetrate even leather gloves and blacken the hands of anyone who touches the document.

One businessman who attended one of the two schools for industrial espionage in Japan in the early 1970s makes it clear whom the techniques were to be used against. "Other companies in Japan were always a possible target," says Ishiawara Watanabe. "But the examples they would use were U.S. [companies]. They would teach us, 'Here is what we can get and how we can get it from IBM or du Pont.' "

Literally thousands of Japanese businessmen have gone through these schools. The techniques are often used and refined on competitors. In one instance, for example, spies made use of the commuting habits of Japanese businesspeople. They identified commuter trains carrying mostly workers from a specific company and then hired students, who were given Walkman-type tape recorders and sent out to gather intelligence. The students recorded the conversations of the employees on the train as they went to and from work. The technique was very effective and has been employed in both Paris and New York, according to a former Japanese corporate spy.

Espionage paraphernalia is quite readily available for purchase in Japan. According to John Quinn, this includes a wide variety of eavesdropping equipment and bugs. "The interesting packaging leads me to believe that they are used widely in Japan," he says. "Some of these are disguised as pens, calculators. One of the more frightening ones looks like a common wall socket that could be plugged in and operated off the power in almost any company for years if it wasn't discovered. They are very high quality." Much of this equipment would be illegal in the United States; a lot of it is purchased by Japanese companies and shipped overseas for use.

Masayuki Taleuchi, an investigator with Tokyo's elite detective agency Kyshimoto Sogo Research Company, Limited, spends much of his time working for clients who think they are being bugged and spied on. He sees a continuing rise in espionage in Japan. "Industrial espionage is becoming common because more people can use the equipment," he says. "The products get smaller and easier to conceal."

William Farnell is the executive director of the American Chamber of Commerce in Japan. A twenty-year veteran of the U.S. Air Force intelligence organization and a former corporate-security consultant, he knows the business of spying and intelligence. For him, the availability of espionage equipment has made corporate spying in Japan very easy: "There's a lot of bugging going on because it's so easy to do now," he explains. "The equipment has become so sophisticated." And often the victims are foreign companies.

Quinn believes that the idea of spying on the competition intensified as Japan's economic power increased during the 1970s and, especially, during the 1980s. He says, "They now have very sophisticated and well-organized efforts."

Perhaps the greatest push in the use of foreign travelers to gather intelligence and spy on U.S. industry began in 1972, with the growing perception that an electronics boom, brought on by the invention of the microchip, was about to begin. Silicon Valley, a fertile strip of land in California once known for its fruit orchards, became the center of a worldwide revolution in electronics. The concentration of computer industries in such a small area made it the epicenter of development—and an easy target for industrial espionage.

It was in 1972 that the Japanese Diet mandated the establishment of an Electronics Industry Deliberation Council to direct the intelligence-gathering effort. Oversight was by MITI, whose Bureau of Heavy Industries set up an Information Room with a Special Survey Group to report on the U.S. computer industry. The effort was intense and highly successful. The Japanese goal was to leapfrog the United States in computer technology. Toward that end, in 1976 Japanese officials established a $250-million government-industry program of Very Large Scale Integration, whose stated aim was the development of all the highly advanced processes, manufacturing techniques, and components that Japan needed in order to be on the cutting edge in computer technology; VLSI included Hitachi, Fujitsu, Mitsubishi Electric, NEC, and Toshiba. MITI's Electrotechnical Laboratory acted not only as the coordinator but also as the information vacuum and spigot. A Committee on Information and Acquisitions was set up in the Electrotechnical Laboratory to direct the acquisition of foreign intelligence on technological developments in the United States. Funds were available to the committee for the purchase of information from individuals in the United States who were willing to sell it, whether legally or illegally. The committee worked with overseas representatives of the five VLSI companies and JETRO, as well as with designated employees at Japanese diplomatic posts in the United States, to seek out intelligence on microelectronic technologies.

Information obtained overseas, which was paid for by the committee, was channeled back to a VLSI "cooperative laboratory," which was located at NEC's facility near Tokyo. There the information was organized and classified and sent to the appropriate research facility to be analyzed and used. The cooperative laboratory focused on basic research. Two other facilities were concerned with potential applications of the research, including the development of so-called fourth-generation computers, whose capabilities were then unknown. One of these facilities worked to develop IBM-compatible computers, coordinating work done by Fujitsu, Hitachi, and Mitsubishi; the other lab organized the work of NEC and Toshiba on non-IBM compatible computer technologies. Representatives from the

MITI Electrotechnical Laboratory were responsible for divvying up the information—to ensure that the information made it to the proper lab and not into the pocket of a particular company.

Besides MITI, the Japanese consulate in San Francisco, and Japanese multinational corporations, the Japanese intelligence operation included a series of dummy corporations, "consulting arrangements" with employees of U.S. computer firms, and the use of electronic eavesdropping equipment to spy on U.S. companies. Like ants in an ant hill, a constant flow of agents traveling to the United States ferreted information out of the valley. "Japanese agents are aggressively gathering information by both overt and covert means," wrote Gene Bylinski for *Fortune* magazine in 1978. "The struggle in Silicon Valley has greatly intensified in the past year or so as Japanese companies, taking advantage of the openness of American business and society, have poured more manpower and money into their spying and buying efforts." From 1970 to 1979, the number of Japanese people traveling to the United States on business visas more than doubled, from 65,000 to 135,000. Several American business leaders were shocked by the aggressiveness of the Japanese spying efforts. "Their intent is quite clear," said the normally low-key Robert Noyce, chairman of the Intel Corporation, a pioneer firm in the development of semiconductors. "They are out to slit our throats and we'd better recognize that and do something about it."

The growth in Japanese business travel to the United States was seen by some in the U.S. intelligence community as part of the Japanese intelligence-gathering and espionage activity. "Let there be no doubt," says one senior official at the CIA. "We knew something was up. There was too much talk going around in Japanese business circles for us not to know." Beginning in the fall of 1980, the State Department, at the encouragement of the FBI, quietly moved to tighten the procedures for granting visas to Japanese citizens being sent by their companies to work at Japanese-owned installations in the United States. The bureau was interested in tripping up the intelligence operations that the Japanese community was running in the United States.

The policy was aimed at Japan alone and communicated directly and without publicity to Japanese companies by American consular offices in Japan, lest U.S.-Japanese tensions increase. According to one State Department official, the policy was meant to "correct abuses" by Japanese companies.

Throughout the 1970s, most Japanese businessmen had traveled to the United States on an E Treaty trade visa, which allowed for a lengthy stay. Businesspeople simply applied to the U.S. consulate, and usually the visa was provided in ten to twenty-one days. The new policy changed all that. Henceforth, most Japanese businesspeople traveling to the United States would be required to get an L-type visa, which required more paperwork and consequently took longer to process. Now applications took forty to sixty days to be approved. The new policy also required Japanese companies to file an application with the Immigration and Naturalization Service, thus allowing U.S. officials to keep better track of the movements of Japanese officials. One INS employee claims to have been assigned the task of tracking Japanese movements in the United States from 1981 to 1983 and then compiling statistics on points of destination and lengths of stay. In an unusual case of State Department candor, officials admitted that the visa problems were singularly Japanese. "Abuses have not been spotted in other countries," said William E. Ryerson, director of the Office of Public and Diplomatic Liaison in the Visa Services of the State Department at the time.

Overseas representatives of quasi-official Japanese institutions are also used to collect intelligence. This effort is coordinated by MITI, which assists in determining targets for espionage. Often the Japan External Trade Organization, a MITI subsidiary, served as a go-between for officials gathering intelligence and MITI. Originally set up in 1951 as a private trade group called the Overseas Trade Promotion Association, it was taken over by MITI in 1954 in order to provide a web by which to organize foreign intelligence collection and espionage activities.

Professor Chalmers Johnson of the University of California calls JETRO a "worldwide intelligence organization." As of 1985, JETRO operated seventy-seven offices in fifty-nine countries with twenty-five of the offices located in "key foreign cities." Two hundred seventy agents are overseas to collect economic intelligence, which twelve hundred analysts back in Tokyo review.

"It's very similar to the way the CIA is set up," said John D. Shea, president of Technology Analysis Group, Incorporated, of San Jose, a firm that does technology forecasting for the Pentagon. "The Japanese have people gathering data and sending it back to a central clearing operation run by MITI and JETRO."

Japanese officials insist that the purpose of JETRO is to promote exports. But Dr. Robert C. Angel, who has worked firsthand with JETRO officials, believes that is "pure public relations." He says, "JETRO is an economic and political intelligence service from beginning to end." And as we shall see, JETRO will go to great lengths to collect the intelligence that it believes is important.

In July 1982, shortly after Hitachi was indicted in the attempt to steal technology secrets from IBM, MITI announced that it would set up regional offices in the United States. The first office was planned for Washington, D.C., to be headed by former Japanese Vice-Minister Naohiro Amaya. Although the ostensible purpose of the office was to promote Japanese trade interests, it was also designed to serve as a base for gathering intelligence on U.S. industry. According to CIA sources, Amaya had a long association with Naicho, the prime minister's Cabinet Research Office, and served as an intelligence agent on previous trips to the United States and Southeast Asia.

The announcement of the opening of these MITI offices caused an uproar at the Japanese Foreign Ministry, according to intelligence sources. Not only did the foreign office feel that the MITI offices would undercut the Japanese embassy, but it also believed the offices would create an institutionalized intelligence apparatus in the United States that would not be out of the embassy's control.

The gathering of intelligence on the United States has extended to the hiring of American consultants as well. Former U.S. government officials and former engineers and managers at many high-tech companies provide Japan with information on how to avoid minefields in Washington, identify threats to their commercial interests, and instruct them on how new developments in their industry may affect them. Dr. Angel worked with such consultants in Washington for several years, and he believes that they are "enormously important" to Japan. "Their basic objective is maintaining the political status quo in which economic relations run." American consultants, he says, keep tabs on individuals in the U.S. government who might harbor "anti-Japanese attitudes" or be considered Japan bashers. And they also help the Japanese prepare for tariff and trade fights in Congress, by helping to determine "just exactly when the volcano is about to go off."

Their success in this field has been enormous, and a list of their names is impressive. By the early 1980s, U.S. consultants for Japan included former CIA Director William Colby; Richard Allen, national security adviser to President Reagan; William D. Eberle, chief trade negotiator for the Ford administration; Daniel Michew, former chairman of the International Trade Commission; and former Assistant Secretary of Commerce Frank Weil. As Clyde Farnsworth of the *New York Times* reported on the intelligence-gathering effort, "The Japanese appetite for economic intelligence extends to such fields as energy, agriculture and Government regulations."

The scope of the Japanese presence in this area is enormous. In 1981, for example, in a Justice Department report on registered foreign agents, a list of Japanese agents filled forty-four pages. In contrast, the lists of British and West German agents ran twenty-three and seventeen pages, respectively. According to former CIA Director Richard Helms, there should be little doubt about the role these consultants play. "Let's put it this way: look at all the consultants here in Washington who are on the Japanese payroll for one reason or another. You don't think any information flows back to Japan? That's totally naive."

Consultants in Silicon Valley often provide intelligence as well. In March 1984, the Gartner Group, a prestigious consulting firm, settled with IBM out of court over allegations that the firm had sold confidential memos to IBM's Japanese competitors. Although not fully admitting guilt, Gartner agreed to refrain from acquiring and selling IBM trade secrets in the future. Japanese corporations have also used American private detectives to gather intelligence that perhaps cannot be obtained in a direct or legal fashion.

The payoff, according to U.S. officials, was enormous in Japanese efforts to leapfrog the United States in terms of computer technology. Executives of high-tech companies in the United States figure that intelligence and espionage operations made major contributions to the VLSI program. Regarding VLSI's achievements by 1979, John Shea said in

December of 1981, "Our estimate is that intelligence operations provided at least 35 to 40% of the base-line data on which [the Japanese] were able to extrapolate and achieve what they did."

Some estimates are even higher. According to an official in the CIA's Science and Technology Directorate, internal agency estimates were as high as 70 percent. "And," he said, "the information that they did gather by, let me say, not-above-board means was the information that made the difference in succeeding as quickly as they did."

The Japanese government itself carries out intelligence operations against the United States and Western European countries from time to time. These operations are directed by Naicho, the country's premier intelligence organization. A small organization, Naicho is under the direct control of the prime minister, providing Japanese leaders with detailed knowledge of foreign intelligence on international affairs. And with MITI, it also takes part in the effort to acquire technological information on the United States.

Naicho acts like a clearinghouse for intelligence operations, both political and economic, carried out against the United States. If MITI is one wing of the operation, the Japanese Defense Agency is another. The Annex Chamber, Second Section, of the Investigation Division of the Ground Self-defense Forces (Chobetsu), coordinates electronic eavesdropping on foreign and domestic targets. With approximately twelve hundred employees, Chobetsu is an efficient organization that intercepts the communications of such countries as China, North Korea, and the former Soviet Union, but it also pays attention to Taiwan, South Korea, and U.S. corporate traffic running into and out of Japan. The operations of Chobetsu are so secretive that even members of the Japanese Diet are not allowed to enter its facilities.

An enormous eavesdropping facility at Shiraho on the island of Ishigaki, northeast of Taiwan in the Ryukyu archipelago, is ideally positioned for intercepting intelligence information on South Korea and Taiwan. Reflecting Japan's emphasis on economic and technological intelligence, many of the circularly disposed antenna array (CDAA) systems home in on corporate communications in both of those countries. The South Korean government, according to one ex-Korean intelligence officer who defends his country's spying on Japan, has from time to time complained privately but bitterly to Japanese officials about this practice.

The Japanese effort to intercept U.S. communications is much more extensive. Electronic stations on Rebun Island and in the Ryukyus at Kikaiga-shima Island are regularly used to intercept U.S. communications going into and out of Japan. The facilities at Higashi Chitose, on the island of Hokkaidō, have a CDAA system similar to the one at Miho and employ as well sophisticated radomes to intercept satellite communications. In recent briefings of U.S. businesspeople traveling to Tokyo, the FBI has repeatedly warned that they should assume they are being eavesdropped on. Noel Matchett, a former senior official with the National Security Agency and a specialist in corporate communications, offers the same advice, saying that "it's more likely to be happening there more frequently than you might think."

The Nippon Telephone and Telegraph Company has a long-standing agreement with the Japanese Defense Agency to eavesdrop on telephone conversations that may be of interest to Japan's companies. Says John Quinn, formerly with the CIA, "I know that Nippon Telephone and Telegraph, Japan's major telephone corporation over here, cooperates with the Japanese government, and their technical capability is very advanced, so they can very easily tap into a phone line. They do not enter the buildings to do so: they can do it from several blocks away; they can do it from a switching station. So tapping a phone is not difficult."

Intelligence at MITI is conducted by a variety of sections, depending on the area being probed. The General Affairs sections of the Secretariat of the International Trade Policy Bureau are primarily responsible for gathering intelligence on foreign trade policies and projected trade postures at international talks. The secretariat works with affected companies when collecting intelligence. The Machinery and Information Industries Bureau does much more detailed work and plays a much larger role in directing Japanese industrial espionage. On certain occasions, MITI has also set up special intelligence operations to deal with specific areas of interest, as, for example, it did in 1972, when it established the Special Survey Group of the Information Room, within the Bureau of Heavy Industries, to report on the U.S. computer industry.

Americans and other foreigners in Japan are often watched quite closely. "Japan has been monitoring foreigners in Japan ever since the first arrival of foreigners in the late 1850s," says Quinn. A Tokyo resident, he explains, "They do keep very tight tabs on American entities here. Especially if you are in Tokyo, there is always a chance of being overheard."

Domestically the Public Security Investigation Agency has been known to conduct bag operations against U.S. business executives in Japan. An agency with two thousand employees, its prime responsibility is to track subversive groups and the activities of hostile intelligence services. But PSIA has strayed from its mandate, carrying out operations in Tokyo and other metropolitan facilities.

The story of one U.S. businessman who traveled to Tokyo in the summer of 1990 is revealing. Staying on the seventh floor of the Imperial Hotel, he awoke one morning and decided to go for a brisk walk before a late-morning meeting. When he returned at approximately 9:15, to prepare for the meeting, he discovered that someone had been through his papers. He made the discovery quite by accident: he noticed it only because in some of the documents he had carried with him, some of the pages had been stapled in upside down. He had discovered the problem on the flight over and was planning to rearrange the pages after his morning walk. But someone had already done the job for him. When he questioned hotel managers about the matter, they assured him only that "criminals" had no access to the hotel. When the American pressed them for an explanation, they shrugged and simply said that if anything had been done, it was done legally, and there was nothing to worry about.

The situation in Japan is so bad, according to security consultants, that several U.S. companies, including Boeing and Hewlett-Packard, now instruct their employees not to let documents leave their sight when they travel to Tokyo.

Ambassador Smith, who often visited Tokyo on official business when he was the U.S. deputy trade representative, says that in Tokyo you always assume you're being bugged. "Certain floors and rooms in major Japanese hotels were always bugged. They always insisted when I visited that I stay on the eighth or ninth floor of a particular hotel. If you wanted to talk about something sensitive, you always went outside."

Bag operations have also been run by Japanese embassy officials in foreign capitals. One such operation was uncovered in Paris during the summer of 1974, quite by accident. At that time, Service 7 of the French secret service was covertly but regularly opening the diplomatic pouches of foreign embassies based in Paris. On one occasion, according to a senior French intelligence official, Service 7 found in a Japanese pouch information on the French optics industry, including confidential memos from two French companies, Saint-Gobain and Michelin. The Service de Documentation Extérieure et de Contre-Espionnage, reluctant to disclose the discovery for fear of having to reveal its operations, grudgingly let the documents pass through.

Beginning in 1984, Japanese government intelligence went through a period of reorganization, an attempt by then Prime Minister Yasuhiro Nakasone to make collection and analysis more efficient. Nakasone appointed a Subcommittee on the Functions of the Cabinet within the existing Administration Reform Promotion Committee. The subcommittee was chaired by Ryuzo Sejima, a senior official of the C. Itoh Trading Company and a trusted Nakasone adviser with an extensive background in intelligence. In June 1985, the subcommittee issued *The Appropriate Comprehensive Coordinating Functions of the Cabinet,* which served as a blueprint for reorganizing the government's national security apparatus and intelligence system.

According to Professor Robert Angel, one of the most important recommendations the report made was to "overhaul the intelligence analysis and distribution structure." Specifically, the subcommittee called for the comprehensive reorganization of the Cabinet Secretariat, the prime minister's executive office. The formation of a Cabinet Secretariat Information and Research Office was a key component in enhancing the coordination of intelligence collection and assessment. This new organization was to be staffed by intelligence personnel lent by the Foreign Ministry, the Japanese Defense Agency, and the National Police Agency, and it was to serve as the central clearinghouse of intelligence collected by the various government agencies. But there was also to be close cooperation and intelligence sharing with large Japanese multinational corporations. This last element of the new secretariat for intelligence was championed by Tosmiwo Doko, former chairman of the powerful Keidanren, the Federation of Economic Organizations. Keidanren was to serve as the new secretariat's liaison in the sharing of intelligence.

In addition to calling for a more centralized intelligence system, the so-called Sejima Committee recommended the purchase of the latest so-phisticated communications technology, as well as more advanced electronic intelligence equipment, including advanced eavesdropping technologies, which would make intercepting communications easier. The result of the Sejima Committee's recommendations and the work of a larger committee headed by Doko was the creation of a new Security Council in February 1986. One CIA official says that the reorganization gave "more direction, ended duplication, and made collection of military, political, but primarily economic intelligence much more intelligent."

A Comprehensive Intelligence Committee was also established to help coordinate the collection of intelligence. Directed by the prime minister's deputy chief cabinet secretary, this committee meets once a month and is under unusually strict security. Members of the committee include the director of the Cabinet Secretariat Information and Research Office, the director of the Security Council, the director-general of the National Police Agency's Bureau of Investigation, the director-general of the Foreign Ministry's Bureau of Information and Research, and the director-general of the Defense Agency's Defense Bureau.

Perhaps the most important component in the Japanese intelligence system is the intelligence activities of the Japanese multinational corporations. These are the most extensive and comprehensive intelligence and espionage organizations in Japan.

Dr. Angel, a Japan specialist and a professor at the University of South Carolina, has worked for more than a decade for semiofficial Japanese institutions in the United States. He worked at the U.S.-Japan Trade Council and later headed the Japan Economic Institute, both of which were funded entirely by the Japanese Foreign Ministry. And he firmly believes that the Japanese government receives "enormously valuable intelligence from corporate spying overseas." He says that the buying or stealing of corporate or technological information is just part of Japanese business. "Japanese companies spend a lot of money on spying," he says. "They do it to each other, but the Japanese assume that foreigners are more vulnerable to spying; therefore, the vast majority of their efforts are directed at their chief competitor, the United States." John Quinn agrees.

He says of Japanese corporations, "These are the closest things that you will find to commercial intelligence agencies." Their interest has been not only in both technology and business secrets but also in classified U.S. intelligence information. Dr. Angel states emphatically that Japanese companies "spend enormous amounts of funds for intelligence."

Dissatisfied with its ability to produce high-quality specialized industrial films, the Mitsubishi Corporation in the mid-1970s sought to gain access to the technology secrets that made the Celanese Corporation of New York a successful industry leader in the field. Mitsubishi scientists simply couldn't match the Celanese formula for making the films. At first, the Japanese company tried to reach an agreement with Celanese to purchase the technology outright, but the company refused. Three delegations from Japan went to New York over a six-month period in 1973, hoping to persuade the American company. The delegations were insistent, telling Celanese officials that if they didn't sell Mitsubishi the technology, it might be acquired "by other means." Celanese still refused, happy to reap its own profits from the technological developments it had perfected. Company officials didn't take very seriously the threat of acquiring the technology by other means. Perhaps they should have. Mitsubishi, unable to tap the secrets to the Celanese method legally, undertook to organize an operation to get access illegally. It is a classic case of how a big corporation, a middleman, and an insider at the target company can work together.

Mitsubishi hired two consulting firms, one in Los Angeles and the other in Chicago, to locate a possible source within Celanese who might be interested in betraying the company for a large payoff. It didn't take long for one firm to identify Harold Farrar, a manager at a Celanese plant in sleepy Greer, South Carolina, as a possible mole. Farrar, Mitsubishi discovered, was unhappy at Celanese. He felt he had been overlooked for promotion; he resented his post in a small town; he was faced with financial difficulties and personal problems that made him a possible recruit—and he had complete access to Celanese secrets across the board, including secrets to the very technology Mitsubishi was hoping to acquire. After being approached to serve as a conduit and a mole, Farrar agreed almost immediately.

For $150,000 Farrar gave Mitsubishi everything it could hope for. In all, he provided company officials with fifty-eight rolls of microfilm covering twelve thousand drawings and nine thousand pages of documents. On at least three occasions, he went secretly to the Mitsubishi chemical plant in Nagahama, Japan, to help interpret the information and offer advice on where to get even more. At least twice, he gave Mitsubishi officials private, after-hours tours of the Greer plant. The visitors were given near free reign of the facility: they took photographs, made notes about the plant's layout, analyzed machinery and equipment, and even rummaged through some company files and papers.

It was not until March 1974 that Farrar's colleagues stumbled across his activities and his relationship with Mitsubishi. By that time, the damage had largely been done, and it was too late to have any hope of preventing Mitsubishi from exploiting the information it had obtained. Farrar was immediately fired by Celanese. Both he and Mitsubishi were taken to court on charges of racketeering and conspiracy to transfer stolen property. Neither of the defendants showed any remorse.

Despite the covert nature of his activity, Farrar claimed he had done nothing wrong. Upon joining Celanese, he had signed a document promising that he would "preserve, safeguard and avoid compromise or disclosure of" company trade secrets; this apparently didn't mean much to him. He even claimed the information he supplied was not that important: "Everything [Celanese] did was common knowledge in the industry." He never tried to explain why, if that were the case, he had gone about his activities so covertly or why Mitsubishi had offered him so much money.

A judge saw the case for what it was: espionage in which the fundamental secrets of a company were undermined by a foreign competitor and a disgruntled employee. He called it a case of "a monumental sellout of the total Celanese technology down to the minutest detail." Mitsubishi apparently agreed with the judge's assessment, pleading no contest to the charges. It perhaps had little concern about being found guilty. The Mitsubishi employees involved in the operation refused to accept court papers from the U.S. marshals who traveled to Japan to deliver them. The company was fined three hundred thousand dollars by the court, an amount that was minuscule in comparison with the estimated value of the Celanese technology: six million dollars outright, plus untold millions in future sales. The operation was, even with the fine, worth the cost as far as Mitsubishi was concerned. As is so often the case in friendly spy operations, it was the insider who paid the highest price. Farrar was sentenced to four years in a federal penitentiary.

The intelligence activities of Japanese multinationals have not been limited to the theft of technology or corporate secrets. The Japanese multinationals have also been voracious consumers of military and political intelligence, which they have been able to gather in Washington, D.C.

According to sources at the National Security Agency, on the morning of July 13, 1982, the NSA had intercepted commercial communications from the Washington office of Mitsubishi to the Japanese Foreign Ministry in Tokyo. The NSA monitors fifty-three thousand communication signals in the United States every day. They usually aren't reviewed by analysts, however, unless the signal carries a message with a signature—a key word or phrase that triggers a computer to transcribe the communication. Any word that might signal confidential or classified government information triggers the transcribing system.

On that hot July morning, to the alarm of NSA and senior U.S. intelligence officials, Mitsubishi was relaying to Tokyo detailed, at times verbatim, information from top-secret U.S. intelligence reports. Mitsubishi transferred to the Japanese Foreign Ministry substantial details from the CIA's top-secret *National Intelligence Daily* reports of July 7 and 9. *NID*s are written for the president of the United States and offer intelligence information on world military and political events. In this case, the reports largely contained military information about the Iran-Iraq War and the troop movements that both sides were undertaking. Also included was political intelligence on the future of the Iraqi campaign and the political vulnerability of Iraqi President Saddam Hussein. The report stressed that Hussein would have to fall before there could be any hope of peace between the two countries. In its communiqués, Mitsubishi simply told the Foreign Ministry that the reports had come from a senior U.S. intelligence official who had passed the information on to a Washington-based consulting firm, which was gathering intelligence for Mitsubishi.

On at least two other occasions, according to NSA officials, Mitsubishi's telecommunications traffic contained details from the *NID* and other intelligence briefing papers. On July 29 and August 4, the company relayed information to Tokyo about political developments in the Soviet

Union. The information came not only from the *NID* but also from other CIA intelligence findings related to the situation there. The flow of top-secret information to Mitsubishi was puzzling and disconcerting for U.S. officials. NSA Director Lincoln Fauer contacted the FBI, requesting that it immediately launch a formal investigation.

Suspicions centered on the vice-chairman of the CIA's National Intelligence Council, Charles Waterman. A CIA veteran with more than twenty years' experience, Waterman had extensive contacts in the Washington community and had been authorized to consult for a Washington firm that provided intelligence reports to businesses doing work in the Middle East. The CIA security office felt that Waterman was the source and should resign. But FBI officials felt that if Waterman had been a source, he may not have been the only one. Although Waterman would know what the *NID* said, some of the other intelligence reports that Mitsubishi had access to were probably too obscure for Waterman to have spent time identifying and tracking down. Probably a more junior analyst at the CIA had been involved as well, according to U.S. intelligence officials.

Waterman eventually resigned from his post, but nothing was ever proved. From that point on, however, according to NSA officials, Mitsubishi communiqués didn't appear to contain classified intelligence information. One U.S. official remains skeptical, nevertheless. "All we know is that they aren't sending the information over a regular communications wire. Who knows if they simply aren't giving them to embassy personnel down the street from their offices."

Japanese corporate intelligence operations have even, in extreme cases, extended to the private homes of Americans. The experience of the Frenches, a family in Costa Mesa, California, is a case in point. During the summer of 1989, Takashi Morimoto rented a room from the Frenches. The neighborhood was like thousands of others across America, and it would seem as though nothing on the tree-lined suburban street would interest Japan enough to conduct a sophisticated intelligence operation there.

Little did the Frenches know, however, that they were being watched by Morimoto. He was, in fact, a specialist in intelligence operations for Nissan and had been employed to do extensive research on "average American" financial and personal habits. The information he collected from the Frenches, including personal financial information, was being used by the carmaker as a piece of marketing research. It would be a definitive study insofar as the family would have no knowledge of Morimoto's research and Morimoto would get an inside look at how an American family works.

He gathered information on everything: family spending habits, preferences, habits, and style. He was very quiet about his intelligence operation, yet he took notes of family finances and photographs of the family's property. One day in August, the Frenches uncovered Morimoto's activities. Outraged, they kicked him out of their home. But by that time, he probably had enough information anyway. The Frenches' experience is probably not an isolated one. Japanese companies are extremely interested in knowing American habits and tastes so that they can build products suited to American tastes. While there is certainly nothing wrong with that, the covert method of gathering the information and the invasion of privacy raises serious questions.

Regarding Japanese students studying in the United States, Professor Angel says that Japanese government and corporate officials will "go to almost any length to get highly valued information and access to secrets"—they will even use students. Professor Johnson reports that several Japanese graduate students at the University of California at Berkeley told him that Japanese consular officials in San Francisco had directed them to provide reports and updates on developments in biotechnology at the university's research facilities—Berkeley is one of the leading innovators in the biotechnology field. A similar incident took place at the Massachusetts Institute of Technology in the fall of 1990. According to a researcher there, several Japanese graduate students were told to join university research teams as lab assistants in order to gather intelligence on biotechnology. "They told me that if they didn't comply, their papers and funds could be pulled," the researcher said.

Most Japanese intelligence operations run in the United States are totally legal. Japanese companies, for example, are some of the most voracious consumers of information received from the federal government courtesy of the Freedom of Information Act. Because the act does not restrict access to government information, it has been a boon to foreign governments and corporations gathering intelligence on U.S. technology secrets (indeed, the fulfillment of their requests is subsidized by American taxpayers, because they pay for the paperwork involved).

Mitsubishi Corporation is a prime example of how the act has been used by Japan. For much of the 1980s, Mitsubishi and other Japanese companies had been attempting to break into the aerospace field, specifically, the areas of satellite and rocketry production. The Japanese government's National Space Development Agency and the Institute of Space and Aeronautical Science are aggressively researching the technology, and part of their effort entails the collection of information from the U.S. National Aeronautics and Space Administration through the FOIA. In particular, they have by some estimates made as many as fifteen hundred requests annually for information on the U.S. space shuttle program and various rockets. These requests have come from a variety of sources: Mitsubishi consultants in Washington, legal firms representing Mitsubishi, and company employees in the United States.

One former Mitsubishi employee in California says that he was twice presented with a letter written over his name and addressed to the FOIA office at NASA: "They didn't ask me or anything. They simply wanted to juggle the names for requests."

Information obtained through the FOIA is believed to have helped Mitsubishi Electric Company substantially in its development of its H-2 booster rocket and its earth resources satellite, ERS-1. File cabinet after file cabinet of NASA and other U.S. government documents obtained through the FOIA are said by some former company officials to be stored at Mitsubishi Electric's Kita-Ithami facility near Tokyo.

The principal firms in Japanese space technology—Mitsubishi Heavy Industries, Nissan, Ishikawajima-Harima Heavy Industries, NEC, Mitsubishi Electric, and Toshiba—talk of cornering 20 percent of the world market in space applications by the year 2000. It was that goal that motivated several of these companies to purchase illegally top-secret technological information on rocketry research being done for the Strategic Defense Initiative. The secrets were bought from a Southern California scientist between 1986 and 1990.

Some U.S. officials believe that Japanese corporate moves in the international telecommunications market offer a potentially tremendous avenue for espionage. According to Robert G. Harris, President of

EconomIncorporated, early in the 1980s, Japan "designated telecommuni-cations as the key strategic industry for the twenty-first century." George Keyworth II, former science adviser to President Reagan, has noted the same intense interest on the part of Japanese companies.

Some fear that this interest might be based in part on the espionage opportunities that dominance in the world telecommunications industry might create. In 1984, Michael C. Sekora, a physicist by training, created and became director of the U.S. Defense Intelligence Agency's Project Socrates, an outfit for monitoring foreign technological developments. Now head of Technology Strategic Planning, Incorporated, he believes that Japan has a well-planned "technological envelopment strategy" for domi-nation of the world telecommunications market. Perhaps this is why Japan has been purchasing companies in the field that develops interlocking technologies: hardware and software technologies that work together and build on each other.

Sekora and his business partner, Henry Clements, fear that the Japanese might dominate world communications within ten years. Tokyo's objective in doing so, says Sekora, is not only to reap the profits of the industry but also to have the capacity and the capability to monitor worldwide banking and financial transactions. Obviously, the value of such information would be enormous. Two companies in the United States communicating over a Japanese-developed telecommunications system could be monitored by the manufacturer. The National Security Agency, in a May 1990 survey of the world telecommunications market, drew a similar conclusion. Although not specifically mentioning Japan, the report noted that laser and optical technologies would make it possible for foreign manufacturers and developers of international telecommunica-tions networks to monitor electronic signals and communications within the United States and between the United States and other countries overseas—and to do so virtually undetected.

The Japanese ability to gain access to industrial and economic secrets from competitors around the world is a marvel to intelligence chiefs around the world. It is a critical factor in the country's future, and it is a likely field for growth. Because of the economic competition and the trade tensions between the United States and Japan, some in the U.S. intelligence community believe Japan is likely to emerge as the major espionage threat of the 1990s.

5

Les Espions Industriels

Economic espionage is a fact of life.
— Pierre Marion, former director of French intelligence

On a cool evening in 1964, Undersecretary of State George Ball headed for his hotel room after a trying day. Ball was in Cannes, France, as the U.S. delegate to the Kennedy Round of Trade Talks taking place in that beautiful French seaside city, famous for its film festival. The Kennedy talks (so-named because they were begun during President Kennedy's administration) were complicated and at a difficult stage. France, the host country, and the United States were at particular odds over several key issues. The hope was for an international agreement that would reduce trade barriers in many countries. Sometimes, however, it seemed as if they were getting nowhere.

Ball headed to his suite in the old-fashioned, continental Majestic Hotel, where many international delegates were staying. He was to try a new tact at the talks, based on consultations with Washington, and in his suit pocket he carried fresh detailed instructions from the president concerning the U.S. negotiating position on such issues as agricultural subsidies and national tariffs. He also carried details of the U.S. fallback position, the minimum that President Johnson would settle for. It was Ball's job to get the most that he could without caving in immediately on several important positions. The secrecy of the U.S. instructions was very important, to ensure that negotiators got the maximum.

Ball was tired from a hectic day. Almost immediately after entering his suite, he prepared for bed. He put his suit jacket over the arm of a chair and crawled into bed. Once under the covers, he was soon fast asleep. Barely two hours after he had turned off the lights, at approximately 1:30 A.M., the door to his suit slowly opened. A pair of eyes peered in, and on seeing the undersecretary fast asleep, a slender figure stealthily entered the room. The hinges on the door to Ball's suite had been heavily oiled hours before the undersecretary arrived, so the door didn't make a sound. The figure knew exactly where to go, heading deliberately to the suit jacket draped over the chair. Slowly a woman's hand searched the jacket pockets, eventually locating the instructions from the president. Out came the important instructions. And as quietly as the figure entered the room, she left.

The figure was no ordinary individual, nor was this a routine theft. Ball's wallet had not been touched. This was a bag operation organized by French intelligence, which wanted a peak at the U.S. negotiating position. And the woman carrying out the mission was no ordinary agent but a French countess who did occasional work for French intelligence. She had been dispatched by Colonel Marcel le Roy, a French intelligence agent with experience in such matters. And according to le Roy, the operation was the idea of then French Prime Minister Valéry Giscard d'Estaing.

The countess, now in the hallway, slipped the papers into her purse and proceeded quietly to the hotel manager's office downstairs. There she was met by Colonel le Roy, who quickly photographed every page. The countess then returned to Ball's room, where she quietly replaced the documents. The next day, when the talks proceeded, French delegates knew as much about the U.S. position as the chief American negotiator did.

In 1969, a U.S. presidential delegation was visiting Paris, a trip during which the newly inaugurated President Richard Nixon would meet his French counterpart for the first time. With Nixon on the trip was a bevy of advisers, including his assistant, H. R. Haldeman. In Paris, the delegation attended a number of official functions, including dinners and receptions. After one such function early in the trip, Haldeman picked up his overcoat from the coat check and left. Unbeknownst to him, French intelligence had attached a small bug to the lining of his coat while he had been dining with French officials. He discovered it only a few days later. "I gave it to the secret service boys, and they shrugged," says Haldeman. "It was business as usual." French officials certainly heard a number of important and private discussions between senior White House officials, many of which reflected the U.S. position and attitude on a number of important issues related to France.

In June 1982, President Reagan was visiting Paris to meet with French President François Mitterand. They were to discuss a variety of issues, some on a cordial basis, others on a more contentious one. The Reagan team was staying at an expensive Paris hotel, where they had two entire floors, for reasons of security and privacy. The president's immediate staff met regularly in a posh suite to discuss several issues that related to the trip and to plot diplomatic strategy for meetings to come. Before the delegation arrived, security officials at the U.S. embassy in Paris had swept the hotel rooms for electronic bugs. None had been found. So when the inner circle met at the hotel, everyone felt comfortable enough to discuss issues candidly and openly. If only they had known. Across the street from the hotel, according to French intelligence sources, the conversations were being recorded. Specialists from Service 7 of French intelligence were firing a specialized laser at the window of the hotel suite in which the inner circle was meeting. The laser was recording the vibrations of the window the conversations caused, and a small computer was translating the vibrations into words. French intelligence was learning quite a bit about what the president and his advisers were thinking on a variety of issues of importance to France.

The French intelligence service is one of the best in the world. And according to both U.S. and French intelligence officials, one of its most important espionage targets is the United States. Not only are government officials like George Ball and H. R. Haldeman targets. So, too, are U.S. business executives and American companies in France. French intelligence operations have even extended to U.S. soil.

"The French have been very active in this area for years," says Raymond Wannall, a former FBI assistant director for intelligence. "They have targeted lots of things, lots of U.S. companies." Dr. Ray Cline, a former deputy director of the CIA, says that French intelligence "regularly tries to penetrate U.S. companies." And former CIA Director Richard Helms tells the same story in an interview: "They have admitted to me in private that they go through the briefcases of visiting businessmen."

French intelligence officials are just as candid. Spying on the United States, particularly for economic reasons, is just standard practice, according to Pierre Marion, director of French intelligence from 1981 to 1982. "It's a normal action of an intelligence agency." This activity extends to the United States, he says, and it is simply a job of the French intelligence service. The French view is that although the United States and France may be political and military allies, friendship extends only to those fields, not to the realms of technology and economics. There we are competitors, so espionage is legitimate. According to Marion,

> I think you have to separate very clearly what are the fields which are not covered by an alliance. It's clear that when you have an ally, you have certain sectors [that are covered]. I'm speaking of armaments. I'm thinking of diplomatic matters where you normally should not try to gather intelligence. But in all other fields where being allied does not prevent the states, the corresponding states are competitors. Even during the Cold War, the competition was still existing. [This] is even more true now, since the competition between states is moving from the political-military level to the economic and technological level.

Marion adds, "I think that even during the Cold War, getting intelligence in economic, technological, and industrial matters [from] a country [with] which you are allied . . . is not incompatible with the fact of being allied." And now that the Cold War is over? "The competition in terms of technology and commerce and industry is stronger than it was during the Cold War. There should be more emphasis put on that, and on industrial espionage."

French intelligence has used a variety of methods to collect information on technologies as well as proprietary information on foreign competitors. Several hotels in Paris frequented by foreign business executives are bugged by French intelligence. Some have employees who offer

French intelligence agents access to the hotel rooms of visiting business executives, no questions asked. Phone lines are tapped. French intelligence agents also work actively to "penetrate" U.S. and other foreign companies. Sometimes this involves nothing more than asking an employee to obtain documents on certain company projects. It has also included more extensive and sophisticated operations, however, including the planting of moles in foreign corporations.

French economic espionage is not restricted to France. Indeed, according to intelligence officials in several countries, including the United States, French agents are active overseas, particularly in the United States, Germany, and Japan. But they have also worked aggressively in countries such as India and South Korea to help French companies win lucrative contracts, by employing "special" methods. According to Marion, "If we were not doing this, we would not be doing our job as an intelligence service."

The French intelligence service commits two hundred agents around the world full-time to the task of economic espionage. These are regular agents of the Direction Générale de la Sécurité Extérieure who are stationed overseas and in France. They are given considerable latitude to collect information, and they generally concentrate on soft business targets. Those acts of economic espionage that require a particularly deft hand are usually conducted by Service 7. It is this unit, a special DGSE "action unit," that carries out most operations involving break-ins, buggings, and covert operations. "Service 7 was made to spy on or, let us say, to conduct very special spying operations and very special espionage operations," according to Marion.

But the activities of DGSE regular agents in the field of economic espionage tell only part of the story. According to former senior DGSE officials, it is a formal and important network of part-time agents, called "honorary correspondents" by DGSE regulars, that magnifies enormously the activities of French intelligence. In addition to French officials, this network includes a surprising number of corporate officials living overseas. Among the ranks of honorary correspondents are French bankers in New York, company representatives in the Far East, and bureaucrats at the European Community in Brussels. Some work for money, but others view their input as part of their regular job. The latter is particularly true of those who work for government bodies or nationalized French companies, such as Air France or the electronics giant Compagnie des Machines Bull.

Perhaps a prime example of the honorary correspondent is Pierre Marion, who worked with French intelligence on a part-time basis while working for several French companies. Marion served for many years as an executive for Air France, a member of the government-sponsored Aerospace Consortium, and the Washington representative for SNIAS.

Marion was particularly active during his stint as the Air France representative in East Asia and the Pacific, a position to which he was appointed in 1963. Indeed, according to one official, Marion took the job with the knowledge that he was expected to cooperate with French intelligence. His task was to collect intelligence in Japanese social circles, particularly as it related to political officials. His residence was a rendezvous point for French intelligence agents, a safe place where they could meet recruits or organize operations. Agents would bring to Marion's home information they had obtained, and it would be transferred back to French officials in Paris via Air France.

Marion was an effective Air France representative in Tokyo, and his activities on behalf of French intelligence made him important friends. As a result, he was appointed deputy director-general of Air France. Back in Paris, he had responsibility for commercial matters. But by 1977, he was overseas again, having left Air France for SNIAS. Two years later he was in Washington, D.C., as SNIAS's representative in the United States. At that time, he maintained close relations with French intelligence officials based in Washington, occasionally passing along information he thought might be useful. So when Marion was appointed the director of French intelligence in 1981, he was not the outsider many might have assumed him to be. Indeed, one intelligence official at his swearing-in ceremony, Colonel Michel Garder, actually paid public tribute to Marion's role as an honorary correspondent, mentioning some of his successes.

The system of honorary correspondents is organized with built-in incentives for participation by both corporations and individuals. The nationalized corporations, such as Air France and Bull, are the most direct conduit for the hiring of nongovernment honorary correspondents. Since these corporations are funded by the government and their decisions are in large part determined by government officials, their senior officials are expected to work closely with French intelligence, especially when it comes to economic espionage. This expectation even includes instances in which local laws may be broken. One French banker recalls how in 1987 DGSE agents instructed him to steal hotel keys from a German colleague staying in London who had recently arrived from Bonn. "Had I been caught, it could have been most embarrassing. After all, this was theft. They wanted these [keys] to get access to the man's room. They wanted to see some documents."

Individuals who work for such companies can and have refused to cooperate. After all, the system is strictly voluntary. But those who repeatedly refuse to do favors for the DGSE risk professional retribution. One former Air France official who now works for a small French company flat-out refused to have anything to do with the DGSE and refused to perform even the most minor favors. Once intelligence officials asked him to take a visiting businessman out to dinner and to keep him busy and away from his hotel for a minimum of three hours. "They wanted to get to the files on his laptop computer. They were made to believe that it would take that long to break the password." He told the intelligence officials that to do such a thing would be unconscionable. "It was a matter of principles." He had refused two previous requests, much to the anger and chagrin of his superiors. They no doubt wanted him to believe that the requested tasks were for the good of his company and his country. His third and last refusal came in August 1983. By the second week of October, he was sacked due to "poor evaluations" by his superiors.

Private French firms also have powerful incentives to cooperate with French intelligence. Although the recruitment of honorary correspondents from large private corporations is not common, it does occur. Firms do not discourage cooperation because in many cases their failure to work with the intelligence service means they will not receive any of the fruits of industrial espionage. "If they do not play it, they will not profit from it" is how one former senior French intelligence official put it.

The information that French intelligence can provide a company may be enormously valuable. After the DGSE acquires the information, it passes it to French government officials. Those officials then determine which companies will receive what. This is a particularly sensitive matter when it comes to intelligence that could benefit many companies. Says

Marion, "Normally, particularly in cases where that intelligence could apply to different companies, different corporations, not only one, then the channel was—and, I think, still is—to transfer that intelligence to the government body which is in charge of that particular sector."

For years, France has collected economic information to assist its industries in the battle with foreign competitors. Initially, this took the form of secret operations performed by Service 7. According to former Service 7 Chief Marcel le Roy, the practice of targeting U.S. corporations was initiated by Charles de Gaulle. American diplomatic bags were regularly intercepted, and U.S. corporate activities in France were monitored. Service 7 conducted notorious operations against U.S. officials, including those targeted at George Ball and H. R. Haldeman. But it also targeted Western business executives. These operations included not only breaking into hotel rooms but also using prostitutes to gain information and in some cases crude attempts at compromising those who possessed particularly valuable information.

At the same time, however, France began an electronic intelligence campaign against her Western allies. Some of what was sought was retrieved by electronic intercepts of diplomatic communications. But economic information about France's competitors, particularly West Germany and Great Britain, was also sought. In July 1967, electronics facilities at Mont Valérien began intercepting commercial traffic between German companies. The facility, directed by the Radio-Electric Communications Group (GCR), was working closely with the French bureaucrats from the Ministry of Industry. A similar relationship was fostered with a communications station at Boullay-ces-Trois run by the French internal security service, the Direction de la Surveillance du Territoire, which began intercepting German as well as British commercial communications traffic in 1974.

It was in the early 1970s that the Service de Documentation Extérieure et de Contre-Espionnage, as French intelligence was then called, began the practice of bugging Air France commercial flights from New York to Paris, London to Paris, and Frankfurt to Paris. In business-class seating, Air France planes were outfitted with extensive electronic eavesdropping systems. Experiments were made in 1974; by September 1975, the experiment became practice. In some instances, Air France planes served as photography platforms for French intelligence agents. Flights over Eastern Europe would at times veer off course in order to allow photos to be taken of sensitive Warsaw Pact facilities. This practice was also applied to commercial purposes at least once. In 1978, an Air France plane went off course over Germany to allow photos to be taken of a West German chemical plant under construction. Such photos can be extremely helpful to chemical companies—they provide important details about production methods and capacity.

But while French economic intelligence was growing in the 1970s, relations between French intelligence and the CIA improved. Under SDECE Director Count de Marenches, who served from 1970 until 1981, some of the more blatant acts of espionage against the United States were ended. De Marenches, a flamboyant French aristocrat who had worked in French intelligence during the Second World War, was pro-American and a committed anti-Communist. Although he believed that spying on the United States was at times still necessary, he felt the practice had gone perhaps a bit too far under Charles de Gaulle. As a result of de Marenches's efforts, relations between the CIA and the SDECE improved. When asked about the warming in relations, de Marenches made this revealing comment: "It was not the SDECE which brought me relations, but, if you will, pardon me saying so, I brought my own relations to the service of France." It was, then, de Marenches's personal relations with American public officials, not institutional relations between French and American intelligence services, that brought warmer relations.

In 1974, technicians from the SDECE began attending courses at CIA headquarters in Langley, Virginia. These officials boned up on their technical skills, from interpreting electronic intercepts to reading photosatellite imagery. The CIA under James Schlesinger, William Colby, George Bush, and then, in 1977, Stansfield Turner, committed itself to assisting de Marenches in his attempts to make the SDECE a more efficient collector of intelligence on the Soviet bloc.

And yet, although de Marenches did shift the focus of the SDECE to the military challenges emanating from the Soviet bloc, espionage operations directed against the United States and other Western economic targets continued. De Marenches, in his 1986 memoirs, admits as much. He writes, "Spying in the proper sense is becoming increasingly focused on business and the economy, science and industry—and very profitable it is. It enables the Intelligence Services to discover a process used in another country, which might have taken years and possibly millions of francs to invent or perfect. This form of espionage prevails not only with the enemy but to some extent among friends, it has to be said." De Marenches continues, "In any Intelligence Service worthy of the name you would come across cases where the whole year's budget has been paid for in full by a single operation. Naturally, Intelligence does not receive actual payment, but the country's industry profits."

The former intelligence chief tells the story of how, through an informer, the French intelligence services "knew for certain beforehand that the Americans were going to devalue the dollar on 18 December 1971." The information was extremely valuable to France, he writes. "Thus the Bank of France was able to put into effect a series of operations which were highly successful. The figures involved, in fact, taken on their own, would have financed the Service for years."

The extent to which de Marenches was able to redirect French intelligence, focusing it more directly on military challenges from the East, was limited by those who served him. In particular, his aides remained committed to continuing intelligence operations against U.S. economic targets, according to former French intelligence officials. Guy Laugère, a veteran member of the SDECE who served as head of counterespionage for French intelligence, did work hard to counter Soviet-bloc intelligence operations in his country, but he was also a firm believer in the widespread use of Service 7 to target Western business executives in Paris. According to a former SDECE official, Laugère's view of counterespionage was particularly broad: "Our actions were not reserved for hostile agents, or provocateurs. I would say, well, that I would spend perhaps one quarter of [my] time, eavesdropping [and] tracking businessmen in Paris." He recalls one instance in particular, in March 1978, when he and the two other members of his team were given orders to bug a flat outside of Paris, in Saint-Cloud. They were given the address and told when the occupants would be away. Bugs were planted, and a listening post was established nearby, which the intelligence official and a colleague monitored. When the occupants returned, the team listened and was astonished to hear American voices—the men had assumed they would be hearing Russian or French. They contacted their superiors and asked for a confirmation of the address and clarification. "The occupants were not spies; they were businessmen, from the company GE."

Another de Marenches deputy was also committed to continued economic spying on the West. Colonel Alain de Gaignernon de Marolles was a graduate of the French military academy and had an extensive background in covert operations. Early on, de Marenches appointed de Marolles head of the Action Service of the SDECE. In that capacity, he was the director of French covert operations, both foreign and domestic. In 1977, happy with his performance, de Marenches promoted de Marolles further, this time to the head of the most important section of the SDECE, which formulated intelligence-gathering policy and made recommendations to the French president and prime minister based on what intelligence was being collected.

De Marolles prided himself in being an expert on North African affairs and was a strong advocate of maintaining close relations with most of the North African countries that had been under French influence. He viewed it as critically important that France, and not any other power, be the preeminent power in the region. "He saw the U.S. as a threat," says one CIA official who was based in North Africa in the late 1970s. "Particularly, he didn't want American companies, specifically oil companies, to supplant the French commercial ties in the region."

De Marolles's suspicions of American intentions were enhanced when the Carter administration began criticizing North African countries for their records on human rights. For de Marolles, the criticism of Morocco was in effect an effort to supplant pro-French regimes in North Africa. And when Washington suggested in 1978 that French arms sales were destabilizing the region, de Marolles said enough was enough. "He wanted to use French intelligence as a tool against Americans," says a former associate.

During the 1970s, the SDECE had approximately twenty-five hundred agents and at least the same number of honorary correspondents, according to a former director of French intelligence. He estimates that 15 to 20 percent of those agents were targeted against the United States, other

Western European countries, and Japan. "And they were tasked primarily for technological intelligence collection." During the second half of the decade, de Marolles constructed a cooperative relationship between the SDECE and the French customs police, one geared toward gathering financial information being held in secret Swiss bank accounts. Some attempts at collecting such intelligence were particularly crude.

In 1980, for example, the French customs police in cooperation with the SDECE attempted to blackmail a Swiss banker into passing on financial information concerning clients at his bank, Union des Banques Suisses. The banker, a Herr Stroehlin, was a technician in the head office of the UBS in Zurich, and French intelligence agents in the Swiss capital had heard that he had recently purchased an old mill in the small French town of Saillerand-les-Bordes. Stroehlin bought the property because it was much cheaper than anything equivalent in Switzerland, and he was hoping to make it a retirement home. French intelligence concocted a plan to blackmail him into passing along confidential financial information on UBS corporate and industrial clients. In early April, the French customs police, with the help of the SDECE, planted a stolen Alfa Romeo at Stroehlin's Saillerand-les-Bordes home. The next morning the French police arrived and accused the banker of having stolen the car. "They told him he was in deep trouble and that he could very possibly spend a considerable stretch in the slammer—not an inviting prospect for a banker," says one Swiss businessman with knowledge of the case.

Stroehlin was aghast. But rather than cave in, the banker vigorously defended his innocence. He said that he had been set up and that he would be willing to do whatever was necessary to cooperate with the police to solve the crime. At that point, French intelligence intervened. While feigning a lack of knowledge of any setup, agents suggested to Stroehlin that they might be able to offer him "a deal." In exchange for the charges being dropped, they asked for an extensive list of names and numbered accounts at the UBS.

Stroehlin paused and with quick thinking said that he did not have direct access to such information, but he certainly knew somebody who did: a certain colleague—whom he called Herr Ralf—might be able to provide it. It would probably require some money, however. After all, Herr Ralf needed incentives if he was to provide the information. French intelligence agreed, and by telephone a meeting was set up. Stroehlin suggested the Hotel Sheraton in Zurich as site for the rendezvous, and French officials again agreed.

At the meeting, Stroehlin and Ralf met with two French customs police officers in the hotel lounge and discussed the matter over drinks. Ralf wanted to know just how much he was going to get for the information. The police informed him that the intelligence service had a "standard fee" of about twenty thousand francs. Ralf agreed that this was a fair price, and the discussion then turned to where they should meet to make the transaction. The French agents didn't want to conduct the transaction in Switzerland, where they might be detected. The bankers, on the other hand, were not about to take the information into France. Finally, to their reluctance, the French agents agreed that the information did not have to be brought into France. The four agreed to meet at the train station in Basel, which was right on the border with France. The meeting would take place in five days, and they would meet in the first-class buffet of the railway station.

On the appointed morning, April 15, the two customs officers arrived at the buffet and sat down. Herr Ralf was there, but Stroehlin was nowhere to be found. A little suspicious, the two French agents proceeded with the transaction. They ordered beers. Suddenly a swarm of thirty Swiss police officers arrived. The two French agents were clearly shaken, but they soon realized they had been set up. Herr Ralf, it appeared, was not a corrupt banker. Indeed, he was none other than Ralf Elsner, the chief of security at UBS. Stroehlin, after he had returned from France, had contacted Elsner immediately and told him about the problem. Elsner, it seems, had contacted his friends at the Swiss police.

Not only were the two French agents taken off to prison, but to send French intelligence a not-so-subtle message, the Swiss held them incommunicado for two weeks. The sensitivity of their mission was no doubt apparent—they had carried no documents into Switzerland, only twenty thousand francs in cash. On April 28, Swiss authorities notified senior French officials of their agents' arrest. The Swiss kept the funds.

The case was not only an example of the lengths to which French officials were willing to go to gain economic information, but it was also a testament to the Swiss commitment to confidentiality. As one Swiss banker told *Forbes* magazine a few months after the Stroehlin case, "We Swiss take these things seriously. Economic espionage, as it's called, is an important crime here." But this crude attempt at obtaining information on Swiss bank secrets would not be the last by French intelligence. Indeed, the French would only become more sophisticated.

Dramatic changes occurred in French intelligence in 1981, and perhaps nowhere more so than in the field of economic espionage. The election of François Mitterand as president and a Socialist majority in parliament meant that the old guard in the SDECE, which was made up largely of military officers and Gaullists, would soon see their agency change. For the first time in more than twenty years, the Socialists would be calling the shots. The man appointed by President Mitterand to bring about a change in intelligence policy was Pierre Marion, business executive and honorary correspondent.

Marion brought with him a view that French intelligence needed reforming; the blunt methods used in the past needed to be made more sophisticated. He believed that the intelligence services should be professionalized, computerized, and focused more on economic espionage. His chief sponsor in the newly formed government was Defense Minister Charles Hernu, who had served in the Aerospace Consortium under the president's brother, General Jacques Mitterand. Like Marion, Hernu was a firm believer in bringing the intelligence services to the further assistance of French industry. "Mitterand, generally speaking, asked me to reorganize the service when I took charge," says Marion. "I did initiate very forcefully an economic intelligence and technological and industrial intelligence program at the end of 1981."

In his first meeting with Marion, Mitterand gave the new director of intelligence detailed instructions, setting them forth in terms of three key priorities. First, he wanted Marion to work to increase French intelligence of the Soviet bloc. Second, he wanted an aggressive domestic campaign to unmask Soviet moles. Third, and perhaps most startling, he wanted Marion to improve the "yield" of economic, technological, and industrial intelligence going to French industry.

To meet this third goal, Marion took a long, hard look at the organization of French intelligence. While Service 7 had performed some tasks of economic espionage, it was not systematic enough for the job. "Service 7 did conduct operations, specific operations, to get some intelligence on technology or industry; that's true," Marion says. "But . . . they were doing that as they were doing other types of activity. They were not oriented specifically [to] technological espionage." What he needed was a specific organization or unit of French intelligence that would engage in industrial espionage. "When I took charge there was no service in the organization agency which was specifically in charge of coordinating, of conducting intelligence in that field. So I created such a special department to do that in October 1981."

Marion created a small group, Planning, Forecasting, and Evaluation, which was responsible for determining industry and technology targets. He appointed Arsene Lux to direct this effort. Lux's job was to determine which Western companies in particular and which research facilities were to be targeted. It was an enormously difficult task, given the group's broad mandate. Planning, Forecasting, and Evaluation relied on French scientific attachés overseas to supply information indicating which companies were delving into which areas.

The group also drew up plans with Marion's newly created economic espionage service to expand economic espionage operations. In January 1982, a joint plan of action was issued by Planning, Forecasting, and Evaluation. It offered the following recommendations:

1. That the French intelligence service create a systematic method for monitoring foreign corporate representatives visiting Paris. This would include not only electronic surveillance but also bag operations. The plan called for the recruitment of honorary correspondents from among the staff of several Parisian hotels frequented by Western business executives.

2. That foreign French agents in Western countries "focus further" on economic and technological information as opposed to "general political intelligence." The paper noted specifically the value of seeking out "non-classified technical information overseas." Such information could be extremely helpful, and its procurement was unlikely to cause a diplomatic incident if detected.

3. That the intelligence service, through the use of overseas agents, actively seek out proprietary information that would be helpful to specific French companies.

4. That the intelligence service develop a computer system that would better enable French intelligence to keep abreast of developments in technology, and that the service create a greater data-base capacity for keeping track of information on foreign companies.

Marion's economic espionage division was a complex one, based on a core group of thirty-five to fifty members at headquarters, which directed operations to be carried out against foreign targets in France and overseas. It was given the authority to instigate operations when it saw fit, without obtaining direct approval from the Action Directorate, the covert arm of French intelligence. These changes and many others brought about a dramatic reform in the SDECE, and on April 4, 1982, the organization vanished altogether. In its place arose the Direction Générale de la Sécurité Extérieure.

One of the earliest and perhaps most spectacular successes of Marion's new economic espionage bureau involved a deal for more than two billion dollars that occurred at the expense of the United States. Throughout the second half of 1981 and early in 1982, the Indian government had been negotiating with the United States, the Soviet Union, and France for the possible purchase of fighter aircraft for the Indian air force. The Indians were prepared to spend two billion dollars for the planes, clearly a beneficial deal for whichever country could get it. All three countries were encouraged to submit private, sealed bids.

In mid-1981, the French intelligence station chief in New Delhi had recruited an Indian civil servant in the prime minister's office to pass along political information concerning internal political developments within the Indian government. The recruitment of the agent was reported to intelligence headquarters in Paris, as was standard. So when the fighter-plane deal was about to close, Marion's new unit swung into action. Lieutenant Colonel Alain Bolley, the deputy military attaché at the French embassy in New Delhi, was contacted by DGSE headquarters concerning the source in the Indian government. Bolley was instructed to use the source to gain access to the American bid. The source did, and France won the contract. "We had an informer inside the Indian chancellery which was making the decision," says Marion. "And we were able to get some intelligence about the proposals by the competitors."

The extensiveness of this French spy network was uncovered by Indian security officials in January 1985. Fifteen officials were arrested, including twelve members of the prime minister's secretariat, the president's office, and the Defense Ministry. Alain Bolley was hurriedly recalled by the French Defense Ministry after it was revealed that he was purchasing secrets from Indian government officials. Two French businessmen fled the country shortly thereafter, having received tips that they would face arrest on espionage charges.

French intelligence managed a similar success in South Korea. There the government was accepting bids for the construction of two nuclear-power facilities. Both French and U.S. companies were bidding. Again, according to Richard Walker, the U.S. ambassador in Seoul at the time, French intelligence had a mole who provided inside information that proved invaluable. French companies won the contracts. "We learned through intelligence sources that the Korean official that was responsible for making contract decisions for [the two facilities] was promised one million dollars and an apartment on the Champs-Élysées by French intelligence agents in exchange for the contracts," says Walker. "Money spoke, and French companies got the contracts."

Along with these successes overseas, the DGSE was actively recruiting permanent honorary correspondents at several prominent Parisian hotels. The DGSE was interested in individuals who would give agents access to the rooms of visiting business executives, help track their movements, and help coordinate eavesdropping operations. The most sought-after employees included those who manned the front desk and the cleaning and maintenance personnel. Personnel at the front desk knew better than anyone when hotel guests were in and out, a critical piece of information if the DGSE planned to run bag operations. Cleaning and maintenance staff offered another important asset: easy access to rooms, often at times when guests were out and about. All of these staff members were important parts of the puzzle.

The bag operations usually worked as follows. A French company negotiating with a foreign entity would contact the relevant government official within the Ministry of Industry and offer details concerning the potential size of the deal, the factors involved, or the potential value of secrets the foreign company might possess. The ministry would then contact the DGSE planning staff, and the DGSE would decide whether it was worth conducting an operation. If the decision was made to go ahead, the DGSE would get from government officials details about when the executives would be arriving, where they would be staying, how many people would be in the delegation, and so forth. It would not tell the French company anything. The matter was private.

The DGSE would then draw up a plan of action based on the information provided. Honorary correspondents at the visitors' hotel would be activated. After the visitors arrived, personnel at the front desk would note their schedules, and DGSE regulars would remain in the vicinity. When the visitors left for dinner or for an extended period of time, the front desk would contact the DGSE regulars, and honorary correspondents among the maintenance or cleaning crew would rendezvous at the room. The correspondents would offer the agents access, and a search would begin. The DGSE agents might photograph documents, photocopy them (if there was time), or simply steal them. The correspondent at the front desk acted as an early-warning system: if the visitor returned before the task had been completed, a phone call would be made to the room, warning of the impending return. All other calls were held, because the guest was out.

One hotel that has been particularly prone to break-ins of foreign business executives' rooms is the Hôtel Nikko in the west end of Paris. In April 1990, GTE officials returning from a late-night dinner party given by French "hosts" found that important company papers were missing from their briefcases. An AT&T team had a similar experience that same year, according to an American security consultant and French officials. And in February 1991, two rooms of NCR Corporation executives were broken into, an act that had all the marks of a typical French intelligence operation. Agents made off with two laptop computers believed to contain valuable corporate secrets.

Under Pierre Marion, more and more employees at foreign corporations based in France as well as overseas were recruited to collect economic information. Marion believes the practice of this recruitment policy is quite legitimate, even between friendly countries. "It's a normal action of an intelligence agency," he says. "To have an informer in the right place in foreign countries, and those right places include government agencies and foreign corporations." The wide use of informers in the gathering of political and military intelligence also makes sense to help an economy compete, he says. "When you have an intelligence service working through a chief of station, which is a station in a specific country, this chief of station tries to create a network of informers which are chosen because they are well located, well placed with information. I don't see why it should not apply to technological or industrial intelligence."

Recruiting informers in foreign government institutions and corporations and their subsidiaries in France became an increasingly important vocation for DGSE agents, one that continues to this day. At its most basic level, this activity includes the recruitment of French nationals who are working for foreign corporations based in Paris. DGSE agents play on two themes when seeking such recruits: money and patriotism. As the security director of an American company in Paris told William Carley of the *Wall Street Journal*, "Our French employees, especially those who have served in the French military, tell us that they are visited regularly by French intelligence agents. Their pitch is patriotism, and their questions are, 'What are your business plans, what are your research projects?' " DGSE agents are usually looking for middle- to senior-level managers or researchers. In some instances—when potential recruits are particularly prized—agents have even signed legal agreements offering the recruits employment should they lose their job as a result of their involvement with the DGSE. Important DGSE targets have included IBM, Texas Instruments, and du Pont, the German companies Bosch, Siemens, and BASF, and the Japanese companies Fujitsu, Hitachi, and Sony.

The DGSE works with the Direction de Renseignement Générale (RG) to identify French citizens who might be recruited. The RG, which is subordinate to the Ministry of the Interior, serves as a domestic intelligence-gathering service for the government. In November 1951, its official mission was described by decree: "It acts for the research and centralization of information about the political, social, and economic order necessary to inform the government." In this capacity, the RG maintains extensive files on several million noncriminal citizens. The intelligence is gathered by mean of an informer network that operates throughout France. DGSE agents rely on RG files to identify potential recruits. Two RG directorates—General Information and Foreigners, and Political, Social, and Economic Information—have the tasks of maintaining specific dossiers on Americans and other foreigners working in France and maintaining files on French nationals working for foreign corporations.

The DGSE also cross-references French military files with those of French nationals working for U.S. and other companies. These files, reflecting the military's interest in access to foreign technology that might be useful to its own defense industry, are fed to the DGSE through the Centre d'Exploitation du Renseignement Scientifique et Technique, Division du Renseignement, of the National Defense Staff. Former officers of the French armed forces are particularly attractive recruits for the DGSE.

The Centre d'Exploitation and the DGSE not only cooperate in identifying potential recruits who are already working for foreign corporations, but in 1984 they also developed a special project, dubbed Chameleon, to plant members of the French military in foreign corporations when doing so was deemed necessary. This activity is carried out particularly in corporations whose technologies are considered to be of critical importance to the French military industry. "Chameleon was designed to be a precise tool," says one U.S. intelligence official. "If a company has been identified and there is an opening, they will dress up a military technician with good credentials and try to get him in." Chameleon recruits were drawn primarily from the specialists within the French armed forces who have substantial technical backgrounds to begin with. One senior French official estimates that Chameleon has been used "perhaps fifty-five to sixty times" since the program began.

At the same time that economic espionage expanded so, too, did electronic espionage. The Directorate for Surveillance of the Territory, formed in 1982, was responsible for cooperating with the DGSE on this front. With the reorganization of the security services, the DST has responsibility for counterespionage and therefore has the tools needed to carry out eavesdropping activities. It was a DST team that eavesdropped on members of the White House staff when President Reagan visited Paris in 1982.

DST targets have also included corporations. Robert Courtney, the former director of data security and privacy at IBM, remembers French eavesdropping well. "There's no question they have been spying on IBM's transatlantic communications," says Courtney. "They tended to monitor everything—phone, telex, faxes—everything. It was a real problem, because even though our messages were encrypted and coded, they had them cracked. We were required to give them the keys to our codes." What they were most interested in, according to Courtney, was technical and proprietary information. He often found himself playing an electronic transatlantic game of cat and mouse. At times he would instruct IBM officials in New York to transmit fake instructions to the Paris office, informing them of a phony price increase. If a competitor in France, such as Compagnie des Machines Bull, boosted its price to the level mentioned in the cable, it was proof that the monitoring was continuing. "You just trip them up," says Courtney. "Then they would be caught wondering if the information they were getting was real or not."

Courtney believes that the French intelligence program for eavesdropping on U.S. and other foreign corporations continues. "It's quite rigorous and intensive," he says. "No doubt it has been enormously valuable for them. And the problem is, there's not a whole lot you can do about it. What are you going to do? Stop sending faxes and talking on the phone?"

According to a former DST official, the intercept program was popular with DST Director Marcel Chalet, who set it up soon after DST was formed. The DST maintains a "hot list" of particularly important targets, companies with information that is of most interest. In 1986, when this DST official was still involved with the program, the hot list included IBM, Corning Glass Works, Texas Instruments, Dow Chemical, General Electric, ITT, and Boeing. "Who we were listening to [was] dictated by the circumstances. If they were to bid, if they were engaging in certain research, or if there might be a merger, teams would—how do you say?—turn on the tap, and monitor communications."

The program continues to this day, say intelligence officials, and is believed to involve approximately forty personnel divided into ten four-man teams. Its success rests on the DST's ability to cooperate with the French national telecommunications and telephone company. "We have direct, easy access by permanent agreement. No paperwork," says one official.

In 1984, the DGSE made another important decision in the field of economic espionage. In March of that year, at the suggestion of President Mitterand, DGSE Director Admiral Pierre Lacoste issued an order to Service 7 to implement a program of intelligence collection within the European Communities. The order instructed Service 7 to recruit French civil servants and other European nationals for the purpose of providing "detailed information on European decision making." The DGSE station in Brussels was directed to implement the program, with the oversight and cooperation of General Roger Emin, then assistant head of the DGSE. Remy Patrand, at that time chief of cabinet to Claude Cheysson, the foreign minister, was briefed by General Emin about the new program in April 1984 at the Foreign Ministry.

Patrand would be particularly helpful in the effort. A graduate of the top school for civil servants, École Nationale d'Administration, he was well tied into the French foreign service, where many potential recruits could be found. Emin sought and received Patrand's cooperation in arranging assignments in Brussels for DGSE officers and civil servants who were willing to work as honorary correspondents. According to several French sources, at least a few important appointments were procured. Remy Patrand was no doubt wise to cooperate with General Emin and the DGSE. Sixteen months later, in August 1985, he was named the new head of the DST.

Recruiting among the "Eurocrats" was not an easy task: a botched recruitment could cause serious problems for Paris. A special DGSE agent named Jean-Claude Vaugnot, who had more than ten years' experience working throughout Europe for the DGSE, was asked to carry out the delicate process. He rented a flat in Brussels and, with the help of the DGSE station chief, began the laborious task of recruiting civil servants in Brussels. Early on, he concentrated on French nationals working for the EC. In many instances, it was simply a case of French employees at the EC being summoned to the embassy, where Vaugnot and the DGSE station chief would discuss the matter. Some, quite naturally, declined. But according to one official, a number of informers were recruited.

According to a senior DGSE official, the groundwork laid by Vaugnot paid off. By 1988, French intelligence had informers in several helpful offices. It maintained honorable correspondents on several directorates within the EC. At that time, there were moles on the science, research, and development directorate. Specifically, there were well-placed individuals in the subdivision that oversees EC policy relating to technical research and new technologies and in the subdivision that oversees EC policy relating to biology and medical research.

But the DGSE also had noticeable successes in gathering intelligence for the critical internal EC debates taking place between the member countries. According to a senior DGSE official, agents had a source in the British delegation to the EC summit at Luxembourg in December 1985: a junior aide on the delegation who had particularly strong pro-EC sympathies. Margaret Thatcher's British government was skeptical of the EC at the time, and the junior aide had approached some French civil servants in September about "assisting them" in accomplishing the goal of a unified Europe. The civil servants turned over the name to the DGSE, which contacted the British citizen through its station in London. After two preliminary meetings between the station and the possible source in late September and early October 1985, the DGSE arranged to fly him to Paris on the weekend of October 12–13. DGSE regulars met the source at Charles de Gaulle Airport and drove him to the Sheraton Hotel in Paris. There the source met with DGSE agents as well as two members of the Foreign Ministry who were working on EC matters. The DGSE agents never identified themselves as such for fear of scaring off the recruit. All the participants were described as French Foreign Ministry officials or "diplomats" in Brussels.

The station in London had attempted to determine what price the possible source wanted for the information he had regular access to. The Englishman insisted that he was not in it for the money and that he was not a spy. He became what French intelligence officials call an *agent bénévole* ("unpaid agent"). "He was motivated by his belief in Europe, not money," says one DGSE official. The DGSE did, however, pay the source for trips to Paris, a nice room at the Sheraton, and his expenses during the weekends in Paris, according to French intelligence sources. The British source made at least one more trip to Paris before the Luxembourg summit in December. The information provided was invaluable and offered Paris the opportunity to walk the diplomatic tightrope with London over the signing of the Single European Act. The act had been tenuously debated at the EC summit in Milan in June, but agreement finally came at Luxembourg.

The British source proved useful in future EC discussions as well. He made at least eleven weekend visits to Paris between the time of the EC summit in Luxembourg and the Brussels summit in June 1987. During that time, tensions between Paris and London were high as the Thatcher government resisted proposed budget reforms and the plan for the Community to be more than just a common market. The source briefed DGSE agents on internal discussions in the British Foreign Office and offered insights into the likely British position on a variety of EC subjects. The information was "invaluable" to Paris, says one DGSE official. Because of the nature of the relationship, the DGSE agents did not ask the British source to seek out information unrelated to the EC. "It was a judgment call," says one official. "The motivation was out of interest for the EC, not France or anything else. We could not risk it."

From time to time at the periodic meetings at the Sheraton Hotel, DGSE agents did try to deepen the relationship between handler and source by offering money, but the British Foreign Service officer always refused. In early 1987, he did make one simple request: he wanted his photograph taken with EC Commission President Jacques Delors. Weeks before the Brussels summit in June, the request was granted. After the photo opportunity in Delors's Paris offices, there was one last meeting at the Paris Sheraton. The British source again gave four French officials an extensive, four- to six-hour briefing based on handwritten notes made during the prior weeks. Then the official announced that the meetings would end. He was being transferred to a new branch in the Foreign Office, one that had little to do with the EC. The DGSE agents tried to convince him that even in his new position he would be of value to them, but he lacked the motivation to continue. In the end, the parting was somewhat bitter. "He believe[d] that we wanted him as [a] spy, which is, of course, really what he was," says one former DGSE official familiar with the case. "He had convinced himself that he was something more noble. The reality, for him, was harsh. A pity."

The DGSE worked hard throughout the 1980s to penetrate not only government institutions in Europe that would protect its interests in the EC, but also those in the United States that would meet the country's technology needs. Often what was sought in the U.S. government was advanced technology that would benefit French industry, particularly the armaments business and the high-tech sector. The program, dubbed Equinox by French intelligence officials, remains a high priority for French intelligence officials in the United States.

When French officials were unable to collect classified, secret technological information, they often settled for nonclassified government information that would offer assistance in seeking the technology from another source. The French calculation is a particularly shrewd one, says John Davitt, former director of internal security at the Justice Department. For many years, Davitt was responsible for reviewing FBI investigations of espionage-law violations in the United States. He says that the FBI investigates most vigorously the sale of top-secret military information. "For an American citizen to give classified, top-secret information is a traitorous act. Americans are therefore more apt to give nonclassified information." It is that American view that French agents have played off in the past. And according to Davitt, such calculations are worth it, because even that sort of information can be enormously valuable.

For several years, the DGSE station in Washington, D.C., had a very helpful relationship with an employee at the Defense Advanced Research Projects Agency. A small, secret government agency located across the Potomac River in Rosslyn, Virginia, DARPA provides U.S. high-tech companies with the funds to conduct research on a variety of cutting-edge technologies, most of which have direct military application. Much of the research taking place on DARPA-funded projects also offers enormous hope for spin-offs into the civilian sector, however.

Between 1986 and 1990, the DGSE station chief arranged to have DARPA-project research summaries and proposals forwarded to Major Jean-Louis Valade, the assistant attaché for armament and procurement at the French embassy. Major Valade, with the help of Pascal Chevit, a scientific attaché, would then interpret the information, make an assessment, and dispatch it to DGSE offices in Paris. There the DGSE tracked DARPA research projects and, on occasion, assigned an agent to the embassy in Washington to visit various DARPA-funded research projects across the United States. Consul officials in the United States were also called on from time to time to collect information on particular companies across the country. In early 1991, officials in Houston got a taste of one of these efforts.

One morning in early May, an unmarked van ventured into the posh

River Oaks section of Houston and quietly drove up to the home of a business executive. Two men jumped from the van, grabbed the trash bags outside the house, and threw them into the back of the van. A guard observed the whole incident, and as the van roared off, he took note of its license plate number. Officials at the company that employed the guard traced the plate to the French consulate in Houston. When company officials approached the French consul general in Houston, Bernard Guillet, he at first denied that the van was anywhere near the River Oaks section that day. But when the guard was shown a photograph of Guillet and identified him as one of the men in the van, Guillet shifted his story. He claimed they were at River Oaks but that he and an assistant were simply trying to pick up bags of grass cuttings for filler—there was a swimming pool at the consulate compound, he said, that couldn't be completed because of a zoning dispute. Guillet simply wanted the hole filled up. FBI agents in Texas were not convinced. Indeed, they continue to believe that Guillet was after documents discarded by corporate executives who lived in River Oaks, documents that might offer insights into DARPA research. Several companies that received DARPA support in 1990 and 1991 are headed by executives who live in River Oaks.

Information obtained from DARPA provided the groundwork for a sophisticated attempt by French intelligence to steal Stealth aircraft technologies from several small companies in 1991. French embassy officials had obtained copies of DARPA research grants to companies working on the low-observable coatings used on Stealth aircraft and their missiles. In August 1991, the DGSE assembled a six-man team of French engineers and briefed them on what was known about the low-observable coatings, which absorb radar, as well as what was known about the companies involved in the research. In the last week of September, the team left for Washington, D.C. Working out of the French embassy in Washington, the French engineers began contacting employees working for the companies listed by DARPA as doing Stealth-technology research. Team members posed as nuclear engineers trying to develop a new nuclear-safety technology based on the coatings. They appealed directly to company scientists to hand over the secret technology. "They tried to bluff . . . more than a dozen companies," said Richard Heffernan, a Connecticut-based security specialist who works with some of the targeted companies. "This was a well-organized information-gathering effort." By early November, the activities of the team, which had by then visited more than three cities, caught the attention of the FBI. Bureau agents confronted the French engineers in Washington and threatened expulsion if the operation continued. The French team quietly returned to Paris in the first week of December.

One of the more elaborate DGSE operations in the United States occurred in mid-April 1988, when a four-man team of technicians traveled to Seattle to monitor secretly flight tests being performed by the Boeing Company. The team included two DGSE agents from Paris who were experts in communications intercepts, a DGSE case officer with a technical background, and a research official named Jean August, who worked for the Aerospace Consortium. On April 11, the men traveled on Air France from Paris to Washington, where they were met by the DGSE station chief at the embassy in Washington and by Michael Badia of the French embassy. For three days, they stayed at the French compound, where they rested and were briefed by officials concerning their task.

France, which was making substantial investments in the European airplane consortium Airbus, was very interested in the tests that its rival, Boeing, was planning to conduct over the next several weeks. "When you think of the competition between Boeing and Airbus," says Pierre Marion, "even during the Cold War it was very strong. And that competition involved getting information on commercial proposals, testing, and technologies."

The assembled DGSE team was to travel to the Pacific Northwest in order to monitor the tests, which they planned to do by eavesdropping on data communications between personnel testing the new 747-400 and the flight-test headquarters on the ground in Seattle. For the task, the team would bring with them some electronics equipment that was matched with other equipment already at the French embassy compound in Washington. It was the team's job to collect the data; it was August's job to ensure that the proper data were being captured.

Knowledge of how the new Boeing 747-400 performed was very important to Airbus. The new version of the jumbo jet possessed advanced navigation electronics that allowed for a two-person crew in the cockpit rather than a three-person crew. A new electronics system was supposed to do the work that used to be done by the flight engineer. In the upcoming battery of flight tests, the performance of the new navigation system would be checked out. Boeing would also be testing a new modified engine, as well as a slightly modified wing design. Results of tests on handling, fuel burn, performance, and stress would be extremely valuable to Airbus. As one Boeing official puts it, the 747-400 was "an airplane of a new type."

Two days after their arrival, the DGSE team at the embassy was met by Georges Pilfrey, an Airbus employee who had been in Seattle for the past three weeks making technical arrangements. In surveying the area, Pilfrey had located the Boeing testing field in Everett, Washington, north of Seattle, as well as the location of the Seattle flight-test organization. Because test data from the plane in flight were not transmitted in a beam, any technical hookup capable of locking in on Boeing's frequency would allow them to read the test data as well. And the telemetry from the test aircraft was not coded or encrypted. Pilfrey made arrangements for the team and took out a six-month lease on a house in Everett. It was that property, with a large hedge and secluded back lot, that would enable the team to make the proper setup.

On April 17, the men flew to the Seattle-Tacoma International Airport with a few bags and some equipment. Pilfrey had the rest of their equipment shipped by air cargo, and it was waiting for the team. Once in Seattle, the men proceeded to the house as planned. In the backyard, they attached a portable satellite dish and pointed it in the direction of the airspace in which the 747-400 would be tested. They then hooked up an advanced-frequency scanner and two portable computers. One computer would interface with the scanner and electronically record and store the signals. The other computer would run a series of complex mathematical functions to make sense of the data that were being recorded. After running a series of preliminary tests, the team proceeded with its second mission, which was to take the necessary steps to intercept the televised conference that would follow the flight tests. The conference was a meeting of Boeing officials at several sites and was to be beamed by a microwave transmitter. They would discuss test results and analyze their findings. Monitoring the conference was a relatively easy task; it simply required the DGSE team to pick up the microwave signals.

In late April, the flight testing began as the giant 747-400 lumbered off the runway and into the sky. Several tests were conducted over the next several days, many of which were of little interest to the DGSE team. But when the tests on the new computerized navigation system began, the DGSE men were listening, and Jean August was ecstatic. According to DGSE officials, the effort was well worth it. The data were given to Airbus officials when the DGSE team returned to Paris. Barely two years later, Airbus was placing a similar navigation system in its latest aircraft—the A340.

Perhaps the most elaborate DGSE operation carried out against U.S. companies took place between 1987 and 1989. It was a plan conceived by two senior officials at the DGSE—Colonel Jean Heinrich, the director of special operations, and General François Mermet, who served as the head of foreign administration—in order to bring the collection of intelligence on specific U.S. corporations to a higher level. The recruitment of employees and the placement of moles had been largely successful, but, according to Heinrich, the information being provided was not always particularly useful. He attributed the problem to two things. First, he felt that the DGSE handlers were not adequately supervising the agents in place: the agents were left largely to collect information as they saw fit. Second, Mermet believed that there was not enough targeting of specific technologies and companies. He told one subordinate in January 1987 that there were "a handful of critical companies" that if "penetrated" could dramatically help France's technological position.

In late January, Mermet appointed a DGSE official named Christophe Defay to identify the high-tech companies whose secrets could most benefit France. By February 8, Defay had identified three companies: IBM, Texas Instruments, and Corning Glass. IBM and Texas Instruments were industry leaders in computer technologies; Corning, in fiber optics. The DGSE took Defay's findings to heart and in March began a campaign to recruit senior-level officials in the French offices of each company. By mid-summer, according to DGSE sources, the operation had succeeded in recruiting individuals at all three companies.

At IBM in particular, the DGSE had tremendous success. An IBM employee named Jean Lucure was a particularly productive source. He also worked with his handlers to help recruit five other IBM employees, all of whom were strategically placed. Two of the five, like Jean Lucure, were in IBM management, a position that gave them access to a great breadth of information—everything from strategic business decisions, financial information, and bids on contracts to high-tech research. The other three were scattered around in other departments—finance, research, and sales. Although it is not fully known how much information made its way to the DGSE, it is known that by the fall of 1987 the information the DGSE did receive was enormously valuable. Indeed, it was so valuable that sometime in the third week of November the DGSE decided to set up a pipeline to the financially troubled state-owned French electronics giant, Compagnie des Machines Bull. French government officials were concerned that Bull, without an infusion of technology, however acquired, would continue to fall dramatically behind the foreign competition.

At about the same time that Lucure and other sources were at work at IBM, four agents were busy at Texas Instruments, and two at Corning Glass. All were passing "volumes of information" to DGSE agents, according to a former senior DGSE official. Indeed, the recruits at the Texas Instruments facility in Velizy were keeping their handlers so busy that an apartment near the Texas Instruments facility was rented by the DGSE in order to store, collate, and copy documents. "They must have had better knowledge of our research and marketing work than senior company officials in the States," admits a Texas Instruments–Europe employee. Robert Courtney says the operation was "very sophisticated. They must have been getting quite a bit to expend such an effort."

Although the operation appeared to be running smoothly, things were slowly starting to unravel. In early 1989, an American CIA official assigned to the U.S. embassy in Paris ran across some peculiar rumors concerning IBM and Texas Instruments. A dispirited DGSE agent with a drinking problem began to speak about his involvement in the operation to an American friend, and the friend took the garbled pronouncements to the CIA station chief at the embassy. When CIA officials went to security officials at all three companies, they found that the security officials had suspicions, too. A joint FBI-CIA team working with security officials from all three companies began to crack the network. After seven months of diligent work, they succeeded. In November 1989, the CIA and the State Department confronted French diplomats with evidence. Employees at all three facilities were sacked. At first, there was denial, but after two weeks of hand wringing the DGSE relented: in the second week of December, it privately admitted its involvement to senior CIA officials visiting Paris.

6

The Mysterious Mr. Spence

This operation was set up with Japanese government connections; that they can't deny.

—Dr. Robert Angel, former director of the Japan Economic Institute

On the morning of November 10, 1989, a cleaning lady at the Ritz Carlton Hotel in Boston tried to enter Room 429 to prepare it for new guests. A Mr. C. F. Kane had been in the room since November 4, but he was supposed to have checked out. She turned the key in the lock and pushed on the door, but it wouldn't budge. She called several co-workers, and they tried together, but to no avail. The door was sealed shut from the inside. She told her superiors, and after they tried unsuccessfully to force open the door, they called the Boston Police and Fire departments.

Only after the fire department sawed the door in half did authorities get in, nearly three hours after the cleaning lady first approached the room. Inside authorities found a macabre, bizarre sight. A king-size bed and a chair had been arranged to block the door. Lying on the bed was a corpse. The body was dressed in a black tuxedo with a white bow tie, white suspenders, and black socks and shoes. On the corpse's face was a blank expression and eyeglasses, and nearby were personal papers, jewelry, and a stack of money. After getting over their initial shock, the assembled police officers and hotel officials began rummaging through the personal belongings, trying to find some clue as to what might have happened. When the police examined legal documents they found near the corpse, they discovered that C. F. Kane was not who he said he was. The man was really Craig Spence, a notorious Washington, D.C., lobbyist and eccentric social host with mysterious connections and strange personal habits. The use of C. F. Kane as an alias was a typical Spence joke: Charles Foster Kane is the name of the main character in his favorite movie—*Citizen Kane*.

On November 13, after examining the body, the Boston coroner's office declared the death a suicide. And given the events of recent months, no one who knew Spence was surprised. In June of that year, he had been implicated by the *Washington Times* for taking part in a notorious Washington, D.C., homosexual prostitution ring that blackmailed its customers and engaged in credit card fraud. He had been summoned before a federal grand jury to testify on the subject. On August 9, he had been arrested in New York City for possession of cocaine and an illegal handgun. He had picked up a male prostitute and brought him to his room at the Barbizon Hotel on the Upper East Side. Police were summoned when Spence burst screaming from the hotel room, saying he was being robbed. Police determined that the gun and the cocaine were his, and it looked as if time in prison would result from the charges. Finally, Spence was under a natural sentence of death anyway. He had AIDS, and he was starting to see its effects.

Spence's suicide dramatically halted a federal investigation of his activities. The prostitution-ring investigation went nowhere, with U.S. officials saying there was insufficient evidence of "financial blackmail." Those who had given Spence and his friends "midnight tours" of the White House in exchange for Rolexes were disciplined and fired. But Spence took secrets with him to the grave. What remained behind—and what was kept from the general public—was Spence's incredible escapades and often sophomoric activities in the world of intelligence and espionage.

Far from being a simple lobbyist, Spence provided his Japanese clients—who represented both the government and large corporations— intelligence on senior Washington officials. He obtained the information in a variety of ways, most often through briefings with U.S. government officials and "profiles." But he had ventured even deeper into the murky world of intelligence, maintaining files on U.S. government officials who frequented a prostitution ring and were practicing homosexuals. And the information was given to his clients.

Dr. Robert Angel, a Japan specialist, remembers viewing the Craig Spence affair from a distance. For seven years, until July 1984, Angel served as director of the Japan Economic Institute, an organization funded by the Japanese government to collect information, and in that capacity he met Spence once. But what interest would Japanese officials have in sensitive information about homosexuals in the government? "Japan was looking for people who were vulnerable—in the White House, and on Capitol Hill," says Angel. "They didn't want anything nice."

Craig Spence was born on October 25, 1940, in upstate New York. He studied communications and broadcasting at Boston University and in 1963 took a job as a secretary in the Massachusetts State House of Representatives. Soon after, he went to work for WCBS in New York City, and then in 1969 he spent the year in Vietnam as a correspondent for ABC News.

While on the job in Vietnam, Spence was known for pulling disappearing acts, sometimes for weeks at a time. Many times his colleagues assumed he had been killed or captured by the Viet Cong while trying to cover a story deep in the jungle. Suddenly, however, as quickly as he had disappeared, he would reappear, always refusing to say where he had been. Spence was forced to leave Vietnam in 1970, after losing his press credentials because he had exchanged his paychecks on the black market.

From Saigon, Spence went to Tokyo, where he worked as a stringer for the ABC radio network. His pay was meager, but he began slowly building a series of relationships that would carry him in future years. They included contacts with prominent Japanese government officials, as well as with several businessmen in the leading corridors of power in Japan. None of these was more important to his future, however, than his relationship with Motoo Shiina, a powerful member of Japan's ruling Liberal Democratic party. Shiina recognized Spence's ability to charm, his penchant for drama, and his driving ambition as characteristics that might be useful to his own business interests and to the interests of Japan.

Spence had always longed to be involved in something secretive and exciting, according to his former friends, and so when Motoo Shiina introduced Spence to his father, the struggling journalist saw it as an opportunity. Etsusaburo Shiina was a powerful figure in Japanese public life. A leader in the Liberal Democratic party, he had been the kingmaker responsible for the rise to power of Prime Minister Miki Takeo. But no matter who was prime minister at a given moment, the elder Shiina was a key figure in his political ascent. He was also a powerful figure behind the creation of the Ministry for International Trade and Industry and had served as the MITI minister immediately after the Second World War. Both the elder and the younger Shiina took Spence under his wing, offering him gifts and money in exchange for information on American journalists in Japan. They were interested in their attitudes toward Japan, as well as their personal views on economic issues.

In 1979, after a three-year relationship, Motoo Shiina offered Spence a position as the Washington representative of a Tokyo-based organization. The Policy Study Group was funded by MITI as well as by several large Japanese companies. A PSG brochure offered this explanation of the group's activities and relationship with the Japanese government. "PSG is based in Tokyo and supported by Japanese industry. It is independent of the Japanese government, although its objectives and activities are endorsed by the ministries of Finance, Foreign Affairs, and International Trade and Industry as a means of generating reliable, unbiased research to aid business and government decision-makers." The brochure concluded candidly: "PSG takes no official position on any of the issues it studies and makes no policy decisions. Instead it functions to supplement traditional sources of information."

In 1979, the PSG list of officers belied the fact that this was no ordinary think tank. Its chairman was Etsusaburo Shiina; its president, Motoo Shiina. Its board of directors included two members of the Diet, Shigesaburo Maeo and Hirokichi Nadao; the director of Nippon Steel Corporation, Tomisaburo Hirai; the chairman of Sumitomo Metal Company, Hosai Hyuga; the director of Nippon Industrial Bank, Sohei Nakayama; and the director of the Idemitsu Oil Company, Keisuke Idemitsu. The financial manager for the PSG was Junpei Nishimura, the president of the Japanese External Trade Organization. Nadao and Nishimura would later play central roles in the broadening Spence story.

In reports filed with the Justice Department as a registered agent, Spence made clear his understanding of what the PSG was all about. He described his activities for the PSG as "representation of Japanese corporations and government agencies in the U.S." Spence's job was to serve as the eyes and ears for Shiina in the U.S. capital, to report directly to him information that he collected concerning U.S. attitudes toward Japan, and to identify key government officials and assess their views. He was paid $12,000 per month by the PSG, and Motoo Shiina also provided him with a loan of $345,000 with which to buy a house to serve as the base of operations. Spence bought an imposing brick building in the Kalorama section, an expensive and exclusive neighborhood where Washington's wealthy and influential live.

Once in Washington, he began to establish himself in the capital's social circles. He threw big parties and held "seminars" in his home, oftentimes with an impressive guest list. Media stars Ted Koppel and Eric Sevareid came, as did William Casey, the Reagan CIA director, and others. Spence attracted many near stars, too, senior government officials or aides to powerful Washington officials. He drew rave reviews for his entertaining talents. In 1980, *Washington Post* social columnist Maxime Cheshire wrote about Spence: "Sevareid was the star attraction at what amounts to the coming-out party of a new Washington host who has already been generating lots of talk. Not since Ethel Kennedy used to give her famous Hickory Hill seminars for great minds in our times during the days of Camelot has anyone staged seminars successfully on a continuing social basis in Washington."

Spence's eccentricities and unique tastes began to shine through almost immediately. He bought a lap dog that he quickly named Winston and was never without. (He even trained the dog to sit so still that he could be hidden in a large shopping bag and taken on airplanes.) He hired bodyguards, who escorted him to parties, although no one could quite understand why he felt he needed them. And he often attended parties dressed in outrageous attire. One of his favorite items was a black cape with a red lining.

And he had a flair for the verbal exaggeration. He told elaborate stories about his past and often bragged about his dealings with intelligence agencies, including the CIA. He once claimed he was going on a secret mission to Central America for the U.S. government. At times he would throw a telephone caller off guard by saying, "This is God. Speak." He told friends that there was much he admired in Asian society. His favorite story about Japan concerned a Japanese food-service manager who, after some of his customers suffered from food poisoning, committed suicide. "Now that's what I call quality control," he would say with a chuckle.

But although he told many a wild tale about nonexistent exploits, Spence was involved in a very real effort by Japanese officials to collect intelligence on American political leaders and to find out other pieces of information in Washington. And despite his flamboyance, he told very few about his precise arrangement with the PSG. Craig Spence Associates, his company, kept a low profile. Its phone number was unlisted, and Spence regularly reported to the Justice Department that his principal job for the PSG was to "provide information," something he never told friends and colleagues.

Concerned about trade and security relations with the United States, the PSG instructed Spence to sponsor private seminars for Japanese embassy officials in Washington. On July 11, 1979, Robert Cassidy of the Senate Finance Committee spoke on "How the U.S. Congress deals with international trade issues." On October 3, Cassidy spoke again; this time, as the new general counsel in the Office of the U.S. Trade Representative, his topic was "The Reorganization of the Office of the Special Trade Representative and Its Effects on U.S. Trade Policy." On October 20, Dr. Roy Werner, the deputy assistant secretary of the army, spoke on "U.S.-Japan Bilateral Security Issues." On November 16, Dr. Richard Kaufman, the assistant director and general counsel of the Congressional Joint Committee on Economics, spoke on "U.S. and Japan Economic Trade Issues." On December 5, Ambassador Elliot Richardson, then the special representative to the Law of the Sea Treaty, gave a presentation on "The Law of the Sea Negotiations and Its Implications for International Trade."

In 1980, the seminars continued. They were becoming an important source of information for the PSG and the Japanese government. On April 9, Dr. Kent Hughs, an international economist with the Congressional Joint Committee on Economics, spoke on "Problems between the U.S. and Japan: From Cars to Computers. The Future of Free Trade: Planning or Protection?" On May 13, Dr. Herman Franssen, the director of international market analysis at the Department of Energy, spoke on "The Politics of Oil."

In 1981, the seminar program grew. On February 4, Carl Ford, a staff member of the Senate Foreign Relations Committee, spoke on "U.S.-Japan Defense Issues." William Lake, Jr., a partner at a Washington, D.C., law and lobbying firm, spoke to Spence's group on April 7 about "Laws and Logistics of Coal Exports to Japan." One week later, on April 14, Dr. Robert Russell, the staff director of the Senate Subcommittee on International Economic Policy, spoke on "Cooperation and Conflict: International Economic Issues Between the U.S. and Japan." On July 7, two senior aides to Michigan Senator Donald Riegle, Jr.—Don Campbell and James Arbony—spoke on "Prospects for the American Auto Industry." A senior partner at a powerful Washington legal and lobbying firm, William Dickey, spoke on October 29 about trade-dumping issues. On December 7, Robert Cassidy spoke yet again, this time in "A Discussion of Emerging Trade Frictions between Japan and the U.S." A similar series of lectures continued through 1982 and into early 1983.

According to a former Spence associate who attended many of the lectures, the speakers were left in the dark regarding the audience. Often Spence would invite prominent friends and specialists to the seminar to make it appear less "Japanese dominated." He never told the speakers that many in the audience were Japanese government officials. Nor did he tell them he was a registered agent for the Japanese government. And finally, he didn't tell them that their presentations and the discussions that followed were being recorded; he always told the speakers that comments were "off the record."

"He wanted [the speakers] relaxed and candid," says the former associate. "He wanted them to give specifics on the topics. Funny, now that I think of it—few questions were asked by the audience regarding the 'big picture,' on the issue. They were all specific. They wanted the names of officials in government and their attitudes on these issues being discussed."

One official who made a presentation before the Spence group remembers much the same. "It wasn't like an ordinary seminar," he says. "It was more like getting questions in a court of law. 'Who is doing such-and-such?' and so on. It became clear to me, but only near the end, that what they really wanted was intelligence on the various positions on issues related to Japan being taken by particular government officials."

Spence's nickname for his seminars was Operation Sunshine, because they were designed to "shed light" on Washington for Japanese political and business leaders.

Another method Spence used to collect information was through another legal means—U.S. journalists. He would approach a journalist, telling him or her that he knew of a Japanese publication that wanted a profile of a particular official in the administration. Among those journalists who wrote profiles for Spence were Ira Allen, Gregory Gordon, and Robert Mackey of United Press International and Sarah McClendon. According to Allen, the profiles Spence wanted would include a summary of the subject's career, political views, and personal interests and habits. The journalists were surprised when they found out that the profiles were not intended for public consumption but, rather, would be added to the dossiers that both the PSG and JETRO were keeping on senior U.S. government officials. As Sarah McClendon put it in a letter about Spence to the Senate Press Gallery, "I filled what I thought was a legitimate professional request from Spence for profiles on permanent officials of the Reagan Administration." When she discovered where the profiles were ending up, she "cut off" her dealings with Spence.

In forms that he was required to file regularly with the Justice Department, Spence was quite open about his activities as a foreign agent because, legally speaking, he was doing nothing wrong. When asked to "describe in full detail your activities and services," Spence wrote, "The registrant arranged meetings, seminars and social occasions attended by representatives of members of the foreign principal [PSG], Japanese government officials, U.S. government officials, U.S. business personnel, and others to discuss political and economic issues." He concluded by noting that "the registrant also provided information to the foreign principal."

Spence was holding two sorts of parties in his Kalorama brick house. The posh, elite parties in which Japanese officials and prominent Americans met and mingled were the public side of his life. Those who regularly attended these parties included a Who's Who of Washington. Besides those already mentioned, there were Senator John Glenn; Senator Richard Stone;

Richard Holbrooke, then assistant secretary of state for Asian affairs; Richard Davies, a former U.S. ambassador to Poland; and journalist Liz Trotta. The parties were impressive. As society-page reporter Phil Gailey of the *New York Times* wrote, "What most impresses, if not benefits his clients, is his ability to master the social and political chemistry of this city, to make and use important connections and to bring together policy makers, power brokers and opinion shapers at parties and seminars."

Spence's private parties were of an altogether different sort. Almost weekly he brought together an assortment of homosexual friends, and the activities would include group sex and drug use. Participants included individuals from various walks of life, including White House and government officials. They, no doubt, wanted to keep this part of their life private, too, something that Spence decided to use to his advantage.

This secret side of Spence's life was known to Shiina and the PSG, and when Spence began providing his clients with information about government officials who were frequenting his off-hours parties, they were most interested. One Japanese official involved in collecting the information was a former Ministry of Finance official who was based at the embassy in Washington, Chikara Higashi. According to Angel, who knew Higashi, he was "quite a supporter of Spence." Higashi made sure that the "sensitive information" Spence was collecting was going to the right people and files were being maintained.

In 1981, Spence's private, secret parties would offer him information that would be extremely valuable in his work for the PSG. A White House official who was a frequent off-hours guest forewarned Spence about the White House view of Richard Allen, the national security adviser. Allen had accepted several wristwatches as gifts from Japanese friends and was in trouble on a conflict-of-interest charge. A full two days before it was known to the general public, Spence informed Shiina that Allen was on his way out. This tip made Spence extremely popular with PSG board members, particularly with Nadao and Nishimura.

Spence's activities continued without trouble until 1982, when rumors about his "private activities" began circulating. Motoo Shiina was clearly not pleased with the public light being shed on Spence. In February of 1983, fearing that it would jeopardize Spence's mission, he went to other officials at the PSG and MITI to discuss the problem. Spence told

Shiina not to worry, that the problem was not serious, but Shiina thought otherwise. Spence was summoned to the JETRO office in New York City to discuss the matter, and senior JETRO officials told Spence that something had to be done. Shiina feared for his own reputation—when he visited Washington, he often stayed with Spence. So in 1983, Shiina wrote to Spence that the relationship had become "a personal burden to me." He exercised his right to cut off PSG funds to Spence, whether MITI thought it a good idea or not. He concluded by saying, "I have also found out that having a representative in a foreign capital is not considered as commendable, but rather dubious behavior."

But while Shiina wanted to sever his personal ties with Spence, he still saw value for MITI and Japan in what Spence was doing. Others at MITI and JETRO agreed, as did PSG board member Hirokichi Nadao. In Nadao's eyes, Spence had certainly proved his value, through the seminars and, particularly, in the Richard Allen case. Spence was providing tremendous amounts of information. The Japanese saw him as a maverick but as an effective man to have in Washington. So although Shiina cut off MITI funds going through the PSG to Spence, the decision was made to maintain the relationship with Spence, minus the PSG as a conduit. Henceforth, funds would come directly from MITI, through its foreign arm, JETRO. The JETRO office in New York put Spence on the payroll, paying him on paper what appeared to be a meager forty-two thousand dollars per year. That was a small amount for someone in Spence's line of work and someone of his value. But according to FBI officials, Spence was receiving much more under the table in the form of cash bonuses. According to federal sources, some of Spence's personal papers subject to inspection in connection with a grand jury investigation after his death indicate that Spence received bonuses of as much as thirty-two thousand dollars in a single payment. In 1985 alone, his records showed seven bonuses with the initials *J.E.T.* written next to them. Officials believe that could only be a reference to JETRO.

But JETRO officials in New York City also worked to pay Spence more by helping him get other clients. In the early 1980s, JETRO officials had suggested to a New Jersey–based health-care company with a plant in Japan that Spence would be a good consultant, one who could generate "access" to officials in Japan. Becton-Dickinson wanted such access, not only to protect its interests but also to pursue ways in which its products could be better distributed in Japan. The company took the advice of JETRO officials, and by 1986 it was paying Spence $250,000 a year for his services. These services were nothing more than getting JETRO officials to meet with Becton-Dickinson officials and having the New York JETRO office arrange meetings with Japanese officials. Although this was something JETRO was supposed to be doing in the first place, the Japanese organization saw this as an opportunity to offer Spence a little something extra. "He really didn't do much," says a Becton-Dickinson company official. "He arranged a few meetings here and there, but that was pretty much it. Where paying Spence helped us was with JETRO. They were suddenly very cooperative in whatever we needed."

Personal relations between Spence and Shiina continued to deteriorate despite the new arrangement. Spence felt that Shiina had been unreliable, and continually sniped about him to JETRO officials and officials he met with. On several occasions, Chikara Higashi took back to Shiina news of what Spence was saying. By 1984, Shiina was fed up, and he decided to take Spence to court. He claimed that Spence had been conducting "private business" in the Kalorama house he'd bought in 1979, and Shiina wanted the house back. Shiina argued that the house was legally his, and he lent the money to Spence to purchase it only to provide a base for the PSG. Now Spence was conducting his own business from the house, so the evidence seemed to be against him. Shiina had a pretty good case: the facts were all in writing. After all, the money in question had been lent to Spence when he was the PSG Washington representative, and the house was to serve as the PSG office in Washington. With the relationship severed, it appeared pretty clear that Spence owed Shiina some money.

In spite of a seemingly air-tight case, the Japanese party boss decided to settle out of court. And in the settlement both individuals signed, Spence was the clear winner. He retained ownership of the house, which was now worth well over twice the price he had paid for it with Shiina's money. (In 1988, Spence would sell the house for a cool nine hundred thousand dollars.) He repaid Shiina only the money that was owed him. How did he manage to achieve this turnaround?

According to Spence's own claims, he won the lawsuit against Shiina through blackmail, by threatening to disclose Shiina's activities in the

United States, including the illegal transfer of funds to this country. Shiina denied that claim, and according to senior government officials familiar with the case, the real reason for the out-of-court settlement was pressure exerted on Shiina by officials who did not want to embitter Spence. He was useful to them, and if his split with Shiina became too great, he might quit or, worse, reveal what he was doing.

By 1985, therefore, Craig Spence had been cut free from Shiina but was still funded by JETRO and JETRO-inspired sources. Perhaps most important, Spence maintained contact and cordial relations with Nadao. The elderly Japanese political patriarch strongly recommended Spence to Mitsuaki Sato, the president of JETRO–North America, which was based in New York.

Nadao was extremely interested in maintaining an alternative source of information in Washington, so as not to rely solely on the Japanese Foreign Ministry, according to a former JETRO employee. He had a long-standing connection with intelligence and security issues in Japan and his views on the subject were well respected. During the Second World War, he had served as vice president of the Naimusho, a secret organization later disbanded by the U.S. occupation forces for "repressive activities before and during the war." In the postwar years, Nadao was involved in the organization of the intelligence, security, and police apparatus under Prime Minister Nobusuke Kishi. Says a former JETRO official who knew Nadao, the Diet member was "obsessed with information" about the United States and its political leaders, particularly regarding decisions on trade and economic issues related to Japan. "He believed that we needed foreknowledge of events because he saw the U.S. government as unreliable and unpredictable."

In 1986, the Japanese government under Prime Minister Yasuhiro Nakasone reorganized its intelligence services, but according to Dr. Angel, it also made a conscious decision to expand the collection of political intelligence. "New . . . emphasis was placed on knowing more about political decision making taking place in important capitals around the world," says Angel. "Washington, of course, was the most critical."

With a new mission to collect political intelligence, Nadao went to Nakasone aide Gotoda Masaharu and talked to him about Spence. Masaharu saw the wisdom of greater political intelligence and had Sato make the arrangements in New York.

According to a former JETRO official, what Sato took to Spence was a three-point proposal. First, Spence would provide political intelligence on Japan-related affairs in U.S. government circles. Specifically, the offer mentioned a set of files and dossiers of all major figures involved in Japan-related issues in both the Executive and the Congressional branches. The reports were supposed to take the same form as those that journalists had previously prepared for the PSG but would also include more details of both professional and personal facets of the subjects' lives. Second, Spence would maintain the highest discretion regarding his new role; he would not mention his new relationship with JETRO to friends or colleagues. Third, Spence would be taken off budget. Henceforth, his financial relationship with JETRO would be covert. He was not to report his JETRO income to the Justice Department, nor was he to register as a foreign agent for Japan.

On November 16, approximately ten days after the offer was made, Spence accepted it unconditionally. He agreed to provide the dossiers on a biweekly basis, to be passed or "dropped" to a JETRO employee who would take the shuttle from New York City to Washington.

Much of what Spence provided was based on gossip and general information he collected from the Washington social circuit. He continued to hold the elaborate parties at his Kalorama home, and they continued to be attended by the famous and the near famous.

There was some dispute, after Spence's death, as to whether Spence had his house bugged so that he could have party conversations recorded. Spence actually bragged in some instances that his home was bugged for "security reasons." Pierre Rinfret, a friend from New York who regularly socialized with Spence, had this to say when reports of Spence's activities began to leak out in 1989: "He always tended to be a bit mysterious. He ran his own intelligence network in the U.S. and Japan." Whereas some, like Rinfret, believe that Spence's place was probably geared for electronic eavesdropping, others are skeptical, dismissing the reports as part of the image that Spence was trying to create. What is known, however, is that those who purchased the house from Spence in 1988 experienced strange problems when they moved in. In one instance, it was confirmed that the phone had been tapped by Spence himself.

Spence also relied on a group of four bodyguards to collect information for him. Guests report that when Spence arrived at a party, his bodyguards would fan out. They would stand in different parts of the room, not speaking to anyone. Sometimes their eavesdropping was so obvious that it drew stares from other guests.

Although the information Spence gathered in this way was extremely useful to JETRO, he also provided information of a more intimate sort, for he was now involved in a homosexual escort service based in Bethesda, Maryland, an exclusive Washington suburb. It was this ring that federal officials would eventually investigate in response to allegations of black-mail and credit card fraud. What Spence wanted from the ring was not just money, but information. The escort service was selective in terms of the clients it took on. The principals involved therefore often knew not only the legal names of its clients but also their professions. Spence was given access to the service's files, which included the names of a fair number of government officials, not only in Congress and in several government agencies, but also on the White House staff. In his regular dossiers for JETRO, Spence included the names and titles of those government officials who frequented the escort service. JETRO officials maintained a special file on those individuals who Spence named as active homosexuals.

Dr. Robert Angel remembers hearing rumors of Spence's activities and the possible involvement of his clients. As early as 1984, he went to friends at the Japanese embassy to talk about the problem. "I warned very senior Japanese government officials about Spence and what he was supposedly involved in," says Angel. "And they said they definitely knew about it, but the decision had been made by MITI, and there was nothing they could do." According to Angel, later claims by Japanese officials that they knew nothing about Spence and his activities were simply not true. "Nothing could be further from the truth. [Spence] was working for Shiina, and [then] MITI. They knew." The clear goal of cooperating with Spence was MITI's hope of "compromising U.S. government officials" and thus blackmailing them for information. "This operation was set up with Japa-nese government connection; that they can't deny. The Shiina effort was to give MITI deniability," says Angel.

Spence worked hard to collect his information for JETRO. The task of forming the files was strenuous and tedious. He collected credit card imprints from clients of the Bethesda ring and often went through federal or Congressional employment directories when it was determined that a client worked for the government. He would keep copious notes about social functions he attended and comments made at parties. Once he had developed a file on an individual, he would alert JETRO that he was ready for a pickup. Spence apparently refused to mail the information, probably fearing that if the package were damaged or opened in transit, he and JETRO would be put in jeopardy.

Late one night in January 1988, Spence called a friend. "Come get me," he said. He'd been picked up for drunk driving and was clearly concerned about something. Once home, his friend says, "he was speaking in sort of waves." Still slightly intoxicated, Spence described a mysterious tale. He had "missed a drop," he said, and "someone's life might have been forfeited."

The friend had heard Spence claim repeatedly that he worked for the CIA, and he figured this was probably just another reference to that claim. But according to one source, Spence's fear that night was real, and it wasn't a CIA drop he had missed. He was supposed to make a drop to a JETRO employee that night, a delivery of two new files. As he drove through downtown Washington, lights suddenly flashed through his rear window. A police cruiser pulled him over. Spence had been to a party earlier and had had plenty to drink. The policeman, on smelling his breath, administered a Breathalyzer and arrested him for driving under the influence. Not only did Spence miss the drop, which was bad enough, but the two files were on the front seat of his car, in an unmarked manila envelope. The police impounded the vehicle. Spence must have wondered what would happen to him if the police stumbled across the files.

The next morning Spence called the JETRO offices in New York City in a panic. He told his main contact what had happened. Horrified, the JETRO official cursed him and demanded that he retrieve the information. "And he warned Spence that if the information was found, JETRO would refute any claims Spence made about their involvement," says one source. Fortunately for both Spence and JETRO, he was able to retrieve his car, with the envelope intact and no questions asked. JETRO officials who knew about Spence's activities on their behalf were outraged at his sloppiness. If it happened again, JETRO would cut him off and deny any connection, they informed him.

Spence's activities continued without incident until February 1989, when federal officials raided the house in Bethesda out of which the prostitution ring was being run. FBI and Secret Service officials stormed the house late one night, making arrests and seizing records and documents. (The presence of the Secret Service was a testament to the concern on the part of some federal law-enforcement officials that the government officials involved might be blackmail targets.) Although Spence was not present when the raid took place, his name was all over the records, not only as a client, but also as a principal involved in the scheme. He continued to maintain contact with others who had been involved in the ring, but he was less successful at collecting information on homosexuals in the government.

Any adjustments to his operation that Spence made after the raid were in vain, because on June 29, 1989, the world came crashing down on him. That morning an article in the *Washington Times* set in motion a series of events that would lead to Craig Spence's self-destruction only a few months later. Under a banner headline, the paper reported that Spence had been a customer of the Bethesda escort service. The paper also reported that the ring was under investigation for charges of blackmail and that Spence was one of those being investigated. The article mentioned that Spence had taken male prostitutes on a midnight tour of the White House on the Fourth of July weekend in 1988, and it said that Spence had "served drugs and sex at parties, [which were] bugged for blackmail." (Some of the claims raised in the piece would eventually prove to be true; others were patently false.)

Suddenly Spence was a social pariah. On June 30, he received a call from the JETRO office in New York. A voice told him that no more pickups would be made from him—not the one planned for the next week, not any after that. Spence was simply cut off. The few other clients he had vanished, too.

Although Spence maintained that the specific claims of the *Times* were false, he did not take the paper to court. According to federal officials involved in the investigation, he probably understood that a lengthy court trial and the paper's right to "discovery" in a libel case would have brought his other activities to light.

If the collapse of his business were not bad enough, his health added to his troubles. His sexual promiscuity had caught up with him, and in early August he was diagnosed as having AIDS. One week later, on August 9, the incident in New York City took place. Chances were now very good that he would be serving time in jail. What led Spence to take his life cannot be fully known. But even in death, mystery surrounded him.

Two weeks prior to the discovery of his body at the Boston Ritz Carlton, Spence sent out a video to some of his select friends. But far from offering clues, the tape only raises more questions. Sitting in a chair, his Maltese dog, Winston, on his lap, Spence seemed to be in some good spirits. "The pressures on us over the past several years have been, let us say, significant," he said. "Keeping a cheerful spirit in the midst of these pressures isn't easy, but Winston's holding up, and I'm working at it." He said that he was making these remarks and sending them to a dozen friends "in case I ever disappear."

In this video communiqué, Spence criticized the *Washington Times,* calling it "a local cult-owned newspaper." But he also made more indirect, mysterious statements. "The government, through its various agencies and ambitious officials, sometimes looks right at the key pieces and cannot or will not see the picture. Worse, it sometimes pockets a piece or two to ensure that the puzzle is never put together." In an ironic twist, Spence went to great lengths to defend his patriotism, which few had ever questioned. But he never denied the allegations of blackmail that had been raised by the *Washington Times.*

At the end of the tape, Spence left this veiled message:

Some of you know when it comes to the intelligence community, there is no such thing as coincidence. Now, I'm not sure I've seen the whole picture myself either.

I'll close by telling you I'm sure that in the end the truth will come out and this too will pass. Now, I may be naive about my optimism, but I'm an American, proud of my country and confident of the fairness of its people. So take heart, good friends, and share that pride and that confidence with me. Good night and God bless.

Two weeks later Craig Spence was dead, an apparent suicide.

7

Monica and Her Sisters

*I know from the organization of the BND . . . that they are extensively
gathering intelligence in the field of economy, technology, and industry.
It is a very important preoccupation of the management of the BND.*
                    —Pierre Marion, former director of French intelligence

In 1981, the West German government issued a booklet about its
federal intelligence service, the Bundesnachrichtendienst (BND). In it, the
government specified what it claimed to be the BND's main areas of
emphasis and study: military policy and armaments in the Eastern-bloc
countries; the war in Afghanistan; the Iran-Iraq conflict; the civil war in
Chad; and energy problems and internal developments in Poland. It also
mentioned, however briefly, the development of new technologies as they
relate to both commercial and military applications.

The booklet described the BND's accomplishments in a number of
instances, including the accurate prediction of Israel's quick victory in the
1967 war and the rise of the Solidarity movement in Poland. It went to
great lengths to point out that the BND had come to be the Western
intelligence service that was most aware of, and best informed on, events
in East Germany and was one of the best in tracking all the events in
Eastern Europe. The survey painted a picture of an efficient and effective
intelligence service with dedicated and proficient employees. No doubt,

that was quite true. But what the 1981 survey failed to disclose was that some of the BND's greatest successes since its formation have included operations carried out against the United States and Germany's economic competitors in Western Europe.

Since the mid-1960s, Germany has been particularly active in the field of economic intelligence and espionage. The BND has assigned agents to spy on research facilities and companies in the United States, France, Great Britain, and Italy. The organization's electronic eavesdropping facilities, along with those of the German armed forces, have been used to monitor international corporate communications. And the German national telephone company regularly monitors the telecommunications of foreign corporations with offices and facilities inside Germany. According to FBI officials, foreign businesspeople traveling in Germany have had their briefcases gone through and had their hotel rooms bugged.

The BND has been particularly active in the United States. According to some sources, the BND has worked to establish agents in the White House. German agents have cultivated moles or spies at U.S. high-tech companies and have even used intelligence-related techniques to collect "background information" for labor disputes in the United States involving German-owned companies. Says Pierre Marion, the former director of French intelligence: "I know from the organization of the BND, which I [knew] more precisely when I was in charge of the DGSE, that they are extensively gathering intelligence in the field of economy, technology, and industry. This is a very important preoccupation of the management of the BND. They collect this intelligence by various means, both overt and covert."

Professor Hayden Peake, a former U.S. intelligence official now teaching at the Defense Intelligence College, finds nothing surprising in the fact that German intelligence works in the field of economic espionage. Says Peake, "Whatever their technology needs are determines what the BND will try to get. Who can blame them?" The reactions of other current and former U.S. intelligence officials are similar. "It has always been a given since the early sixties that the Germans had agents working in the realm of technology and economics in the hopes of stealing secrets that will aid German industry," says a former U.S. intelligence official who served as the CIA station chief in Bonn. "When the CIA thinks about the

BND, it thinks about the work it has done in Eastern Europe (what we used to call the Soviet bloc)—and economic espionage pure and simple."

To trace Germany's move to a sustained program for gathering economic intelligence on its competitors through economic espionage, one must go back to the early 1950s and early 1960s and Bonn's experience with the Allied administration of the country. Britain, the United States, and France had a broad variety of rights in West Germany as part of the 1954 convention (the German Treaty). Among them were the rights to tap wires and inspect mail for "a definite purpose—the security of Allied forces." The Allies had insisted on these rights of surveillance as a means of safeguarding their military forces stationed in Germany. But according to U.S. and German sources, the Allied powers abused those rights on several occasions for commercial advantage.

In January 1968, a ranking member of the West German government publicly accused the Western powers of engaging in economic espionage. Martin Hirsch, a member of the Bundestag and the deputy chairman of the Social Democratic party in the lower house, claimed that the Allies' rights of surveillance of West German communications had produced a steady leak of confidential industrial information to companies in the United States, France, and Great Britain. Hirsch said he knew of at least two incidents in which American companies had received confidential business information from U.S. forces stationed in Germany. An internal U.S. Army investigation in June of that year revealed that, indeed, information had been leaked. The report disclosed that two junior army officers had offered information on the German optics industry to a U.S. company in exchange for two thousand dollars.

According to German and U.S. intelligence officials, as well as former French officials, the French monitoring program was much more extensive. The French intelligence service, then the SDECE, systematically monitored German companies for commercial information that it would then pass along to the relevant French companies. The program, nicknamed Onyx, was the brainchild of Étienne Burin des Roziers, a trusted aide to Charles de Gaulle. It was instituted "to take advantage of a unique opportunity which we had in Germany, and to make it pay for France," says a former SDECE official now living in the United States.

Among the most important recipients of the information obtained through Onyx was the French conglomerate Schlumberger. Under Schlumberger head Jean Riboud, the company received important updates on developments in the German oil industry. Riboud, officials say, particularly relished the thought of receiving such confidential information on Germany, for during the Second World War he had joined the French resistance and had been captured by the Gestapo and sent to Buchenwald; at war's end, he emerged ridden with tuberculosis and weighing ninety-eight pounds. Riboud firmly believed that Nazism and Hitler were not an aberration of German history but the logical fruits of it. And so he took advantage of the opportunity to obtain valuable secrets at Germany's expense. He received detailed information on the German oil concern Deutsche Erdoel-Aktiengesellschaft, and its search for oil in Libya and other parts of North Africa.

Other French companies received information on the German engineering concerns Eisenwerk-Gesellschaft Maximillanshutte; Farbenfabriken Bayer, Aktiengesellschaft; and Entwicklungsring-Sud. One German builder, Generbebautraeger, repeatedly had its bids passed on to French contractors and in several cases lost to French companies as a result of information they had obtained.

The plans for a fully integrated economic espionage program were developed in 1967, under Chancellor Kurt Georg Kiesinger, who had been alarmed by the reports of French spying on German industry. General Reinhard Gehlen, head of the BND at the time, was an advocate of such a program. Like Kiesinger, he saw espionage as a powerful tool in Germany's efforts to gain economic strength.

"Politically we are one of the middle states, while in economics and trade we are in the top group," Kiesinger said shortly after becoming chancellor. He saw economics as the fulcrum by which Germany could influence world events while developing a world-class economy and achieving prosperity. But he was concerned about the extent to which the other economic powers might restrict Germany economically. Specifically, he was concerned about U.S. ownership of certain companies in Germany and the effect of such ownership on Germany's sovereignty and economic livelihood. "The great economic power of the United States is a problem for us," he said. "We want United States participation in German industry, but we do not want control passing into the hands of foreigners. We have no single institution that knows who has what."

Kiesinger wanted that disadvantage corrected. So he instructed Gehlen to institute a program to monitor foreign corporations operating in Germany. The program would be run by the counterespionage department within the BND. Gehlen suggested that the effort include the German national telephone company. He forcefully argued that if French firms were benefiting from eavesdropping in West Germany, then French firms and French business executives in Germany ought to be subjected to a similar fate. He also argued for greater political intelligence in the United States. Finally, Gehlen argued for a program to target specific technologies about which the BND should collect information. Gehlen's plan was ambitious, and Kiesinger saw merit in it. He briefed members of a special Bundestag committee that included officials of all three political parties. And he then began the implementation of a new program for economic espionage.

A special detachment of the BND's counterespionage unit was assigned to the German public telephone and communications company, to oversee the regular monitoring of foreign companies in West Germany. The unit worked out of a regional office in Munich and implemented a program to target specific companies at particular times. "In one instance, for example, we knew that an American company was planning to make some important changes with regard to West Germany," says a former BND official. "So the unit made a point of monitoring all of their calls." Dr. Ray Cline, who was the CIA's station chief in West Germany from 1962 to 1969, remembers BND eavesdropping operations. "They were careful to do what they were instructed to do. They certainly listened in on foreign businessmen in Germany. They had an elaborate system. The BND then left it up to the federal government as to which German companies would get which information, if any."

Other plans within the BND laid the groundwork for foreign intelligence operations for economic purposes.

In early 1968, BND headquarters learned about a unique opportunity regarding the collection of intelligence in the United States and the possibility of influencing a future presidential administration. Agents had come in contact with a man who was eager to work closely with West Germany. Daniel Edwin London, a wealthy San Francisco businessman well connected in the Republican party, was the senior vice president of Western International Hotels and a financial backer of fellow Californian Richard Nixon. According to early reports filed by BND agents, the American had expressed support for Germany's position and had expressed a favorable attitude toward Kiesinger's policy of *Ostpolitik*, or greater openness to the East. He even promised to instill in Nixon a "pro-German" point of view. BND officials created a file on London but did not pursue the matter further.

The replacement of BND chief Gehlen with Lieutenant General Gerhard Wessell in 1968 brought about a renewal of interest in London. Wessell was a strong advocate of intelligence operations in the West. And along with Wessell came a new chief of operations for the BND, Dr. Karl Winterstein, alias Dr. Kurt Weiss, a man who wanted BND operations to expand on several fronts. He saw the need for greater covert operations in East Germany and in the rest of the Soviet bloc as well as in the West—particularly in France, Great Britain, and the United States. In a memo to General Wessell in 1969, Winterstein outlined the importance of "understanding the intentions and political machinations of those we rely on for our security"—a reference to the United States, Great Britain, and France. He went on to argue that only by economic and technological success would Germany continue to gain independence from, and reduce its reliance on, the other major Western powers. And so he pushed for "economic operations" to aid German industry.

The Federation of Metal Industrialists in Northern Württemberg and Northern Baden was an early beneficiary of the BND effort. Beginning in 1968, it received information at regular intervals regarding the French steel industry and the status of contracts. Several managers at French steel companies were recruited by the BND station chief in Paris to provide intelligence on company bids and sales, particularly those to other European countries and West Germany. The operation was marginally successful.

What Winterstein had in mind, however, was more advanced and more sophisticated. He wanted operations in the cutting-edge industries, fields in which German firms could prosper in the future. He also favored more intelligence collection in the United States, particularly as it related to economic decisions being made in Washington.

BND contact with Daniel London continued, despite a decision by headquarters not to activate him. Dr. Hans Langemann, a balding, jovial BND operative, identified London in a November 12, 1968, secret document as someone who was willing to "influence Nixon for the benefit of Europe." He also wrote that London would be "influencing the President of [the] necessities of Germany." The report to BND headquarters went on: "The connection with London is therefore especially valuable, through which it is possible to aim political information direct to Nixon without official filtering, and through him to influence and prepare wishful political projects."

Langemann had been making regular visits to the United States in 1967–68 and would play a key role in recruiting London. The BND resident agent, code-named Danko, was also a key figure in the recruitment plans, as well as in the plans to launch a wider operation.

Nixon's election in November of 1968 led to an internal debate within the leadership of the BND regarding whether the service should activate London and use him or avoid doing so because the potential risks were too great. Winterstein argued aggressively in favor of activating the American, while other BND officials, particularly those responsible for international liaisons, resisted. A wavering Wessell finally came down on the side of Winterstein. According to a former BND official, the decision was probably based on two primary calculations. First, because London was not being directly paid for his services, the operation would not appear so sinister to the Americans if it were uncovered. Second, Winterstein and the BND knew from past experience with agents of influence that because these agents were simply trying to influence decisions rather than collect information, they were particularly hard to identify. Wessell concluded that the chances of London's ever being discovered by the Americans were extremely low. But the approach would not be made until later.

Even in 1968, when the BND had made the commitment to collect more intelligence concerning the United States, the operations were limited. After all, the BND was in part the creation of the CIA, and its ranks were filled with individuals who had close personal, as well as professional, ties to the CIA. In October 1969, however, that all changed. Willy Brandt, head of the Social Democrats, became chancellor in a coalition with the Free Democrats. Brandt was both ambitious for Germany and nervous about U.S. policy in Europe. He proclaimed that the U.S.-European Atlantic relationship was evolving and sought a reduced U.S. role in Europe. "Nothing in the world remains unchanged forever and, it would, therefore, be an absurdity to believe that the United States engagement in Europe will stay unchanged," he said.

Brandt wanted a more assertive and a more independent Germany and Europe, a Germany and a Europe that were less dependent on, and beholden to, the United States. He proclaimed that he foresaw a "quadrangular" structure of world power, with Western Europe as a fourth corner, instead of "a triangle" of Washington, Moscow, and Beijing. Brandt wanted greater independence in foreign affairs, and he made clear that German policy would be more independent under his tutelage. As Brandt put it, "The United States has to take a more global look at things and calculate how they fit together. . . . But as a loyal member of the Western family, we have to take care of our own interests."

Central to Brandt's vision of a more independent Germany were his plans for *Ostpolitik*. The chancellor saw that German interests would be well served by warm relations with the Soviet bloc, and he conceived of a policy of normalizing relations with the regime in East Germany, as well as with such countries as Poland and the Soviet Union. "If the West German government succeeds," he declared, "the way will be clear for a serious attempt to reduce the strain of confrontation in Europe."

Brandt was a shrewd leader, and he understood that his policies were fraught with problems—a virtual minefield of them when it came to relations with Washington. His early pronouncements were met there with coolness both publicly and privately. And a number of important bilateral agreements between Germany and the United States were being contentiously negotiated. The offset agreement, in which Bonn helped offset the costs of maintaining American troops in Germany by purchasing American goods, was unpopular in Germany and increasingly expensive. By 1969, the annual cost to Bonn was $950 million. Brandt and his finance minister, Alex Moller, were of the strong opinion that West Germany simply could no longer afford the arrangement. The then-current bilateral agreement between Washington and Bonn for stationing U.S. forces in West Germany was set to expire in June 1971, and negotiations were becoming increasingly tense. Reducing the cost for Bonn was one of Brandt's top priorities.

Against this backdrop of Brandt's foreign policy ambitions and the complicated offset agreement, the chancellor was aware of increasing pressure in the United States to reduce the American commitment to defending Western Europe. In the Senate, Mike Mansfield was leading a movement to adopt an amendment to the defense budget that would dramatically reduce the number of U.S. troops stationed in Western Europe. Brandt, of course, didn't want any of that, at least not so soon. And while the Nixon administration had come out publicly against the Mansfield amendment, Bonn feared that the White House might use the threat of its passage to gain an advantage in their bilateral talks and negotiations. So Brandt had to tread carefully, lest he prompt a crisis with Washington.

Brandt's views concerning the United States and his plans for *Ostpolitik* led to his decision to reshape the BND and to redirect some of its assets, focusing them more on collecting intelligence on Washington. According to Dr. Cline, Brandt was "devious and double-dealing" when it came to intelligence matters relating to the United States. Despite Brandt's taking money from the CIA when he was a political leader in the 1950s, says Cline, "he didn't particularly like the U.S. And when he became chancellor, he wanted to put that imprint on the BND and what it did." One former BND official concurs. "Brandt was suspicious of the Americans. He came to conclude that [in] the realm of politics and economics, we needed to have bigger ears in Washington. This decision meant by May 1970 the addition of at least two more agents assigned to the BND station in Washington." Brandt appointed a Social Democratic politician, Dieter Blotz, to be deputy director of the BND and gave the organization a mandate to seek more intelligence in the United States. Blotz was a key advocate of extensive intelligence operations in the United States, particularly as they related to Germany's economic and political position.

In January 1970, Blotz made an extraordinary decision: to activate London as an agent of influence. Danko and other officials at the German embassy in Washington encouraged London to maximize his influence in the presidential administration. "We always emphasized to London that he was one of those few officials who understood Germany and what we were trying to do," says a former BND official. In February 1970, London sought out and was given the post of chairman of the State Department's National Review Board Executive Committee. While the post was advisory, it did give London insight into the thinking of State Department officials concerning Brandt's policy of *Ostpolitik*.

A former member of the National Review Board Executive Committee, while saying he believes it is doubtful London was working with the BND, does remember London's being "consistently pro-Brandt" in his views on Western Europe. "Whether that reflected his true feelings or some connections with German intelligence, I wouldn't know," the former committee member says. But whether his feelings were "true" or not is largely irrelevant, for according to German intelligence documents and former BND officials, London volunteered to work with the BND to serve German interests, which he believed were not antithetical to U.S. foreign interests.

When Daniel London visited Washington, D.C., in his capacity as a member of the State Department review board, he regularly met with BND and embassy officials. On at least two occasions, in March and June of 1970, BND agents met with him in San Francisco. Both times they met at the Saint Francis Yacht Club, where London was a member. At those San Francisco meetings, BND agent Rolf Grunter asked London to draw up a list of officials in the administration who could be viewed as hostile to Brandt's *Ostpolitik*. Those named by London included not only the national security adviser, Henry Kissinger, and Secretary of Defense Melvin Laird, but also more junior State Department officials whom he had contact with or had heard about. Martin Hillenbrandt, a State Department expert on Germany was also on the list.

London's motive for working with the BND was not financial but, rather, reflected his honest assessment that Germany's view had merit and Washington ought to give it more credit. In exchange for his work, he received no money, only official accolades, and those in ways that would not be too obvious. The German government awarded London its Order of Merit, an award to foreign nationals who could be regarded as friends of Germany. German embassy officials also arranged through contacts in the Austrian embassy to have London named honorary consul general of Austria for northern California and northern Nevada, an almost comical title that London retained from 1971 until his death in 1974.

While in the State Department, London regularly collected information and briefed German embassy officials about administration views on German policy. According to a former BND official, London helped identify key officials in the administration who opposed Brandt's policies. He also attempted, as best he could, to influence the deliberations of the National Review Board, to push the State Department view of Brandt in a positive direction.

At the same time that Dieter Blotz activated London, he decided to move on another front as well. Since November 1969, Danko had been reporting to headquarters that he was developing social relationships with two White House staff members, one at the National Security Council and the other in the Office of the Special Trade Representative. Both were becoming good friends of Danko's, and both were described by the BND agent as "free talkers." They regularly spoke with him at Washington social events about a variety of subjects. In one report submitted in early December, Danko reported having dinner with each of them and that both complained about their lack of pay and status at the White House. (White House staffers, then and now, are notorious for working long hours for pay that is not competitive with other government jobs at a similar level.) The German agent reported the dinner as part of his regular intelligence briefings that he sent to the BND.

In January 1970, Danko's orders arrived via diplomatic pouch in handwritten form. The instructions were broad in nature but specific to his relationship with the White House staff members. He was instructed to "institute [an] effort for enhanced collection of intelligence." Specifically, he was to "seek out and recruit said individuals. Clarify first."

"Clarify first" meant Danko was to inform headquarters of when he planned to make the approach and what his exact language would be. Given the sensitivity of such an operation, the BND chief wanted to exact complete control over recruitment. Danko was surprised by the suggestion, especially in light of the fact that although London had been activated, he was a volunteer and was primarily an agent of influence—and therefore difficult to detect.

Danko sent a simple coded message, "Repeat level A." He wanted the message and orders sent to him again, to ensure that they were genuine and came from the BND chief. It was generally assumed that the BND had been penetrated by Soviet and East German intelligence, and Danko thought it conceivable that he had been given false orders, in the hopes of provoking an incident between Washington and Bonn. But a coded message was sent back three days later: "Proceed 464." The numbers were the director's code, which was known only by the station chief he was sending a message to. Each station chief was given a different secret number that only that station chief, the BND chief, and his top advisers knew. Four hundred sixty-four was the correct number. Danko proceeded with his work.

All that is known about the approach Danko made is that it was not a conventional one. A conventional approach, it was thought, would be rejected by the staff members, who did not seem, in ordinary terms, the type to sell secrets to a foreign power. So Danko simply asked them both if they would serve as "consultants" to the embassy, to foster closer U.S.-German relations. He made clear that he did not want actual documents or top-secret, classified information but simply their impressions of White House attitudes on key issues. The line, of course, was a fine one. After all, the information they would be providing would be based on secret, sensitive information. But the distinction was fine enough for both of the White House staff members: they accepted Danko's offer for a fee of one thousand dollars per month. The first monetary transaction took place in January. Because the men were part of the larger effort to collect intelligence in the United States (which had been dubbed Operation Monica), the BND nicknamed the NSC staff member Monica's Big Sister and the staff member in the Office of the Special Trade Representative was called Little Sister.

Almost immediately Big Sister and Little Sister proved to be extremely valuable to the BND and Willy Brandt. This was particularly the case when it came to complex U.S.-German diplomatic issues. The new chancellor had his first meeting with President Nixon in early April 1970. It was critical that Brandt get an accurate reading of the U.S. position on *Ostpolitik,* the issue of troop reductions being debated in the Senate, and the administration's negotiating position on the offset agreement. At the time, Brandt was working toward signing diplomatic treaties to normalize relations with Poland and the Soviet Union, and he wanted to proceed without risking the wrath of Washington.

Big Sister provided summaries of the private NSC view on a number of important matters, often in the form of six- to eight-page memorandums. And what Big Sister provided was critical to the April meetings. The source confirmed that although Washington was not pleased with Brandt's apparent attitude toward the Soviet bloc, it was unwilling to do anything about it. Indeed, Big Sister showed that the Nixon administration felt its own dealings with Moscow were too important to risk a showdown with Brandt.

Little Sister passed on to Danko detailed information concerning the deliberations of the Office of the Special Trade Representative Executive Committee, as well as summaries of the office's position on trade liberalization within the European Economic Community and the offset agreement. One solution Washington proposed for the offset agreement was well-known to Bonn before the administration even put it on the table, thanks to Little Sister. (The proposals were specifically related to asking Bonn to restrain EEC farm prices and subsidized surpluses, which were reducing U.S. agricultural exports to Europe and the Third World.)

On April 10, when Chancellor Brandt went to the White House to meet with President Nixon, he was very well briefed concerning the White House view on all the substantial issues facing American-German bilateral relations. He knew that although the White House was skeptical of *Ostpolitik,* it was not willing to see U.S. forces in Western Europe reduced, as the Mansfield amendment proposed—the White House had quietly left the issue of troop reductions in Western Europe stewing in the hopes of maintaining some leverage over Bonn and to gain some assurances concerning *Ostpolitik.* And although, in the words of the *New York Times,* Brandt's policies were "greeted with public coolness and private questioning in Washington," the German chancellor stood firm, knowing that the Nixon White House was unprepared to challenge his policies. "We knew that Washington was unwilling to risk relations with the Federal Republic over these [policies]," says a former BND official. Brandt aggressively stuck to his positions.

Big Sister and Little Sister kept the BND and Brandt informed on the

U.S. attitude toward Bonn throughout 1970. In November, for the first time, Big Sister provided his handlers with actual copies of NSC documents, particularly those relating to the treaties Bonn had been negotiating with Poland and the Soviet Union. Both informers also provided details of the U.S. attitude toward specific commercial deals that Bonn was negotiating with the Soviet bloc. Both Big Sister and Little Sister forwarded information to Danko concerning the Mannesmann Company of Düsseldorf, which was negotiating the sale of $330 million worth of seamless, large-diameter pipeline to Moscow.

When Brandt visited Washington for a second time, in June 1971, he was again well briefed on the U.S. position before his meeting with President Nixon. On June 15, Nixon and Brandt met in the White House for almost two hours. One of the major issues of contention was the offset agreement. In the Senate, the Mansfield amendment was gaining momentum, and, as Brandt had feared, the administration was using the threat of its passage to secure a more favorable position in the talks. The administration warned that if Germany was unwilling to help alleviate some of the costs to the United States, the Senate might vote for the amendment, forcing the administration to follow suit. What the administration failed to realize, of course, was that Big Sister and Little Sister had passed to Danko the private opinions of the NSC on the matter, particularly those that had been articulated by Henry Kissinger. "We knew that they would fight [the Mansfield amendment] at all costs, based on the internal deliberations at the council," says a former BND official. "We knew this was a ruse."

The BND's relationship with the two White House staff members ended in late 1971, when a close call almost lead to their discovery. In early November, a BND agent assigned to the Washington station had gone to the botanical gardens in northwestern Washington to make a pickup of documents. According to the routine, the BND courier would identify the source and then circle around the meeting point, keeping approximately twenty yards away. This was done to ensure that the source was not being watched or followed. After making certain that the coast was clear, the courier would then make the approach, take possession of the documents, and leave. (The payment, surprisingly, was delivered by mail.)

It was particularly busy that day in the gardens, and as the courier reached for the document, a voice shot out from some forty feet away. It shouted Big Sister's name. Courier and agent made eye contact but stood perfectly still, not knowing what to do next. The voice in the distance came closer: "Hey, it's me!"

The Big Sister's co-worker arrived, and the men exchanged pleasantries. The co-worker, by coincidence, happened to be at the gardens that day. He looked over to the courier. "Aren't you going to introduce me?" he asked Big Sister.

Big Sister froze. The BND used different couriers at different times— he didn't even know the man's name! The courier then interrupted, introducing himself. When the co-worker asked how the courier and Big Sister knew each other, the two conveniently sidestepped the question.

Nothing ever came of that awkward and nerve-racking moment. But when the concerned courier reported it to the BND station chief, Operation Monica and the relationship with the sisters came to an end. Big Sister clearly indicated he wanted out of the whole thing. According to one former German intelligence official, the incident raised too many concerns and worries in the BND. Had the co-worker seen the papers and become suspicious? What if he reported it, even casually, to other co-workers?

All contact with the two agents ended by early December 1971. Neither of the sisters knew about the other's existence. Big Sister severed all ties with the BND. Little Sister was never contacted again. He probably appeared at the appointed place on the evening of December 4, 1971, and waited in vain for his courier. He was probably never told that the relationship was ending.

Inside a looking-glass-covered professional building on a wooded lot on the outskirts of Frankfurt, important work is taking place that could revolutionize the field of economic intelligence and espionage. Approximately thirty-six computer specialists and senior intelligence officials are working on a top-secret project to bring computer hacking into the realm of spying and intelligence. They hope that through the use of sophisticated computers and specially trained personnel, German intelligence agents will be able to enter computer data bases of corporations and foreign governments around the world. And the access could be achieved while the agents remained thousands of miles away.

The few scholars who have ventured into the field of professional computer hacking by national intelligence agencies give the Germans high marks in this area. A paper delivered by computer specialist Wayne Madsen to a computer-security conference in Helsinki in 1990 provides a rating of each of the world's national intelligence services in terms of its capabilities to hack as a means of engaging in computer espionage. Madsen rated German capability "excellent."

The German effort was dubbed Project Rahab, named for the harlot who helped the Israelites infiltrate Jericho. The concept of bringing computer hacking into the world of intelligence was developed under then-BND Director Eberhard Blum in 1985. In 1988, the idea was developed further and became an experimental program.

The original plans for Rahab were drawn up by a BND official named Christian Stoessel. An expert in computers and computer security, he had been working for the BND for eight years, tracking the activities of West German computer hackers and learning about ways in which foreign intelligence services might try to penetrate BND data bases. He had taken a particular interest in a Hamburg computer hackers' club called Chaos and was impressed with its technical proficiency and the technological reach it had achieved with ordinary computers. "He wanted to harness the power [of the computer] to serve our intelligence ends," says a former colleague.

In August 1988, Stoessel issued an eighteen-page paper concerning his findings and the feasibility of using hacking for intelligence purposes, and he submitted it to senior directors of the BND's Division II. He proposed that the BND establish a hybrid project to explore the possibility of developing an arm of Division II that would be devoted to entering systematically the data bases of foreign governments and companies.

Although neither Stoessel nor senior officials of Division II spoke about potential targets while in the conceptual stage, U.S. intelligence officials are adamant that the focus of the main effort was intended to be Germany's Western allies. "As much as they may like the claim that they wanted a worldwide capability to target anybody, that claim just doesn't hold water," says a senior U.S. counterintelligence official. "No one in what at that time was the Soviet bloc really had the sort of computer network that could be entered. In the U.S., France, Britain, Japan, and every other Western industrial power, it's another story. Everybody is linked somehow and therefore accessible."

Stoessel's proposal was approved by the BND director on November 17, 1988. A directive was issued, calling for a development project—Rahab—to determine the feasibility of systematic entry into computer data bases as a tool of intelligence. The directive specifically emphasized determining Rahab's viability in assisting in the acquisition of technological intelligence.

The development project was a joint effort by BND Division I, which is primarily involved in the collection of human intelligence by means of agents; Division II, which runs signal and electronics operations; and a small component of Division IV, the BND's central office. As a matter of policy, Rahab was installed outside of Frankfurt. This was because senior officials feared that the hybrid nature of the project might lead to turf battles. Division I, with its focus on human intelligence and operations, had traditionally been at odds with Division II, where technological wizardry and electronic gadgetry made intelligence more a technical drama than a human one. It was hoped that placing Rahab at a distance from the other BND offices would lessen interdivisional competition. It was also hoped that this location would serve to cover any links between Rahab and well-known BND facilities. Officials believed that if entry were made, for example, to a computer network at a U.S. military installation and the Americans were able to determine the site from which entry was gained, then it should be a "nontraditional" site, one that would arouse few suspicions regarding the BND.

Along with BND personnel from Divisions I and II, Rahab was made up of a number of key employees from other branches of the German scientific and technological community. At least fourteen of Rahab's estimated sixty-six employees came from a variety of outside institutions, including the German army, government research institutions like the one outside Jolich, and private companies. The German Defense Ministry's Office for Radio Monitoring (Amt für Fernmeldewesen Bundeswehr) assigned several specialists from its headquarters at Bad Neuenahr-Ahrweiler near Bonn, and from a facility near Hof. Two observers were also sent by the Federal Armed Forces Intelligence Office (Amt für Nachrichtenwesen der Bundeswehr). And senior officials from the federal office of the Protection of the Constitution (Bundesamt für Verfassungsschutz), an organization somewhat akin to the FBI, have tracked the development of Rahab from the beginning in order to consider countermeasures for German government and corporate data bases.

In the initial months, Rahab was focused almost exclusively on gleaning as much as possible from earlier hacker cases. Stoessel used the files he had developed for protecting BND networks to learn more about how to enter other data bases. Rahab officials established an internal, detailed computer network to replicate those they might be attempting to enter. The operation was concerned not only with data base entry, however, but with all that might be of use to the BND.

Because of an expressed interest in the possibility of using the Rahab network against the Soviet bloc during a crisis or a war, in April of 1989 the network was subjected to deliberate attempts to replicate a computer virus that had been created by a West German hacker named Bernd Fix. Like all such viruses, this one had two parts: a code that infected other programs by duplicating itself with those programs and a function that, once planted, could erase or damage magnetic data or interfere with normal computer operations.

Fix's virus attracted the Rahab team because it was particularly powerful. It was capable of destroying all the information in a large mainframe computer in a matter of minutes. If widely used, it could render national computer systems useless in the course of a few hours. But it was also dangerous. By their nature, viruses cannot be contained, and Rahab officials recognized that for all practical purposes using the Fix virus against a potential enemy could eventually lead to Germany's being infected, too. And, finally, the Fix virus was incredibly complex. Once the program was reproduced by the Rahab team, it would take twenty hours of programming to recreate it from start to stop.

BND agents, with the cooperation of the BfV, did extensive research on other hackers, including individual members of the infamous Chaos Club. According to one German official with knowledge of Rahab, BND officials were truly shocked at what they learned: "They discovered that they knew very little about hacking." They learned, for example, that it was not technique that mattered so much as understanding one secret: few legitimate owners of information install computer security products properly. Once you figured out the flaw in the installation, you could easily defeat them.

Rahab specialists made their first forays into foreign data bases in early 1989, according to CIA officials. The targets included corporate data bases in Great Britain and the United States. This effort was undertaken by a Rahab team led by a computer engineer named Hans Mulricht. According to intelligence officials, the team on at least four occasions breached passwords and electronic data security systems at three separate sites, two in Great Britain and one in the United States. The tests were successful and proved the feasibility of running an intelligence operation by hacking.

In May 1989, Rahab received the go-ahead, thus becoming a funded program—a top-secret component of the BND's Division II. A scientist named Rolf Hecht was made responsible for carrying out and administering Rahab. As a full-fledged BND program, Project Rahab was given a broad mandate to gain access to electronic information that related to German "national security, essential commerce, and economic welfare." According to intelligence sources, Rahab agents have accessed computer systems in the Soviet Union, Japan, France, the United States, Italy, and Great Britain. During the dramatic collapse of Soviet power in Central Europe, Rahab agents successfully accessed Soviet government computer systems in a search for information pertaining to Soviet intentions.

But it is in the post–Cold War era that Rahab may bear the most fruit. According to a senior FBI official who has been tracking the German operation, in the fall of 1991 Rahab was being reconstituted to focus increasingly on economic, technology, and corporate targets. "Western economic targets are softer and probably a lot more fruitful, too," he says. According to this official, Rahab is most likely directed toward a cluster of industries, including chemicals, computers and electronics, optics, avionics, and telecommunications. What occupies Rahab agents most is establishing "roadways" and "maps" to particular data bases and networks. "They want numbers and codes for certain companies in the U.S., Japan, and Europe," says another intelligence official. "They are cataloging everything they find out to make entry easier next time."

In March 1991, Rahab employees hacked their way into a key private computer network known as SWIFT, run by the Society for World International Financial Transactions. This high-speed computer link carries instructions for most global international bank transactions. Rahab officials entered SWIFT at least three times in March, according to U.S. intelligence officials, in order to establish a roadway to ensure easy access for the time when such access is deemed necessary. By tapping into SWIFT, U.S. intelligence officials say, the BND will be able to track a number of international financial transactions between companies and countries as well as other intelligence that few other nations know about.

Although Western intelligence services have, from time to time, attempted to enter government data bases in allied countries, never before has an operation on the scale of Rahab been conceived and carried out. Rahab hacking, directed at companies in the United States, Western Europe, and Japan, continues to this day, U.S. intelligence officials insist. And it in all likelihood will augur an era in which state-sponsored computer hacking becomes every bit the intelligence tool that spy satellites have been for the past thirty years. It offers the benefits of an agent on the inside without the costs inherent in his potential unmasking. German intelligence has seen the future, and it lies with Rahab.

8

The Liaison

Economic intelligence is clearly the primary target for the BND as Germany seeks to maintain its position as one of the world's industrial powerhouses.

—Colonel William V. Kennedy

It was on a particularly overcast day, December 7, 1989, that Karl Heinrich Stohlze landed at Boston's Logan Airport on the shuttle from Washington, D.C. A full-figured man in his late forties with wire-rimmed glasses and a slight beard, Stohlze took a taxi from the airport and checked into the Sheraton Hotel, in the heart of the city. This trip was to be the pinnacle of many months worth of work.

Stohlze described himself as a commercial attaché at the German embassy on Washington's embassy row or, alternatively, as a scientist, depending on whom he was talking to. The fact is he was neither. He was not trained as a scientist and rarely set foot in research laboratories. He was not on the embassy payroll, nor was he employed by the German foreign service; he did not have diplomatic immunity. But he was employed by the German government, serving as a special agent for the West German federal intelligence service, the Bundesnachrichtendienst.

Stohlze traveled to Boston that day on official business. He was a special agent connected to Division I of the BND, as part of a special program dubbed Economic Technical Collection/USA. According to U.S. counterintelligence sources who pieced together Stohlze's activities later in 1990, after having been contacted by a Boston-based biotechnology company, Stohlze's trip was one of many in search of American high-tech companies' technology secrets. He actively recruited employees at several companies and even maintained a liaison with one female researcher in the hopes of ferreting out important secrets of biotechnology research being conducted at her firm.

Stohlze on this trip was meeting his contact to collect information concerning biochip research taking place at a Boston-area high-tech company. The idea behind the research was to develop a computer chip that would incorporate genetic engineering as a means of making the chip more efficient and magnifying the power of its memory. It was a merging of two scientific disciplines, biology and electronics, and was therefore extremely difficult. Nonetheless, there was, and is, a worldwide race on among perhaps a dozen companies that hope to create the ultimate computer chip. The technology was of interest to several German electronics companies, not the least of which was Siemens, an electronics giant that had a project under way to develop technologies for the so-called fifth generation of computers that are expected to make their appearance in the 1990s. The project, called MEGA, was enormously ambitious and expensive for the company and included some biochip concepts.

Although it is unknown whether Siemens did end up with any of the information Stohlze eventually acquired, U.S. intelligence sources identify it as a "logical beneficiary" of the secrets. According to these sources, the BND and Siemens have an informal relationship, which was established by Siemens's chief executive officer, Dr. Karlheinz Kasile. The relationship was forged in the early 1980s, when the research director at Siemens at that time, Karl Heinz Beckhurts, advocated and negotiated an informal agreement. Beckhurts had worked for a government research facility prior to joining Siemens and was well-known in BND circles. (In 1986, he was brutally murdered in a car-bomb attack by the radical Red Army faction.)

Stohlze's task when he was sent to the United States was to act as the eyes and ears for Division I of the BND when it came to biochip research and to gauge what successes, if any, U.S. companies might be having. He was picked in part because he had a seemingly inherent knack, say former colleagues, for identifying and gathering useful scientific information, despite his lack of any real scientific training. His only college study had been a year and a half at the Free University of Berlin in the 1960s. Fluent in English and French, Stohlze was an experienced agent, having served as an operative for the BND in Switzerland, France, and the United States. According to a former colleague at the German intelligence service, Stohlze was the consummate professional. It is believed that his portfolio included a number of daring attempts at economic espionage in France and Switzerland. He also had a limited reputation in Division I as some-thing of a Casanova—as someone who had charm and could use it to his advantage. And although he was not encouraged to do so, he had used this talent to get out of trouble.

In 1984, the Institut Merieux, a subsidiary of France's largest chemical company, Rhone-Poulenc, had joined forces with the famous Institut Pasteur of Paris to conduct biotechnology research. In the second half of 1984 at the Institut Merieux, based outside of Lyons, Stohlze recruited several workers in order to discover what sort of work was being done and what sort of progress was being made. Stohlze once bragged to colleagues that one Rhone-Poulenc plant manager, named Jacques Cornilliant, would give him anything he wanted. Stohlze's BND colleagues were skeptical, however, because the information he collected was not detailed enough to warrant the continuation of the operation. In June of 1985, Stohlze was removed from the project, only after an internal debate in Division I that opted against expanding the probe into the chemical company's research. "The conclusion reached was that this was not worth any more [resources or effort]," recalls a former BND official.

Stohlze's second known exploit before coming to the United States was carried out against an IBM research laboratory in Zurich in December of 1986. At that facility, there had been pioneering work going on that could revolutionize the computer industry. Research was being done on superconductors, the potentially perfect source of conductivity. Unlike the semiconductor, which, as the name implies, conducts only part of the energy passing through it, superconductors conduct electricity with no loss of energy. Researchers at the IBM lab were hoping to make superconductors more practical by getting them to work at warmer temperatures. Prior to their research, superconductors had been found to work only at extremely low temperatures ($-459°$ F).

For two months, Stohlze stayed in Zurich, where his mission was to observe the workings of the facility, follow and track its employees, and establish a plan for tapping into the facility's secrets when the orders were given to do so. He was not to make direct contact with employees or attempt to recruit them but only to find out the facility's vulnerabilities and the habits and activities of key plant personnel. According to one former BND official who was briefed by Stohlze, the approximate course of action that Stohlze recommended included seeking to recruit native Germans working at the facility; tapping several external lines running from the facility, including telephone lines and systems for microwave communications; and possibly bribing several plant employees who appeared to be wanting financially.

What brought Stohlze to the United States in the spring of 1989 was his peculiar knowledge of the country and his strong command of the English language. Because of his work with Rhone-Poulenc's biotechnology effort and IBM's superconductor research, he had operational background that would be ideal for the biochip project. According to a former colleague, Stohlze was particularly happy with the assignment because he had a strong affinity for U.S. culture, especially American movies, food, and music. The director of Division I personally assigned Stohlze to the task, which was no doubt a sensitive one. When Stohlze left Frankfurt in April 1989, he took with him three tools provided by the BND.

First were a series of detailed instructions describing the facilities on the U.S. eastern seaboard that deserved to be examined. These were U.S. high-tech companies that were conducting research on biochips, considering such programs, or working on related technologies. By one estimate, the list included four companies, all located in the Route 128 corridor near Boston or in North Carolina's Research Triangle. Though not comprehensive, the list was a starting point. Stohlze's instructions were to find out (through largely open sources) which other U.S. companies were doing research in the field and to size up the facilities on the list in terms of penetrability. Once he had filed an initial report, he would receive instructions on how to proceed and whether to attempt to penetrate the facilities.

Stohlze's second tool was a bank-account number and a cash card from Manufacturers Hanover Trust Company in New York City. The account had been opened several years before by personnel at the German embassy in Washington, D.C., for special purposes—like Stohlze's operation—and was replenished from time to time via wire transfers from Germany. The account was preferable to having Stohlze carry funds himself, a situation that would cause problems with U.S. Customs if discovered.

Finally, Stohlze took with him a small card, about half the size of a business card, to carry in his wallet. On it were the name and phone number of an employee with the West German mission to the United Nations. The employee worked for the BND, largely to collect intelligence from the staffs of other delegations at the UN. He was to be contacted only if Stohlze found himself in trouble on account of his activities.

Stohlze left well prepared and ready for his work. After his arrival at Kennedy Airport in New York City, he headed for the apartment that had been rented for him on the East Side, one that the German government paid for to house German members of the UN delegation and "visitors" such as Stohlze. After staying at the flat for a week or so, Stohlze moved to the Boston area to begin working his way down the BND target list. The first name on his list was that of a company performing delicate research on biochips.

Stohlze made arrangements for a one-month stay at a hotel near the facility. He then went about his business of probing the company to find out how best to discover what progress they were making on the chip and how to gain access to some of the results. His first task was to examine the setup at the company and learn as much as possible about the facility and its personnel.

He found out about local hangouts and even infiltrated a company social event. He did this by calling a secretary at the facility and telling her that he planned to throw a surprise birthday party for his brother, who, Stohlze said, worked for the company. "Could you possibly send me a copy of the company's phone directory so I can invite his friends?" he asked. She agreed, no questions asked. "Could you suggest where I could hold the party? I'm just visiting from out of town." The unsuspecting receptionist said she could and gave him his first crack at getting through the company's door. A party for a departing employee was being planned at a nearby club. "It's a great place," the receptionist told him. "Maybe you should just drop by and see it for yourself." Stohlze thanked her for the information and made plans to make his first move. With a simple phone call, he had managed to gain entry into the company and get his hands on a company phone directory.

In late October, Stohlze attended the party and quickly identified a possible source. At the party, but not really of it, was a fortyish woman, dark haired, who sat quietly by herself. On her face was a look of extreme self-consciousness and insecurity. In her expression, he saw an opportunity. He asked her if he might join her, and they struck up a conversation. Stohlze engaged her with questions meant to portray a genuine interest in what she did, who she was, and where she was from. She soon told him that she was a middle-level administrator at the company. The German agent found her to be frustrated and lonely. He described himself as a researcher for a West German company but was vague about where in the Boston area he was working. Later, according to former colleagues, Stohlze bragged that he had given the appearance of deep fascination with her story in spite of his extreme boredom with it and that he had feigned a certain warmness when she complained about the unfairness of her life. Stohlze was extremely lucky, in fact, because he had made contact with a potentially valuable source—a midlevel administrator who dealt with research data on a regular basis and had access to all of the company's records and facilities, including those relating to work being done on biochips. Stohlze asked to meet her again, and they set a date.

The relationship with the administrator quickly accelerated into a romance. The woman had never been married and appeared to be greatly in need of affection and companionship and was therefore vulnerable to Stohlze's advances. His success came so quickly and the opportunity seemed so ripe that he opted to devote most of his energies to this company. This decision met with BND approval. It was decided that Stohlze should limit his activities to the Boston area and forgo the planned operations in North Carolina.

During their early courtship, Stohlze learned quite a bit about the company's operation and progress in biochip research. According to a former colleague, Stohlze's information was very useful in determining the company's progress. His information lacked details about the research, however, especially details of the company's cutting-edge work on the application of genetics to electronics. What Stohlze needed was to advance beyond talk and gain access to research documents. He felt the woman would probably provide them, but only under the right pretense. Thus, in late November, Stohlze made an important operational decision: he would try a false-flag ploy to get her to steal information for him. Although frustrated, she didn't seem to Stohlze to be the sort who would, out of a sense of vengeance, betray her company. But he thought she might do it to please him. She might be especially eager if she thought she risked losing him. Since Stohlze had been effective at convincing her that he was a consultant for a German firm doing research in the same field, he decided to suggest that she "acquire" some information for him. As a motive, he would use the prospect of his being transferred to another city.

In the first week of December, he put on a sullen face and told her that his work had not been going well, that he had been stumped by a series of research problems. "I can't seem to solve some of the puzzles that we have been facing," he said. He told her he had been depressed about the matter for several weeks and that his company was not pleased with his performance. Unless he was able to come up with something, he might be reassigned somewhere else, possibly even back in Germany. He played up the idea of their being separated and his inability to resolve the "scientific problems" he was facing. "I wish I could do something to help," she murmured, clearly with the thought that another romantic disappointment was about to arrive. Stohlze paused and then—picking up her utterance as a cue—began to make his pitch. "Actually there is." He said he had run into several of her co-workers and had heard from them about the work being done at her company. Stohlze and his target talked in general terms about the research they were doing. "Your people appear to have solved the problems that have been perplexing me," he told her. Then, with a lengthy proviso in which he made clear that he understood the awkwardness of what he was asking, he popped a question he had been waiting to say since they had first met: "Could you maybe get this information for me?"

There was a pregnant pause—she seemed almost shell-shocked. Stohlze no doubt figured he had made a tactical mistake. After what must have been ten seconds of silence, she told him that she cared for him but she wasn't capable of doing such a thing. "There's got to be another way," she said.

"Forget about it," Stohlze said, quickly changing the subject as if he had made a mistake. But he wasn't done with her. The pause must have indicated to him some hesitation, some indication that she might just do it. He planned to tighten the emotional screw even further at a future rendezvous.

Two days after he made his approach, he called his source at her office. "I'm sorry," he said. "My company is not happy with my results, and I must go to Washington to discuss a reassignment." Stohlze later bragged to colleagues that he had purposely called her at work—something he usually avoided doing so as not to raise any suspicions—to remind her of the connection between her job and the information he needed in order for them to stay together. "I don't know how long I will be gone. Do you remember what we discussed?" he asked.

"Yes," she confided.

"Well, don't think another thing of it. It was wrong of me to ask."

They exchanged the required "I will miss you" and "take care," and he ended the conversation with another subtle hint: "If you want to reach me in Washington, just to talk, this is my number."

While in Washington, Stohlze did some research on the other targets and made some other inquiries, but he was also waiting for her to call. On December 4, she phoned. The moment he picked up the receiver, the automated tape recorder clicked on. If she agreed to get the materials and then later backed out, he wanted to retain the option of blackmail.

"What is the news?" she asked. "Have they made a decision? Are you being transferred?"

He told her calmly that it didn't look good and that he might be transferred to the West Coast or even back to Germany. When he did come back to Boston, he said, it would likely be only to pack his belongings. After a few minutes of detached chatter, she uttered the words that he had patiently been waiting for. "Remember what you asked me to do for you? You know, get some information from work? Well, I've thought it over, and I'm willing to do it for you."

Stohlze was pleased, and he told her that if he was able to get enough from her, then he could probably stay, and they could be together. "I'll fly up on the shuttle tomorrow. Can we meet tomorrow night for dinner? Could you have some materials for me that soon? Time is of the essence. They will be making a final decision on my status shortly. I can only delay them for so long." She promised to go to work in the wee hours of the morning and provide some more sensitive and useful documents. They agreed to meet at a restaurant on the evening of December 5.

At the meeting, Stohlze played the grateful friend, overcome with the joy of her willingness to help. He bought champagne, and she brought him the first in what he hoped would be many documents on the biochip research being done at her company.

Another meeting was set for the next evening, at a different location. She told him she planned to return to the company that night and secure some more information. Stohlze agreed that that was advisable. It also fit into his plans to move their relationship from a sexual one to a purely professional one. According to a former co-worker, "He believed that in the long run blackmail would be a more powerful weapon to wield in getting her to supply documents. After several meetings he was planning to make that clear to her."

The first packet she brought was pretty ordinary. It included a roster of research projects, internal memos on the progress being made, and a list of proposed alternative methods for doing specific DNA research. It was a good start for Stohlze, but only a start.

On the evening of December 6, they met again, this time later in the evening. She seemed a bit more nervous than she had on the previous evening. "I'm afraid someone might find out," she said. "Lord knows what will happen if they do."

Stohlze tried to calm her a bit. "No one will discover what you are doing. They would never think it was you."

She didn't seem mollified by his comments. "Maybe this should be it. This should give you enough to stay on here in Boston. Let's just stop with this."

Stohlze was surprised that she was trying to back out so quickly. He considered whether he should try to persuade her to acquire more by emphasizing the romance or radically shift the relationship by reverting to blackmail. He did, after all, have the tape of her offer. After brief reflection, he decided to try to use a hint of both, inventing a co-worker he named Hans. "That might create problems," he began. "I don't have enough information yet. I need more—more details of the research—in order to stay here. I would hate to think that we've gone this far and we end up losing each other anyway because I am reassigned. What you have given me so far is good, but I need much more specific and detailed information on research. Besides, there is a slight problem. I may have made a mistake. I told one of my associates in Washington what you are doing for me."

She looked at him with a certain horror. "I had to tell him. His job is on the line, too, and I thought he should know." He paused for just a moment and then uttered a veiled threat: "The trouble is that Hans is crazy. He does not want to be reassigned; his family is settled here. I fear that if the information stops coming, he might contact your company and show them the documents, just to get even with you." She sat stunned, as it became apparent to her that she was boxed in.

Stohlze let her sweat a bit and then made a pitch to reiterate his care and concern for her. "I must return to Washington tonight, and I will try to talk to him. Maybe if you can just keep the information coming for a while, we can get enough, and then we will put this whole thing to an end and we can think once again about our romance." He had, of course, no intention of letting her off so easy.

The next morning, December 7, he took an early shuttle back to Washington to begin transferring back to BND headquarters in Germany the information she had provided. He had—by some estimates—perhaps four computer disks and two thousand pages of documents and other assorted materials at this point. It was not his responsibility to sort through all of it but, rather, to skim it and write a two- or three-page "finding" on where the information came from and what it was all about and add any observations that would be useful to BND analysts and the companies that would receive the information.

That morning he took the documents to the German air carrier Lufthansa and had the materials sent to a BND front company in Hamburg so that the service's Division II could have a look at them. After he returned from Dulles Airport at about eleven-thirty in the morning, he found a message on his answering machine. "They have been asking questions," she said. "I'm scared and I don't know what to do."

When Stohlze received the message he was preparing to leave for the airport to catch the shuttle back to Boston. He did not dare return her call, for fear of being exposed. The thought did cross his mind that perhaps her superiors had gone to her, confronted her with the facts, and forced her into setting him up. Their meeting planned for that evening could be trouble. The night before, she had promised him she would deliver "very important documents" that would be "very useful to him." He figured they might be worth the effort, even with the risk he faced. He decided to arrive at the meeting place earlier than they had agreed, to watch to see what happened.

When he arrived at Logan Airport, he decided to be cautious. Rather than go to his regular hotel, he checked into the Sheraton. He didn't want to be surprised at his flat if something indeed was wrong. He then proceeded to their meeting place, an hour and a half before the set time. Stohlze waited and waited. Three hours passed, and there was no sign of the woman. He decided to drive by her townhouse to see whether he could find any sign of her or—perhaps more important—the documents. He had to keep his distance because he wasn't sure what she had told her superiors.

At approximately nine-twenty, he drove by her townhouse. There was no sign of her car, and the lights were out. He thought of going in (she had told him where in the bushes she kept an extra key), but he elected to drive to the company. There he saw her car, sitting in its assigned spot in the parking lot. Some of the lights in the building were on. He noticed several other cars in the lot. Was she being questioned? He decided to wait and see what would happen next. He wanted to know whether she had got the materials and whether she had been detained. With no one around, he went slowly to her car to look for the papers. He didn't see them, so he concluded that she either had them with her and she was telling the company officials everything or she had left them at her townhouse. He let the air out of her tires and did the same to the other cars in the lot. He then proceeded to her townhouse, to search for the materials. If they weren't there, he would leave town. The risk of being caught was too great.

He scanned her block and, noticing nothing unusual, headed up the walk of her townhouse. He reached into the hedge; the keys were there. He turned the key in the lock and quietly entered the house. He knew the place well, having spent many evenings with her there. He scanned the first floor and found nothing. He rambled up the stairs and headed for her study. Atop her desk, he saw a series of manila envelopes with numerical codes on the corners. He also found several floppy disks. He glanced inside the envelopes and saw they were the documents she had taken. He tucked them under his arm and placed the floppy disks in his pocket. After checking the street from the study window, he proceeded down the stairs, out the front door, and into the night.

On and off for two and a half hours, Stohlze's source was grilled by her superiors about missing documents and reports that she had come to the office at unusual hours and left with some envelopes. They asked her whether she had been in contact with any individuals who had asked for information about the research being done at the company. Upset and distraught, she asked at one point to be excused from the meeting to go to the ladies' room. After ten minutes or so, two employees forced their way into the room and discovered her lying on the floor unconscious. On the counter was a nearly empty bottle of pills. Although the suicide attempt was a real one, her methods fortunately were flawed. Corporate security officials were able to induce vomiting, and she was revived. No authorities were called, according to company officials, for fear that the inquisitors might be pressed to explain what had forced the woman to such drastic lengths.

The following morning, with their mole resting in a company sickbed, company superiors were led through the labyrinth of Stohlze's penetration of the company. She explained what she had given her lover and whom he said he worked for. Only when company officials contacted the FBI did they discover that Stohlze was no researcher but an agent of the West German government.

According to company officials, the employee was let go, and no charges were filed. The company continues its efforts to develop the biochip in the hopes of reaping enormous benefits from its development. Some of the company's best information is in the hands of the German intelligence service, and Karl Heinrich Stohlze is reportedly on another case, somewhere in Western Europe.

9

The Diamonds

South Korea gets enormous economic benefits from spying.
—Dr. Ray Cline, former deputy director of the CIA

On an unusually cool and windy May evening in 1989, Joe Elliott was sitting quietly at his home in suburban Ohio. A technician at the local General Electric plant, Elliott never thought the sort of things about to happen to him were the kinds of things that happened to ordinary people like himself. That night he received an unexpected phone call from a man he had never met. Someone identifying himself as Mr. Larry King of Sanyang Engineering Services was on the other end of the line. He asked to speak to Joe, who got on the line.

In a low, methodical voice, Mr. King said that whereas Joe wouldn't know who he was or anything about Sanyang, he certainly knew a lot about Joe. The mysterious caller went on to describe in detail Joe's work at GE and his important knowledge of the company's process for manufacturing and refining artificial diamonds. Mr. King praised Joe for his depth of technical knowledge and proficiency at his job. He also told the GE worker that he felt sorry for him. He said Joe was being taken for granted by GE: he deserved more pay and more promotions; his skills and knowledge were worth a fortune to GE, yet he was receiving only a fraction of his net worth. Then the mysterious caller dropped a bombshell in the form of an offer that he believed Joe couldn't and wouldn't refuse. "Mr. Elliott," he said, "how would you like to double your $40,000 salary? How would you like a $20,000 cash bonus and two months of vacation? All this can be yours if you consider my offer."

Joe was so stunned he didn't know what to say. The offer had come so suddenly, and from someone he knew nothing about. Joe was silent, and so Mr. King continued. He proposed that Joe consider a job for a South Korean company that just happened to be interested in entering the lucrative synthetic diamond market in which GE was dominant. "This is a once in a life opportunity," King wrote Elliott in a follow-up letter. "Please do not pass it by."

Mr. King's fateful phone call to Joe Elliott on the night of May 28 was a strike of boldness, but also a strike of arrogance. If it had not been for that call, Chien Ming Sung might still be at large today. As one of the most successful peddlers of secret information in the United States, Sung (alias Larry King) transferred millions of dollars in industry secrets from General Electric and Norton Electric to South Korean companies. And whether Sung was aware of it or not, he was one part of a larger plan organized, coordinated, and directed by the South Korean intelligence service to steal U.S. industry secrets.

Sung was a Horatio Alger, making it in America by hard work and ingenuity. Born in China's Fukien Province in 1947, he moved his family to Taiwan to escape Communist persecution and seek greater economic opportunities. Showing exceptional mechanical and scientific ability at a young age, Sung saw his gift as a ticket to the land of opportunity: the United States, a place he had always dreamed of living in. Drawing on his technical brilliance, he came to this country as a graduate student in 1972. He attended the prestigious engineering school at the Massachusetts Institute of Technology, where to this day he is remembered for his talents.

When he first arrived in the United States, things were difficult, but he soon mastered the hurdles he faced. "He arrived with an English problem, but he cracked that quickly," said his adviser, Professor Roger Burns. At an institution where exceptional abilities were the rule, Sung still received numerous academic awards and honors. His hard work, intense concentration, and tremendous problem-solving skills were recognized by professors and classmates alike. If he chose to, he seemed destined to have a promising career with a good salary at a major U.S. high-tech company. His break came in 1977, when General Electric, impressed by his brilliance and determination, hired him to work in an important and demanding division of the company. GE promised him rich financial and professional rewards for a job well done. He worked first at the GE synthetic diamond plant in Worthington, Ohio, a jewel in the company's crown. Worthington is a facility critical to the company's future because it reflects GE's hopes of breaking into new technologies and thus broadening its product base. It is the same plant that Joe Elliott would go to work for a decade later.

While at GE, Sung worked almost exclusively on saw-grade diamonds, which a variety of industries use for numerous tasks. These diamonds are nearly as hard as naturally occurring diamonds but, of course, can be purchased for a fraction of the cost. Sung became very popular with his superiors when he developed a way to raise the efficiency of synthetic diamond production. He developed methods for increasing the number of carats per diamond and producing larger synthetic diamonds. Both of these developments resulted in greater profitability for Sung's division. He was an instant star. Let there be no doubt, says Lowry Manson, a GE manager and a former colleague of Sung's, he "put a lot of money in the bank for GE." In exchange, Sung got large salary increases and fat bonuses. GE even pulled a few strings to help Sung get U.S. citizenship. Had he wanted to, Sung could have spent his whole career at GE.

The engineer was growing restless, however, and wanted to move on. The same old surroundings and tasks were beginning to bore him. By 1984, Sung's star had risen so high that GE competitors began to learn about him. One, also in the diamond-manufacturing business, managed to lure him away with a lucrative offer. Norton, an old-line manufacturer based in Worcester, Massachusetts, saw in Sung the perfect recruit to strengthen the research staff at its center for synthetic-diamond technology in Salt Lake City. Norton was hoping to move into the business of synthetic diamonds in a big way by expanding both production and research, and management understood that young specialists like Sung would provide the intellectual horsepower to make the expansion possible. Norton had long been one of GE's biggest customers in synthetic diamonds, and so the loss of Sung to Norton was a big one for GE, not only because the company would miss his talent, but also because that talent would now be used by a competitor.

Subsequent events would reveal that the loss of Sung's talents was only part of GE's loss. For Sung had managed to take with him critical information worth hundreds of millions of dollars. Before his last day in Worthington, Sung did the near impossible: he made off with a virtual library of GE information on the diamond-manufacturing process. It was the near impossible because the GE Worthington plant is surrounded by a twelve-foot chain link fence electronically monitored by an array of sensors and cameras. Guards man security gates twenty-four hours a day, randomly searching the cars of visitors and employees as they leave the facility. "It's like Fort Knox," says one competitor. But those security precautions didn't hamper Sung. They were apparently inadequate, ill-suited to the activities of a determined insider. The GE employee came up with innovative ways to smuggle out the critical documents. Sometimes he hid them under a false bottom in the trunk of his car or within compartments inside the passenger seats, locations impossible to detect in a cursory search. Security personnel clearly didn't anticipate that such elaborate methods might be used to spirit company secrets out of the plant.

Norton gave Sung a good job, a six-figure salary, and plenty of professional freedom. But for some reason, it wasn't enough. Sung never told Norton about the GE documents he had taken. He reckoned wisely that had he done so, they would have reported him. Besides, he had bigger plans for the secrets he now possessed. Almost immediately he began gathering documents from his new employer, just as he had done at GE.

Less than two years after joining Norton, he laid the groundwork for his scheme. In January 1986, Sung set up a secret company innocuously named United Machinery, Incorporated, while continuing to work for Norton. It was one of many fronts that Sung would establish in order to sell secrets to foreign companies. United Machinery was involved in everything: selling technology, offering consulting services, and importing diamonds into the United States. The secrets he took from GE and the ones he was gathering at Norton figured prominently in the services United

Machinery would eventually provide. The information he could offer foreign competitors was first-rate and, at the right price, was available for the asking. GE was the industry leader, controlling 45 percent of the worldwide artificial diamond market, and Norton was engaged in cutting-edge research in the field. To any competitor, Sung's knowledge and intelligence, as well as this information, would be an enormous boost.

Sung's first big client was a company from his native China, the Shenzhen Asia Diamond Company, which paid him $1.6 million for GE documents, diamond-manufacturing technologies, and equipment. The deal offered the government of China an opportunity to become independent in diamond manufacturing and the hope of exporting synthetic diamonds to lucrative markets all over Asia. The deal between Sung and Shenzhen was sealed when Shenzhen representatives traveled to San Francisco to make arrangements for the transfer of the materials to the Chinese mainland. Xia Wong and Mahmutsha Sing stayed in the posh Four Seasons Hotel in the heart of San Francisco while making shipping arrangements. During their ten-day visit, word of their business trip reached the streets and eventually reached Sung Syung Rhee.

Born in Inch'on, South Korea, Rhee was a chain-smoker and a lover of old Bruce Lee movies. A thin, balding, bespectacled man, he had moved to the United States in 1981 and had worked at various jobs in San Francisco's Chinatown. He eventually became mildly successful in the import-export business but maintained a life-style that exceeded his regular income. He traveled often to exotic locales, according to FBI sources. He wore expensive clothes and ate out frequently, at San Francisco's best restaurants. And he never seemed short of money. According to an FBI official in the bureau's counterintelligence division, Rhee lived the way he did by working as a snoop for South Korea's intelligence service, an organization with an international reach, once feared by most Koreans living in the United States but beloved by those like Rhee who made good money passing secrets and information to South Korean operatives. By some estimates, Rhee made one hundred thousand dollars a year off the South Korean National Security Planning Agency. His specialty was technology secrets and information that would be coveted by the NSP and passed along to large Korean conglomerates.

When Rhee stumbled across information about the deal Sung had struck with Shenzhen, he knew almost immediately it would be of interest to his handlers. He phoned the South Korean consulate in Los Angeles, and his contact moved quickly to alert several South Korean companies to Sung's secrets and their apparent availability to those willing to pay. Rhee received a hefty ten-thousand-dollar finder's fee for his efforts. His tip culminated in February 1988, when Sung signed a one-million-dollar contract with the Iljin Corporation, a South Korean manufacturing company interested in producing diamonds. By then, diamond production was a five-hundred-million-dollar-per-year industry, in which GE was the leader. Iljin wanted to try to get a share of the market.

The information Sung supplied saved Iljin from having to invest millions of dollars and man-hours in researching and perfecting a "recipe" for making diamonds. What had taken GE years of research, development, and hard work came to the South Korean company with relative ease. "The information from Sung was critical," says one FBI official. "It made a great deal of difference."

The form in which Sung provided the information surprised Iljin's officials. It reflected Sung's confidence that he would never be caught by GE or Norton. He almost flaunted his treasure trove of documents, offering a catalog of items. Indeed, he was so brazen and cavalier in his approach that he barely bothered to change the GE documents that he had stolen when he sold them overseas. "Mr. Sung merely took the GE process instructions, cut out the GE logo and proprietary legend and pasted materials onto letterhead from one of his own companies," said Harold Bovenkerk, the manager of technology and planning at the GE Worthington plant.

This same brazenness extended to Sung's intelligence activities at Norton. Seniority gave him access to the company's technology and research facilities, where he regularly collected information. Between what he had obtained at GE and what he was gathering at Norton, Sung had access to virtually all the important secrets in the field. Because he was so deeply involved in the development of diamond-manufacturing technologies, Sung put the pieces together easily and made sense of them for his foreign buyers. His value, no doubt, was recognized by his clients. He was, by some accounts, making more than one million dollars a year from his relationship with Iljin.

Sung's work was beginning to strain him, and he had a difficult time juggling his espionage activities with his work at Norton. "[Mr. Sung] tells me he was a man who led virtually no personal life, was working round the clock," Sung's attorney, William Crowe, would later say at a court hearing. He was constantly searching for more information, and as he became more senior at Norton, the demands and responsibilities of his job there were increasing enormously.

The strain was also growing because of the nature of Sung's activities. Despite his supreme confidence, his was a high-risk operation, and the need for company documents and the connections with foreign firms, most specifically Shenzhen and Iljin, were complex activities that required delicate handling. His clients, in offering him large fees, insisted on a constant flow and a large volume of up-to-date information. So Sung was forced to include more people in his scheme, gather more intelligence, and juggle more deals. It was this pressure that, in the end, was his downfall. He might never have been caught had he not placed that call to Joe Elliott.

It was out of the blue, a cold call to someone about whom he had only a limited amount of professional information. But it was a call he felt he had to make. Elliott was critical to Sung's plans. Gordon Andrew McKay, a private investigator for GE, later stated in a legal affidavit, "Elliott's expertise was required to actually commence the [diamond] production process." Iljin wanted someone with inside knowledge of GE's processes to oversee the process at their facilities in Seoul. They thought Elliott was the perfect candidate: a middle-ranking GE employee who might just sell out his company for enough money. Unfortunately for everyone involved in Sung's scheme, they thought wrong.

On May 30, when Sung followed up his call to Elliott with an employment application, the GE employee's suspicions and concerns were simply too great to be kept to himself. He contacted his superiors, and a trap was set. Elliott agreed to meet with Mr. King and Kyuseop Kim, the president of Imec Corporation, a U.S. subsidiary of Iljin. The meeting, under the guise of a job interview, took place at the Marriott Marquis Hotel in New York City on June 14.

The palatial hotel formed a backdrop for the first act in what would be the beginning of the end for Sung. Elliott arrived with a man he introduced as his attorney, Gordon Andrew McKay, who was actually a private detective hired by GE. They feigned interest in the job opportunity and subtly but systematically pumped Kim and Mr. King for information about what Iljin wanted from Elliott. It was clear almost immediately that Iljin was desperate for Elliott's help. The company needed his expertise and his knowledge of the GE process in order to bring Iljin into the diamond-manufacturing business on a strong footing. Things at GE had changed since Sung had left in 1984. Only up-to-date expertise would do. Kim hinted that without Elliott, Iljin would be unable to make a go of it. By getting Kim to outline the situation, Elliott and his "lawyer" had discovered the paper trail that led from GE to Iljin courtesy of Sung.

Having gathered the information he needed, McKay returned to GE headquarters to brief company security officials. Norton was soon brought in, on the grounds that Sung was a Norton employee. GE officials assumed, correctly as it turned out, that Norton was a likely victim of Sung's operation, too. Meanwhile, Kim and Mr. King were persistent in their efforts to recruit Elliott. On June 26, Kim sent Elliott a round-trip ticket to Seoul along with a note encouraging him to explore the opportunities available in Korea. Elliott, on the advice of McKay, returned the ticket the next day, telling Kim he wasn't interested. But Mr. King didn't take the hint. Not giving up easily, he contacted Elliott by phone, asking whether he might consider working for Iljin as a consultant while on "vacations." That way Elliott could stay on at GE and supplement his income by working for Iljin on the side. King promised a fat consulting fee and other perks. Could he, King asked, perhaps pass along some new information about a relevant GE technology if they made it worth his while?

Sung's persistence forced GE and Norton to recognize the seriousness of the campaign to steal their technology. The persistence of both Sung and Iljin was evidence enough that the South Koreans had already invested plenty to gain access to company secrets. It indicated, too, that they already had almost all the pieces they needed. The only ingredient missing was someone with up-to-date knowledge of the GE process, someone like Joe Elliott. That GE and Norton agreed to work together was a potent symbol of the risks both companies felt they were facing. After all, by working together each company would give the other access to the secrets Sung had.

A special investigative unit was formed, made up of specialists and security officials from both companies. Several consultants were also brought in. An in-depth investigation of Sung's activities and his liaisons with the South Koreans was launched.

After weeks of monitoring Sung's movements, the unit made its move. On a balmy night in July of 1989, the special GE-Norton unit approached the trash cans at Sung's home on Indian Meadow Drive in Northborough, Massachusetts, where he was living after having been transferred from Salt Lake City. Things seemed quiet in the house, Sung's residence and the base of his operation. The GE-Norton team was looking for hints of the operation. Slowly, quietly, and systematically the men began going through the trash cans on the sidewalk in front of the house. The team's method, which entailed professionally dressed men sifting through trash, was perhaps unusual, but it was certainly effective, offering GE and Norton incredible insight into United Machinery and the activities in which it was involved.

Sung didn't shred all of his documents. That was a critical mistake. The paper trail the special team uncovered was invaluable to the investigation. Along with discarded food containers, rotten banana peels, and old shoes, they found evidence that Sung had thousands of pages of documents from both GE and Norton, detailed classified documents worth a fortune to any competitor. This trash-can search was also a completely legal operation. Because Sung had placed his trash cans on the street and not a few feet away in his own yard, anybody had legal access to it. This was another critical misstep of Sung's.

Armed with the testimony of Joe Elliott and Gordon Andrew McKay, as well as the documents culled from Sung's trash, Norton security officials and lawyers went to court. Arguing that Sung held GE and Norton documents that were not legally his, Norton lawyers asked for a civil writ of seizure, which grants citizens the same right of search and seizure that is far more often granted only to police and law-enforcement officers. The judge, overwhelmed by the information Norton officials had obtained, gave the company the right to search 146 Indian Meadow Drive on September 18. The civil writ offered GE and Norton the opportunity to repossess the documents they rightfully owned without involving law-enforcement officials and without forewarning Sung.

With the writ in hand, an unmarked, windowless van with twelve

Norton and GE security officials inside waited on the corner of Indian Meadow Drive on the morning of September 18. After Sung departed for work, they descended on his home. Officials began searching his home and hauling out documents by the boxful. The take was enormous; by one estimate, fourteen file cabinets worth of documents were taken that morning. Security officials were perhaps too thorough: they accidentally came away with Sung's slides from a family vacation in Newfoundland. After they finished, they climbed back into the van and left as quickly as they had arrived. The mission was accomplished, and the leak was plugged—without incident.

Returning home that evening, Sung was shocked to discover his file cabinets empty. Everything was gone; his operation was ruined. He broke into a cold sweat. After wandering around the house for twenty minutes, he began to see the writing on the wall. He quickly began to cover up the operation and salvage what he could. The next morning, according to security officials, he directed his wife to transfer $1.3 million from their accounts in the United States to several in Asia. He suspended all communications with his clients for fear that GE and Norton or law-enforcement officials might be tapping his phone. He also began burning and shredding documents relating to his work that had not been taken by the security team. He did not even bother to call the police.

In response to rumors of what the security team had found, Sung claimed to be innocent of any wrongdoing. "I had to bring some documents home relating to my work," he told a local reporter. But Sung's attempt at damage control, and his efforts to cover his trail, came too late. On September 20, he was fired by Norton and slapped with a lawsuit filed by both companies.

10

The Laughing Bird

When you think about South Korean intelligence, subtlety is not a word that comes to mind.

—William Colby, former director of the CIA

For its size, no country in the world has the intelligence capability of South Korea. The Korean Central Intelligence Agency, renamed the National Security Planning Agency in December 1980, has been active around the world, providing a variety of intelligence and espionage services for Korean interests. These have included not only gathering information on North Korea, China, and the Soviet Union but also spying on Koreans overseas and carrying out operations against South Korea's allies. The United States and Japan are two countries in which South Korean intelligence agents and operatives have been most active. Political, economic, and technology secrets have all been targets of South Korean espionage operations. In many respects, say U.S. intelligence sources, the NSP is more efficient and more effective than Israel's famed Mossad, often regarded as the premier intelligence organization for its size. The NSP boasts technically proficient agents, enormous financial resources, and a well-organized cadre of informers who, for a fee, supplement the work of agents.

The Korean Central Intelligence Agency was established in 1961 to function as the military government's central source of security information. Though named after its U.S. counterpart, it did not resemble it in form or in deed. Under the Central Intelligence Agency Law of June 1961, the agency was charged with the mission of supervising and coordinating "both international and domestic intelligence activities and criminal investigations by all government intelligence agencies, including that of the military." It was given sweeping powers to "direct and supervise" the personnel of other government agencies as well. The agency was not accountable to anyone in South Korea save the South Korean president.

Overseas, KCIA operatives were often posted to the South Korean embassy as members of the diplomatic staff. But from time to time they also used Korea's enormous industrial conglomerates—like Hyundai, Samsung, and the Lucky Group—as cover. According to former Korean intelligence officers, these companies were at least some of the time aware of the presence of intelligence agents working out of their corporate offices. "They would get [a] call [from government officials], and it would be arranged easily. Most times, no questions would be asked by them," says one former South Korean intelligence official. The KCIA encouraged its agents to gather political, economic, military, and technology secrets simultaneously rather than specialize in specific fields. Unlike their counterparts in other intelligence services, KCIA agents were assigned to specific geographic regions overseas with a responsibility for everything in the region—surveillance of opponents of the government, political spying, and technological espionage. Often members of the Korean community in the United States were manipulated by, or blackmailed into cooperating with, KCIA operatives working in the United States.

Tongsun Park was an awkward but intense schoolboy when he arrived in Washington, D.C., in 1956 to attend Georgetown University. Knowing only broken English, he quickly began having academic problems and at one point was suspended for "academic deficiencies." In 1960, however, he graduated from the Georgetown School of Foreign Service.

Far more important to Park than his studies was his growing friendship with a new powerful and ambitious leader in South Korea. General Park Chung Hee, a steely man who would become president of South Korea in 1961, became Tongsun Park's good friend. A professional relationship based on mutual respect and ambition soon developed between the two men. General Park told Tongsun Park that "new opportunities" would be available for people like him who wanted to make a contribution to South Korea's economic and political success and had an understanding of important countries like the United States. The general made it clear that these opportunities were intertwined with plans to establish a powerful government institution in South Korean society, an intelligence service that would be Park's eyes and ears around the world. It would track events in Korea and in the rest of the world, especially in the United States, South Korea's patron and sponsor.

In January 1960, General Park established a small working group of advisers, aides, and supporters to discuss the idea of an intelligence service. It was a typical thing for the rising political star to do: talk of establishing an intelligence service even before he was president. But his respect for intelligence matters was so great that this made sense. After all, having knowledge of his political rivals' doings had proved critical to his rise to power in the first place. Once he assumed power, General Park received the active support and assistance of the U.S. Central Intelligence Agency in organizing and creating the Korean Central Intelligence Agency. Unbeknownst to his sponsors, however, one of the KCIA's earliest and most important missions was to spy on the United States.

In the summer of 1960, Tongsun Park returned to Washington no longer the clumsy Georgetown student he had been four years before but now a young enthusiast for his country. Tongsun Park was valuable to the Korean government. General Park had been impressed with the young man's knowledge of Washington. His credentials were different from those of most of the other possible recruits to the forthcoming intelligence organization. The others were former military officers, who might do well tracking military developments in North Korea and the rest of Asia but knew little about the social nuances that would be critical in serving as an intelligence operative in a foreign capital. With his improved English, Tongsun Park had the odd mix of charm and cold, hard calculation that made him one of the best and brightest prospects for the KCIA. He already knew many Americans in Washington quite well socially. And the business ventures that brought him to Washington would make the perfect cover for an intelligence operative.

Tongsun Park learned early about the importance of mixing the social and the professional in Washington. He also discovered that the social set that included some of the most important members of the Washington political and economic establishment was a cohesive group, one whose members swam together like a school of fish. If some key members of the establishment moved one way socially, many others would follow. To gather influence and power for both his business interests and those of the KCIA, Tongsun Park decided to launch a social club, which he would control and direct. The Georgetown section of Washington he well knew to be the locus of most social activity, and it made the most sense as the location of his club. With the direct financial support of the South Korean government, Park leased an elegant townhouse in 1961 that would eventually become the George Town Club.

For years, the wealthy and powerful of the Washington social elite flocked to Park's club. The club, with its deceptively modest green facade at 1530 Wisconsin Avenue Northwest, had powerful and well-known members and guests and catered to their culinary and social tastes with success and elegance. In the early 1970s, guests included senior elected officials as well as such cabinet members as Secretary of Defense Melvin Laird, Attorney General William B. Saxbe, and even Vice President Gerald Ford.

The club, with its grande dame fashion, reeked of good taste: seventeenth-century English wall paneling, Oriental antique jade, oil paintings, and a ceramic collection; English pewter, Sheffield silver, and crystal goblets; and one of the finest wine and liquor collections in the capital. The food was also some of the city's finest: lobster in garlic butter served with white wine; steak *au poivre* with red wine; the finest Stilton and French cheeses; and free-flowing champagne. The Washington elite came to the George Town Club to play, enjoy, and casually talk business. A powerful tool with which to influence U.S. policymakers and gather intelligence, the George Town Club was in fact a KCIA front operation and, in the eyes of one former KCIA agent, was "the best investment that the agency ever made."

Park's search for members was critical. Harnessing his charm, money, and a touch of boldness, he persuaded several members of the Washington elite with whom he was acquainted to become members. They provided the stamp of approval the club needed to attract even more members. And the more who joined, the easier it would be to collect intelligence. Founding members included a veritable *Who's Who* of the Washington political elite: Robert Gray, a cabinet secretary of President Eisenhower's and a prominent Republican fund-raiser; Thomas G. Corcoran, affectionately known as Tommy the Cork, who was a member of FDR's brain trust and by the 1960s was an influential Washington attorney; Air Force General Fred Dean, who commanded the U.S. Air Task Force on Taiwan from 1957 to 1960 and went on to hold key staff and command positions in Washington and Europe; George Murphy, who at the time of the club's founding was serving his one term in the U.S. Senate; Congressman Clark Thompson, a senior conservative Democrat who served twenty-two years in the House; Mrs. Robert McCormick, wife of the late publisher of the *Chicago Tribune;* Louise Gore, a member of the Maryland State Legislature and an unsuccessful candidate in the 1974 gubernatorial contest; and Anna Chennault, a Washington socialite and widow of Claire Chennault.

In all, with the help of friends and through what one early member would later recall was his "charming charm," Park managed to sign up 160 initial members. They came from all the corridors of the Washington establishment: government, business, law, and the military. For Park, says another one of the club's early members, Henry Preston Pitts, Jr., these 160 were all that he needed "to get the snowball rolling."

With membership growing, the Korean socialite and intelligence agent began his job as entertainer and host. The club became legendary. New members, including members of Congress and senior administration officials, flocked to it. Members often brought important friends, who also became permanent fixtures at the George Town Club. And with Park at the center, making sure their needs were attended to, many members began to trust him and count him as one of their own. They told him all sorts of things. They discussed marital and personal problems, troubles at work. Some even inadvertently discussed classified government information in front of him. "He was like your kid brother," says one former member. "You knew he couldn't do anything about it, but it helped you to tell him anyway."

But Park was no innocent little brother. While he was running the George Town Club, he was also serving as an intelligence officer in the KCIA, with a mission to collect intelligence and act as an agent of influence. He began keeping files and assembling dossiers on members of Congress, senior administration officials, lobbyists, businessmen, and military leaders. In October 1962, according to CIA officials, he planned the visit of KCIA Chief Kim Jong Pil, who had helped bring General Park to power in a 1961 coup. Tongsun Park and Kim held several private meetings, during which they exchanged information about events in Washington. Park briefed Kim on what he knew about the key officials in the Kennedy administration and what they thought about Korea. He also made suggestions that could be taken back to General Park, regarding how much aid the administration might be willing to give, which members of Congress should be regarded as friends, and what secrets Park held that could be used to blackmail officials at a critical moment.

Kim was impressed by Park's operation and his ability to move easily in Washington social circles. The amount of intelligence he provided his handlers surprised the Korean officials. "We did not believe we could acquire such information so easily," says one former KCIA operative now living in the United States. "It seemed to be so easy for Park." And the quality of intelligence, due to his access to senior government officials, was surprising to Korean officials, too. His early success and the positive impression he left on Kim Jong Pil led to even closer cooperation. In May 1965, the KCIA upped its financial support of Park, providing him with $260,000 a year to fund his activities. According to Kim Hyung Wook, the late ex-KCIA director who defected to the United States in 1973, these funds were transferred from Seoul to Park through the diplomatic pouches of the South Korean embassy in Washington. Park was also tossed a golden plum by Seoul: a contract to serve as the agent for Korean rice purchases in the United States. It would allow him to earn large commissions that would supplement his income and give him the resources to expand already-existing intelligence operations. Many of the rice purchases were funded in part by U.S. Food-for-Peace grants, perhaps the first time in history that a foreign intelligence agent spying on the United States was being partially financed by U.S. taxpayers.

These additional funds from Seoul were crucial to Park's plans for the George Town Club. They allowed him to purchase the club building. That transaction, in turn, allowed him to add a technical sophistication to his intelligence collection. As long as someone else had owned the building, electronic eavesdropping was too risky. As his sole means of retaining information, Park had relied on his memory and furious note taking every night after club guests had departed. Now electronic eavesdropping equipment could be installed. In the months after the purchase of the building, renovations were made to enhance the clandestine collection of information. They oftentimes took place during odd hours so as to avoid arousing the suspicions of Park's business partners and club members. At one point, however, the activity did arouse some curiosity. One club member noticed work being done at two-thirty one October morning and asked Park about it. The quick-thinking club owner justified the work schedule on the grounds that electrical problems that couldn't be put off had been plaguing the club and he didn't want the renovations to interfere with the club's social activities.

According to a former KCIA official who participated in the bugging of the club, the process was designed to look as if general renovations were taking place. But the renovations were not aesthetic. Dozens of eavesdropping devices, including cameras and bugs, were planted in the club's luxurious private rooms. "We even put [bugs] under the urinals," the official claims. The goal was a net of eavesdropping devices that would cover the entire club but could be quickly detached and removed when structural renovations were made to the building. The wires for the eavesdropping equipment were run alongside the rest of the wiring, to prevent easy detection by handymen who might be called in to make minor repairs from time to time. The electrician was a friend of Park's and was paid by the KCIA.

The George Town Club was a perfect observation post from which Korean agents could collect enormous amounts of information. Comments were filed by subject and topic as well as under the name of the principal involved. Files on the personal habits and problems of club members were also maintained by Korean intelligence officers at the embassy. One former KCIA agent believes these were kept in order to retain an option for blackmail.

In the summer of 1966, Park created a unique opportunity for showcasing the club's effectiveness as a front for espionage. An event took place that both highlighted the club's potential and demonstrated the ease with which the highest reaches of the U.S. government might be entangled in Park's eavesdropping web. Just months after the renovation, the rehearsal dinner preceding the wedding of President Johnson's daughter Luci was held at the George Town Club. The choice of Park's club was not an accident but was made covertly by Park for the First Family. For all its popularity in Washington social circles, the George Town Club was not the president's first choice. Indeed, according to a former KCIA operative, Park bragged about how he created the conditions that gave the Johnsons no other choice than to have the dinner at his club. Through his circle of friends who were members of Washington high society, Park had learned of the First Family's plans for a wedding months before it was publicly announced. Using this tip, he began to contact local clubs and other facilities, booking them up for the evening that the dinner was planned, thus leaving the First Family with little choice but to hold the event at the lesser known—and now extensively bugged—George Town Club.

The public record seems to support Park's claims. Bess Abell, the social secretary in the Johnson White House, said that a routine selection process was used to pick the site. The George Town Club was picked, she said, because older, better-known clubs were all mysteriously booked up. Through his cleverness and charm, Park hosted the rehearsal dinner and delivered a coup to his KCIA handlers. On September 2, 1966, he presented a visiting KCIA deputy director with something that could hardly be believed back in Seoul: an audiotape of the First Family and close friends in private conversation at Luci's rehearsal dinner.

The Johnson event opened up new avenues of contact for Park. He continued to recruit members, in an effort not only to serve as an agent of influence but also to gather intelligence. He also began seeking information directly from members, particularly when the opportunity presented itself.

U.S. Marine Corps General Graves Erskine, who commanded the

Third Marine Division at Iwo Jima and from 1953 to 1961 served as assistant for special operations to the secretary of defense, was a "good source" for Park, according to a former KCIA operative. Erskine was well connected in the Washington intelligence and security communities. His post at the Pentagon included the areas of intelligence, counterintelligence, communications security, CIA relationships and special operations, and psychological warfare operations. Erskine was closely connected with Park and often met with him privately at the club after hours, according to a former Korean agent. He provided elaborate information on the U.S. campaign in Vietnam, an issue that provoked serious concern in South Korea. According to this agent, "Park would say, 'The general likes to tell things—all the things he knows.'" Through consulting arrangements, Erskine maintained informal and formal contact with many senior Pentagon officials throughout the 1960s and offered Korea "detailed information about American plans in Southeast Asia," according to an FBI official familiar with Park's operations.

Park also used the club and his social connections as means to gain influence with members of Congress and other elected officials. His hope was to influence officials and gather intelligence indirectly through subtle questioning in a relaxed social atmosphere in which champagne and liquor often flowed freely. He held lavish dinners and fund-raisers for members of Congress. He befriended Thomas P. ("Tip") O'Neill, Jr., when he was the House majority leader, and he held two lavish birthday parties for him, in 1973 and 1974. Speaker of the House Carl Albert also attended parties at the club, as did numerous other members of Congress, including Thomas Foley. Gaining influence with members of Congress was an important mission for Park.

Both O'Neill and Foley were unwittingly helpful to Park in his clandestine intelligence-gathering operations and in his efforts to promote South Korean interests. On at least two occasions, according to a former Park associate, the club owner received valuable information from O'Neill by plying him with liquor. Park once told colleagues that his assessment of O'Neill was "drink, drink, drink, then talk, talk, talk." One evening during the first week of June in 1974, Park and O'Neill sat at a corner table on the second floor of the club, splitting a bottle of champagne—the last in a long series. On this evening, Park wanted information on legislation before the House concerning trade with South Korea. Park wanted to know whether the legislation would make it out of committee, how the votes were lining up, whether something could be done to stop the legislation if it were passed in the House. O'Neill was apparently very forthcoming, believing he was sharing the information with a friend, not an intelligence officer.

Tom Foley, then a relatively junior member of Congress, was also caught in Park's web. A recipient of a Tongsun Park five-hundred-dollar political donation in 1970, Foley was being watched by the KCIA as a possible source, like Tip O'Neill. The quiet native of eastern Washington State was invited to, and attended, several Park parties at which the host and at least one other operative tested his potential as a source. Although there is no direct evidence that Foley ever did become one, the federal indictment of Park claimed that "in or around 1971 or 1972 in the District of Columbia the defendant, Tongsun Park, did cause Congressman Foley to call an official in the executive branch of the United States government."

According to a former KCIA official, the call was made to the U.S. Department of Commerce in September of 1971 and regarded difficulty that the South Korean Hyundai Group was having with several unnamed American companies over a contractual agreement. The American companies felt they had been shortchanged in a joint-production agreement and had gone to the Commerce Department for moral backing, hoping political pressure might circumvent the need for legal action. Foley called to get a clarification of Commerce's position, which ended up being indifference despite the claims of the U.S. companies. Foley then relayed Commerce's attitude to Park, who, via the KCIA station chief in Washington, contacted Chung Hee Yung, son-in-law of Hyundai Group Chairman Chung Ju Yung.

Park also managed to recruit agents in the U.S. government. One of his best recruits was Suzi Park Thomson, a senior aide to the speaker of the House, Carl Albert. Thomson was named in U.S. intelligence reports as a KCIA operative and was considered by KCIA agents involved in White Snow to be an effective and loyal agent. One FBI report outlines her role as that of "a channel of information on individuals and policy." Although she denies any involvement with the KCIA, her role was apparently to act as hostess at small, informal parties, where she could introduce her congressional friends to Korean diplomats and KCIA operatives.

Korean intelligence, according to former agents, reportedly had a list of congressional staff members whom they hoped to recruit or compromise, their goal being the establishment of an elaborate network of informants on Capitol Hill. Thomson was to be the hub of, or linchpin in, the network. At its most ambitious stage, the KCIA envisioned a network that would include informants or sources in important Senate and House committees, such as those on foreign relations, commerce, and science, space, and technology. It is unclear how far the plan ever got or how much success Thomson had. What is known is that she was privy to valuable information, and she had the complete trust of the House speaker. She made several trips to South Korea, according to intelligence officials, including one with Carl Albert in August 1971. According to U.S. intelligence sources, Thomson's presence on that trip caused serious tensions between the U.S. embassy in Seoul, which was aware of her connections with the KCIA, and Albert.

The CIA station chief in Seoul had several times prior to the visit identified Thomson as an agent for the KCIA and shared his findings with the U.S. ambassador to South Korea, Philip Habib. When Albert and Thomson visited the U.S. embassy for a briefing and a private meeting with the ambassador, according to intelligence sources, Habib objected to Thomson's presence at the meeting and asked her to leave. She refused and looked to her boss for support. The speaker, unconvinced and perhaps a little insulted, insisted that she remain. At the meeting, Thomson received important access to high-level and current information regarding the U.S.–South Korean military and trade relationship and American thinking on these subjects.

Other Thomson trips followed, in 1973 and 1975, during which she was again privy to embassy meetings and probably also attempted to influence delegation members. In both instances, she traveled with members of Congress, including Robert Leggett, with whom, it was eventually disclosed, she was having an affair. Some U.S. intelligence reports, according to an FBI official, listed Leggett as compromised for that very reason. There is no evidence, however, that he had any direct connection with Korean intelligence.

While in Washington, Thomson was a regular hostess, throwing parties with guest lists that included senior congressional staffers and, on occasion, even congressmen themselves. A regular attendee at these affairs was Yung Hwan Kim, the KCIA station chief in Washington until he defected to the United States in 1976. Thomson claims she didn't know who Kim was until she read about his defection in the *Washington Post.* Kim claims otherwise. Another former KCIA official corroborates Kim's story, claiming that part of the station chief's job was to work with Thomson in identifying possible sources of intelligence and maybe even in recruiting agents.

Park's efforts to gather valuable intelligence as well as influence important elected officials were not restricted to Washington. He developed a financial and friendly relationship with Edwin Edwards, a Congressman from Louisiana who was elected governor in 1971. According to federal officials, Edwards received ten thousand dollars from a Park agent, Jay Shin Ryu, during his campaign for governor. The money was given in two five-thousand-dollar installments, the first in December 1971 and the second in January 1972. Edwards's wife, Elaine, also received ten thousand dollars from Park in 1971. The relationship between Edwards and Park was cordial as well as social. Edwards attended parties at the George Town Club and was a common fixture at Park's social affairs. This relationship gave Park access, which often translated into political horse-trading that benefited the South Korean government as well as Edwards's district in Louisiana. At one point, Park asked for, and received help from, Edwards in securing more aircraft for the South Korean air force. In exchange for Edwards's delivering four Phantom F-4 fighters on the budget bill, Park promised that South Korea would begin to purchase more Louisiana rice rather than the California variety it had been buying for years.

Interest in Edwards continued once he was installed in the governor's mansion in Baton Rouge. When the KCIA listed "petrochemicals—technical features" on a hot list of desired intelligence in late 1970, Park contacted his old friend Edwin Edwards. Louisiana had several petrochemical facilities, and the state government had direct information that would be helpful in developing the South Korean petrochemical industry. According to a former KCIA official, Park asked for, and received from Edwards, blueprints and details concerning the layout of a new petrochemical facility outside of Baton Rouge. Two petrochemical complexes in South Korea, one in Ulsan and another at Yosu, were built in part on the basis of secrets learned courtesy of Governor Edwards, according to KCIA officials.

By 1973, the Park campaign was considered an unqualified success in the eyes of the KCIA. Park had gathered an enormous amount of intelligence on U.S. political and military developments. He had been able to use his connections with members of Congress and other officials to act as an agent of influence to protect South Korean interests in the United States. His success led to a KCIA decision to institutionalize further its intelligence operations in the United States and to broaden them not only in terms of the number of intelligence officers involved but also in terms of areas into which previous operations had never gone.

In April 1973, Jal Hyon Lee, an information officer in the South Korean embassy in Washington, attended a secret meeting at KCIA head-quarters in Seoul. At that meeting, according to Lee, plans were laid "to seduce and buy off—that's about the closest I can translate the Korean—the Congress." The private meeting, attended by about twenty senior KCIA officials, was chaired by the director of the KCIA, Lee Hu Rak, an official known for his zeal and a penchant for rooting out enemies of the KCIA—real and imagined—in overseas allied countries. Another participant in that meeting, Huin Bok Po, recalls that the KCIA's plans were to step up its intelligence gathering on American officials and to begin building a network of agents at the White House. With a network on Capitol Hill already under way, the White House seemed the next logical place to go for the ambitious leaders of the KCIA. They were particularly interested in recruits at the staff level of the National Security Council and the Executive Office of the President. KCIA officials were optimistic that some staff recruits at the White House could be found.

Foremost among the priorities for South Korean intelligence operations in the United States was the continuation of the U.S. commitment to military support of the Park regime—specifically, the continued presence of U.S. forces in South Korea to deter an attack from North Korea, military and other forms of assistance, and continued arms sales. Criticism of Seoul's human-rights record and America's pending withdrawal from Vietnam concerned the KCIA and Park, who feared an abrupt U.S. withdrawal from South Korea might be imminent. The expanded spy operation was planned in part because of Seoul's vulnerability to U.S. pressures. In October of 1972, when President Park seized additional power in his country, the Nixon administration withdrew thousands of U.S. troops. Seoul feared that South Korea would be left alone on the Asian continent to face the challenges of North Korea, the Soviet Union, and the People's Republic of China.

According to Po, Operation White Snow was given an important economic and technology component as well. By 1973, South Korea had shown itself to be competitive in a variety of manufacturing fields, including steel and consumer goods. But for Lee Hu Rak as well as for President Park, there was "a new wave" of technological development that South Korea needed to master to ensure greater prosperity and national stature. Microelectronics, still a virgin territory, and chemicals, a difficult field to master, were critical to the future of South Korea, the KCIA concluded at its April meeting. The consensus at the meeting, says Po, was that South Korea needed to excel in some of these fields in order to ensure economic prowess and prosperity. "Mastery in some sectors was believed to be very important to the future of South Korea," says Po. President Park was fond of saying (indeed, it might have been put on his tombstone as his epigraph), "In human life, economics precedes politics or culture."

But the KCIA and Park also feared the loss of markets in the United States due to growing calls from protectionists. South Korea's economic success had come in industries in which there were strong labor constituencies in the United States—textiles, footwear, steel, and shipbuilding. The recession of 1973–74 was a particularly strong one, and Seoul feared that South Korea might be fingered as a threat to those industries and therefore targeted with tariffs or trade quotas. South Korea's powerful Economic Planning Board identified protectionist measures in the United States as a serious threat to South Korean national security. Accurate intelligence on this problem was critical for South Korea's economic strength. White Snow would therefore be concentrated on Washington, but it would also include other parts of the United States that had particular technological significance.

At the meeting, key operational decisions were made. Operation White Snow was to be directed by Han Byung Ki, then deputy ambassador to the United Nations and President Park's son-in-law. Ground-level intelligence work would be left to the KCIA officers in the South Korean embassy in Washington and Tongsun Park. Han's oversight would ensure political control by President Park. It would be Han's choice to approve or reject proposed operations; the KCIA station chief in Washington would be responsible for planning them.

An elaborate system of code words was established to avoid detection of the operation by the U.S. intelligence community. President Park was code-named Patriarch; the KCIA was Catholic Father; and Han was Socket. Individual operations were likewise given code names.

From time to time, when an outside, fresh face was needed, Korean businessmen traveling to the United States would be brought into the operation. It was decided that the more difficult and delicate covert tasks carried out against targets outside of Washington would be conducted by Steve Kim, a KCIA officer stationed in Mexico City and the brother-in-law of one of Tongsun Park's top aides. Kim was picked because he was an aggressive and highly effective operative who specialized in espionage activities. Because he could travel frequently to the United States to visit relatives or conduct business, his movement was easily covered. And his station in Mexico City was perhaps ideal, being near the United States but outside the country's jurisdiction, thus providing him with an escape hatch in case a plan went awry. In Mexico City, KCIA officials believed, Kim could easily find refuge if he needed it, with the help of corrupt Mexican officials.

Kim was also picked because of his keen tactical mind. He was in many ways the ideal agent to run covert operations. Discreet yet capable of persuading people around him to do what he wanted them to do, he was described as having an uncanny ability to get things done even in environments with which he was unfamiliar. He was charged with recruitment and other activities.

Tongsun Park's high-profile activities in Washington were drawing attention by late 1974. Calls for an investigation of his lobbying and influence peddling were being made, and it was feared that his activities might undermine the more important task of establishing an intelligence network in Washington. Says Po, "Lobbying and influence were of secondary concern. What was important was intelligence operations."

In November of 1974, the KCIA was forced to make a conscious decision to phase out their most successful overseas agent. Tongsun Park was becoming a liability. He was being watched, and high-ranking American officials who had once spoken freely with him began to clam up. Park was to be phased out. But the KCIA hoped to keep his operations intact and build off his accomplishments with a new, low-profile figure. They saw the continuing need for a guiding spirit to act as tactician for Operation White Snow, and so they recruited another South Korean businessman in Washington, Hancho Kim, to replace Park. Kim was, it appeared, an ideal choice. While Park was getting increasingly unfavorable press coverage in the United States because of his lobbying and influence peddling, Kim was gaining respectability, having been named a trustee of the American University and having made a number of influential friends. Kim was, according to former KCIA officials, an eager recruit who showed a strong willingness to serve his country and President Park.

In June 1975, Hancho Kim received the first of two payments that year through the KCIA station chief in the Korean embassy in Washington. Both were for three hundred thousand dollars, and both came through the diplomatic pouch, according to former KCIA officials. The funds were to be used by Kim to begin where Park would soon be leaving off. Plans were to have Kim not only continue the influence-peddling campaign on Capitol Hill but also expand the much more important task of developing and sustaining a broad-scale intelligence-gathering operation in Washington.

At the same time that Hancho Kim was recruited, the KCIA sought new avenues for intelligence activity and economic espionage in the United States. As a result of the meeting at KCIA headquarters, a program was instituted with the Korean Traders Association in New York City, an organization registered as an agent of the South Korean government. According to former KCIA Director Hok, the Korean Traders Association served as an outlet for money laundering, allowing funds to be brought into the United States ostensibly for business practices but, more important, to serve as a conduit for intelligence activity. The Korean Traders Association would be the stop-off point or the link between Korean businessmen visiting the United States and conducting intelligence operations here and KCIA officials stationed here. By relying less on the embassy and more on the Korean Traders Association, it was believed that the operation was less at risk. Business travelers from Korea were common visitors to the association. In Japan, the Korean Traders Association in Tokyo served a similar function, according to an ex-KCIA official, directing intelligence operations and determining targets in Tokyo and other industrial centers.

Operation White Snow was successful in the short run, but in a sense it never got off the ground. U.S. intelligence, which had been tracking the operations of KCIA agents in the United States as well as the dealings of Tongsun Park and his relationship with the South Korean embassy in Washington, slowly moved in on the operation. The result was the Koreagate scandal of 1977, in which several members of Congress were indicted on charges of bribery. No Koreans ended up serving time for bribery, and yet from the KCIA's perspective the damage was done. The principals of the intelligence network were exposed, and the prospects of establishing a successful network were dimmed. Koreagate effectively paralyzed the ability of Korean intelligence to conduct or even plan such an extensive operation in Washington. "It is [a] common mistake in America to believe that all we wanted were Congressmen in our pockets," says one KCIA agent involved in the operation. "Our plans were more subtle and also more ambitious than this."

Following on the heels of the greater scrutiny in Washington and the closer monitoring by the CIA and the FBI that were brought on by Koreagate, South Korea was plunged into crisis. On the night of October 26, 1979, President Park was assassinated by a KCIA gunman while he dined in a KCIA building. The coup had the backing of the Korean intelligence service and the armed forces. Both institutions felt compelled to overthrow Park due to the dramatic decline of the economy and growing political tensions. Inflation in South Korea was above 30 percent, and the country's annual oil bill of three billion dollars had doubled, creating financial difficulty. Korean competitiveness was affected by the increase in wages, and exports declined. In May 1980, deeper tensions in society led to armed clashes between the military and students in Kwangju.

KCIA officials feared that economic instability might mean that the left-wing politics championed by radical students would find support in the middle and working classes. These two realities—economic weakness and political uncertainty—created difficult circumstances for South Korea internationally. Many foreign bankers and businesspeople adopted a wait-and-see attitude about loans and investments at a time when Seoul was extremely dependent on foreign capital. One week before the coup, the nation's powerful Economic Planning Board had warned of a serious financial crisis unless foreign banks were more forthcoming in offering loans. In an effort to forestall possible economic collapse, the new Korean leader, General Chun Doo Hwan, undertook to attract foreign investment in his country. Officials at the Ministry of Finance estimated that the country needed $7.7 billion for the year to stave off a severe economic crisis, and General Chun considered the KCIA a valuable resource in the effort to secure international loans on the most favorable terms possible.

In September of 1980, two critically important meetings took place in Seoul that could have determined the country's financial future: David Rockefeller, chairman of the Chase Manhattan Bank, and William Spencer, president of Citibank, came to discuss the extension of new loans to the government. In both instances, the meetings took place against a backdrop of KCIA operations being carried out against the American banks, including the monitoring of Rockefeller's and Spencer's communications while they were in Korea. According to a KCIA officer who left the agency in 1983, President Chun's effort to attract international bank loans was paralleled by a KCIA campaign to monitor electronically both international banking institutions and domestic banks, collect from individual informers intelligence on the banks' financial statuses, and even monitor some private phone conversations of senior American banking officials.

It was the Korean Development Bank that helped identify Chase and Citibank as the chief targets of a KCIA operation. Representatives from the two American institutions in Seoul were regularly monitored and eavesdropped on. Two-man units were assigned to track their movements over a four-month period. The KCIA's Sixth Bureau (Special Missions) was even charged with developing dossiers that could be used for blackmail. Communications to the United States were regularly monitored by KCIA officers with the cooperation of officials from the telephone and telegraph company. In at least one instance, according to the former KCIA official, KCIA officers entered the office of the Chase representative in Seoul following his transmission of a report to New York concerning South

Korea's industrial prospects and his recommendations for loans. The break-in took place in July 1980. The motive was to discover the full contents of the private report and obtain a copy.

South Korean consulate officials in New York and embassy officials in Washington were also involved in the campaign. Case officers in both places were held responsible for collecting intelligence overtly and covertly. They would regularly consult with officials at Chase and Citibank who were willing to talk, posing as South Korean businessmen wondering about the banks' attitudes toward the government in Seoul. On at least one occasion, in August 1980, days before an important Chase meeting to discuss loans to Korea, KCIA officers paid cleaning crews at the corporate headquarters in New York to grant them access to several executive suites. Although this access apparently didn't net anything devastating or particularly useful, it did provide some indication of Chase's plans and terms for new loans.

The renewal of loans from Chase Manhattan and Citibank, two leading American banks, was critical to the international perception of South Korea as worthy of financial support. One official remembers KCIA thinking at the time as being that "they were the important ones to get. If we got them to commit, others would follow."

In early 1980, the new government of President Choi Kyu Hah made a conscious decision to redevelop and redirect the function, organization, and structure of the Korean Central Intelligence Agency. Choi had been impressed by the organization's effective in gathering information overseas, particularly in Washington. It had performed admirably, given its mission. But he also saw the KCIA as reflecting the political interests of former President Park, who had used substantial KCIA resources to track dissident Koreans overseas and had conducted operations to serve his own interests. President Choi and General Chon Too Hwan, the strongman in the armed forces, sought a new KCIA, whose mission would be not only to protect Korean interests overseas but also to advance the country's economic interests. Chon, in particular, saw intelligence as a means of strengthening South Korea's economic stability, a key determinant in the country's power and independence. Under Chon's temporary stewardship of the KCIA, from April to July of 1980, and, more substantially, under his handpicked replacement, General Yu Hak Song, changes were made to enhance the industrial espionage capability of the Korean intelligence service.

The new intelligence director, General Yu, was suspicious of both the United States and Japan. Responsible for the defense of the strategically important northern corridors leading to Seoul, he was a no-nonsense military officer with military instincts and interests. And yet he viewed the world with remarkable depth, understanding that South Korea's economic success or failure was critical to the country's standing internationally. He believed that most important to South Korean security were the prevention of war with the North and a strong economy.

General Yu continued a sweeping purge of the KCIA that had been begun by General Chon, ousting more than three hundred senior officials for corruption or incompetence. Most were military officers who had been placed in the organization to protect President Park's personal political interests. In General Yu's KCIA, there would be no room for these officials. Yu was interested in intelligence professionals. Rather than replace them with military officers such as himself, he sought out officials who would be helpful in his efforts to remake the KCIA into an entity that would serve national political, economic, and military ends. Economists, scientists, and senior government bureaucrats were brought in, not only to ensure civilian dominance of the agency at the senior levels but also to ensure expertise.

In the past, the KCIA had used an enormous amount of its resources to protect President Park from his domestic enemies and his international critics. The organization was accused of kidnapping South Korean students from West Germany in 1967 and of abducting Kim Dae Jung, a prominent political dissident, from a Tokyo hotel in 1973. Agents had been regularly assigned to travel to the United States to harass South Korean citizens living in this country who opposed the government of President Park. In South Korea itself, the KCIA routinely kept watch over various departments of the government as well as churches, civic organizations, universities, and newspapers and other media. Businesses were also routinely monitored. General Chon, when he began the reform of the KCIA in April 1980, declared that "a time has come for the agency to make a fresh start as an organization modest and loyal to the people and dedicated to the nation's security." General Yu declared that the KCIA would no longer engage in political activities but, rather, would concentrate on "political and economic security."

In September 1980, at General Yu's behest, an internal committee was established within the KCIA to reevaluate the agency's goals and objectives. The Yu committee, as it came to be known, met in the chandeliered offices of the presidential Blue House. Its seven members were drawn from the office of the KCIA's assistant director for external affairs, the Economic Council, and the Defense Security Command. It was given sweeping authority to remake the KCIA anew. One result of its work was a secret report calling for a new emphasis on technological espionage to aid South Korea's economic development. Specifically, the committee called for four major reforms.

First, the Yu committee called for dramatically expanding the resources and personnel assigned to the agency's Sixth Bureau (Special Missions) and the Seventh Bureau, Foreign Operations (Intelligence), at the expense of the KCIA's Second Bureau, Domestic Affairs (Surveillance). Second, the committee called for the creation of a small board to establish objectives and targets for these operations. This committee, named the Intelligence Directive and Coordination Group, was attached to the administrative office of the director of Korean intelligence. Third, the committee called for a new approach to relations between the intelligence service and Koreans living overseas. Rather than viewing overseas residents as potential threats, they were to be viewed as possible recruits and allies, particularly in countries where they are a troubled minority. Japan was specifically mentioned in the report as an ideal location for such new relationships. A special fund, to be managed by the Sixth Bureau, would be established to encourage Koreans living overseas to cooperate with the Korean intelligence service. Finally, the committee recommended consolidating the assets assigned to the task of economic espionage. These consolidated assets would then be concentrated on gathering intelligence on technological developments in the United States and Japan.

These and other committee recommendations were endorsed by the president's cabinet in a closed session on December 17, 1980; on December 23, the committee's recommendations became law. The name of the

KCIA was changed to the National Security Planning Agency, with its main functions modified to focus on the planning and coordination of intelligence affairs. The new agency would be governed by a Consultative Council on Intelligence Coordination within the NSP, whose mission was to deal exclusively with national intelligence policies, their direction and operation. The new agency has two deputy directors, one of whom shares responsibility with the Intelligence Directive and Coordination Group for overseeing what would become one of the NSP's most successful and profitable operations against the United States and Japan, one that is still being conducted today: Operation Laughing Bird.

Named after a joke that General Yu was fond of, Operation Laughing Bird was conceived and designed to gather technological and industrial information in a systematic way to support South Korean industry. It has entailed numerous methods of industrial espionage, including electronic eavesdropping, the planting of agents, the use of organized-crime syndicates in Japan, and the attempted recruitment of American and Japanese workers to act as moles and agents. Officially instituted in February 1981, Laughing Bird includes more than two hundred agents drawn from the Sixth and Seventh bureaus, according to a former KCIA official, with perhaps hundreds of informers in both target countries, who cooperate actively in these intelligence and espionage activities. Industrial espionage has been an important element in Korean economic success. Says Ray Cline, "South Korea gets enormous economic benefits from spying." He says the country has been "extremely active, trying to get, grab, and steal technology that will benefit their industry."

Laughing Bird has been perhaps most extensive in Japan. Its proximity to Korea and the presence there of a large, stigmatized Korean minority have made it a particularly lucrative and fairly easy target. An estimated eighty to one hundred agents have organized an extensive campaign to steal Japanese technology and industrial secrets from a variety of sources in that country.

John Quinn, a former CIA official in Tokyo, remembers well the NSP in Japan. "I know they are all over Tokyo," he says. "I remember one . . . source warning about Korean night clubs being heavily staffed with hostesses who were tasked by South Korean intelligence." He notes, "I know they direct a lot of their intelligence tactics against the Japanese because of the strict and very severe competition between Japan and South Korea."

The Korean minority in Japan has been a natural ally in conducting Laughing Bird, and the NSP has found many eager recruits. Brought over to Japan as workers and laborers when Korea was a Japanese colony (between 1910 and 1945), the Korean community today is marginalized in Japanese society. Ethnic Koreans face systematic discrimination in education and employment. Many Japanese institutions, such as the police department and the public school system, discriminate against Koreans in some subtle and not so subtle ways. By Japanese standards, Koreans are poor and are stigmatized socially. Though they number more than 650,000 they are largely ignored politically and economically. Both official family registers, which are organized by the Japanese government, and private information-gathering agencies allow employers and parents of marrying children to eliminate members of the Korean minority from consideration. Despite the fact that most Koreans living in Japan today were born there, until 1991 they were required to submit to fingerprinting every five years under the Alien Registration Act and were issued identity cards.

These practices and others have caused serious tensions between the Korean community in Japan and the Japanese government. In May 1985, widespread anti-Japanese protests were held in Tokyo and South Korea after Lee Sang Ho, a nursery school teacher and leader of an anti-fingerprint campaign in Kawasaki, was arrested by Japanese police for failing to comply with the fingerprint law. There were bomb threats against Japanese businessmen in Korea and threats to the government in Tokyo (presumably phoned in by Koreans in Japan).

Many Koreans in Japan hold marginal jobs, as cleaners, maids, and workmen. A surprising number work in Japanese organized crime (the *yakuza*), one of the few Japanese institutions in which they can prosper economically. In part by design, Laughing Bird, when operating in Japan, relies on the support of the Korean minority to act as informants and, in some cases, as agents. In cities like Kawasaki and Tokyo ethnic Koreans have carried out, or have assisted in carrying out, bag operations against Japanese corporations and American companies based in Japan.

For several years, according to a former Korean intelligence agent,

NSP operatives in Japan ran a sophisticated ring based on the work of a Japanese researcher assigned to a management role at the Agency for Industrial Science and Technology, a division of the Japanese Ministry for International Trade and Industry. The researcher, financially and personally troubled, was paid approximately two thousand dollars a month to pass information about AIST's Sunshine Project to the NSP. The Sunshine Project, which involved research on the development of new energy technologies, was of particular interest to Korean government officials, who are concerned about their country's continued reliance on foreign oil. In July 1987, MITI quietly dismissed the source at AIST in response to allegations of spying. Before he was caught, however, he provided what one former NSP operative calls "very detailed" information on Sunshine. He had managed to recruit a brother-in-law who was a member of one of the research teams; to this day, that man has never been identified.

Other Laughing Bird acknowledged successes have taken place in Tsukuba, a city of approximately 170,000 with some fifty-two research institutions. NSP agents made arrangements with Koreans who were cleaning many of the facilities in off-hours to grant them access at night. In one instance in 1984, NSP agents bragged about having complete after-hours access to a research facility in Tsukuba that was conducting research on the flexible-manufacturing-system complex with laser.

Laughing Bird has also included efforts at electronic eavesdropping on Japanese firms engaged with Korean firms in bidding for foreign contracts. Between 1985 and 1988, according to a former NSP official, operatives in Japan regularly monitored the bids that Ishikawajima-Harima Heavy Industries Company and Mitsubishi Heavy Industries were making on international shipbuilding and ship-repair contracts. Communications at the Ishikawajima-Harima Tokyo office, at its Yokohama shipyard, and at its Aichi ship works were regularly intercepted using nonattached bugging devices that NSP agents had smuggled into the country via the embassy. Communications at the headquarters of Mitsubishi Heavy Industries and its Nagasaki shipyard were likewise monitored. The information obtained was enormously helpful to South Korean shipbuilders. In several instances, these acts of espionage are known to have borne fruit—for example in the sale of tankers to an Indonesian-based fleet in 1986 and on a ship-repair contract for the fleet of Hong

Kong shipping magnet Pao Yue-Kong. In both instances, bids were altered and contracts won with the help of information provided by Korean operatives in Japan.

In the United States, Laughing Bird has been concentrated on high-tech companies in Silicon Valley and along the Route 128 corridor near Boston, as well as on petrochemical companies and steel corporations. In many instances, Laughing Bird agents simply wait for information to come to them. It was on the wings of Laughing Bird that GE secrets found their way to Iljin in 1989 and 1990.

Laughing Bird has also been involved in bugging and eavesdropping on U.S. trade officials and business executives traveling to Seoul. According to Ambassador Michael B. Smith, a former deputy trade representative, the South Koreans were widely known to bug American visitors. "I know the Koreans were doing it to us," he says. U.S. businessmen have reported the same.

Richard Walker, who was ambassador to South Korea from 1981 to 1989, says that targets of South Korean bugging attempts include President Reagan. In 1984, when Reagan was making plans to visit Seoul, the Korean government insisted that the president stay in a particular hotel. "They really wanted the president to stay there," says Walker. "The place was completely bugged. They had a switchboard downstairs that would plug them in to anywhere in the hotel." According to Walker, the U.S. government flatly refused, insisting on another hotel. Says Walker, "We only learned about it because we had penetrated the operation at the hotel. Needless to say, the president ended up staying elsewhere."

The rise and dramatic fall of Tongsun Park shocked many in the United States when revelations of KCIA operations came to light. But the discovery of Park's network did not end Korean intelligence operations in this country, nor did it lead to less ambitious operations. According to Walker, Korean intelligence remains very active in the United States and other friendly countries. "Very little has changed since the stuff in the 1970s," he says.

11

Mr. X and Mr. Y

They were more active than anyone but the KGB. . . . They were targeted on the United States about half the time and on Arab countries about half the time.

   —John Davitt, former director of the internal security section at the Justice Department

On December 1, 1985, Secretary of State George Shultz placed an urgent phone call to Israeli Prime Minister Shimon Peres. It was three-thirty in the morning in Tel Aviv. The call was unexpected, and Peres had to be awakened by his staff. But George Shultz didn't seem to care much. Things, he must have felt, had already gone far enough. Jonathan Pollard, an analyst in the Naval Investigative Service, had been picked up outside the Israeli embassy in Washington, D.C., barely a week before. He had been suspected of spying. Growing evidence indicated that Pollard had been spying, and not for an adversary like the Soviet Union but for a close ally, Israel. Shultz was so outraged when he received a conclusive FBI report on Pollard's activities that he decided to phone Peres and demand an explanation. Shultz was undiplomatic and blunt. He wanted the truth. And if Pollard had been run as an Israeli spy, Shultz wanted to know who in the Israeli government knew about it and, more important, who was responsible. He also wanted an official public apology from the state of Israel.

Peres was surprised by the sudden call and offered his apologies to Shultz while feigning ignorance about those who had recruited Pollard. "They were, I assure you, rogue operatives," the prime minister told Shultz. The next morning Peres did indeed issue a public apology: "Spying on the United States stands in total contradiction to our policy. Such activity, to the extent that it did take place, was wrong, and the government of Israel apologizes." Peres went on to declare that "those responsible will be brought to account, the unit involved will be completely and permanently disbanded, and necessary organizational steps will be taken to ensure that such activities are not repeated."

In the U.S. intelligence community, the Israeli apology was met with a mix of cynicism and outright laughter. Peres's attempts to distance the Israeli government from the Pollard affair was particularly ironic. Pollard had been recruited by agents of a small intelligence unit connected to the Israeli Ministry of Defense. The unit was so secret that few Israelis or Americans knew of its existence, let alone what it did, how it operated, or what its purpose was. The unit is known as LAKAM, and it was formed, organized, and developed in 1957 under a deputy defense minister who just happened to be named Shimon Peres. Until 1957, the responsibility for obtaining technical and scientific information had lain with the Aman (the Israeli FBI) and the Mossad (its CIA). LAKAM was an attempt to bring industrial and technological espionage to a higher level, making it more thorough and more systematic. The very existence of LAKAM was a closely guarded secret, even in the highest level of Israeli politics. But what the U.S. intelligence community knew for sure was that no one in Israeli politics probably knew more about LAKAM than its creator, Shimon Peres.

Intelligence officials were skeptical of Israeli claims of innocence for another reason. It was well-known that Israel regularly carried out intelligence operations in the United States, not only against the government but also, and especially, against companies and research facilities. According to John Davitt, former director of the Justice Department's internal security section, in a number of instances over the years Israeli diplomats suspected of espionage have been quietly asked to leave the country. At the same time, dozens of other Israeli citizens (nondiplomats) believed to be engaging in espionage have been quietly but forcibly removed from U.S. shores.

According to Ambassador Richard Walker, a member of the CIA's Senior Review Panel and a consultant to CIA Director Robert Gates, "Israel is one of our most difficult counterintelligence problems." But, says Walker, "the subject is so sensitive we don't write it down when discussing it; we only talk about it."

Despite U.S. knowledge of some intelligence operations, the Israeli efforts can largely be considered successful. And no institution in Israeli intelligence has been more successful in the United States and possibly in Western Europe than LAKAM. What LAKAM has accomplished goes far beyond Jonathan Pollard. Since its formation, LAKAM has been one of Israel's most effective and efficient intelligence organizations, stealing technological and scientific information for the benefit of the Israeli defense and civilian industries. Its name bears this role out: LAKAM is the Hebrew acronym for the Israeli Defense Ministry's Scientific Affairs Liaison Bureau. Its reach is enormous. LAKAM agents have operated in the United States, Japan, France, Germany, Italy, Great Britain, Switzerland, and Sweden. And they have stolen secrets worth hundreds of millions, perhaps billions, of dollars.

Oftentimes LAKAM's targets have been companies that deal in military-related technologies or senior government officials with access to technology that is relevant to the military. But Israeli security is not the only motive for acquiring such information. Arms exports are a big business in Israel. Israel Aircraft Industries, the defense contractor and a major recipient of stolen information, is Israel's largest exporter. In 1989, it made foreign military sales worth more than $800 million. According to official Israeli records, Israel's total military sales came to more than $1.4 billion. Hard economics drives these exports. Says David Ivry, director general of the Israeli Defense Ministry, "Foreign policy is one reason to approve a contract, but no one is even asking permission if it isn't economically wise."

Jonathan Pollard received twenty-five hundred dollars a month from LAKAM to pass information about U.S. military secrets to Israel. But LAKAM's farther-reaching role is intelligence on American and European technological information. It is here, U.S. intelligence officials insist, that Israeli agents have been most active. "When you think economic espionage, Israel almost immediately comes to mind," says security consultant

James Lamont. U.S. intelligence officials agree, and they believe that Pollard was an aberration. Regarding LAKAM agents, a former CIA deputy director for counterintelligence says, "They have been extremely active in the U.S. When you look beneath the surface and see Pollard for what he is—a relatively unimportant fluke, there is a lot—I mean a lot—going on that perhaps matters even more."

LAKAM agents, run from Israel's embassy in Washington and two "shops," one in Los Angeles and the other in New York City, have been successful in acquiring a vast array of information. Some of LAKAM's biggest beneficiaries include the state-owned Israeli industries in aerospace, chemicals, and electronics—for example, Israel Aircraft Industries and Tadiran. And despite the problems that the Jonathan Pollard case brought LAKAM, an active remnant of that bureau still exists today, contrary to Israel's claim that it was disbanded.

LAKAM operations in the United States are believed to include thirty-five full-time agents, with perhaps several dozen informers who—for a fee but sometimes for free—regularly pass on to LAKAM information that might be useful. LAKAM agents are assigned, and serve, as scientific attachés at the Israeli embassy and consulate. In the past, they reported directly to LAKAM headquarters on Carlebach Street in Tel Aviv. Today U.S. intelligence believes offices at Israeli air force headquarters are being used. But LAKAM also makes use of deep-cover agents—businesspeople and scientists living in or traveling to the United States. Some are motivated by money, others by ideology. Contrary to what many might think, most are not Jewish. "Israeli intelligence would much rather use non-Jews as agents," says a senior FBI official. "Then if they are caught, the American Jewish community is not put under a cloud like it was with Pollard."

LAKAM officials in Tel Aviv have direct access to the prime minister and are accountable to no one except the prime minister and the minister of defense. According to U.S. intelligence officials, LAKAM offices and missions overseas regularly communicate with the Ministry of Defense by telephone and telex. But when particularly valuable information (at times covertly obtained) needs to be transmitted to Tel Aviv, Israeli diplomatic pouches have been used, with little questioning by Israeli diplomats.

The extent to which Israeli intelligence spies on the United States for technological intelligence was outlined by the CIA in a forty-seven-page secret report issued in March 1979. Entitled *Israel: Foreign Intelligence and Security Services,* the document offers an overview of the Israeli intelligence system: its workings, its chief targets, and estimates of its size and internal procedures. Most interesting, perhaps, is the CIA's assessment of its priorities. Perhaps not surprisingly, the Arab states surrounding Israel and posing a serious military threat are the number-one target, according to the CIA. These "confrontation states," such as Syria and Iraq, are of the most interest to Israeli intelligence, according to the CIA report. But the second and third primary targets, according to the report, are the "collection of information on secret U.S. policy or decisions, if any, pertaining to Israel" and the "collection of scientific intelligence in the U.S. and other developed countries."

The document outlines a number of ways in which Israeli intelligence operates overseas, particularly in the United States and in respect to U.S. targets overseas. For example, Israeli intelligence "plays a key role" in exploiting scientific exchange programs, according to the CIA report. Compromising Americans and recruiting individuals with financial difficulties are other techniques. The report concludes that "the Israelis devote a considerable portion of their covert operations to obtaining scientific and technical intelligence. This has included attempts to penetrate certain classified defense projects in the United States and other Western nations."

The report makes clear the CIA view that Israel has used its intelligence services to "promote foreign trade deals" and Israeli "commercial enterprises." It also paints a picture in which a significant portion of Israel's intelligence assets are being directed toward the United States. The report made no mention of LAKAM, however, a tribute to Israeli intelligence in keeping secret the structure of its U.S. operations.

When Shimon Peres established a science and technology intelligence service in 1957 that would eventually become LAKAM, its focus was exclusively on nuclear issues and technologies. Binyamin Blumberg, a former official of Shin Bet, the Israeli counterintelligence service, was assigned to head the organization. In its early days, it was housed at the Ministry of Defense and was simply named the Office of Special Assignments. By the mid-1960s, however, it was renamed LAKAM, and the headquarters were moved to an undercover location on Carlebach Street.

After the Six-Day War in 1967, LAKAM was dramatically changed. The war convinced Israeli officials that technology was more important than ever before, but Israel faced new difficulties in the field of military technology: foreign sources suddenly began to dry up. French President Charles de Gaulle imposed an embargo on all arms exports to Israel after the war, including not only future orders but also those already paid for. This cutoff caused a serious problem for Tel Aviv, for France had been one of Israel's chief sources of high-tech weaponry. Other foreign sources also restricted their exports to Israel. Israeli officials, mindful of their vulnerability, decided to do something about it.

Thus Israel speeded up its plans to develop a domestic arms industry, and economic and technological espionage was seen as the place to start in assisting that effort. At Blumberg's encouragement, the Israeli defense minister expanded LAKAM's mandate to include not just nuclear technologies but other fields in science and technology as well. Enhanced operations carried out against new targets, such as the electronics, avionics, and ballistics industries, were funded by those in Israeli industry who stood to gain the most financially from LAKAM's exploits, including, most specifically, Israel's state-owned defense industry. Since the industry is state owned, financial transfers to, and cooperation with, LAKAM were simplified. Israel Aircraft Industry, the high-tech weapons-development firm Rafael, and Israel Military Industries, state owned companies all, made regular financial contributions to LAKAM to subsidize espionage. Only very senior company officials knew where the funds were going.

Industry support for LAKAM was not only financial. From time to time, industry captains learned that their companies would be used as covers for LAKAM operations, although they were never briefed on specifics. And because almost every defense company in Israel is headed by a former military officer, the task was simplified and LAKAM was assured of a sympathetic cadre at these corporate offices. LAKAM agents would pose as consultants to or representatives of these companies when traveling overseas as case officers. Regular LAKAM agents were particularly likely to use such cover on special assignments, when the embassy might be watched by domestic counterintelligence services or their movements might be regarded with suspicion. Almost every time a company was used as a cover by LAKAM agents, industry officials were uninformed, largely to protect the security of the operation but also to prevent the company from being implicated directly in espionage activities. This was particularly true when it came to operations carried out in the United States. Many of the Israeli defense firms being used as covers by LAKAM were competing for contracts or were trying to reach agreements with the Pentagon and American contractors. They did not wish to risk those agreements by finding themselves implicated in intelligence operations carried out against those same organizations.

The move to expand LAKAM's operations, particularly in the United States and Europe, had the general support of the other Israeli intelligence organizations, particularly the most important one: the Mossad. That might seem a bit surprising, given the tendency of bureaucracies to fight for turf. But the Mossad, Shin Bet, and Israeli military intelligence did not see LAKAM as a threat. Although LAKAM might have in some ways become a competitor of the Mossad, the agency did not resist the expansion, largely because it didn't wish to put its relationship with the CIA in jeopardy by participating in extensive espionage operations in the United States. The 1951 intelligence-sharing agreement between the United States and Israel, along with subsequent amendments and modifications, was extremely valuable to the Mossad. Senior Israeli intelligence officials purposely restricted Mossad activities in the United States that might seem ordinary in any other country in order to maintain access to U.S. intelligence resources, including satellite photoreconnaissance intelligence and U.S. intercepts of Arabic communications, or signals intelligence (SIGINT). Senior Mossad officials considered a critical error in spying in the United States to be too risky. LAKAM, unknown to the Americans and detached from the traditional institutions of Israeli intelligence, could run the risk of carrying out operations in the United States. Its agents would be outsiders and their operations oftentimes unknown to the Mossad agents stationed in America. Intelligence cooperation could continue while, on a different plane, operations could be carried out against U.S. and European targets in the sphere of high technology.

Heightened Israeli espionage activity after 1967 did not go unobserved in the United States. Senior intelligence officials, particularly at the FBI, noticed the growing number of Israeli experts and business executives visiting this country. Reports started filtering back from U.S. business executives who had been approached by LAKAM agents. Beginning in 1968, according to former bureau officials, the FBI began keeping a closer watch on scientific delegations visiting from Israel and the activities and movement of Israeli embassy and consular scientific attachés. The program was dubbed Scope, and was supersecret. The bureau was even reluctant to share information about Scope with the CIA, which was keen to have further, deeper cooperation with Israeli intelligence and would likely not have thought too highly of the program. A flurry of activity in 1968–69 led the FBI to expand Scope in 1969 to include the wiretapping and bugging of the Israeli embassy in Washington, D.C. As a result, dozens of Israelis were quietly asked to leave the country. The campaign was ended in November 1973. A combination of CIA pressure and concern over civil rights complications (Americans who had contact with certain Israelis were being watched, too) meant the death of Scope.

But the problems of stopping Israeli agents went beyond simple counterintelligence work. Even if the perpetrators were identified and caught, the cessation of their activities was not guaranteed, say frustrated counterintelligence officials. For all those who were rooted out, many remained, due to the conflicting interests of the FBI and the CIA.

The experience with Professor Yuval Ne'eman is a case in point. During his frequent visits and lengthy stays in the United States, the FBI tracked Ne'eman, a former colonel in Israeli military intelligence. They watched him as he visited the U.S. government's Livermore Laboratories outside of San Francisco, high-tech research facilities at the University of Texas, and research facilities in Pasadena. FBI officials believed they had conclusive evidence that Ne'eman was working for LAKAM. At one point they confronted him in Pasadena. They demanded that he register as a foreign agent of the Israeli government or risk expulsion from the United States. When he refused, they outlined everything they knew about him. Ne'eman knew that his registering as an agent would cut off access to numerous U.S. research and technology facilities, so he decided to circumvent the FBI. He went to the Mossad station chief in Washington, D.C. (an old friend), and asked for help. Ne'eman was lucky. The CIA and the Mossad had been negotiating an intelligence-cooperation deal at the time. A Mossad appeal to the CIA's counterintelligence office did the trick: the agency told the FBI to leave Ne'eman alone so that the agreement wouldn't be put at risk. "As was typical," says a former FBI deputy director for intelligence, "intelligence cooperation superseded effective counterintelligence here to protect our secrets. The Israelis knew that was our tendency, and they took advantage of it."

The importance that the CIA placed on Israel as a source of critical intelligence has led the United States to turn a blind eye to Israeli espionage in this country, even when the evidence was substantial. The groundwork of cooperation was laid by James J. Angleton, a powerful figure in the CIA hierarchy for twenty years. Until 1974, he served as the head of CIA counterintelligence and of the office responsible for liaison with the Israelis. For years, the United States received its best human intelligence on the Soviet Union from debriefings of Jewish émigrés who traveled to Israel from behind the Iron Curtain. Israel was also an important base for covert assistance to U.S. allies in Africa. Several African intelligence agencies were trained by CIA officials in Israel. Beginning in 1971, the United States and Israel began the formal exchange of information on terrorism. And Israel, like other countries, recognizes and takes advantage of this U.S. reliance on its allies for the collection of intelligence.

One of LAKAM's greatest early successes within its broadened mandate occurred not in the United States but in Switzerland. In that peaceful, neutral country, LAKAM penetrated a company manufacturing engines for the French Mirage fighter plane. Israel was working on a fighter aircraft of its own, and with the French arms embargo in effect, an opportunity to steal French secrets was one Israel would take advantage of.

A Swiss engineer, Alfred Frauenknecht, was disgruntled with his job. He had been passed over for promotions, found his current position boring, and needed the money to keep a mistress. Early conversations with Israeli agents had revealed that he was sympathetic to the predicaments the country faced during the Six-Day War. Although not Jewish, he did have strong sympathies for Zionism and the state of Israel's security needs. After a brief meeting with Israel's military attaché in Paris, Colonel Dov Sion, Frauenknecht agreed to serve as a LAKAM agent.

He began copying documents and blueprints for the Mirage. He even recruited a nephew who also worked at the company to collect documents for him. The shear volume of information was impressive, but Frauen-knecht's behavior led to suspicions by company officials and his eventual arrest. On April 23, 1971, a Swiss court found Frauenknecht guilty of spying and espionage. A sympathetic judge sentenced him to only one year in prison.

The information he provided saved Israel hundreds of millions of dollars in research and development. By the fall of 1971, barely six months after Frauenknecht's trial, Israel was flying a new warplane, the Nesher, whose production had benefited greatly from the stolen Mirage designs. But that was only the beginning. On April 29, 1975, Israel unveiled the Kfir fighter, which appeared to be a nearly complete replica of the Mirage. It had been built almost entirely on the basis of the stolen blueprints. (Frauenknecht actually attended the ceremony for the Kfir's inaugural flight.)

More than an aircraft was at stake for Israel during the Kfir's maiden flight. The plane's success opened up a new era in the Israeli aircraft industry. For the first time, Israel Aircraft Industries had produced an advanced military aircraft as good as many others in the world and in so doing offered the prospect of self-sufficiency when it came to military affairs. The success of the Kfir also meant that Israel could compete in the worldwide arms-sale market. And on the success of the Kfir and other advanced weapons, it did. In 1967, arms sales were barely fifty million dollars. By the mid-1980s, they were estimated to have mushroomed to more than one billion dollars annually. Arms became one of Israel's largest and most important exports.

At the airfield on that April day was a man who had a great deal to do with the Kfir's success. He also vowed to remember the lessons learned by LAKAM's success in Switzerland. His name is Al Schwimmer. At the time, he was the head of Israel Aircraft Industries and a veteran of the Israeli air force. Born in the United States, Schwimmer had taken to airplanes at a young age. He saw in aviation a measure of national great-ness. In Schwimmer's mind, if any country, including Israel, wanted great-ness, security, and prosperity, aviation must play an important role. He had seen what a difference LAKAM had made for the Kfir, a project he considered essential to Israel's security interests. And he vowed that the lesson would not be lost. Barely a decade later it would be Al Schwimmer who would help push LAKAM to pursue a similar operation involving advanced aircraft technology, only this time the operation would take place in the United States.

When Ariel Sharon became Israel's defense minister in August 1981, he opted for expanding LAKAM's operations even further than Blumberg had done in 1967. Sharon was even more skeptical of using foreign sources to meet Israel's needs for advanced weaponry. He also believed that a thriving defense industry and arms-export business could be a boon to the Israeli economy. But to achieve that, Israel needed even more foreign technology than it was already getting.

Sharon replaced the long-term LAKAM chief, Binyamin Blumberg, with a close friend, political ally, and confidant, Rafi Eitan. An intelligence operative with more than thirty-five years' experience refining his craft, Eitan brought a professionalism to LAKAM that it had previously lacked. Although the organization had achieved some notable successes under Blumberg, LAKAM was not a systematic collector of technological intelligence; its operation as an agency for economic espionage was haphazard. As director of LAKAM, Eitan hired more agents, intensified activities, and made operations more efficient. According to some observers and intelligence officials, in a few short years Eitan achieved a tenfold increase in the quantity of foreign technological information LAKAM was acquiring without experiencing a decline in the information's quality. The biggest help in this regard came from greater clandestine operations carried out against "soft targets" in the West. Eitan's taste for greater espionage was paying off.

The desire for more extensive use of covert intelligence operations was a manifestation of Eitan's character as well as an effect of his past. It was Eitan who had been responsible for the Israeli effort to track and kidnap the Nazi war criminal Adolf Eichmann. It was also Eitan who masterminded the theft of two hundred pounds of plutonium from a nuclear-power plant in Pennsylvania in 1968.

According to a declassified FBI document, "Rafi Eitan, chemist, ministry of defense, Israel, born 11/23/26" was part of a four-man Israeli team that asked to travel to a Nuclear Materials and Equipment Corporation uranium-processing plant in Apollo, Pennsylvania, in September 1968. An FBI assessment of the visit later concluded that Eitan was part of a LAKAM effort to divert uranium from the NUMEC plant to Israel. During routine investigations by the Atomic Energy Commission in the late 1960s, it was discovered that two hundred pounds of enriched uranium—enough to make six atom bombs—was missing from the Apollo plant. The FBI conducted an internal investigation of NUMEC's founder, a nuclear scientist named Zalman Shapiro, and Shapiro's alleged connections with Israeli intelligence agents, including Eitan. No formal charges were ever brought against him.

It was in Jonathan Pollard that Eitan had his best-known case, one that demonstrates LAKAM's ability to seek out possible recruits and successfully co-opt them. Eitan had been encouraging LAKAM case officers to increase their contacts with Israelis and Jews overseas. Usually agents did not identify themselves as LAKAM agents but, rather, described themselves as students or, alternatively, as representatives of an Israeli company. Eitan's new foraging policy paid off in 1984, in a man named Jonathan Pollard.

It was not a LAKAM regular who first spotted Pollard. Instead, it was businessman, Steven Stern, who first came in contact with him and brought him to LAKAM's attention. Stern met the disgruntled Navy employee in early 1984 and in May of that year introduced Pollard to a friend of his named Aviem Sella. Whether Stern knew it or not is unclear, but Sella was a colonel in Israeli air force intelligence, ostensibly in New York City to study computer science at New York University. According to FBI officials, that was only a cover. Sella was really a LAKAM case officer, who in Pollard found a willing volunteer to spy for Israel.

Pollard provided the Israelis with hundreds of thousands of pages of secret information relating to terrorism, U.S. weapons policy, Middle East military planning, and other sensitive documents. Pollard, while insisting that his spying was motivated by his Zionist convictions, was paid by his handlers. In the end, his zealousness in providing huge quantities of information was his undoing. Co-workers began to notice that numerous documents were missing for periods of time. And when investigators started closing in, Pollard tried to flee to the Israeli embassy for protection, only to be captured by federal officials. After questioning by U.S. security officials, he admitted his guilt and told intelligence officials everything he knew. Nonetheless, questions remained.

Early on in the Pollard investigation officials concluded that the American was not the only agent the Israelis had inside the U.S. government. The other agent, dubbed Mr. X by government investigators, has never been caught. Evidence of a Mr. X exists in something Pollard told U.S. officials after his arrest: that his Israeli handlers often specified by date and control number the highly sensitive documents they wanted him to acquire. At times, his handlers showed him top-secret documents, ones that U.S. investigators established Pollard himself never could have had access to. They had to have come from someone else. Mr. X, the FBI concluded, must have provided the index and other documents that Pollard was shown. The FBI believes that only a senior Pentagon official could have provided those papers. "He must have been so highly placed . . . that he could not regularly gather and collect information for LAKAM," says one senior FBI official.

At the same time that Pollard was being arrested, a far more senior navy official was in LAKAM's sights. Because the secrets involved in the case were related more to military technology than to sensitive intelligence secrets, this navy official did not receive much attention. In some respects, this case is even more startling than Pollard's. It was through a series of brushes and encounters with a wide array of Israeli intelligence officials that Eitan and LAKAM came to see a corrupt senior Pentagon official as a possible source for commercial secrets that would dramatically help the Israeli defense industry. That man was none other than Melvyn Paisley, assistant secretary of the navy.

An ex–fighter pilot and a larger-than-life figure, Paisley was a tough-nosed individual with a strong technical background in aviation. He had joined the aircraft manufacturer Boeing in 1954, eventually working his way up to the position of head of international marketing. He was regarded by some colleagues as an unscrupulous individual who would stop at nothing to gain an advantage, climb the corporate ladder, or make a business deal. He was constantly pushing beyond the limits of ethical behavior, and he bragged about it. "Usually every major company has one guy who does the dirty work," recalls one former co-worker. "He was that guy." Paisley repeatedly boasted to co-workers about his no-holds-barred attitude, which at times included illegal activity that he took part in on the company's behalf. He bragged, for example, about how he bugged a competitor to find out what it was bidding for a lucrative contract with Pan Am; Boeing won the bid as a result of his handiwork, according to his version of the story. He related stories of his bribing U.S. military officers overseas and offering payoffs to third parties in order to make sales. He recalled with a smile how he sometimes used prostitutes to promote Boeing's interests. All evidence indicates that his superiors were unaware of many of his activities. Paisley would have won few popularity contests among his co-workers and subordinates, but senior Boeing managers saw him as someone who got consistent results for the company. So co-workers feared taking him on, despite the evidence and his bragging about his "creative methods."

Paisley in all likelihood could have stayed with Boeing and had a quite successful career in business. But in January of 1981, he made a decision to go to Washington to work for the incoming Reagan administration. It was a fateful decision, one that would lead to the selling of secrets, his arrest, and his eventual imprisonment. Paisley rose quickly in the Navy Department, by December of 1981 becoming the assistant secretary for research, engineering, and systems. At this post, Paisley had de facto control of navy procurement, research, and weapons development. He dealt with a wide range of contractors on multi-billion-dollar projects, from warships, to missiles, to aircraft. The Reagan administration's ambitious plans for a six-hundred-ship navy gave Paisley a large budget and the authority to make the difference in determining which defense contractors would receive billion-dollar contracts and which would not. During his six-year tenure as assistant secretary, Paisley earned a reputation as an official who ran roughshod over contractors and admirals. He seemed to revel in his position and the authority it brought.

Paisley saw to it that the Navy Material Command was eliminated entirely. The only existing branch of the department that might have challenged his decisions on procurement and research was thereby gone. He now had almost complete authority on many critical procurement decisions. Paisley critic and former Assistant Secretary of Defense Lawrence Korb later remarked that the navy under Paisley was "a bureaucracy run amok" whose rules for procurement were, in many cases, different from those of the Defense Department. Paisley was playing by his own rules in a game that was designed to advance not the interests of the U.S. Navy but his own. As an investigation would later reveal, Paisley was interested in making money and getting rich, and he was willing to sell government secrets to do it.

A two-year-long investigation by the FBI and the Naval Investigative Service entitled Operation Ill Wind would reveal to federal authorities in 1987 that Paisley was passing critical Pentagon information to large U.S. defense contractors. Companies like McDonnell Douglas and Unisys received classified information on contracts, Pentagon procurement plans, and documents on the technological specifications of competitors' proposed weapons systems. According to Pentagon and industry sources, rumors about Paisley's schemes began circulating in U.S. industry circles in early 1985. One person who heard these rumors was a LAKAM agent under deep cover, Yaacov Shai, who was intrigued by the idea that Paisley might be selling information on the navy's most advanced weapons systems to companies for a price.

Shai and LAKAM were interested in several navy projects at the time, including the navy's advanced tactical aircraft (ATA), an aircraft-carrier-based bomber that was supposed to be a cut above anything the United States currently had. Although Israel had no aircraft carriers of its own, LAKAM wanted to know about the project because the ATA was based on advanced design concepts and technologies that were of interest to the Israeli aircraft industry. In the summer of 1985, Shai reported the rumors about Paisley to LAKAM headquarters in Tel Aviv and gave a detailed account of the projects Paisley might have information on. Shai had learned from a defense contractor based in Potomac, Maryland, what the projects were and that Paisley had several "black budget" projects that were so secret they weren't even listed in the Pentagon's budget.

LAKAM chief Eitan saw the report and was impressed by the details Shai had been able to amass on the navy's research programs. He decided to approach Al Schwimmer and get his views on the matter. Schwimmer's involvement in the application of Frauenknecht's stolen Mirage plans to the Kfir fighter in the late 1960s was legendary in Israeli intelligence circles. In November 1984, while serving as prime minister, Shimon Peres had tapped Schwimmer to act as a private adviser. Schwimmer, according to FBI sources, made some inquiries of his own in the international defense market and found Shai's rumors repeated. A few weeks later Schwimmer contacted Eitan and said that the rumors were being taken seriously in the U.S. defense industry. He made a point of reminding Eitan of the Kfir case and how the stolen Mirage plans had been so useful. Israel was in the midst of developing a new generation of fighter aircraft, the Lavi. "Perhaps Lavi could benefit as the Kfir did," Schwimmer told Eitan; some of the principles being applied to the ATA might apply to the planned Lavi fighter as well. He also offered to arrange a meeting with Paisley, using a subsidiary of Israel Aircraft Industries to make contact, ostensibly to discuss the procurement of Israeli weapons systems.

At the same time that LAKAM took an interest in Paisley, the Department of Justice and the Department of Defense's Naval Investigative Service began acting on the same rumors concerning Paisley's activities. The NIS launched a formal investigation into allegations that Paisley was trafficking information to American defense contractors in return for consulting contracts and financial payoffs. Several agents were put on the case and began looking into Paisley's on-the-job performance as it related to handling contracts. These preliminary investigations eventually evolved into the full-blown investigation that was dubbed Operation Ill Wind. The investigation culminated in 1988, when agents, acting on information obtained from wiretapes, raided dozens of offices around the Washington, D.C., area. What the NIS found was a paper trail linking Paisley financially to a number of defense contractors during his tenure with the navy. For a fee, Paisley and a business partner, defense consultant William Galvin, passed Defense Department classified information to defense contractors such as Boeing, McDonnell Douglas, United Technologies, and Unisys, information that would help these companies win lucrative contracts.

Agents also found documents linking Paisley to Mazlat, a subsidiary of Israel Aircraft Industries, Israel's largest defense company and one notorious for working with Israeli intelligence, often as a cover. It was Mazlat that provided the bridge between LAKAM agents and Assistant Secretary of the Navy Melvyn Paisley.

Though it was a critical part of the Ill Wind scandals, Paisley's involvement with Mazlat has been overlooked, in part because the U.S. media was more interested in the domestic side of Melvyn Paisley. Senior

Pentagon officers receiving payments from defense contractors in exchange for favors made juicy copy, especially in light of the defense buildup of the 1980s. The Paisley connection to Mazlat, in contrast, was much more Byzantine. The Israeli company was not just interested in a Pentagon contract; Mazlat wanted more than that. As one senior U.S. official told Barbara Bradley of the *Christian Science Monitor,* "the kind of information-passing evident in this investigation has totally broken down all the control the government has instituted to insure that sensitive, highly classified information does not fall into foreign hands. Nobody knows what damage has been done."

The Mazlat connection and what it meant were also not played up by the bureau. According to one senior FBI official, "On a series of fronts we were forging a cooperative relationship with the Israelis in the area of counterterrorism. The conventional wisdom at the bureau was—especially after Pollard—what do we gain by pulling off the covers this time? And more [important], what might we lose?"

It was in October 1985, barely two weeks before Jonathan Pollard was arrested, that LAKAM made its first contact with Paisley. Yaacov Shai, the LAKAM agent, and General Zvi Schiller, president of Mazlat, made an appointment to meet with Paisley. Mazlat and its principals must have been known to Paisley: Schiller had served as defense attaché at the Israeli embassy in Washington during the early 1980s, and another major player at Mazlat, Major General Uri Simhoni, had also once served as the military attaché. Both of these officials had strong ties to Israeli intelligence.

At Paisley's suggestion, Shai and Schiller met him at his home in McLean, a wealthy Virginia suburb of the capital. The reason for the meeting was ordinary, although the location was not. Schiller had come to speak with Paisley about the Mazlat GCS 2000 ground-control station and its remote-piloted vehicles for aerial reconnaissance. Mazlat was one of the best manufacturers of such systems in the world, and the navy was buying millions of dollars' worth of them every year. Schiller was interested in a contract. Yaacov Shai had come for another reason, however. Whether Schiller knew it or not, Shai was along to look for indications of whether Paisley might be of use to LAKAM. It was Schwimmer who had called Israel Aircraft Industries to have Schiller set up the meeting with Paisley and to arrange for Shai to go along as a consultant. LAKAM and Schwimmer had instructed Schiller to leave open the possibility of a kickback for a navy contract. Such a tactic had worked for IAI and Mazlat in other countries. LAKAM apparently wanted to get close to Paisley any way it could. But how much Schiller knew didn't matter—he was visiting Paisley to make a deal, pure and simple.

At the meeting, Shai and Schiller asked Paisley about the prospects of the navy's buying the Mazlat GCS 2000 and its reconnaissance drones, and they offered to have the system demonstrated for him. Paisley, however, seemed uninterested and detached. He told them the navy had a good supplier already. "What's so good—or should I say—what is the advantage of buying your system?" Paisley asked. Schiller was at first straightforward. He told Paisley that Mazlat drones were regarded as some of the best in the world and that Mazlat could offer a very good price. He emphasized that they wanted the sales mostly to achieve economies of scale (producing greater volume to cut the per-unit price) for the systems the Israeli military would buy. Therefore, a large profit wouldn't be necessary: the price would be low. That was an appeal to Paisley's instincts to save the navy money.

Then Schiller put out a feeler concerning Paisley's personal financial interests and the possibility of his setting up a contract for a kickback. Shai would be interested to know, too, since it would offer evidence of Paisley's willingness to pass technological information to LAKAM. "You will not be in the Pentagon forever," Schiller began. "When you leave, we will probably be looking for a special consultant or agent for Mazlat and IAI here in Washington, one with great experience. You would make a good candidate." Schiller was careful not to draw too close a connection between the sale and the "consulting agreement," in case Paisley took offense at the suggestion. But Paisley clearly had the picture. While never directly picking up the idea of a consulting arrangement, he suggested that Schiller consider retaining the services of a defense consultant named William Galvin to compete for the navy contract.

Paisley explained to his visitors that he worked closely with Galvin and that if Mazlat retained Galvin's services, Mazlat's chance of getting a contract would be greatly enhanced. He explained that Galvin was in the process of forming a new company called Sapphire Systems, Incorporated, which was to be incorporated in December of 1985 and would be able to help Mazlat. What was never spelled out—though clear to Schiller and Shai—was that Paisley himself had a silent financial interest in Sapphire. Paisley's hidden message was that by paying Galvin through Sapphire, Paisley himself would benefit. Paisley suggested Schiller contact Galvin in the early part of 1986 about retaining his services.

Paisley's bluntness was not founded on carelessness or stupidity. According to FBI sources, prior to his meeting with Mazlat, he had the CIA files on Schiller and Mazlat pulled for his examination. The agency maintains an enormous collection of dossiers on foreign officials and government institutions, including large defense contractors like IAI and Mazlat. In the file, according to sources, Paisley found a sketchy record of IAI and Mazlat business dealings. He discovered that there were in the companies' histories repeated cases of the use of bribes and financial inducements to advance business interests. This was particularly true when it came to IAI dealings in Latin America.

Schiller and Shai left the meeting stunned by Paisley's frankness and his openness to a deal. They returned to Tel Aviv at once. In keeping with LAKAM policy, Shai did not inform the LAKAM deputy station chief, Ilan Ravid, or his assistant, Irit Erb, in the Israeli embassy in Washington about the Paisley meeting. Instead, he returned immediately to consult with Eitan. Schiller returned to his offices, contacted Schwimmer, and consulted with officials at IAI, who also came in contact with Schwimmer. Plans were made to propose a deal with Galvin and Paisley.

The timing and the decision to move ahead on Paisley were remarkable, in retrospect. Barely a week after the decision was made in Tel Aviv to approach Paisley, Jonathan Pollard was arrested in Washington on suspicion of spying for Israel. And yet, in January 1986, Schiller and Shai returned to Washington to seal a deal with Paisley and Galvin. As instructed by Paisley, they contacted Galvin, who arranged a meeting with Schiller, Shai, Paisley, and himself. This time they met at Galvin's private and secluded home, which was an hour's drive from Washington. A large house in Front Royal, Virginia, with a swimming pool and tennis courts, Galvin's home formed the backdrop to a deal that promised the Israelis a virtual treasure trove of information on America's most highly guarded military technology secrets, as well as a Pentagon contract.

Schiller's proposal, made on a freezing evening amid the Shenandoah Mountains of northwestern Virginia, was that in exchange for Paisley and Galvin's help in securing several navy contracts for Mazlat's pilotless reconnaissance drones, Mazlat would pay a finder's fee of one million dollars, which the two men would split. For reasons of security, especially in light of the Pollard case, he proposed that the funds be placed in a Swiss bank account, in their names. Paisley and Galvin agreed, and they shook on the deal. Paisley explained that he would act on the agreement in March, and Mazlat could expect to have a navy contract for the sum of twenty-five million dollars by April of 1986.

Schiller, Paisley, and Galvin also agreed to establish a consulting arrangement whereby Mazlat would receive information on advanced U.S. military weapons systems, particularly those using advanced technologies. Schiller mentioned specifically his interest in the ATA and a secret Marine Corps project dubbed Killer Egg. During the same conversation, Paisley and Galvin dropped a bombshell: would the Israelis be interested in documents from the Department of the Air Force concerning advanced technologies? Schiller and Shai answered affirmatively and offered to arrange a consulting agreement with Sapphire. It is unclear whom Paisley and Galvin had as a source. According to some FBI officials, a certain amount of suspicion rests on Victor D. Cohen, then deputy assistant secretary of the air force. Although there is no direct evidence linking Cohen to Mazlat, FBI sources believe he might have been the source Paisley and Galvin had in mind. In December 1989, as a result of Operation Ill Wind, Cohen, Paisley, and Galvin, were named by the Loral Corporation as the Pentagon officials who had secured Navy Department contracts for Loral in exchange for a $578,000 fee.

The uncovering of Jonathan Pollard in December 1985 brought big changes to LAKAM. The outcry in the United States led the Israeli government to disband LAKAM formally. Eitan was removed as LAKAM's head and given the chairmanship of Israel Chemicals, the largest state-owned industrial company (and, ironically, a company that is believed to have benefited for years from LAKAM activities). LAKAM offices in the Ministry of Defense were closed. But according to U.S. counterintelligence sources, its core functions continue to be carried out by LAKAM regulars overseas and the organization's remnants are managed by the Israeli air force and the prime minister's office. To this day, scientific and technical attachés overseas continue to collect intelligence in those fields.

In April 1986, Mazlat received its contract for twenty-five million dollars, just as had been promised. In exchange, Schiller wired the first installment of the one million dollars to a Swiss bank account in the names of Galvin and Paisley. But Schiller also did something else, something he wasn't supposed to do. Along with the first payment to his two friends in the States, he wired one million dollars to another Swiss bank account, this one set up in his own name. According to FBI officials, Schiller apparently convinced his superiors (including Schwimmer) that Paisley and Galvin had upped the price a week before the navy contract was granted. He even offered as proof a fake telex Galvin had allegedly sent over a "secure line."

Only several months after the navy began receiving the Mazlat drones did technical difficulties arise. The drones suffered mechanical malfunctions and massive electrical problems; several of the vehicles were lost at sea. By the fall of 1986, the rate of failure was so great that the Navy Department began investigating the problems. Paisley resisted his subordinates' attempts to confront Mazlat. He managed to hold off investigators until February of 1987. By that time, a total of $268,000 had been transferred to the secret Swiss bank account. With the mechanical problems continuing to mount, navy officials suspended Mazlat's contract. The payments to the Swiss bank account stopped just as suddenly. According to FBI officials, Paisley frequently expressed concern about how he would get the money from the Swiss bank account into the United States.

The cancellation of the Mazlat contract strained the Paisley-Mazlat relationship. Schiller and Shai pressed Paisley for a means by which the contract could be completed, and Paisley angrily scolded them, through Galvin, for Mazlat's poor quality. There wouldn't have been any problems if it hadn't been for Mazlat's lack of quality control, said Paisley. Schiller and Shai hoped to maintain the relationship with Paisley and Galvin despite the contract blunder. They told Galvin they were still interested in technical information pertaining to the ATA and other aviation projects. In February 1987, Galvin promised them some information "soon."

Two months later, in April 1987, Paisley resigned from his navy post. He decided to devote his full attention to Sapphire Systems and a new company he established five days after leaving the navy, Paisley Associates, Incorporated. But his resignation did not mean he wanted to put an end to the sale of government information to his "clients." Paisley hoped to continue to provide his services to defense contractors for large fees well into the future.

Critical to his plans, however, was continued access to Pentagon technology and contract secrets, the sort that would fetch top dollar from domestic companies like McDonnell Douglas and Unisys as well as foreign companies like Mazlat. By the time he left his Pentagon offices for the last time on March 27, he had managed to spirit out dozens of critical documents. Among those he took were those that Mazlat had requested, including information on the ATA, technical-briefing materials on upgrades to the Pratt and Whitney F-404 jet engine, and information on Killer Egg. He also had persuaded navy officials to keep him on as a consultant. As a result, he would maintain his security clearance and retain access to information involving even the military's most secret "black budget" projects.

Paisley seemed all set up to begin his scheme of selling secrets when suddenly, twelve days after he resigned, the new assistant secretary of the navy, James Webb, decided to cancel his consulting contract. Paisley was in trouble. With no secrets to sell, he would lose big fees; the lucrative contracts he had planned were in jeopardy. Desperate for a way to tap into Pentagon secrets on contracts and advanced technological systems, Paisley turned to a source on the Pentagon's Naval Research Advisory Committee, a secret, prestigious group of academicians and industry leaders who met regularly with navy officials to discuss sensitive military programs. The body had access to a wide variety of classified information concerning the latest in navy technological developments. Paisley had appointed many of the committee members himself during his six-year tenure as assistant secretary. This improvisation proved to keep Paisley supplied with enough critical navy documents to entice foreign and domestic buyers of his services.

By the spring of 1988, things had begun to unravel. In Israel, Schiller was confronted by senior IAI officials over the funds transferred to the Swiss bank account. And in the United States, Ill Wind investigations were proceeding at full speed. The investigation net included taps on hundreds of phones, including those of Paisley, Galvin, Cohen, senior Pentagon officials, industry executives, and various other consultants. According to FBI officials, Paisley's contact with several foreign embassies was also probed. Investigators accumulated an incredible amount of information.

On the morning of June 8, 1988, Melvyn Paisley's world came crashing down on him. At approximately 8:00 A.M., FBI agents armed with search warrants raided dozens of locations around Washington, D.C., including Paisley's offices at the Watergate office complex and his home in McLean. They uncovered thousands of pages of sensitive technological information in Paisley's possession, including information in which Schiller and Shai had expressed an interest: technical specifications on the Pratt and Whitney F-404 engine upgrades, the ATA, and Killer Egg. Federal officials have never been able to determine whether copies of these documents ever made their way to Israel. "It's anybody's guess," says one senior official.

Also uncovered by FBI agents was Paisley's relationship with the head of another Israeli-owned defense contractor. Pocal was a Scranton, Pennsylvania, company owned by Israeli weapons maker Shlomo Zabludowicz and his son Chaim. Pocal had received Pentagon contracts between 1981 and 1988 to build plastic dummy artillery shells. Chaim Zabludowicz had a long-standing social relationship with Paisley. According to the New York Times, Paisley's ex-wife told the New York Times that Melvyn Paisley took a trip with Chaim Zabludowicz in 1983 or 1984 to Sun Valley, Idaho, where Paisley had a condominium.

Paisley's relationship with senior Israeli defense officials, including Al Schiller, led some in the FBI to speculate that maybe Paisley was the mysterious Mr. X of the Pollard affair. Whether he was Mr. X or not is unclear. He certainly had access to the documents that Mr. X had provided to Israeli intelligence. He also had social dealings with a Pocal official, as well as social and financial dealings with officials from Mazlat, a government-owned defense contractor, according to published accounts. Perhaps Paisley, so willing to sell secrets to defense contractors, did the same, knowingly or unknowingly, to LAKAM? Paisley was placed on a Justice Department Mr. X subject list in 1988, and he remains on the list to this day.

But even with the arrest of Paisley, Galvin, and Cohen, serious questions remained unanswered. Evidence had surfaced indicating that Israeli intelligence had obtained classified U.S. documents relating to a high-tech tactical intelligence system called the joint services image processor (JSIP), a system being developed by the U.S. Air Force that would presumably speed the transmission of data from intelligence reconnaissance flights to a sophisticated ground station. Advanced computers at the ground station would then weigh the data with other available intelligence from a variety of sources. The system's technology is extremely sensitive and has a variety of military, as well as commercial, uses.

In September 1986, Israeli government officials showed the documents in question to officials from a U.S. defense contractor, Recon Optical, Incorporated. The Israelis told the Recon officials that the plans were part of an Israeli intelligence program known as the remote imaging system (RIS). Recon executive John Whyte later received a detailed, unclassified briefing about the American JSIP and concluded that the RIS was so similar to the American system that it was "extremely likely" the similarities were more than "mere happenstance." When Whyte told Pentagon officials about the common elements, the Defense Investigative Service launched an investigation.

The JSIP project was top secret, and it had a specific no-foreign prohibition. General Kenneth Israel, who oversaw the project from May 1985 to May 1989, says he doesn't remember "ever giving the country of Israel any information" about JSIP. So the question remained: how did Israeli air force officials get documents on the top-secret project? The FBI had hoped to find evidence when its agents raided the homes and offices of Paisley and Cohen. After all, as senior Pentagon officials, both would have had easy access to the information. The troubling answer was there was not one shred of evidence to indicate that either man had passed the information to the Israelis. There is only one explanation: another senior Pentagon official must have passed it to the Israelis. To this day, there are no leads in the case. The FBI has dubbed the mysterious official Mr. Y.

† † †

Israeli intelligence activities in the United States and Europe are not limited to machinations in Washington involving government employees. According to U.S. intelligence officials, Israeli agents have been active in a variety of areas.

In the summer of 1986, the U.S. Customs Service and the Justice Department began investigating charges that Israel had tried to obtain technologies that would enable it to build cluster bombs. The investigations involved two U.S. companies, including the Vector Corporation, which uses the same equipment to compress and coat the drug capsules it makes as can be used to make cluster bombs. According to FBI officials active in the investigation, an operation run by Israeli intelligence began in 1983, after Congress banned the export of cluster bombs to Israel. (Reports that Israel was using the bombs in its invasion of Lebanon led to the ban. When the United States first sold the weapons to Israel, it was on the condition that the weapons be used only for defensive purposes and only against organized Arab armies.)

Several members of Israel's defense mission in New York and the commercial attaché at the embassy in Washington, D.C., carried out the plans. FBI officials now believe that the commercial attaché's office in Washington was serving as a cover for LAKAM agents, and the operation did not involve regular embassy staff. In response to a request by Israeli Defense Minister Ariel Sharon, Rafi Eitan ordered the compilation of a list of companies in the United States that produced technologies relevant to cluster bombs. In September 1982 LAKAM agents began tracking the companies, and in March 1983 agents in Washington began traveling to several of them. One of the firms the Israelis had identified was Assembly Machine Industries in Erie, Pennsylvania.

Posing as employees of Israel Military Industries, the agents toured the plant and purchased machinery that would be helpful in the production of cluster bombs. When the U.S. Customs Service blocked the export of the machinery in July 1986 on the grounds that it would be used for making the bombs, LAKAM agents got access to blueprints and sample parts of Assembly Machine Industries equipment and brought them back to Tel Aviv. By late 1986, Israel had begun producing a cluster bomb domestically. In large part, by Israel's admission, this was made possible by the technology acquired from the United States.

Israeli agents have also carried out a variety of industrial espionage operations in the United States and Europe over the last twenty years, for purely commercial benefit. Targets have included high-technology companies large and small, some of which have maintained business relations with the Israeli government for years.

Recon Optical, for example, had done business with Israel since the early 1960s, and in October 1984 the Barrington, Illinois, company signed one of its largest contracts yet with the Israeli military: a four-year forty-million-dollar contract to produce aerial reconnaissance cameras to be used by the Israeli air force for security purposes. As part of the agreement, Israeli officials from IAI were to be present from time to time during the development and production of the system. But according to Recon Optical's chief executive officer and president, Larry G. Larson, things started going wrong when suspicious activity on the part of several employees was noticed.

Three officers from the Israeli air force who were working at the plant began spending prolonged amounts of time going over the camera system's technical specifications. In May, the Israeli officers attempted to ship back to Israel some fourteen cartons from the plant. Recon security officials stopped them and demanded to see what was inside. When the Israelis refused, Recon security officials opened the boxes themselves. Inside they found important Recon documents as well as papers in Hebrew describing plans to steal Recon's secrets. Evidence seemed to indicate that the Israeli plans included giving the Recon technology secrets to an Israeli defense firm named El Op, or Electronics-Optics Industries, Limited. It was hoped, apparently, that El Op would not only produce the system for Israel but manufacture it for export as well.

For a company of 1,150 employees with annual sales at the time of about one hundred million dollars, the loss of the forty-million-dollar contract presented a dilemma. At first, Larson went to the Justice Department to request an investigation, but he got nowhere. According to senior FBI officials, the Justice Department went to the State Department for guidance because the case involved what it characterized as the "sensitive nature of Israeli-American relations on security issues." The federal investigation quickly bogged down as diplomatic concerns grew. As one federal official told Bernard Gwertzman of the *New York Times*, "The State Department has a vested interest in this, and so does the Justice Department."

One senior FBI official with responsibility in the field of foreign espionage is even more blunt. Having reviewed the file in 1986 he concludes, "There is no doubt in my mind that there was something going on at Recon Optical. Had it been the Sovs or the Chinese, we would have acted on it immediately. But this involved a close U.S. ally so State told us 'hands off.' We listened." In May 1986, the company filed suit against the Israeli government in federal district court, charging that the government was in breach of contract and was stealing company secrets.

The Recon case went to private arbitration soon after the lawsuit was filed. In February 1991, the arbitrators reached a sealed decision. They concluded that the Israeli agents had used "elaborate subterfuges" to steal Recon's secrets, they decried the "sordidness" of the affair, and they ordered Israel to pay Recon three million dollars in damages. The arbitrators also noted that the Israeli government never reprimanded the agents involved. The three-man arbitration panel also concluded that the Israeli air force was working in cooperation with El Op. The Israeli military even dressed an El Op employee as an air force officer simply to give the company an inside look at the Recon operation. The information clandestinely collected by the military officers stationed at Recon was transferred to Israeli air force intelligence officials in Tel Aviv and passed to El Op management, according to the arbitration panel. El Op then made specific requests of air force intelligence, which passed the orders on to the officers at Recon.

One of the key individuals representing the Israeli air force at Recon, and named by the arbitrators as one of the "direct perpetrators" in the case, was a trained engineer named Motti Hankabi. When the espionage ring was exposed in 1986, Hankabi was not punished by his government. Rather, as an example of stubborn arrogance, the Israeli air force gave him a pay raise and a new job: trying to obtain the information on the same system from another U.S. company, Loral Fairchild.

In August 1986, another case of probable Israeli industrial espionage emerged when an employee of the Israeli consulate in New York was arrested for attempted burglary. Ronen Tidhar, a twenty-five-year-old, was found on the roof of a building in Mineola, on Long Island. Tidhar and another Israeli not employed by the consulate were caught by police trying to pry open a skylight in a building owned by an aviation parts and technology company. Tidhar and his partner refused to talk with police and instead insisted that the Israeli consulate be contacted. Two days after Tidhar's arrest, the consulate issued a statement. Said Barukh Binah, the press attaché at the consulate in Manhattan, "I don't know what he was up to, but it was no business of the Israeli government."

Yet the way in which the Tidhar case was handled indicates that in all likelihood the young man was acting with some official sanction. Although the consulate did dismiss him, it threatened to invoke diplomatic immunity if his case went to trial. Tidhar had been an associate of Joseph Yagur, who was the science attaché at the Israeli consulate and in 1986 was named by the Justice Department as a co-conspirator in the Pollard case. After his return to Israel, Tidhar was retained as a consultant by the Israeli Foreign Ministry until he found employment in industry. One former deputy director of the CIA for counterintelligence calls the Tidhar case "a textbook example of Israeli industrial espionage in action in the United States."

Perhaps Israel's best LAKAM agent in the United States was a California computer expert named Richard K. Smyth, who passed to LAKAM handlers an enormous amount of technological information over a fifteen-year period. Smyth, an apparently successful businessman who taught part-time at the University of Southern California, was not someone who would be considered a likely suspect for recruitment. He was the proud father of five children, including a son who won a silver medal in sailing at the 1984 Olympic Games. He was a well-known fixture in his Huntington Beach community. A yacht-club member, friendly neighbor, and man with a great many friends, he was the president of his own company which did consulting work on advanced computers and other related technologies. But only after a mistake, a costly one that led to an FBI investigation, did the truth about Richard Smyth appear—as he sought a safe haven in Israel.

Smyth's relations with LAKAM and Israel began in the early 1970s, when he was working for the Rockwell Corporation, the southern California defense contractor. At the time, Smyth was a chief engineer in its avionics division and traveled to Israel to set up a Rockwell subsidiary there. According to former associates, Smyth was the company's "point man with the Israeli government." While in Israel, Smyth met a number of LAKAM officials as well as a flamboyant Israeli playboy named Arnon Milchan. Milchan at the time was firmly connected with the Israeli military and defense establishment. His business was arms sales, and he was clearly good at it, penetrating markets that had been difficult for Israel to crack, including those in South America. (Milchan later went on to a second career, as a Hollywood producer; his work includes the futuristic film *Brazil*.) In January 1973, while still working at Rockwell, Smyth founded his own company, Milco, which was funded by Arnon Milchan.

One of Milco's first duties, in late 1973, was to order several barrels of a butyl compound, which is used to bind explosive powders in solid-rocket fuel. At the time, Israel was working to perfect a solid-fuel tactical missile known as Jericho, which could carry nuclear warheads. Milco shipped the barrels to a Milchan front company in Houston, which in turn shipped them to Israel.

In 1975, Smyth quit Rockwell and went to work for Milco full-time. The company struggled financially until 1980, landing several contracts for less than twenty-five thousand dollars apiece with NASA and the Department of the Air Force for studies on computer software for avionic systems in advanced aircraft and the MX and Patriot missiles. Smyth performed several tasks for LAKAM during this period, according to federal officials, passing the Israelis information on several systems he was researching.

In 1980, Smyth got a break that substantially increased his value in Israel's eyes. He was asked to join the Air Force Department Scientific Advisory Panel, which was concerned with advanced technological systems. The appointment gave him access to top-secret Pentagon technological information and research programs. Not coincidentally, Smyth's financial condition improved dramatically as a result of the appointment. His income rose to about one million dollars per year.

While on the air force panel, say FBI officials, Smyth almost certainly passed his Israeli contacts top-secret information on a variety of advanced avionic systems. The Kfir fighter was still in production, technologically upgraded to be marketed for export. But Israeli officials were ambitiously planning for the production of a newer and more advanced fighter aircraft, the Lavi. By mid-1981, Smyth had contracts with the Israeli Heli Trading Company to acquire technology related to the Lavi fighter plane, according to Milco records. In early 1983, Milco won a contract to provide "research support" on Lavi flight-control systems.

Smyth was also working at the time to export to Israel nuclear-related technologies, including critical timing devices known as krytons. By late 1982, he had shipped more than two hundred krytons to Israel, labeled as something else on the shipping licenses.

But in early 1983, Smyth's world started to crumble. In March of that year, someone broke into Milco's offices and took several thousand dollars' worth of computer and software equipment. Because Smyth was doing classified government work as a Pentagon consultant and member of the Air Force Scientific Advisory Panel, he was required to let the Pentagon and the FBI know about the theft immediately. The trouble was that if the equipment were discovered by federal authorities, the FBI might start asking questions about his dealings with Israel, the details of which were recorded in those computers' memories. So in his report to the Pentagon, Smyth admitted that he may have "bent the rules" when it came to his business dealings with Israel. He was not specific, and he clearly hoped that the admission might give him a few points should the FBI find his computers.

Little did Smyth know that the FBI and the CIA had been suspicious of his activities for quite some time. According to U.S. intelligence sources, an Israeli businessman had tipped off the CIA station chief in Tel Aviv about Smyth's relations with LAKAM and Israeli intelligence in 1982. He had apparently heard about Smyth from friends in the Israeli defense industry and was hoping to exchange the tip for U.S. help in securing emigration papers for his relatives still in Eastern Europe, so they could join him in Israel. (True to its word, the CIA did get State Department assistance, and the man's relatives reached Israel in 1985.)

With Smyth's admission that he "bent the rules," the CIA took the opportunity to move in. CIA officer Ron Romano was dispatched to the Milco office, where he conducted an in-depth and sometimes testy questioning of Smyth. Soon after, Romano returned with U.S. Customs Service officers and a warrant to search the premises. Nothing firm was uncovered, but the FBI, the CIA, and Customs maintained a watch on Milco and Smyth, convinced that while they had no smoking gun, the operation Smyth had going was more than it seemed.

For the next two years, the California computer expert, despite the close call over the computer theft, continued to maintain his relationship with LAKAM and Israeli intelligence. He continued to ship krytons and passed along information he obtained as a member of the Air Force Scientific Advisory Panel. In April 1985, he even received the Pentagon's prestigious Meritorious Civilian Service Award. The citation mentioned that his work as a member of the panel "directly affected programs vital to the Air Force and has significantly enhanced the defense posture of this nation." He was cited for making contributions in advanced electronics, mission-critical software, and replacement weapons for the nuclear-tipped "genie." Smyth, it seemed, was at the top of his profession.

Yet the FBI-CIA-Customs team had continued to monitor Smyth's activities, and on May 16, 1985, it decided to move. On that day, a federal grand jury, in reviewing the evidence the team had collected, indicted Smyth on charges relating to the illegal export and transfer of technology. Smyth was awestruck and shattered. Fearful that he might have to serve time, he fled the country almost immediately. "He was convinced he was going to jail," said Milco's attorney, Brian Carter. Despite the indictment against him, Smyth found easy refuge on the run. Richard Smyth and his wife turned up in Israel, where they remain to this day.

Israel's reputation for possessing an aggressive and highly successful intelligence service is well deserved. And in its efforts to protect and advance its national interests, Israel has consistently targeted the United States, especially in the area of high-technology military secrets. Israel's equally deserved reputation as an arms manufacturer is also important to the national interest and is an economic bonanza when it comes to foreign sales. Extensive spying on the world leader in this field is a high-priority endeavor, and Israeli officials plan to keep it that way.

12

007 Joins the Firm

Spying, or industrial espionage in the corporate world, is an everyday fact of corporate life.

—Robert Redmond, Security Consultant

In 1982, Bernard Mayles joined the pharmaceutical giant Schering-Plough with great promise, serving as a director of the project for the development of interferon, a drug that is effective against hepatitis and certain forms of cancer and was promising to be an important advance in medicine as well as a big money maker. Mayles had responsibility for overseeing the fermentation process that is necessary to produce interferon, as well as for supervising a team of microbiologists who used genetic engineering to make the microbes that are needed for fermentation. Although generally competent in his oversight of the fermentation process, Mayles ran into serious conflicts in his management of the microbiologists. They complained to their superiors that he was autocratic and paranoid, always suspicious of them and their work. Says Francis Bullock, Schering-Plough's senior vice president for research, "[They] were coming to me saying this guy didn't know what he was doing. We almost had a palace coup on our hands." The tensions were a real problem for the company. Bullock and other senior officials were concerned that

Mayles's behavior might disrupt the production of interferon or hurt productivity. Morale was already low. And so in early 1985, management decided to do something about it. Using the excuse of a company reorganization, Bullock moved the microbiologists to another division, away from Mayles's control. Because he was now heading only the fermentation team, Mayles was also demoted two pay levels, and he was cut out of senior-level management meetings.

Mayles did not take the news well. According to colleagues, he seemed depressed and angry. He was bitter with the company, with his superiors, and with his co-workers. He complained that he was the victim of jealous colleagues who didn't have the talent he had. So it came as no surprise when he quit Schering-Plough in early 1987. But what would eventually surprise his co-workers was the lengths to which he went to get even. For in the weeks prior to his resignation, he had managed to take with him reams of confidential and extremely valuable information on the interferon process. There can be little doubt that he planned to hurt the company and help himself by selling the secrets to Schering-Plough's main competitors. But things never worked out that way, fortunately for Schering-Plough. Mayles's action would eventually set off an FBI sting operation along the eastern seaboard, extending from Philadelphia to Atlanta. It would entail dummy front companies and unscrupulous individuals involved in the lucrative black market for industrial secrets, where enormous profits are to be had.

Bernard Mayles was considered a bright student when he enrolled in West Virginia University's doctoral program for microbiology. He did so well that upon the completion of his course work and dissertation he received a plum job offer in 1971 from the chemical-manufacturing division of the pharmaceutical giant Merck. By 1977, he had so impressed the company that he was promoted to senior research director at Merck headquarters in Rahway, New Jersey. There he joined a team developing an advanced drug called Ivermectin, which kills an assortment of parasites in cattle and heartworm in dogs. As a member of the team, Mayles made several important research contributions. The drug was first marketed by Merck in 1981 and went on to be one of the company's crowning successes. By 1990, Ivermectin was the biggest-selling animal-health product in the world, with sales running at nearly eight hundred million dollars annually. With Mayles's contributions to the development of Ivermectin came more job promotions and salary bonuses. Then in 1982, he got the offer from Schering-Plough.

Mayles did not leave Merck an entirely happy man. The promotions, it seems, had not come fast enough, nor the praise loud enough. He believed that he had made large contributions to the development of Ivermectin that had gone unnoticed. So before he left he took with him a vast assortment of valuable company documents pertaining to Ivermectin and other projects he had worked on. In a way, he believed the secrets belonged to him: after all, he had been an important part of the research team. But even if Mayles felt he had a right to the information, he clearly knew it wasn't legally his. Indeed, he smuggled out the documents under his coat and in his briefcase during off-hours, to make sure no one saw him take them. It is unclear whether Mayles already intended to pedal the valuable secrets on the international market. But it is known that Mayles's decision to take confidential company secrets with him would be a fateful one.

By 1987, Mayles was without a job but in possession of information worth hundreds of millions of dollars to any number of drug companies around the world. For two years, he tried to develop business ventures as a consultant and independent researcher, but he failed almost entirely. He did not have one substantial success to carry him through. By 1989, he had two mortgages on his house in suburban New Jersey, and he was desperate. Throughout those years, his bitterness had only grown.

During those two years of frustration and financial difficulty, Mayles had slowly developed a working partnership with an Italian chemist named Mario Miscio. Whether Mayles knew it or not, Miscio was rumored by many to be in the business of selling valuable pharmaceutical secrets to companies around the world, particularly in his native Italy. He had many contacts there, having immigrated to the United States in 1970. Italy was a gold mine for international pharmaceutical spies, who would sell valuable secrets for multimillion-dollar fees. For years, Italy had a "humanitarian clause" in its patent law, which meant that Italian drug companies would not be prosecuted for violating international patents of products like pharmaceuticals.

There had already been several well-known cases in the pharmaceutical industry concerning the sale of drug information to Italian drug companies. In 1965, Dr. Sidney Martin Fox, an ex-employee of American Cyanamid, sold antibiotic cultures to several Italian drug companies. Cyanamid's loss was approximately thirty million dollars a year. At the same time, Robert S. Aries sold information about some of Merck's most valuable drugs, which he had received from a young chemical engineer at the company, to one French and several Italian firms.

Mario Miscio was an energetic and lively man. He knew about the secrets Mayles possessed, and when he saw Mayles's desperation, he proposed that they "market" the secrets on the international industrial espionage market and split the fee fifty-fifty. Miscio proposed using his own small company, Biopharm Research, Incorporated, of Hazlet, New Jersey, as a cover for their scheme. Miscio, says a former colleague, often joked about becoming a "shorter, darker version" of Aries. (He did in a way; both have spent time in prison.)

Whether it was just fate or dumb luck, one of the first individuals Miscio approached was the owner of a small chemical business who had been involved in questionable deals with stolen information in the past and wanted a way out. This time rather than purchase the information and peddle it overseas, the company owner informed Edward Stiffler, who was a former Merck security director. Stiffler, when he heard the story, dutifully passed the information along to Merck and Schering-Plough. When the two pharmaceutical giants heard what Miscio and Mayles were selling, they were stunned. They knew that if the two found an international buyer (which they would assuredly do, given enough time) the costs to their profits would be enormous, running into the hundreds of millions of dollars per year. Thus both companies decided to go to the FBI with their story. Their highest priority was to preserve their secrets, but they also wanted to bring Miscio and Mayles to justice and put a dent in the international pharmaceutical black market.

The value of the information Mayles and Miscio were offering to sell was valuable because it was unique. Given the structure of modern drugs and pharmaceuticals, what competitors need in order to duplicate the products easily and effectively is insight into the production method, not simply the drug recipe. And that insight is what Mayles and Miscio were offering.

In order to snare the two men, Merck and Schering-Plough (with the cooperation of the FBI) had to arrange the attempted sale of the illegal documents. The business owner approached by Mayles and Miscio agreed to cooperate in a sting operation on two conditions: he wanted his identity kept secret, and he wanted his 1960s conviction on a trade-secret case involving American Cyanamid reviewed by a law firm, with the understanding that it might be overturned. Merck and Shering-Plough agreed to the conditions and offered to pay the legal fees for the review.

Under the direction of the FBI and the U.S. attorney's office in Newark, New Jersey, the business owner arranged to meet with Mayles and Miscio regarding the possible purchase of the secrets. He told them he had a potential buyer in mind and that he wanted to serve as broker, for a fee. In January 1990, the three met at Biopharm Research, along with a "prospective buyer" of the stolen secrets. Described by the business owner as "a friend," Edward Stiffler posed as an international broker whose international clients regularly bought stolen information. Stiffler said he needed to know whether the information was on an "important drug."

"We have information for sale on a very important product," opened Miscio almost immediately after the initial handshake.

"Oh, what product is that?" Stiffler asked.

"Well, I have several products ready to go. What interests you?" Miscio retorted smugly.

Stiffler wasted no time. He needed to know whether they really had the information or were just bluffing. "Do you have anything in the cancer line?"

"Oh yes," said Miscio with a chuckle. "We can offer interferon."

Miscio was very candid in the meeting, probably because of his knowledge of how widespread the market for stolen secrets was. But in this instance, his openness was a mistake. Not only was Stiffler listening to what he had to offer, but so was the FBI. Stiffler was wearing a hidden mike, and two agents were sitting a block away from the office, quietly listening to, and recording, the conversation.

Stiffler probed Miscio regarding what else he had available for sale. The Italian chemist leaned back in his chair and added further mystery to the case. "Ah, we also have another Merck product, an anticholesterol product called Lovastatin. It's pretty good stuff."

Stiffler struggled to hide his shock. He knew that Lovastatin was developed largely after Mayles had left Merck. That meant only one thing: Mayles and Miscio had someone inside Merck passing them information. It was a leak Stiffler and Merck hadn't imagined existed.

After Stiffler gracefully recovered from his surprise, he told Miscio and Mayles about a business associate in Atlanta who would be interested in talking about a deal. Stiffler described him as an international broker who could market the secrets even more widely than he could, especially to leading Asian and European drug companies. Miscio and Mayles said they liked the idea, because U.S. companies were "too stupid" to take advantage of the information. Stiffler and Miscio set up a meeting at the Marriott Hotel at the airport in Philadelphia, in which the Atlanta broker would participate. The decision to set up the next meeting in the City of Brotherly Love was both deliberate and critical to the sting. Miscio and Mayles had to transfer stolen property across state lines in order for their crime to be a federal matter and a felony.

At the next meeting with Miscio and Mayles, Stiffler was joined by FBI agent Paul Hayes posing as the business broker from Atlanta. Hayes, a dark-haired man with a steely stare, played his role perfectly. He described to Miscio his contacts with drug companies in foreign countries like China, Poland, and Italy. He acted cool and businesslike, as if the purchasing of such information were routine. He left telling them he would consult a contact named Hugo and he suggested they meet again. He left Mayles his business card, which gave the name of a brokerage firm in Atlanta that was, of course, an FBI front.

The sting seemed to be going perfectly for Merck, Schering-Plough, and the FBI. They had tapes of Miscio and Mayles offering to sell stolen information. They had lured them out of state, making it a federal case. And they had apparently peaked the interest of both men so that they were enthusiastic about concluding the sale. But then a big problem erupted. A few days after the Philadelphia meeting, Paul Hayes got an unexpected phone call from Bernard Mayles. After they exchanged pleasantries, Mayles confronted Hayes. He accused him of not being registered to do business in the state of Georgia.

Hayes was mortified. After a brief moment of silence, Mayles explained that he had called the office of the Georgia secretary of state to see whether Hayes's firm was registered. (Why Mayles, who knew he was peddling stolen documents, was so concerned about the legitimacy of his buyer's business is anyone's guess.)

"We got to be," Hayes responded, acting surprised and confused. "I know we're registered."

"Well," retorted Mayles, "I called down there to the secretary of state's office. After all, when I do business, I like to know who I'm doing business with, you understand. I called the secretary of state's office, and they checked it by computer. And all I can say is that you're not there on it."

Hayes recovered from his initial surprise and acted as if it were no big deal. More than likely, he told Mayles, it must have been a mistake. You know how government bureaucrats are, and besides, you know computers. "You ever heard of GIGO—'garbage in, garbage out'—in computers?" By his quick thinking and fancy verbal footwork, Hayes saved the sting from a minor bureaucratic mistake that might have undone hundreds of hours of work. An FBI bureaucrat had failed to pay a fifteen-dollar annual fee to the state of Georgia to renew the dummy company's incorporation registration.

Several other preparatory meetings were held between Hayes, Mayles, and Miscio. One took place at the Biopharm Research offices in New Jersey, another at a New York City hotel and another in a Newark restaurant. Hayes wanted the deal to appear realistic, so at some of these meetings he dickered about the price and at times pretended to be skeptical about whether Mayles and Miscio actually had what they claimed to have. At all three meetings, Hayes was wired: a small mike had been woven into his clothing.

At the restaurant meeting in Newark, the case almost fell apart again. Hayes, with a small tape recorder attached to his back, had tucked in his shirttail too firmly, snagging the on-off switch and making it impossible to turn the thing on. And a small piece of wiring was exposed. Fortunately, Hayes realized the problem and during appetizers excused himself and headed for the men's room. In a stall he corrected the problem and returned to the meeting.

That evening the sting reached a critical juncture when, after much haggling, they agreed on a price of $1.5 million for the Ivermectin formula. To prove they had the genuine article, Mayles and Miscio sold a few pages of the information and several diagrams of the formula for $2,500. "This shows the actual production process, and sure as heck no one can get that from anyone but Merck," says an FBI official.

With the Ivermectin deal closed, Hayes opened up discussion about the purchase of information on interferon technology. This was raised in part to probe Mayles and Miscio regarding what else they had to sell. At that point, no one quite knew the quantity and quality of information the men had in their possession. The fact that they had a source at Merck led the FBI to believe they might have even more information than had previously been imagined. But Hayes also raised the prospect of a deal on interferon in order to keep Mayles and Miscio preoccupied. "That was to keep them thinking about as many things as possible so they couldn't focus on any slipups in the sting," said Hayes after the operation was over.

To lure in Miscio and Mayles, Hayes told them he knew of a foreign buyer who would be willing to pay top dollar for the interferon formula. "He throws money around. . . . He said, 'Anything up to ten million bucks will probably work out OK.' "

Mayles said only one thing: "Wow."

While Hayes was negotiating with Mayles and Miscio and promising to make them a fortune on the stolen secrets, the FBI investigation was proceeding on other fronts as well. Miscio's phone was tapped to pick up any hints as to whether he had contact with the other source at Merck. The bureau also considered the possibility that Miscio had several other sources at both Merck and Schering-Plough, and agents discussed the matter with security officials at both companies, so that they would be alert to the possibility of other leads. At the same time, FBI agent Richard Smith was going through Mayles's trash. In return for several cases of beer, garbage collectors handed Mayles's trash to Smith, who was waiting in a nearby van. Mixed in with household scraps and rotting food, Smith and his colleagues found small telltale signs of the scientist's activities. But one day they found something as good as a free invitation to his home. In one bundle of newspapers was a classified ad that had been circled. Smith checked it out and found that the phone number was Mayles's. The suspect was trying to sell his home. Three days later two FBI agents posing as a husband and wife interested in buying a new home called Mayles to set up an appointment to look at the house. Mayles gave the couple a tour himself. Inside the agents picked up some more important clues when they spotted stacks of confidential pharmaceutical papers in the study.

The FBI now had enough evidence to move the sting into its final phase. A date for the exchange of information for money was finally set. Mayles and Miscio promised to hand over a twenty-nine-page report that would include all the information they had on interferon. Hayes suggested they meet in a private conference room in an Atlanta bank building, and Mayles and Miscio agreed.

On August 10, 1990, Mayles and Miscio arrived on time, Miscio clutching a black patent leather briefcase in his right hand. Hayes was waiting with a briefcase that contained the cash. The three men sat around the long, shiny conference table and got down to business. Mayles handed the report to Hayes, sliding it across the table toward him.

"I think this is what you've been waiting for," Miscio said with a grin.

Hayes glanced at it briefly and then slowly stood. "I want it confirmed by an expert," he said. "He's just outside—he'll review it briefly for the buyer. Just give me two minutes."

The bureau wanted to be sure the information was genuine and confidential. Hayes casually exited the conference room and handed the report to his "expert"—another FBI agent, who quickly took the document to a portable fax machine. He punched in a number for Merck and Company in Rahway, where a team of scientists was waiting to confirm its authenticity. When the team in Rahway concluded that indeed the documents used in the report were authentic, Hayes returned to the conference room—with a team of muscular FBI agents behind him.

Mayles was shocked. It became clear right away that he had been set up. Miscio, on the other hand, reduced the arrest to sad, comic opera. He got to his feet, protesting the presence of unknown faces. "This is a private meeting, a private meeting! You guys get outa here!"

The nearest agent kindly pushed Miscio back into his seat. "We're the FBI," another said, "and you're both under arrest."

Hours after Miscio and Mayles were led out of the Atlanta bank building in handcuffs, FBI agents descended on Mayles's home in suburban New Jersey. Inside they found reams of Merck and Schering-Plough documents, many dating from his tenure at both companies but numerous other documents dating from after 1987.

In September 1991, Judge Alfred Lechner found Mayles and Miscio guilty of transporting stolen documents. Mayles, fifty-seven, was sentenced to nine years in prison; Miscio, to five years and three months. Their inside sources at Merck and Schering-Plough have not yet been caught. Both companies fear other secrets may already have been taken and could be circulating on the international industrial espionage market for stolen secrets.

Intelligence and espionage, once the exclusive occupations of monarch and government, have become an important component of international business. No longer are spies employed only by national intelligence services. Large corporations around the world, particularly in Western Europe and Asia, now hire sophisticated agents to gather intelligence on competitors and other countries. "Intelligence," says former CIA director William Colby, "is being privatized." Some of these corporations field networks of agents that, according to one former CIA director, "rival those of middle-sized countries." Other major companies, while not employing intelligence agents full-time, retain consultants or hire private detectives when a situation lends itself to espionage. "Some companies are just too tempted, and they cut corners to get information," says Colby. Arion Pattakos, a security consultant, warns companies, "There is a real threat. Their motive is big dollars . . . to exploit sources both legal and not legal to gain another's secrets. There is plenty of opportunity to exploit those sources and exploitation methods abound."

In some instances, company intelligence officers are simply business executives with a flare for collecting information, an ex-police officer, private detective, or ambitious security official who branched into this more lucrative field. But in Asia and Western Europe (and also in the United States), companies are more frequently hiring former intelligence agents from any number of nations. "For former practitioners it can be and has been extremely lucrative," says one former official who has done some work for U.S. companies such as Motorola. August Bequai, a business lawyer who has handled trade-secret theft cases, says companies can buy a lot on the open market. "If you're willing to spend the money and criminality doesn't bother you, you can pretty much buy anything you want." One Japanese business publication predicts, "As the Cold War becomes an historic relic, the electronic spy gadgets that its heyday spawned will be increasingly used in the field of corporate espionage."

Companies are increasingly prone to engaging in industrial espionage because it is so profitable. As Richard Greene of *Forbes* magazine put it, "Crime, at least in the form of stealing trade secrets, can pay handsomely." Few industrial spies get caught because the problem is usually discovered only long after the fact. But losing secrets can destroy a company. Security consultant Robert Redmond warns, "Keeping sensitive information secure . . . is an essential element of business success."

Industrial espionage takes a variety of forms and includes multiple targets. Companies spy in order to win bids on important contracts, uncover a competitor's business strategy, or gain access cheaply to research and development data that a competitor may have just paid handsomely for. By collecting such information through espionage, companies can save tens, or even hundreds of millions, of dollars. This is largely a result of the increasing value of information. In a technological world, trade secrets—formulas, designs, marketing plans—are the new gold of the marketplace. As a result, says Redmond, "Spying, or industrial espionage in the corporate world, is an everyday fact of corporate life."

In many foreign countries, greater latitude is given when it comes to acquiring information from competitors. What is patently illegal in the United States is readily acceptable in other parts of the world. Says Admiral Bob Inman, former director of the National Security Agency, "We do know that many foreign companies aggressively try to find out what their competitors are doing, and their standards are often different from our own."

Many companies discover they have a problem only after they have been victimized repeatedly. Ambassador Richard Helms, who served as the director of the CIA under President Johnson, is no stranger to the world of espionage. But even he was surprised when a California-based oil-drilling company came to him with problems it was having with bids on international contracts. Helms investigated and eventually discovered that a Japanese company had been buying the American company's bids from a disloyal employee. "It was a plain, simple act of bribery, a betrayal for money—industrial treason, if you will."

Corporate spying need not be illegal. Indeed, many experts argue that an immense amount of intelligence can be collected aboveboard by the clever corporate spy. In April 1986, the Kellogg Company closed its Battle Creek, Michigan, plant to public tours when it learned that two industrial spies sent by two German competitors had gathered valuable information during such visits. The plant had just the year before been outfitted with five hundred million dollars in modernizations and new technologies, and Kellogg's competitors wanted to find out what the company's latest methods looked like. So they took the tour several times, armed with cameras.

In July 1989, a du Pont chemical plant in Delaware was the site of a professional, well-orchestrated espionage scheme. Visitors from a German chemical company were taking an informal tour of a plant that produces synthetics when one of the visitors, looking over a laboratory table, accidentally dropped the tip of his tie into a vat of liquids. Company officials were at first apologetic. They offered to replace the stained tie with a new one and dispatched someone to purchase it. But the visitor insisted on keeping the old tie, claiming it was a gift from his family, and he was attached to it. Only after an experienced company security official protested quietly to company leaders that the accident was more than likely a scheme to get a chemical sample did company leaders insist on keeping the old tie.

Corporate industrial espionage occurs in almost every sector of the economy. According to Raymond Wannall, a former FBI assistant director for intelligence, "The phenomenon of industrial espionage is not confined to high-tech industries. It includes every place there's money to be made."

Noel Matchett, a former communications specialist with the National Security Agency who now consults for U.S. corporations, believes espionage can be useful to any business, regardless of its field. He advises that all companies doing business overseas are "at risk" of being spied on by another company. "It's not relegated just to high-tech companies," he says. "A lumber company bidding on a contract overseas can be a target. Wherever there is a profit to be gained, a real risk exists." Companies that fail to grasp this will face real challenges in the 1990s. He warns, "The ability of an organization to survive in the increasingly competitive global marketplace of the 1990s depends in large part on the security and control of its information. An organization's capability to successfully leverage its proprietary technology, execute partnerships and acquisitions, and win major procurements is continually threatened."

Intelligence operations run by one company against another can take a number of legal and illegal forms. Professor Claude Olney, who has studied the phenomenon of corporate spying, notes that "industrial espionage [between companies] is as serious and as sophisticated as that which is carried on between governments." Some companies are active participants in the international stolen-information market, willingly purchasing from anyone—rank amateurs like Bernard Mayles and professionals who have been in the business for years. Electronic eavesdropping, bugging, examining the contents of briefcases carried by visiting business executives, buying information from disgruntled employees, and other forms of information gathering are used by a surprising number of companies. Perfectly legal means of gathering intelligence are even more common. Some companies purposely try to lure away their competitors' senior employees in the hopes that they will bring and share valuable information. Others make use of the Freedom of Information Act and other government-disclosure provisions.

Business espionage is difficult to detect because it is often conducted by professionals. Sometimes businesses can only ponder what has happened. Says Jan Herring, a consultant with the Futures Group of Glastonbury, Connecticut, "You find companies that lose by $600 on a $5 million bid and ought to wonder why."

Most companies that strive to compete in the international market often do so against an industry leader. Depending on who that may be and how much of the market it controls, they have a difficult time matching the competitor with money or technology, and so they are tempted to dabble in the international stolen-secrets market. "That's why U.S. companies are target number one," says Richard Helms. As early as 1962, BusinessWeek referred to "the existence of a formalized international market in stolen industrial secrets, ready and eager to snap up any item." International information brokers, the magazine noted, were bringing "a rising wave of industrial espionage [that] is threatening a vital U.S. commercial asset: the productivity of its research and development." What was true in 1962 is even more true today.

According to business leaders and security consultants, there are currently two world centers for stolen industrial secrets: Geneva and Tokyo. Both are international in scope, catering to companies around the world. Unlike the economic espionage of intelligence agencies, these international networks sell their information to anyone who will pay the price. In several instances, victimized companies have entered the market and bought back the information that was taken from them, paying a high price. These informal centers where the peddlers of secrets congregate include a myriad of consultants, brokers, and attorneys who, by maintaining formal or informal relations with employees or consultants of major multinational companies around the world, buy and sell information.

In Japan, the Institute for Industrial Protection is the most visible example of that country's thriving international market in stolen information. In addition to teaching the skills described in Chapter 4, the school trains students how to take photographs in sensitive conditions and how to approach potential recruits. A similar school exists outside of Geneva.

Around the world, companies are engaged in a shadow war of spy versus spy as companies seek information on their competitors and access to their secrets. The lucrative pharmaceutical market is an area in which industrial espionage is common. According to a study by Tufts University, it takes an average of twelve years and $231 million to bring a new pharmaceutical product to market in the United States. But almost without exception, drug makers in Thailand, India, and Brazil manage to bring the same products to market a few months after their appearance in the United States. Tufts estimates that this problem alone costs U.S. companies four billion dollars annually. Companies in those countries can often reproduce a drug by simply dissecting a sample. But at times, when the drug is complex, these companies resort to fairly sophisticated intelligence operations to obtain the production recipe.

Robert Courtney, a former IBM security official who now consults for U.S. companies, traveled on business to Italy in 1989 for a major American pharmaceutical company. "There are people who have had their briefcases gone through in Italy," he says. "I'm one of them. One of the best ways I know [is] when they copied my stuff on an office copier. They screwed things up and gave me back some of the copied pages and some of my originals." In 1990, a senior representative of the pharmaceutical company Courtney consults for had the same thing happen.

In surprising numbers, foreign companies are often able to find a Bernard Mayles or a Mario Miscio out there who will sell them the information readily. Some Thai and Indian companies are said to hire private detectives to "cruise" American pharmaceutical-company circles in search of secrets. This activity usually includes regular social contact with company employees at parties and restaurants or through mutual friends. Such representatives regularly funnel to their foreign clients information concerning employees in financial difficulties or those leaving a company disgruntled. If the opportunity is ripe, an approach will be made to propose the sale of information.

A similar problem exists in the U.S. chemical industry. U.S.-designed chemicals are counterfeited in large quantities abroad, cutting into three billion to six billion dollars in sales annually. German, French, South Korean, Japanese, Israeli, and Taiwanese chemical companies, at times in cooperation with their government, work hard to procure information on the American chemical industry and on each other. Free-lance consultants are paid hundreds of thousands of dollars a year to track technological developments in this U.S. industry. The methods of collecting information include both the complex and the mundane. A surprisingly common method is flying over chemical plants, particularly during their construction or renovation. "You can get an enormous amount of information on processes, techniques, and methods of chemical production with some good aerial photos," says one security consultant whose clients include Dow and du Pont. "Whenever a new plant is under construction, the number of private flights in the area almost always goes up."

Satellite technologies can also be used to obtain detailed photographs, according to Arion Pattakos, who uses the SPOT Earth-Resources Satellite. The September 1990 issue of *Defense Electronics and Computing* showed a detailed photograph of the U.S. Navy base at Norfolk, Virginia. The picture was taken by the SPOT satellite and enhanced by computer imaging. As the magazine notes, "The quality was such that even a nonprofessional photo interpreter would be capable of deriving valuable intelligence." A similar set up for use on commercial targets could be enormously helpful.

Espionage in lucrative foreign markets is an even more common practice than that between U.S. companies. Following the collapse of the

Central European Communist regimes in 1989 and that of the Soviet Union in 1991, those countries' domestic and foreign intelligence services have been either disbanded or restructured, with the dismissal of thousands of intelligence agents. It has been estimated that in East Germany, eighty-five thousand full-time employees of the Stasi (the Ministry of State Security) lost their jobs overnight when the intelligence service was disbanded. Similar fates awaited numerous agents in Poland, Hungary, and Czechoslovakia. Some "defected," trying to sell information they had in exchange for a comfortable life in the West. Many others have had trouble finding jobs or have taken menial ones just to survive. But those with an entrepreneurial spirit are "marketing their specialized skills abroad," as one Western intelligence publication has put it. A recent classified ad in the *International Herald Tribune* read, "Former KGB agent seeks employment in similar field. Tel.: Paris 1-42.40.66.76." Says security consultant James Lamont, "If I were a former East European intelligence agent, I'd be going to German companies offering my services."

Some of these agents possess a variety of skills—knowing how to strengthen and intercept international communications, deploy effective surveillance or countersurveillance, recruit agents, cross borders undetected, and establish false-front companies and bank accounts, for example—that multinational corporations would find extremely useful. A number of developing countries have already retained the services of these former agents. Iraq and Syria, which maintained intelligence links with the Eastern-bloc intelligence services through the 1970s and 1980s, have reportedly hired some agents from the Romanian Securitate and the Stasi. Israel, according to the *Independent* of London, reportedly offers "less money but better benefits" than Iraq. Oil-rich Saudi Arabia has also hired some former Stasi agents, particularly those previously stationed in the Middle East.

A number of ex-agents from Eastern Europe have also been hired by multinational corporations around the world. Some companies have found a powerful business tool in the use of former Eastern-bloc spies, especially when it comes to doing business in their countries. Says intelligence expert R. D. Henderson, "A number of these intrusive skills are adaptable to commercial and industrial espionage, or conversely as an aid for devising enhanced protection of their own secrets." Henderson sees growth in this field: "Multinational corporations also may be interested in hiring those personnel with technical expertise for encryption and decoding. With the escalating need for secure global communications, these international entities are both vulnerable targets for economic intelligence gathering and increasingly interested in intelligence collection in their own right. The acquisition of even a few world-class cryptologists could qualitatively enhance their access to the secret communications of their commercial competitors, as well as of some foreign governments."

Several Western and Japanese multinational corporations have already sought out such former agents, who sell their knowledge of local affairs and in some instances act as "contract finder" agents or "government liaison" consultants. Large companies seeking assistance in gaining entry into the emerging free markets of Central Europe and the former Soviet Union have hired former agents to perform a variety of functions. According to German intelligence sources, several German companies have hired former agents from the Polish intelligence service to help them smooth their entry into the Polish market. One German electronics company is known to have hired three agents in Warsaw to track the business deals of its competitors. And in another instance, a German company hired a Slovak who was a former member of the Czech intelligence service, Statni Bezpecnost. The agent apparently collected intelligence on Czech companies to determine which one might be prime for a buyout. "Collection" included breaking into one company's headquarters and bugging the home of an executive from another. The availability of intelligence agents from the former Soviet bloc represents a new threat of espionage in the European marketplace.

Many companies in the United States, Asia, and Europe are hiring intelligence experts in their own countries in an attempt to gain a competitive advantage. American companies such as Eastman Kodak, Motorola, American Telephone and Telegraph, MCI Communications, Xerox, McDonnell Douglas, Ford, Digital Equipment, and Corning have all hired former U.S. intelligence officers in recent years to collect intelligence on competitors. The attitude of David Whipple, president of the Association of Former Intelligence Officers, is typical in U.S. business circles these days. "The French, the Germans and the Japanese spy on U.S. companies. Our companies should organize something similar to even the playing field."

258

A growing number of U.S. companies have created formal intelligence units. Motorola has set up one that bears a striking resemblance to the CIA's National Intelligence Council. The similarity is not so surprising, for it was organized and developed by former U.S. intelligence agents and officials. Members of the committee do everything, including debriefing the company's own executives each time they return from an overseas trip. Corning asks all of its employees, from the janitor up to the chief executive officer, to send tidbits on rivals to a central data base. Intelligence analysts then cull through it, classify it, and maintain detailed files on other companies. Du Pont recently hired James Geer, a former chief of counterintelligence at the FBI, to beef up security in order to guard against industrial espionage. Other companies, such as Pfizer, IBM, and International Paper, are doing the same.

William Colby is one of the growing number of former senior intelligence officials who consult with U.S. businesses about setting up in-house intelligence operations. He offers any U.S. company four rules of thumb: "First, establish a clear set of ethics. Second, centralize the intelligence collection. Third, pick one guy to circulate around the company to debrief other employees. And fourth, make use of a wide array of information services available to the company."

At times, companies engage in campaigns against each other that they carry on for several years. The Japanese film and camera company Fuji victimized Eastman Kodak for years by repeatedly gaining access to sensitive, secret information concerning the technology and methods used to produce cheap, single-use cameras. Fuji acted on the information quickly, managing to introduce its thirty-five-millimeter disposable camera in Japan before Kodak was even close to marketing its own invention. Kodak lost millions.

After this instance and several prior experiences, Kodak decided to turn the tables. It sought out and hired consultants to collect intelligence, several of whom had formerly worked for the CIA. With their help, Kodak uncovered Fuji's secret plans to launch a new version of the throw-away camera in the United States. This time it was Kodak who moved on the information, quickly rushing a matching model to market. In the United States, Kodak beat Fuji to the market.

By 1988, Fuji may have tried again to get critical Kodak information. That year a Fuji employee tried to enroll in several advanced courses at the University of Rochester, where hundreds of Kodak employees were taking courses. A Kodak spokesman told the university that it feared the prospective student might gain access to "proprietary information" that could be of enormous value to his employer, Fuji. After the controversy became public, the Fuji employee elected to go to MIT instead.

For every American company's success, there are many more failures. "American companies, more or less across the board, are three to five years behind their counterparts in Europe and Asia when it comes to business or competitor intelligence," says Herb Meyer, formerly of the National Intelligence Council. According to Michael C. Sekora, who once headed the Defense Intelligence Agency's Project Socrates, the real problem is attitude: American companies don't realize the United States is in an "economic war" with foreign competitors. Meyer more or less agrees. "American companies can be alarmingly naive about what foreign competitors may be willing to resort to," he says.

It does not appear that American businesses are unaware of the espionage being carried out around them. According to a May 1988 study by the University of Illinois at Chicago, *A Study of Trade Secrets Theft in High-Technology Industries,* the vast majority of businesses are aware that it takes place on a regular basis. Of the 150 companies responding to the survey, 48 percent reported that they had been victims of trade-secret theft at some time in the past. Of those, more than 90 percent reported incidents in the last ten years, and over 80 percent reported incidents in the last five years. In terms of targets, the survey found that information and data on research and technology were most frequently targeted (86 percent), followed by customer lists (28.8 percent), financial data (21.2 percent) and program plans (24.2 percent).

American businesses tend to believe they are victimized as a result of circumstances, not that they are part of a systematic effort on the part of foreign competitors to gain an advantage. Says one former director of the CIA now working as a business consultant, "Corporate America doesn't understand that intelligence—or, more bluntly, spying—is a business tool being used by most major companies around the world." Robert Courtney says that senior management "may know there's a problem, but they just don't know where the heck it is coming from."

American companies by and large do not engage in industrial espionage because it is not accepted practice. "Domestically, there's not a major problem," says Courtney. "U.S. companies don't operate that way." Herb Meyer concurs: "Call it puritanical, or whatever you like, but American companies tend to play aboveboard. It goes against our instincts to accept spying."

One reason for the growing level of corporate espionage is the increasing availability of technology, which makes spying so much easier. As *Technology Review* recently put it: "Sophisticated electronic bugs are no longer the exclusive bailiwick of government intelligence agencies: they're making their way to the private sector, too. With a few thousand dollars and a little know-how, it's now possible to build an assortment of electronic gear that will read computer screens from one hundred feet away, intercept phone calls, scan radio frequencies used by cellular telephones—and fit into an attaché case or two." Noel Matchett says, "I can go out and for five thousand dollars buy a computer-controlled signals intelligence intercept system. Commercial equipment can now be bought that ten years ago was available only to professional intelligence services."

U.S. companies such as General Electric have been repeatedly victimized by foreign eavesdroppers. According to GE sources, the company lost a number of bids in Europe during 1987–88, many by only a few thousand dollars. Consultants hired by the company eventually discovered that the company's satellite communications were being monitored by European competitors. So in November 1988 and early 1989, GE invested in one hundred STU-3 secure telephone units. "The phones cost us about three hundred thousand dollars, but we're winning bids in Europe again," says one GE official.

Corporate espionage against U.S. companies is also continuing to rise because of the increased availability of professionals willing to carry out spy operations. During the 1980s in particular, there was a dramatic rise in the number of private investigators going into business. And although the majority of them work aboveboard and within the limits of the law, thousands are willing to step over the line and work for foreign companies in a variety of capacities. More than fifty-five thousand private eyes are at work in the United States today—a 50-percent jump since 1980. In a recent study, federal law-enforcement agents posing as business executives approached 115 private detectives to see whether they would be willing to do something as simple (and illegal) as tap the telephone line of a business competitor. One in three agreed to do so—no questions asked—for fees ranging from thirty dollars to five thousand dollars. Of the 67 percent who said no, 40 percent offered instead to train someone else to do it properly, or suggested do-it-yourself phone taps and explained how to install them.

A detective who used to do bugging operations in Philadelphia and New Jersey for several German, Dutch, and French companies but now insists he has gone legitimate claims to have made quite a comfortable living planting bugs and installing wiretaps in the mid-1980s. Easy wiretaps were installed for twenty-five hundred dollars. Placing a bug in a corporate headquarters would cost a company ten thousand dollars. His techniques for bugs went from the basic (delivering a flower arrangement with a bug on it) to the more creative. In 1987, he appeared in an office posing as an office-supply delivery man and left a stapler with a bug in its base in the corporate boardroom the Friday before an important Saturday board meeting. That same year he entered another company, a regional office of Eli Lilly, posing as an electrician. He planted a bug in the power socket of the vice president's office. It was the perfect location: not only did the bug pick up everything, but it drew its power from the socket itself!

He was often contacted by phone by a company representative. "They wouldn't identify their company by name, but I could usually guess at it. Depending on which company they wanted done, I could then deduce who they were," he says. Once it was determined when the bug had to be in place and where it had to be located, he would draw up a plan of operation, including a price, and the deal would be made. "About 75 percent of my business was repeat customers." Transactions were strictly in cash. "Taxes weren't something you bothered paying with that sort of arrangement, and the money was really good."

Using private detectives is preferable to using company personnel, so many foreign companies have private detectives they use on a regular basis for a variety of illegal and legal tasks. Nothing is ever put in writing, so if he is caught, the detective is on his own. Nothing can link the act to the company directly. "Call it a perfect arrangement for plausible deniability," says the private detective. "If the private dick snitches, the word gets around, and he'll lose clients. So you usually offer a trade for information in exchange for no charges. The companies usually take it, figuring they're so smart that they'll catch you again the next time."

The growth of corporate intelligence as a tool has been enormous. According to Herb Meyer, "Throughout the world of commerce and industry, intelligence is on its way to becoming a key management tool for corporate chief executives and their top policy-making lieutenants. Indeed, the development of business intelligence and the subsequent emergence of business intelligence systems is the most striking and potentially important business trend of our time."

John Quinn, a former CIA specialist on the Far East, believes that intelligence is one key reason for Japan's economic success. Giant Japanese companies like Mitsubishi, Mitsui, Sumitomo, and others "are the closest thing that you will find to commercial intelligence agencies," he says. For cutting-edge industries like high-definition televisions and liquid-crystal displays, economic intelligence is "a very high, if not top, priority," according to Quinn. But, he says, even in less advanced industries "economic intelligence in general is regarded as a high priority." These commercial intelligence networks are massive, involving, in some instances, hundreds of employees. According to Herb Meyer, "The Mitsubishi intelligence staff in New York takes up two entire floors of a Manhattan skyscraper." Such networks collect vast amounts of information, most of it legally, to keep track of competitors and key business developments.

Intelligence can also be used by large corporations to acquire materials on the international black market. Legitimate businesses from time to time enter this world to save the millions of dollars that it would cost to buy the articles legally. Nowhere perhaps has this been more true than in the world of microelectronics and computers. In the early 1980s, the German electronics giant Siemens saved tens of millions of dollars every year by purchasing the services of Tony Maluta, a former intelligence officer for the U.S. Air Force who at one point had been stationed in Germany, performing duties that required top-secret clearance.

Maluta was part of a three-man ring that was apparently involved in the theft of thousands of advanced computer chips and then in their resale to large German electronics companies, including Siemens. One of those working with Maluta was a German businessman named Werner Bruchhausen, who had extensive business contacts in German industry and was on good terms with some senior Siemens officials. At times, he told Siemens about the availability of goods that could be acquired well below market price.

In November 1979, about ten thousand chips disappeared from the Intel Corporation's Santa Clara warehouse. The disappearance of the chips was not easy to detect. All ten thousand could have easily fit into a suitcase. The loss was discovered a month after the theft took place.

Intel was the industry leader at the time, and its prized 2732 chips were selling for about one hundred dollars apiece. Each one was capable of storing thirty-two thousand bits of data on its fingernail-sized surface, and they were being used by numerous companies in dozens of products—electronic games, copy machines, radar-jamming equipment, and missile-guidance systems. There was a two-month waiting list to purchase them; Intel couldn't make enough.

The chips were lifted by an Intel reliability technician who delivered them to John Henry Jackson, a five-time convicted felon who regularly sold stolen goods. Over a period of several years, Jackson had also trafficked more than one million counterfeit Intel chips. One of his buyers of stolen chips was a Tarzana, California, company called Mormac Microtechnology. At Mormac, an official named Patrick Lyle Ketchum was the "moneyman," according to law-enforcement officials, someone who marketed the stolen chips on the international black market. Two of Ketchum's associates were Tony Maluta and Werner Bruchhausen. His goal was to establish a pipeline to large foreign companies such as Siemens. Maluta and Bruchhausen had been in contact with Siemens officials through the late 1970s, knew of the company's interest in good Intel chips, and were aware of the fact that the company had dabbled in the lucrative gray market in computer chips, as had so many other large reputable companies. Siemens officials agreed to buy the chips, and a procedure was established.

The first batch was sent to an Arlington, Virginia, firm, Republic Electronics Corporation. Republic, in turn, sold the chips to a German firm, EBV Elektronik. While both firms deny knowing that the chips were stolen, a number of interesting facets of the sale should have at least raised their eyebrows. The transaction was in cash, pure and simple, which was not common business practice, and the chips were sold for six dollars apiece, or 6 percent of their market value. EBV was not a fly-by-night operation but an important supplier of Siemens's. Siemens also bought chips directly from Bruchhausen, who acted as an informal buyer on the gray market. Siemens got the chips for one third the price Intel itself was charging the German company.

By mid-1980, Intel was on to the fact that someone was stealing its chips by the hundreds of thousands, if not by the millions. The theft was costing the company millions of dollars every month, not only because of the lost merchandise, but because companies like Siemens were getting chips off the black market or the gray market rather than directly from Intel. So in cooperation with sheriff's deputies, the company began to delve into the murky world of the Silicon Valley stolen-chip market.

The Intel investigation went nowhere until late in 1980, when company officials received an interesting tip, a tip they really should never have received. One of Intel's preferred customers—Siemens—began complaining that some of the chips it had received had an abnormally high failure rate. Obviously, the managers at Siemens would never have complained had they been aware of the chips' dubious source. But in making their complaint they revealed the truth about one of their suppliers. It was the information Intel needed. Company officials knew that several thefts had taken place prior to the chips' going through quality control. Thus they reasoned that the Siemens chips were stolen. The company went to the Santa Clara sheriff's office with the information. It proved to be critical.

Intel officials almost immediately contacted Siemens purchasing agents to find out the names of their suppliers, particularly those who sold the batch of chips that were failing at a higher-than-normal rate. Siemens, to the shock and anger of Intel management, flat out refused to give the names. The German company stated that the suppliers were confidential and asked that the defective chips be replaced. Internal Intel memorandums reveal that Siemens said it was "reluctant" to name its suppliers out of "concern for the loss of their source of product." Bruchhausen and his cohorts had proved very valuable to Siemens, and the company wasn't about to give up the pipeline.

Intel management was outraged. After all, Intel was the source of the product—and had been the victim of a theft. And some Intel senior officials felt that Siemens was a willing participant in the black market. For a full month, Intel waged a quiet war against Siemens. It threatened to cut off all sales of its 2732s, which were critical to the German company. It considered seeking damages from Siemens in a U.S. civil court. It even considered asking the German courts to confiscate all Siemens products containing the black market chips, an action that, if successful, would have disrupted the entire Siemens distribution system, and that, in a sense, was the point. Intel was determined to make the German company's stubbornness as costly as possible. Finally, under pressure and fearful of legal action, Siemens "burned" its sources: it gave Intel the names of Bruchhausen and EBV.

The gray market in microelectronics is booming. Many companies participate in it because it offers an inexpensive means by which they can buy the components they need, and the major companies that participate usually suffer no retribution. A number of foreign companies hire consultants (including a surprising number of former intelligence officers) to find "suppliers" on the gray market. It is they who will face any legal repercussions.

U.S. concern about such technological espionage led the FBI and the CIA to establish a temporary task force in Silicon Valley in 1982 to track the relations that foreign multinationals were forging with gray-market participants. In early 1983, the task force concluded that numerous foreign companies, along with the Soviet-bloc countries, were "willful and visible participants in the market." The task force still exists today, operating out of San Jose.

In October 1982, the U.S. attorney for the northern district of California (which includes Silicon Valley) formed a "critical technology task force" to concentrate on corporate theft and espionage. The office hoped victimized companies would lend the support needed to prosecute the foreign companies and governments involved. But many U.S. companies have been unwilling to cooperate. The choice largely stemmed from self-interest, for many Silicon Valley companies are either doing research for or selling products to the federal government. The Pentagon and other government departments constantly watch such contractors to evaluate their security. As Lieutenant Robert McDiarmid of the Santa Clara Sheriff's Department put it, "If you report a theft, you could lose your defense contract."

Foreign companies collecting economic intelligence in the United States use a wide variety of legal means. Says Herb Meyer, "You can learn an incredible amount legally, especially if you are creative."

In 1980, the American Association for the Advancement of Science sponsored a visit to Silicon Valley. The trip included tours of a number of high-tech computer companies involved in a variety of projects. Of most interest, perhaps, was a half-day tour of the Hewlett-Packard integrated circuit processing laboratory and a similar lab at Fairchild Semiconductors. The tour was planned in conjunction with the annual January AAAS meeting, which was to be held in San Francisco.

Suspicious activities soon raised concerns in Silicon Valley circles. Fairchild noticed that after the tour was announced in November 1979, a number of employees of companies in Japan and Europe joined the AAAS and requested to go on the tour. Fairchild asked that advanced registrants note their citizenship, and AAAS agreed.

At first the annual meeting seemed to be going smoothly. The number of participants was up, and the seminars at the San Francisco Hilton were popular. The bus tour went ahead, apparently as planned, with Hewlett-Packard as the first stop. The participants got an extensive tour of the facility, including access to the company's processing laboratory. At particularly interesting and important parts of the tour, several foreign participants took numerous photographs. By some estimates, hundreds of pictures were snapped. (The camera of choice was the Nikon FM-2, a favorite of corporate-intelligence collectors; its shutter speed of 1/400th of a second allows the user to take photographs without worrying that the camera is vibrating.)

This activity did not go unnoticed by a Fairchild security specialist who was along on the tour, undercover. He quickly became extremely nervous. "They were snapping photos left and right of anything and everything involving the HP process," he says. "That's what we were afraid would be the problem for us." About three quarters of the way through the tour at Hewlett-Packard, the Fairchild employee asked to be excused and was escorted from the plant. He quickly found a pay phone and contacted his superiors. The Fairchild tour was canceled; the company claimed that the AAAS group was "behind schedule and would disrupt work at Fairchild."

Other legal methods of collecting intelligence include hiring consul-

tants and "representatives" who can provide information. What is important is not so much what skills or abilities the consultant has but what he
or she knows about a competitor or U.S. government policy. Such consultants are often former executives of U.S. companies or former government
officials. Sometimes the link is direct and clear-cut. According to a study
by the Center for Public Integrity, more than twenty senior U.S. trade
officials have registered as foreign agents. Forty-seven percent of the
former senior officials in the Office of the U.S. Trade Representative are
registered as foreign agents or work for consulting firms that represent
foreign companies or countries. In some instances, very little is done to
camouflage this effort.

The case of Walter Lenahan perhaps best demonstrates the power
that this sort of activity can give a foreign company. As a senior negotiator
for the Commerce Department, Lenahan was involved most specifically
with Asian countries, helping to establish textile quotas, quality-control
specifications, and classifications of which apparels would apply under
which tariffs. He knew what U.S. policy was and what it would be. He also
knew, no doubt, how one could maximize one's exports to the United
States by manipulating the system. Overnight he went from representing
the United States to representing the same foreign interests he had been
negotiating with. On Friday, February 7, 1986, Lenahan had been involved in sensitive textile talks on behalf of the United States. By Monday,
February 10, 1986, however, he had a new employer. On that day he
began working for several Hong Kong textile companies with large interests in the U.S. talks.

David Olive is another example. On January 1, 1990, Olive quit his
job as a State Department economic and commercial officer at the Japan
desk. At his post, he had worked on a variety of technology policies
relating to Japan, including the U.S. negotiating position on bilateral talks.
Within days, he was working for Fujitsu, the Japanese conglomerate, as
deputy general manager of the company's new Washington office.

No doubt Lenahan and Olive brought these foreign companies talent
and ability. But they also brought intelligence and information about the
U.S. position on a variety of trade and technology issues. The intelligence
was worth potentially hundreds of millions of dollars if used correctly.
Lenahan could tell the Hong Kong companies the U.S. negotiating fallback

position as well as the points to push on and challenge. What Olive brought Fujitsu was perhaps even more lucrative: he had reportedly been involved in the development of the negotiating strategy that the United States would take with Japan on high-technology issues ranging from semiconductors and space stations to superconductors and high-definition television. Olive was open about what he knew the job with Fujitsu included. "It's the company's embassy in Washington," he said about his office. "I'll be reporting on what's going on to those executives who want to know more about Washington and its processes."

Edward Gottfried perhaps best demonstrates how easy it is for foreign companies and countries to buy information and services in Washington. When he resigned in 1985, Gottfried had been a U.S. government employee for more than thirty years, having served his last ten years as the deputy director of the Commerce Department's Office of Textiles and Apparel. In that capacity, he had developed positions on, and represented the United States at, several trade negotiations. When Gottfried left the government, he set up Trade Consulting Services, a consulting firm for foreign countries and companies. His specialty remained textiles and apparel.

In 1989, after serving foreign companies for four years, Gottfried went back into government service, as a special textile adviser and negotiator in the Office of the U.S. Trade Representative. He headed textile-negotiation teams that hammered out agreements with a number of countries, including Pakistan. The agreement with that country, according to the U.S. Information Service, "enables Pakistan to ship much higher volumes of textiles to the U.S. in many product categories." The bilateral agreement became effective on January 1, 1990. By mid-April, Gottfried had left the government again. This time he went to Pakistan, to collect a fee for his services.

What concerns many American companies is not only that government officials have access to government information but that they also have access to a vast array of corporate information as well. R. Michael Gadban, a Washington trade lawyer who represents the U.S. semiconductor industry, said after the Olive case, "We are reluctant to give the U.S. government basic data because it will go straight to the Japanese. It's a problem."

But hiring former U.S. government and business officials is not the only way foreign companies gain access to U.S. corporate secrets. As noted in Chapter 2, one of the most popular forms of economic intelligence collection is through the use of the Freedom of Information Act. The FOIA has gone through a remarkable transformation since it was enacted in 1966. It was envisioned as a means by which journalists and private citizens could acquire information that would help open debate on public policy and form a more accountable government—it was supposed to promote the public interest. But today the act is more likely to be used for commercial interests, and many of those commercial interests are likely to be foreign companies. The FOIA gives the same rights to foreigners as it does to U.S. citizens. If a French or Italian drug company wants information on a drug produced by a U.S. company, it need only file a FOIA request with the Food and Drug Administration. (The fact that the FOIA gives foreign citizens access to U.S. secrets perhaps reached its absurdest point in 1981, when the Ayatollah Khomeini filed a FOIA request seeking access to CIA information on the then-exiled shah of Iran. The search was performed at taxpayers' expense.)

The number of commercial requests for information that are based on the FOIA is enormous. According to Stephen Markman, a former assistant attorney general at the Department of Justice, "Agencies all too often are required to devote substantial FOIA staff resources to the processing of requests from business entities which seek information solely for the purpose of gaining a commercial advantage over a competitor." No other country in the world offers anything similar to the FOIA.

More than 80 percent of the FOIA requests filed with the Food and Drug Administration originate with companies or persons working on their behalf. More than two thirds of the requests filed with the Federal Trade Commission come from corporations or their law firms. Similar attention is paid to the Environmental Protection Agency. Thousands of requests are made for documents relating to chemical compounds and information on production facilities, which must meet certain federal standards and therefore disclose their manufacturing processes. Numerous requests are also made to the EPA's Environmental Photographic Interpretation Center, whose staff of fifty pilots, photographers, and map readers are involved in taking and interpreting photographs of chemical facilities across the United States. These photos provide a cheap source of mapping information to corporations who simply file FOIA requests to obtain copies of them.

The damage done by the FOIA can often be immense. As one court noted in a dispute over the release of FOIA documents, FOIA information "could easily have competitive consequences not contemplated as part of FOIA's aim of promoting openness in government." No one needs to tell that to the U.S. chemical giant Monsanto. After spending several years and millions of dollars, Monsanto developed a herbicide that helped it dominate a $450-million-per-year market. The company jealously guarded its product's formula, but in 1982 the unimaginable happened: the EPA released the formula to a foreign competitor, which was represented by a U.S. lawyer. Said Monsanto spokesman Tom Slocum after the incident, "To develop and test a pesticide takes ten years and $25 million. The value of this type of information is not just money, it is also time and methods and procedure."

The number of foreign requests for information on research being conducted at government labs was so great in the 1980s that in 1987 President Reagan moved to suspend the FOIA, so that valuable technological research taking place in government laboratories would not have to be revealed to foreign requesters or the U.S. subsidiaries of foreign firms. (The policy change was not approved by Congress.) "Commercial espionage use of the act is expanding," says James O'Reilly, a lawyer for Procter and Gamble. According to the U.S. Chamber of Commerce, the use of the FOIA by foreign competitors has become "a way to cut research and development costs." A number of U.S. companies, including Sikorsky Aircraft, Air Cruisers, Dow Chemical, Honeywell, and Boeing, have "seen their products copied elsewhere because of this problem."

The number of foreign requesters is difficult to establish. According to Stephen Markman, the government does not keep track of requests by foreign entities. The problem is complicated by the fact that many foreign companies make their requests through U.S. consultants, lawyers, or representatives, who do not need to disclose whom the request is for. Other foreign companies subscribe to "service companies," which gather information through the FOIA and then sell it. One of the more successful of these is FOI Services, Incorporated, of Rockville, Maryland. The company files more than eight thousand requests annually with the FDA alone.

Mergers and acquisitions are another fertile area for the collection of intelligence. As former CIA (and FBI) Director William Webster has warned, mergers can be an effective means of collecting intelligence. Admiral Bob Inman regards purchasing small U.S. companies and turning them into subsidiaries as a "highly effective means of acquiring technology secrets." It's a "scurrilous but legal practice," he says, that is simply a way of "scooping up the technology secrets and taking them home to their countries, for their use." John Quinn concurs. He notes that mergers and acquisitions mean access to technological and corporate information. "The Japanese find this a very practical way to acquire needed technology from the United States. Frequently this is a critical technology." He believes it is no coincidence that foreign mergers and acquisitions "are primarily in the high-tech fields."

Japanese companies are not the only ones to use mergers and acquisitions as an intelligence tool. In 1988, several French companies secretly attempted to acquire one of the Boeing Company's subcontractors. It was a medium- to small-sized company involved in the production of specialized machine tools used to produce the wing components of Boeing's commercial aircraft. The French companies were actually attempting the acquisition for the European consortium Airbus. Boeing managers found out about the scheme and headed it off by proposing an alternative buyout. "Had they succeeded," says one senior Boeing official, "they would have known an enormous amount about production processes, capabilities, costs, specifications, and future plans. It would have given them a lot of help and a leg up." In August 1990, the French national computer company Bull announced plans to purchase Honeywell Federal Systems. According to Herb Meyer, the purchase was "an amazing display of French gall." The Honeywell unit provides computer systems integration products and technical services to the U.S. government itself.

What makes mergers and acquisitions such a useful method of collecting intelligence and gathering technological information is that they offer a foot in the door to a private meeting. An outsider can suddenly learn every technology secret that the company possesses, and it can gain access to critical information concerning any firms the company may have dealt with. Because many blue chip high-tech companies rely on numerous small contractors and subcontractors to supply them with goods and services, those critical suppliers are vulnerable targets for buyout by a rival. "We are quickly seeing an economic war between the major industrial powers develop," warns one former director of the CIA who consults for American business. "Mergers and acquisitions are a great way to buy off your rival armies, just like the Italian princes did to each other in the sixteenth century."

13

Reaching for the Stars

These software modules no doubt substantially aided Japanese efforts to challenge us in the space business.
—Senior official, Space Applications International Corporation

On February 20, 1990, Steven J. Bosseler was sitting in his southern California office, quietly going over paperwork. Bosseler, a special agent in strategic investigations for the U.S. Customs Service and a veteran of the CIA, was expecting another ordinary day. Then the phone rang. He picked up the receiver, and on the other end an individual who asked to remain a confidential informant began to tell him a tale. It was a story about Ronald Joshua Hoffman, a rocket scientist who until recently had been working for Science Applications International Corporation. It was a story of how Hoffman was selling top-secret advanced computer software for space systems to foreign entities, not to America's military rivals but to a friend: Japan.

The caller described his suspicions, based on what he knew about Hoffman's activities. The caller went on to describe the information that he and his wife had accumulated on the rocket scientist. The wife had worked for two and a half years as an office administrator under Hoffman, who had been a general manager for SAIC until his forced resignation in

January 1990. The source went on to describe in great detail Hoffman's activities at SAIC on behalf of several Japanese corporations.

What Hoffman was working on at SAIC was not an ordinary project. Indeed, he was the SAIC general manager on a secret research project under contract with the U.S. Air Force armaments laboratory at Elgin Air Force Base. SAIC had been hired to research and produce a computer software system module called CONTAM, which was used to study the plume (that is, the missile exhaust) emitted by a rocket engine lifting a payload into orbit. By studying the exhaust, design engineers are able to make modifications and improvements in the design of rockets and missiles. It also enables the user to identify and categorize "signatures" of individual rocket engines by their exhaust. With this capacity, a target would be able to identify the type of rocket or missile that has been launched and determine how best to counteract it. Thus CONTAM has also been used in the Strategic Defense Initiative's research. In addition, the technology proved to be particularly helpful in the design of advanced satellite surveillance systems, particularly the U.S. Air Force Defense Support Program, which detects enemy launches of ballistic missiles worldwide through a network of global satellites and provides warnings to national command authorities.

Hoffman had worked for SAIC since 1978 and was a productive employee, overseeing several important projects during his tenure. But he was also dissatisfied with his financial position. Recalls one former co-worker, "Ron was always down about money. There was never enough, as far as SAIC was concerned." And so in the early 1980s Hoffman elected to start a side venture, one that would provide him with extra income—substantial extra income. It would also prove to be a wonderful vehicle through which foreign entities could gain access to some of America's most critical technology secrets.

Hoffman set up Plume Technology, Incorporated, and ran it out of his home. PTI was a business that would not have existed had it not been for Hoffman's work at SAIC. Indeed, most of what PTI was pedaling was SAIC research, much of it secret and classified. It was not surprising that when Hoffman offered materials on the market, he found eager buyers.

The availability of the CONTAM technology could not have come at a better time for several Japanese companies that in 1986 had made a decision to enter the space technology business aggressively. According to the *Economist,* six companies—Mitsubishi Heavy Industries, Nissan, Ishikawajima-Harima, NEC, Mitsubishi Electric, and Toshiba—set a goal of cornering 20 percent of the world market for space applications by the year 2000. Mitsubishi in particular began investing millions in its rocket program. Mitsubishi Electric, a prime contractor for Japan's Earth-Resources Satellite (ERS-1), looked to diversify its space-technology program. It planned to develop an advanced lightweight spacecraft that would revolutionize space exploration. The design and production of a new booster rocket, the H-2, was also in the works. Perhaps the most ambitious part of Mitsubishi's vision was the development of an international space station for the twenty-first century, to be built in conjunction with other Japanese contractors.

But Mitsubishi Electric and the other companies knew they had a long way to go before they could see their plans fulfilled. At the time, Mitsubishi Electric was a contractor for thirteen satellites in Japan and a subcontractor for nine others around the world; it could hardly be regarded as a cutting-edge company in the aerospace business. Most of the other companies also had little experience in the space-applications field and had a significant technological gap to close before they could begin to compete effectively with the U.S. and European leaders in the field. And whereas much of the gap would be closed by ambitious research and development, great progress would also be made with the help of technology secrets these companies would purchase from Ronald Hoffman. In all, Hoffman would receive over $750,000 between 1986 and 1990 from four Japanese companies for the sale of this secret advanced technology, a small price for the companies to pay, given that the development of CONTAM cost U.S. taxpayers tens of millions of dollars. According to a SAIC official, the research would have cost the Japanese companies more than one hundred million dollars to replicate.

Hoffman's relationship with the Japanese companies began in 1986, when he contacted them, telling them what he had for sale. He began the slow and laborious process of marketing the information by writing the companies and even visiting Tokyo. In a brazen manner, he often had his subordinates at SAIC help with the administrative tasks of putting together the PTI proposals. According to Steven Bosseler, "Hoffman routinely used the SAIC administrative staff, telephones, address, fax machine, office equipment and other necessary business paraphernalia to conduct PTI business. This business included the sale to various Japanese firms of the CONTAM module, including data, components and systems, expertise in the field and training for employees in use of the system."

It didn't take long for Hoffman to find an interested buyer. And despite the fact that the companies almost certainly knew that CONTAM was classified and secret, they didn't seem bothered by the knowledge. Indeed, it probably made the information all the more alluring. The first company to bite was the Nissan Motor Company. Nissan was a relatively new entrant in the space technology business, and it undoubtedly saw in CONTAM a great opportunity to catch up. After four months of tenuous negotiations, on September 9, 1986, Hoffman exported to Nissan the CONTAM software. For the sale, Hoffman received a wire transfer of more than fifty-six thousand dollars, sent to the Security Pacific National Bank in Century City, California, to the account of Plume Technology, Incorporated.

The second sale to Nissan was outlined in PTI proposal 88-12, according to Hoffman's records. Dated May 15, 1988, the agreement provided for the sale, export, and delivery of two important components of CONTAM software, TCC and TMIP, which would offer Nissan direct help in the area of rocket design, an area in which the company was lagging. These two modules would allow Nissan to forgo extensive testing, in effect using the test results that were incorporated into the modules. The software was shipped to a front company in Los Angeles, KBK, Incorporated. Nissan wanted the software sent to KBK in case there were problems with the export and to avoid a direct link to Hoffman.

The CONTAM software was delivered on July 1, 1988. Hoffman also agreed to arrange for training on use of the software. Nissan paid Hoffman thirty-six thousand dollars for the software and seventy-five hundred dollars for installation and training. It was a bargain. According to Assistant U.S. Attorney Stephen A. Mansfield, who investigated the case, the technology Nissan bought had been developed "at a cost to taxpayers of millions of dollars."

CONTAM offered Mitsubishi Electric, the space-industry leader in Japan, a step up, allowing it to move to a higher level of technological development at minimum cost. Hoffman's connection with Mitsubishi was more detailed and more consistent than that with any of the other Japanese companies. "They, perhaps more than anybody over there, understood the value of CONTAM," says one SAIC employee. Hoffman sold CONTAM to Mitsubishi Electric on September 30, 1986, for $44,393.

Mitsubishi Heavy Industries of Nagoya, Japan, stepped up to the counter in 1987. This company was interested in some of the more advanced CONTAM software programs Hoffman was offering. They in particular wanted Monte Carlo and Chemkin, two programs that served important functions in the assessment of rocket design. PTI proposal 87-79 gave officials at Mitsubishi Heavy Industries four options for CONTAM software modules.

Once the word got around in Mitsubishi circles, everyone involved in space research wanted information from Hoffman. The Mitsubishi Research Institute in Tokyo was very interested in what the rocket scientist had to offer. The institute does extensive research for Mitsubishi companies on a variety of technologies, most of which are part of the company's efforts to broaden its standing in the space technology business. So when officials at Mitsubishi Heavy Industries mentioned what Hoffman was selling, the research institute was all too interested. PTI and Mitsubishi Research Institute agreed to a package that included basic CONTAM software as well as training and consultation in the setup and use of the modules. In total, the Mitsubishi Research Institute paid Hoffman $65,400 for the software: $39,000 for its delivery on May 26, 1987; $19,800 shortly thereafter for a "training workshop"; and $6,600 on completion of a follow-up consultation on January 22, 1988.

At the same time that Hoffman was negotiating with Mitsubishi Heavy Industries, he was also negotiating with Ishikawajima-Harima Heavy Industries for the sale of CONTAM. IHI was very interested in the CONTAM software, and Hoffman was all too eager to do business. Indeed, he was so willing to please that he even offered to sell IHI a sweetener: programs that had just become available to NASA. On May 18, 1988, he sent a letter to IHI stating that a new module of CONTAM software known as TRASYS was expected shortly by NASA. He offered IHI the option of waiting for the release of the software to ensure that they receive the most "up to date module available." The two parties eventually came to terms on a price and signed a contract. But the contract was not clear on whether the new TRASYS software would be among that which IHI was buying. When IHI took delivery of the package on May 31, 1988, and the TRASYS was not included, company officials were upset.

The correspondence that ensued is instructive in delineating exactly what IHI was expecting from the deal. On October 2, 1989, Hoffman sent a letter to IHI officials stating that "it was our intent to give IHI the best possible product, that is, the new version," but, he noted, the new version of TRASYS had come out after the two companies agreed on the final contract. Hoffman further noted that "IHI was aware that PTI was not the author of TRASYSII"—IHI knew Hoffman was not authorized to be selling the software modules in the first place. IHI was frustrated, but the software was simply too valuable to pass up. The relationship continued despite the disagreement.

Meanwhile, Mitsubishi officials were undoubtedly pleased with what they were getting from Hoffman. In early 1989, they began negotiating for the latest software packages available in the CONTAM modules. The research at SAIC had been proceeding, and more recent versions were available. Hoffman said he would be happy to provide them. In particular, what Mitsubishi officials were most interested in was Chemkin and Monte Carlo as well as a module code-named PLIMP. According to a senior official at SAIC, "These software modules no doubt substantially aided their efforts to challenge us in the space business."

For the advanced software, Hoffman wanted a big fee, and Mitsubishi was willing to pay it. On November 1, 1989, Mitsubishi headquarters in Tokyo sent Hoffman a fax stating the company's intention to pay him $372,400 by the end of December. A final payment of $72,000 would be made at the end of February 1990. Hoffman counteroffered. He asked for $100,000 on November 25, $72,000 on January 1, and the balance to be sent on January 15. Mitsubishi agreed, and the deal was sealed. In the third week of November, Hoffman sent the valuable secret software directly to Mitsubishi headquarters—by Federal Express.

In addition to selling the secret software packages to Japanese companies, Hoffman also attempted to make sales elsewhere around the world.

According to Steven Bosseler, there are documents that link Hoffman to companies in Germany and Italy. Hoffman also approached the Israeli

Defense Ministry about the possible sale of CONTAM software. Specifically, on January 14, 1987, he submitted a proposal to Defense Ministry offices in Haifa concerning the sale of a vast assortment of CONTAM software modules, installation of the software, and the provision of a training workshop. His price: $423,000.

Hoffman tried to interest MBB Erno Raumfahrttechnik GmbH of Germany, offering modules as well as training workshops. The asking price was ninety thousand dollars. He also spoke with Italy's Aeritalia, in Corso Marche. In April 1986, he met with Aeritalia officials to discuss the possible sale. On May 25, 1987, he wrote the company, offering updates on pricing. In this letter, Hoffman stated that the prices were somewhat higher than originally discussed due to the significant upgrades in the CONTAM software since the meeting a year earlier. He also offered the sale of two additional modules, TRASYS and VNAP2. "There are no documents available reflecting whether or not a sale was made," says Bosseler; only Hoffman and the companies involved would know.

Between 1986 and 1990, Ronald Hoffman made an excellent living by selling CONTAM secrets, earning more than $750,000. And yet each of the buyers got a bargain. The foreign companies received the most advanced modules for rocket and missile design available at a fraction of what it would have cost them to develop the software independently. And because of Hoffman's position at SAIC, they were assured continual upgrades. So when the cozy relationship started to unravel in January 1990, the companies were not pleased.

On January 2, 1990, the confidential informant and his wife went to Dennis Heist, chief counsel for SAIC in La Jolla, California. They told him what they knew of Hoffman's dealings. The wife revealed that she regularly saw evidence of Hoffman's activities on behalf of Japanese multinationals. To support their claims, they brought with them actual memos and faxes concerning the sales. In late December 1989, the couple had gone to SAIC offices late one night and started to photocopy documents concerning PTI and Hoffman. The rocket scientist had carelessly left incriminating documents lying on his credenza, including faxes confirming wire transfers from Mitsubishi to his PTI account.

Based on this information, Heist confronted Hoffman the next day about the sales to the Japanese multinationals. Hoffman promptly resigned from SAIC and left the premises immediately. For Heist and SAIC, the problem appeared to be solved—until three days later, when Heist was unable to locate a number of original documents pertaining to CONTAM software. Checking for clues, he reviewed tapes maintained by the company's security department. Sure enough, the film showed Ronald Hoffman late on the evening of his resignation, leaving his office with boxes of documents. Hoffman was apparently still in business.

Despite that midnight haul, Hoffman still wanted more from SAIC. On March 22, 1990, he persuaded Carl Maag, an engineer employed at SAIC's Century City office, to meet him after work. Hoffman pleaded with Maag to give him the latest CONTAM software codes; Maag refused. On April 2, Hoffman telephoned another SAIC office, this one in Torrance, California, and spoke with Rich Ziskind, the division manager. He told Ziskind he was being poorly treated by his ex-colleagues and asked him to send CONTAM software and documents to his residence. Ziskind flat-out refused and hung up.

With Hoffman still very much in the business of selling CONTAM software and with him aggressively seeking CONTAM upgrades, Steven Bosseler and an officer of the Air Force Office of Special Investigations became involved in an undercover operation designed to bring Hoffman to justice. The two posed as international brokers who wished to purchase CONTAM software on behalf of a client in South Africa. Bosseler told Hoffman that the South African firm was in the aerospace business and was attempting to launch a rocket booster and communications satellite into space.

On April 26, 1990, the three men met at the Stouffer Concourse Hotel on Century Boulevard in Los Angeles. Hoffman presented Bosseler with a proposal. Bosseler said he would look it over and get back to him. A second date was set, for May 3, again at the Stouffer. At the second meeting, Hoffman and Bosseler discussed the terms of the sale, and Bosseler pressed Hoffman about the legality of the proceeding. When Bosseler said the CONTAM was really intended for the South African Defense Ministry and not for an aerospace company, Hoffman said, "I'm not going to write that down."

Jorge Urquijo, a special customs agent on assignment with Bosseler, pressed Hoffman on the legality of the sale as well. Urquijo wondered if there might be repercussions in "backdooring" the law. Hoffman side-stepped the issue. "I don't want to put it in those terms at all," he said. "I think from this point on, we all need to be very careful about the terms that we use." Hoffman clearly didn't care what the law said, only that he make the deal.

The deal was consummated, and another meeting was set. On May 22, the three men went through the details of the exchange: where the software would go, and where the training would take place. Since South Africa was out of the question, they agreed that West Germany would be a good place to "sidestep" the law. After nearly two hours, the terms and arrangements were finalized.

The transaction was to take place on June 14. Urquijo and Bosseler met Hoffman at the Los Angeles International Airport at 12:15 P.M. Hoffman drove them to the Stouffer Concourse Hotel, where they signed the contract. At 1:45, Hoffman drove Bosseler to the Federal Express office on Imperial Highway near the airport. Hoffman promptly put the CONTAM software into a Federal Express shipping box and sealed it. He then handed it to the clerk and gave Bosseler the shipping form. Hoffman had written that the carton contained "business documents" and "magnetic tape." Destination: "Bonn, FRG." The two men then returned to the hotel, where they met up with Urquijo. Bosseler handed Hoffman a check for $150,000, which Hoffman graciously accepted. At that point, he was arrested.

In April 1992, a jury in Los Angeles found Ronald Hoffman guilty of export violations and the sale of secret government technology. He was sentenced to six years in prison.

14

Socrates and Snowflakes

It has been known for quite some time that economic espionage takes place. But only now people are starting to talk about it. The real question is what do you do about it?

— Richard Helms, former director of the CIA

One day during his tenure as the director of the CIA, Admiral Stansfield Turner gathered together seven senior agency officials to discuss the possibility of a new role for the agency. Turner was interested in perhaps developing an economic espionage capability. He recalls, "I said, 'Even if an agent stumbles across some information that might be useful to a U.S. company, they couldn't do anything with it right now.'" He asked the senior intelligence officials what they thought of the plan. "Six of the seven assembled told me it would never work. One of them told me, 'Agents will risk their lives and perform dangerous missions for their country. But they won't do the same for General Motors or IBM.'"

Throughout the Cold War era, America's chief intelligence mission has been to learn more about the Soviet Union and its allies while using covert action to thwart their advances against U.S. and Western interests. The U.S. intelligence community did not perform flawlessly, but there can be little doubt that it substantially helped the United States and the West during major crises and in the face of threats to our security. "Our number-one mission during the Cold War was countering the Soviet threat," says Herb Meyer. "And I have to say I think we did a pretty good job."

Like a medical specialist who has assisted in the eradication of the disease he has studied for forty years, the U.S. intelligence community is groping for a new mission. With the Soviet threat vanquished, the intelligence community must redefine itself and its mission to meet the new challenges facing the United States, or it risks dramatic cuts or even extinction. After all, the U.S. intelligence community as we know it today—with its technical gadgetry and large budget—was born in the early stages of the Cold War. Senator Daniel Patrick Moynihan of New York has already called for the elimination of the CIA as well as dramatic cuts in other intelligence agencies in light of the collapse of the Soviet Union. Says one former deputy director of operations at the CIA, "Like that singer put it, 'Times they are a-changin'.' But change will not come easy."

The intelligence agencies are directed by programs and personnel to focus primarily on the now nonexistent superpower rivalry. "It is difficult to exaggerate how thoroughly the gathering of information on the Soviet Union, and especially its military power, has dominated U.S. intelligence operations since the Cold War began," Turner wrote.

When the Berlin Wall fell in November 1989, senior officials at CIA headquarters in Langley, Virginia, began thinking about the world of intelligence in a post–Cold War era. The view of former CIA (and FBI) Director William Webster and his immediate aides was that the security threats to American interests had not dissipated but, rather, were changing. And Webster set in motion a period of soul searching that is likely to continue well into the mid-1990s. The agency is exploring new missions and means by which intelligence can be applied to the protection of U.S. interests. A renewed debate has also been brewing in intelligence circles over the same issue raised by Stansfield Turner during his tenure as CIA director: should the United States develop an industrial espionage capability? The debate pits advocates against skeptics in the debate of the sort of role U.S. intelligence can play in a world in which economic competition and rivalry have become increasingly important. "The new importance and central role that economics is now playing in world affairs is going to dramatically affect the world of intelligence," says Dr. Ray Cline, a former deputy director of the CIA. "There's probably going to be a new spy race heating up," says Raymond Wannall, a former assistant FBI director for intelligence. The question is where the United States will fit in.

The debate over economic espionage is taking place because espionage threats remain despite the collapse of the Soviet Union—and they reflect the new form of competition between countries. Rather than emanating from the KGB, espionage now comes from Third World intelligence services and those of our leading allies. And rather than serving military interests, espionage is being used as a competitive tool. Senator David Boren, Chairman of the Senate Select Committee on Intelligence, explains that "the spy race is heating up against commercial targets in the U.S." He believes the situation merits a review of American intelligence policy: "We are going to have to think about the role we want our own intelligence service to play in terms of protecting America's economic and commercial interests around the world."

In the face of economic espionage by our competitors, and with a large and effective American intelligence apparatus available, some are pondering the previously unthinkable: spying on our friends and allies for the sake of U.S. industry. The fact is the U.S. intelligence community could offer help to U.S. industry were it to engage in economic espionage. Says Michelle Van Cleave, deputy director of the White House Office of Science and Technology Policy, "Clearly the Intelligence Community has the ability to provide commercially useful information such as details about competitor firms, advanced plans for major foreign projects, financing arrangements and government and industry research projects." But for her and many others the real question remains, Is it feasible?

There can be little doubt that economics and technology will loom larger in the future of intelligence collection. The general consensus appears to be that the U.S. must, and will, redirect its intelligence assets, focusing less on military issues and more on economic and technology issues. The realities of the post–Cold War era largely account for this change. The faded Soviet threat frees up intelligence assets. Agents, satellites, and eavesdropping facilities will now be deployed against a wider array of targets.

But the collapse of the Soviet Union has also given U.S. intelligence officials the freedom to deal more boldly with a continuing and troubling problem: the activities friendly agents are carrying out against U.S. businesses and government. Minus the pervasive threat of the Soviet Union, the issue of economic espionage can now be addressed and discussed. Quite simply, fissures or disagreements within the Western alliance no longer have the dangerous consequences they might have had during the height of the superpower struggle. "We won the Cold War," says former CIA Director Richard Helms. "Now this subject can be aired out." He adds, "It has been known for quite some time that economic espionage regularly takes place. But only now people are starting to talk about it. The real question is, What the heck do you do about it?"

The big question is the way in which the intelligence community should approach the economic issues. Should U.S. intelligence agencies simply track general global economic trends, or should they target specific industries and companies? Should the U.S. response be limited to blocking the economic espionage of allies through counterintelligence, or should it include active operations to acquire foreign secrets covertly? And can or should the information acquired be shared with U.S. companies to make them more competitive?

Despite persistent denials, the U.S. intelligence community has spied on friends and allies in the past. This has largely taken the form of passive collection of information—making sure to note information when it is encountered. In reevaluating U.S. intelligence cooperation with its allies in 1981, the Reagan administration took information compiled by the CIA under Stansfield Turner and ordered intelligence agents around the world to begin systematically watching the intelligence activities of friendly countries on a regular and orderly basis. This was to get a coherent and up-to-date sense of what friendly intelligence services were doing and how they were using their resources. "We wanted and needed to know what exactly our allies were doing, most specifically to us," says a former U.S. intelligence official.

In August 1981, the Defense Intelligence Agency sent out orders from the Pentagon to all DIA personnel and defense attachés at foreign embassies. A similar set of orders went out to CIA agents overseas. All were stamped NOFORN, meaning not to be shown to any foreigners. The message instructed U.S. defense attachés and other intelligence officers to report on a continuing basis about the intelligence services of Canada,

Israel, West Germany, France, South Korea, and thirty other countries, all friendly or neutral. This was a low-key but persistent monitoring program aimed at getting a better understanding of the operations of friendly intelligence services. The orders specifically sought "details" on the services' "locations, operations, capabilities, intentions and operations conducted or planned against U.S. targets. These include government as well as private sector American targets."

Whereas the initial purpose of the orders was to track the activities of certain foreign intelligence services to understand them better, in the end they were used in attempts to modify the behavior of these services. Then CIA Director William Casey used some of the information collected by U.S. agents to challenge allied governments to use their intelligence assets more wisely. Casey regularly told friendly countries that their assets were not being used against the enemy but, rather, were being wasted on the United States. "It was a bully pulpit," says one former CIA official. "Casey wanted them to quit wasting their assets on us and focus rather on the main enemy." Casey ended the orders in 1986, but the exercise served to heighten U.S. awareness of, and concern for, friendly spying. It was some of the information compiled on Israel during those years that led the United States to come down so hard during the Pollard case.

During the same period that the United States began watching these intelligence services more closely, the CIA also began focusing on the technological developments achieved by this country's economic competitors. According to Michelle Van Cleave, "Beginning about ten years ago the intelligence community began to devote additional resources to examining science and technological developments outside the traditional target countries. . . . Recently we have seen a significant increase in Science and Technology intelligence products with an economic competitiveness focus."

The Defense Intelligence Agency's Project Socrates, launched in 1984, was somewhat similar to the CIA effort. Its purpose was to track the developments and technology strategies of economic competitors such as Japan, Germany, France, Great Britain, South Korea, and Taiwan. Socrates focused on high-tech and so-called strategic industries, noting significant mergers and acquisitions involving foreign companies, national technology policies, and technology strategies. According to a former DIA official,

Socrates was a "substantial, comprehensive and valuable intelligence tool" for understanding the international technological competition shaping up among the United States, Western Europe, and Japan. It in some instances accurately predicted the moves and strategies of other countries, using computer simulations. But in 1990, President Bush canceled Project Socrates, saying it reeked of an "industrial policy."

Despite the setback at the DIA, in recent years the U.S. intelligence community has grown increasingly interested in taking an active intelligence stance against economic espionage carried out by allied countries as well as in the possibility of collecting intelligence on this country's competitors.

In July 1990, William Webster, then director of the CIA, announced that the agency was beginning to think about how to reorient its activities in the post–Cold War era. "Increasingly, economic interrelationships affect stability and, hence, national security," he said. "We want to be on top of the trends, the resources and constraints of nations and regions, financial transactions, and technology. That means, both overtly and covertly, collecting economic intelligence to permit our policymakers to make wise decisions and to keep the playing field as level as possible. Knowing what our competition is doing and being able to confront it or confound it, whichever the case may be." But then Webster cautiously stepped back and made clear that he did not plan to get into the business of engaging in economic or industrial espionage. "We're not turning to the business of spying on business," he insisted. "What we are turning to is a better and richer understanding of those economic trends that affect us all." Mark Mansfield, a CIA spokesman, said shortly after Webster's speech, "Our focus in the future will be in three areas. Economic capabilities and constraints, trade and financial strategies, and technology."

Soon after his speech, Webster instructed senior agency officials to begin working with the Office of the U.S. Trade Representative, the Commerce Department, and the Treasury Department to explore ways in which to increase cooperation in making intelligence more readily available to policymakers in those bureaucracies. But he also wanted the information made more relevant. "We wanted intelligence that was good and relevant," says an official in the Office of the U.S. Trade Representative. "We wanted the sort of information that we could take to trade negotiations just like our arms negotiators had during the Cold War. Slowly but surely, that is starting to happen."

At the same time, the CIA has made a conscious decision to focus more on economics when seeking new employees. The agency has become less interested in military and political specialists and more concerned with persons who have knowledge of technology and economics. Tellingly, this applies to both analysts and operatives. "We will need greater human capabilities and personnel equipped with economic expertise," announced Senator David Boren in early 1990. The decision was based on the opinion of CIA Director Webster and President Bush that economic questions have a "new importance" in American interests. President Bush specifically called for "a new emphasis on broader global economic and trade issues" in the interests of keeping the United States competitive.

At the same time, an economic-competitiveness task force was created at CIA headquarters. It was made up of senior CIA officials as well as some outsiders, mostly former intelligence officials now involved in consulting for major corporations. Significantly, the task force included three officials from the agency's Operations Directorate, which is responsible for clandestine operations overseas. Its establishment indicated that although he was publicly saying the CIA had no interest in economic espionage, Webster was a thorough director of the agency who wanted all aspects of a topic explored.

What Webster wanted the task force to do was look into questions concerning the sort of intelligence-collection methods the CIA could feasibly engage in when it came to economic and technological intelligence. Would it include only the use of open—that is, public—sources? Could technical means—communications intercepts and satellites—be effectively used? What about the thorny question of agents and clandestine methods?

Webster instructed his Science and Technology Advisory Panel to look at the other side of the issue. From that group, he wanted to know what sort of intelligence would be most useful, whether economic intelligence or espionage would offer much help in making the United States more competitive, whether it would be possible to share intelligence with U.S. corporations, and what sort of counterintelligence policy was feasible in a technology-oriented economy.

During his confirmation hearings in the fall of 1991, Robert Gates, now director of the CIA, was very blunt about what he saw as the problem of economic espionage. "We know that foreign intelligence services plant moles in our high-tech companies," he told the Senate Select Committee on Intelligence. "We know that they rifle briefcases of our businessmen who travel in their countries. We know they collect information on what we're doing."

In a December 1991 interview with the *Washington Post,* CIA Director Robert Gates sounded a tone similar to Webster's as far as prescriptions were concerned. But he also—ever so slowly and slightly—opened the door concerning the role the CIA might take in economic intelligence. Although Gates expressed concern that economic intelligence is "potentially a bottomless well for the intelligence community," he did note that there were two areas in which U.S. intelligence could make a "unique contribution." The first, he said, was in uncovering foreign economic espionage in the United States, and the second was in gathering information about the attempts of other governments to violate international trade agreements and other basic rules of fair play. For the first time, a director of central intelligence linked CIA policy and operations to U.S. competitiveness.

Richard Kerr, deputy director of the CIA, said much the same in another interview: "We have done a fair amount in terms of competitiveness issues, where countries are using in an either illegal way or in an unfair way practices that disadvantage us. Where you're talking about governments and industry working together to disadvantage another government or industry in a competitive arrangement, we will continue to work that." But he added, "I don't see us getting into what we'd call industrial espionage. We aren't going out to steal secrets of companies."

Perhaps the most vibrant announcement on a U.S. role in economic espionage came not from Langley but from senior officials at the supersecret National Security Agency, who in May 1990 began talking among themselves about shifting the NSA's global electronic eavesdropping network to nonmilitary activities. Among the new targets considered were international financial transactions between banks and other financial institutions, world trade deals, and potential mergers and acquisitions involving foreign companies.

Vice Admiral William O. Studeman, in a remarkably candid speech for an NSA director, warned that his agency might soon begin turning its massive electronic spy systems on the economic and corporate affairs of our friends. Studeman noted that a new role was probably ahead for U.S. intelligence. "The area of economics is now becoming the area of principal concern to the American citizen . . . [and] more people are concerned about economic competitiveness than they are concerned about military problems." Studeman was fairly specific about what the NSA's role might be in economic espionage: it would include eavesdropping on specific foreign companies to learn about everything from new product lines to sealed bids and new technologies, but it would also include eavesdropping on friendly countries, to discover secrets about their national economic policies. Studeman's statement had serious implications. Because its ability to collect intelligence is enormous, such a program could be massive. "When it comes to eavesdropping," says James Bamford, author of *The Puzzle Palace,* a study of the agency, "the NSA has the world wired." Studeman's remarks were unusual for an NSA director, and he no doubt understood that. As he murmured as he exited the stage after delivering his speech, "We'll see how much my butt gets burned as a result."

Studeman's remarks sent alarm bells ringing across the Western world as concerned companies and governments speculated about when and if the NSA would begin to redirect its antennae toward them. Most knew that few international (or even national) communications would be safe. "My allies are asking me lots of questions on a day-to-day basis about NSA spying on our friends," admits Studeman.

The possibility of a U.S. intelligence program designed to steal the economic secrets of our competitors has been taken up by the small and influential President's Foreign Intelligence Advisory Board. The board, made up of business and public officials as well as former intelligence officials, is appointed by the president and expected to offer general advice concerning intelligence matters. It includes a small staff on the third floor of the Old Executive Office Building, adjacent to the White House. In late 1990, the board spent three and a half months studying issues related to economic espionage and intelligence. According to a source at the PFIAB, the study's findings were mixed. He summarized them as follows: "Is there a significant problem out there? Could the U.S. intelligence community help our competitiveness? The answer to both is yes. Should it start to do so right now? No, because as a country we aren't ready yet."

On Capitol Hill, there has also been a growing chorus of calls for a greater role for U.S. intelligence in the field of economics. As the Senate Select Committee on Intelligence put it, "Intelligence agencies have for some time examined world economic trends, strategic materials, and commodities, and specific sectors of the world economy. Sweeping political reform in Eastern Europe and a reduced Soviet bloc military threat have placed new emphasis on economic issues, especially U.S. economic competitiveness." In July 1990, the Senate Banking Committee pushed to the Senate floor a bill that requires the CIA to keep track of foreign efforts at making inroads into U.S. high-technology markets. (The bill failed.)

For advocates of U.S. industrial espionage, timidity on the part of the U.S. intelligence community makes little sense. "The preeminent threat to U.S. national security now lies in the economic sphere," wrote Stansfield Turner. "We must, then, redefine 'national security' by assigning economic strength greater prominence. That means we will need better economic intelligence." Turner believes that Webster and Gates are right about the need to chart international economic trends and protect U.S. economic interests. But he adds, "If the objective of collecting economic intelligence is to buttress national economic strength, then that requires making our businesses more competitive in the global marketplace." That means not only charting broad global business trends for policymakers but also tracking individual foreign companies and helping certain U.S. firms. For Turner, there should be nothing surprising in that, given the new reality. "The United States would have no compunction about stealing military secrets to help it manufacture better weapons. Why the objection to this?"

Stansfield Turner believes that a hierarchy of possible U.S. intelligence policies relating to economic espionage can be established, from the least intensive policy to the most intensive policy. At the lowest level is pure and simple counterintelligence used to combat industrial espionage carried out by this country's economic competitors. It would involve the use of "existing intelligence mechanisms" to prevent U.S. secrets from being stolen.

At the second level are clandestine intelligence assets used to determine whether foreign countries are cheating on international trade agreements, be they multilateral agreements such as the General Agreement of Trade and Tariffs or bilateral agreements between the United States and specific countries.

At the third level are efforts aimed at "helping the American business community learn about the world economy and where it is going." It would encompass general trends, as well as "industry-specific intelligence," including the collection of intelligence largely through open sources but also through the use of satellites.

At the fourth level is America's substantial satellite, electronic, and signals intelligence capability used to listen in on specific foreign companies. The information obtained in this manner would be shared with specific U.S. companies.

The fifth level of economic espionage involves helping American companies with all of the above as well as using U.S. intelligence agents overseas. "If a chief of station learns from one of his undercover agents what three foreign companies were bidding on a contract, it is shared with a specific U.S. company," says Turner. He tends to think that the United States should consider instituting the first four levels of policy at the present time. "Technical collection makes the most sense at this point and time," he says.

Raymond Wannall believes the United States ought seriously to consider engaging in economic espionage and collecting business intelligence because of what he calls the "new challenges" facing the United States. "At the very least we need to track what foreign competitors are doing here, in terms of economic spying. We need to be tougher on them, and we need more counterintelligence resources." Economic espionage, says Wannall, "makes good sense, and it's probably feasible for the U.S. in the long run." Security consultant James Lamont adds, "We should do it as a defense mechanism. Right now we are getting hammered. But if we start doing it, we can use it as leverage to get them to stop."

What there seems to be little debate about is the extent to which other countries engage in economic espionage and how helpful it has been to them. Three former directors of the CIA see it as a serious problem. Turner is "very worried" about the problem and how it affects U.S. competitiveness. Richard Helms warns that "everybody's trying to steal our secrets" and says it's "a real problem." Herb Meyer, former vice chairman of the CIA's National Intelligence Council, believes that economic espionage offers our competitors "an enormous advantage": they learn not only what their competitors are doing but also what new technologies are being developed, and thus they have an idea of what they ought to be doing.

John Quinn, who tracked Japanese developments for the CIA before going into the consulting business, believes that for Japanese companies economic intelligence has been "decidedly advantageous." Noel Matchett, formerly with the NSA, says that economic espionage unilaterally hurts U.S. companies because "we do not share our national intelligence as a matter of policy with our industry. Most other nations do, and the advantage that can give is absolutely tremendous." A former deputy director of operations at the CIA says that "it's a serious problem; they're stealing us blind." He believes that economic espionage "is a valid and good idea as long as it doesn't supersede other things."

Ambassador Michael B. Smith, a former U.S. representative to the General Agreement of Trade and Tariff talks, says, "Other countries have active intelligence programs directed against our companies to give their companies a leg up. We ought to emulate them." After all, he says (with a grin), "All is fair in love, war, and trade." Smith believes that intelligence compiled from open sources would be enormously helpful to U.S. companies competing overseas as well as to those competing against foreign companies in the United States. The current level of economic intelligence is pitiful, he says. "We have an outstanding intelligence community, but we don't even know who owns what in this country." In his view, U.S. intelligence should be redirected toward economic targets, and he believes the problems that such spying may cause are overstated. He notes that "in trade negotiations we are users of intelligence. We used to get classified intelligence reports [on foreign companies] all the time, and there is no way they collected some of that information except by clandestine means." Even if the United States doesn't decide to spy on its economic competitors, Smith believes that "economic counterintelligence is very important." Economic espionage needs to stop.

General William E. Odom, a former director of the National Security Agency, believes that questioning the value of economic espionage for some countries is pointless. "If it weren't very advantageous, they wouldn't take the risk. Why take the risk, and use limited intelligence assets, if it's not getting you something?"

The debate is not over whether allies regularly engage in espionage against the United States or whether such activities hurt U.S. competitiveness. Rather, it is over the feasibility of a U.S. economic espionage program, the extent to which it would benefit U.S. industry, and whether it violates the principles of the American intelligence community. Leo Cherne, a member of the President's Foreign Intelligence Advisory Board for more than forty years, has long been ringing the alarm bells concerning the U.S. need for interest in economic intelligence. "We are living in a world in which our interdependence increases more quickly than we are able to assimilate the significance of that interdependence. That interdependence involves manufacture and trade, commodities and credit communications, vital resources and ideas," he said in a speech before a private group on February 18, 1986.

> Now the challenge! The actors in this new international drama are not only governments, but they include industries, labor unions, universities, banks, stock and commodity exchanges. Intelligence has thus far been essentially limited to informing other government sectors. We impose understandable limits, and they are sharp, to keep the world of foreign intelligence and our domestic life apart. We also have our antitrust laws. We do not, as the Japanese do, have an instrument like MITI which performs some of the coordinating and judgmental functions for Japanese industry. Yet, how do we meet the manifold challenges of the information age? How do we share essential intelligence with the private sector of our society, the sector upon which tomorrow's eminence depends?

For Cherne, the problems with a U.S. program for economic espionage are numerous: "The U.S. is truly handicapped by its culture, laws, the nature of our society and our belief in the market economy in our dealings with foreign countries to whom all this is quite alien."

NSA Director Studeman comes to largely the same conclusion:

This country does not have, if you will, the business ethic and the arrangements that some of the other Western countries have that do engage in economic intelligence collection. We do not have a large, vertically integrated support structure in the sense that the Japanese have. And we certainly don't have, let's say, the structure that the French have in terms of the close affiliation that exists between the government and a lot of their major industries.

One of the chief objectives made by skeptics of a policy of economic espionage concerns the sharing of the information once it is obtained by U.S. intelligence. This country has on its books antitrust laws that prohibit the government from favoring or aiding particular companies and industries. As Cherne points out, it is simply not the custom in the United States, as it is in much of the rest of the world, to have close cooperation or relations between industry and government. But assuming this cultural impediment could be overcome, problems still remain.

If the CIA steals an industry secret from another country, do they give it to GE or to Westinghouse? Given the realities of American business, if one received it and the other did not, news would eventually leak out, and outrage would result. Sharing the information with all relevant companies poses problems, too. Says Michelle Van Cleave, "If the intelligence we collect were made fairly—which may well mean widely—available, wouldn't that very availability decrease its competitive value?"

There is also the problem of determining exactly who would be given access to such intelligence. If foreign companies were not eligible, what about companies that are 20-percent foreign owned? What about U.S. subsidiaries of foreign companies? "The question of what defines a U.S. company is not easily answered," says Van Cleave.

The other problem associated with sharing intelligence with the private sector revolves around the protection of U.S. intelligence sources and methods. Over time there would develop a general awareness of the availability of certain information, and interested parties would conclude that it could have been collected only in particular ways by particular persons.

Even if these problems were solved, others would remain. Herb Romerstein, a former staff member of the House Select Committee on

Intelligence, believes that economic espionage "provides an economic advantage, but it's an incredibly dangerous thing to do. It could very easily lead to corruption and influence peddling." Senior intelligence officials might be bought by companies trying to corner the information market, or they might serve parochial interests by favoring particular companies. A "revolving door" could be the result, with agents peddling information for a price. Romerstein believes the United States "should have a counterintelligence response, not an emulation response."

Advocates of economic espionage don't pretend to have all the answers. But many, both inside and outside the intelligence community, share Ambassador Michael Smith's view that the question of distributing the information is "a bit of a red herring." "I'm not satisfied to just say, 'Well, it's a good idea, but we haven't discovered how to distribute it yet.' That's a cop out." Smith believes that complete answers may take time to come up with, but there are solutions out there. He notes that some critical industries consist of only a very limited number of producers. In such a situation, sharing intelligence with all producers would not be difficult. "In the case of commercial aviation, you are really talking about Boeing and [McDonnell] Douglas. They're a huge industry that could be helped, but only by dealing with two companies," he says. In cases where U.S. companies are the victims of theft, he believes information would rightfully go only to the victims. "No one else really has a right to know."

Stansfield Turner admits he doesn't have all the answers to this either, but he does believe the problem can be overcome. "A lot of defense secrets have been entrusted to U.S. companies in the past, and they did a pretty good job of protecting them. Perhaps we need to give business more credit," he says. Turner thinks that perhaps the secrets could be shared with company representatives at a private Commerce Department briefing. Companies would be included in such briefings if they could make use of the secrets.

Cord Meyer, a former CIA deputy director for plans (and an opponent of a U.S. economic espionage program), also believes that sharing intelligence with companies is not the problem some people make it out to be. He recalls that the CIA regularly passed classified information to U.S. industries when it came to military-related technologies. "In the past, we've given information we had to businessmen. If the Soviet aircraft industry made a breakthrough and we found out about it—even clandestinely—we would pass it along to U.S. company executives."

Herb Meyer believes it is impossible to discuss an American espionage program and the passing of intelligence information to business executives absent changes in the U.S. economy. Unless the United States adopts an industry policy, he says, economic espionage doesn't make sense. "Intelligence itself is a tool of policy, which means a country without a policy cannot ever make good use of intelligence. Because the U.S. has never really had an industrial policy, it has never been able to use intelligence effectively to achieve commercial goals."

With an industry policy, the problems usually associated with the transfer of intelligence to private companies would not occur because the government would play an important decision-making role, creating an atmosphere in which passing information to the private sector is expected. The transfer of information under such circumstances would be based on the premise that some companies or industries are worthy of government support.

To prove an economic intelligence program workable and worthwhile, American business would have to be willing to collaborate with intelligence agencies, something several senior intelligence officials with business experience doubt. "The initiative really has to come from business," says Richard Helms, who has yet to make up his mind about the soundness of an American economic intelligence program. "You really can't foist it on them. They need to approach government and ask for help in this area to make it work."

William Colby thinks this is unlikely to happen. As a former director of central intelligence now consulting for business, he sees in the U.S. business community a legitimate skepticism about the extent to which the government can help. "Most businessmen want to be left alone. They think the government is always lousing things up. What's that joke: 'What are the ten scariest words for a businessman? I'm from the government and I'm here to help you.' That's the attitude of the business community."

Economic espionage also creates potential problems in that the major targets would be our chief economic competitors—who also happen to be our major friends and allies. Countries such as Germany, France, Japan, South Korea, Britain, Taiwan—any country with valuable technology and industry secrets—would be the target of a U.S. economic espionage campaign. That would create diplomatic problems. "When engaging in foreign espionage of any sort, you are violating another country's laws," says William Colby. He believes that consideration should not cause us to eliminate all U.S. espionage overseas but that it should make U.S. intelligence officials think about three questions: "First, you have to ask, how important is the information, and how important is it to learn about it secretly? Second, how great are the risks of exposure when the operation is being conducted? And third, when the matter is exposed (and it will eventually be uncovered), what will the consequences be?"

For Colby, the consequences of carrying out economic espionage against major allies is "so negative that it's not worth it." He and others point to the consequences when the operation is eventually exposed. The United States remains reliant on its allies for a wide array of intelligence support. Listening posts and eavesdropping facilities in allied countries, as well as information from allied intelligence services about terrorist groups and regional threats, remain important to the CIA and the NSA. Were the United States to begin an economic espionage campaign, says Colby, these benefits would be put at risk, and some facilities overseas would be shut down.

Admiral Turner is not so certain the consequences would be so dire. According to Turner, our allies need the United States every bit as much (perhaps even more) than we need them. "Cooperation between countries is so important today that countries would be ill-advised to launch public campaigns about friendly spying." He believes countries would handle evidence of American espionage "quietly." The Pollard case was the exception to the rule because it was so blatant, and the Israelis had gone too far. "Remember, too," he says, "they're spying on us. If I go public [with a case of espionage], I'm also cutting myself off from spying."

Ambassador Smith agrees but also thinks it's a question of fairness. "They do it to us all the time, but we're afraid to do it to them because of the diplomatic consequences? That doesn't make any sense." Others believe that an economic espionage program would perhaps raise our allies' eyebrows, but in so doing, it would challenge them to reconsider their own activities. Eventually it could force them to strike a bargain with the United States. Ray Wannall believes that only if the United States develops an economic espionage capability will allies be open to discussion about limiting their operations. "It's probably a good—no, the *only*—bargaining chip we have."

Dr. Robert C. Angel has a different solution and different suggestions for using intelligence to aid American business. A professor at the University of South Carolina and a specialist on Japan, Angel knows the Japanese economic intelligence system well, having worked for both the Japan Trade Council and the Japan Economic Institute, both funded by Japan's Foreign Ministry. He has been a long-time advocate of the establishment of a new U.S. intelligence service, similar to that of the Japanese External Trade Organization. And he believes there should be "more economic collection—both overt and covert." He says the CIA is the "wrong tool for the right task" and that the government ought to establish an "economic intelligence organization that is an economic and political intelligence service from beginning to end." He envisions a semiofficial service headed by a "high-profile figure, a retired senator or former vice president," who would be stationed at an office overseas—in Tokyo. Beneath this figurehead would be two career intelligence officers, but not former CIA officials. These careerists Angel nicknames "the piranhas," because it would be their job to eat up every piece of information in sight. They would be tough and effective and would maintain a low profile. Below each piranha would be two or three more agents, who would collect the information.

The sorts of methods used to collect information would depend on local laws, says Angel. In a country such as Japan, the methods would be "quite legal but effective." "They have a much more flexible definition of legal collection than we do," he says. So in Japan the new intelligence service could gather gray material (which in some instances is illegal to collect in the United States) and could even purchase information from "sources." The agents would maintain a list of informants, "to keep the information flow going." The information they obtained would be shared with any U.S. company that subscribed to the service. No foreign companies would be allowed to subscribe.

Richard Walker, who served as the U.S. ambassador to South Korea from 1981 to 1989, believes that more than anything, U.S. diplomats and intelligence sources overseas should be used to push for fairness in economic and business dealings. He recalls that during his tenure as ambassador in Seoul, several international companies were competing for lucrative contracts to build nuclear power plants in South Korea. U.S. intelligence agents discovered (quite by accident) that contracts were being given to French companies because of bribes and other promises being made by the French ambassador. "We learned through intelligence sources that the Korean official who was responsible for making contract decisions for plants nine and ten was promised twenty million dollars and an apartment on the Champs Élysées in exchange for the contracts. Money spoke, and French companies got the contracts." Walker, outraged at the whole affair, vowed to use his office and the CIA station in Seoul to win contracts for American companies for plants eleven and twelve. "We used both overt and covert methods," says Walker. "The French ambassador was steaming mad."

In a growing number of instances, the United States is beginning to use its intelligence assets to its economic advantage. In 1990, the CIA station chief in Djakarta received a bit of information from a source within the Indonesian government. The source reported that the government was about to award a contract for roughly one hundred million dollars to the Japanese electronics giant NEC. The contract was for the modernization of the national phone system, which was old, inefficient, and plagued with problems. The project had been open for bidding, and companies from around the world made offers. What was of most interest to the CIA station chief was the information he received concerning why the contract was going to NEC. According to the source, AT&T's European subsidiary had a more attractive bid: its price was lower, and the specifications of its proposal would have made for a better phone system. Under normal circumstances, said the source, AT&T would have received the project. But Tokyo used the threat of reducing its more than $2.1 billion in foreign aid if the contract were awarded to another company. "It was a pretty stark quid pro quo," says one intelligence official familiar with the case.

In the past, the station chief might have passed the information on to CIA headquarters in Langley, where it would have simply ended up on someone's desk. But this time things were different. The report was sent to headquarters, and senior CIA officials inserted it into the *Top-Secret President's Daily Brief,* which the president reads every morning in the Oval Office. George Bush, at the urging of then Chief of Staff John Sununu, acted on the information, writing a candid letter to President Suharto of Indonesia. His letter spoke of America's "long-standing commitment and strong commercial ties to Indonesia, that should not be overlooked." Two weeks later President Suharto split the contract fifty-fifty between NEC and AT&T.

According to senior U.S. intelligence officials, these sorts of commercial problems are going to become a greater concern for intelligence officers stationed overseas. With increasing frequency, the CIA's planning office is instructing its stations overseas to collect and report on commercial, economic, and technical events that in the past would have been largely ignored by agents. Already there are signs that information similar to that from Indonesia in 1990 is making its way into the hands of senior government officials.

The *National Intelligence Daily* is a classified intelligence newspaper put together by the CIA to keep American officials in a variety of departments abreast of foreign events. The *NID* includes "briefs" that are a full page or longer, "notes" that take up a couple of paragraphs, and "snowflakes," which are no longer than four lines. According to several readers of the *NID,* there are a growing number of snowflakes and even a few notes on commercial and technological subjects having to do with competitor countries. These usually take the form of reports on the bidding process for large contracts in which foreign pressure has been asserted or reports on technological breakthroughs made by foreign corporations. The information is confined to government use, but it reflects a shift—however slight—in the targets of choice of U.S. intelligence agents overseas.

In the summer of 1989, CIA agents in Paris began running across some peculiar rumors. An agent assigned to the U.S. embassy heard from a dispirited DGSE agent about operations his government was carrying out against IBM and Texas Instruments. The French agent had a serious drinking problem and was prone to talking about his exploits while under the influence. The American agent was, by coincidence, a neighbor in the same apartment building and had built up a friendship with the Frenchman over the course of two years. After the French agent repeatedly told the American wild stories concerning DGSE agents in these companies, the CIA station chief in Paris, on orders from Langley, made contact with security officials from both companies' Paris offices. What the CIA discovered was that both companies were suspicious of several employees. The two companies joined with both the CIA and the FBI in an attempt to root out the moles. Through a number of sophisticated means, a joint FBI-CIA team working out of the U.S. embassy in Paris eventually identified the culprits. The employees were fired, both companies undertook a series of new security precautions to prevent the same from happening again, and the U.S. government sent a letter of protest to President Mitterand. The level of cooperation between U.S. intelligence and the two American companies was, according to a senior CIA official, "unprecedented in agency history."

There has also been a change on other fronts at the CIA. At its Langley headquarters, the agency maintains a small, secretive department called the National Collection Division. A small subsection of the NCD is a clandestine, little-known department called the Foreign Resources Division, whose purpose is to recruit foreigners in this country to work as agents of the CIA when they return home. Since its inception and throughout the entire Cold War, the Foreign Resources Division has concentrated on recruiting diplomats from the former Soviet bloc, as well as individuals from certain developing countries, such as India and Argentina. The program has been enormously successful and has been credited with recruiting a surprising number of agents. While it was only an unwritten rule, "friendlies" were basically off limits because of what was seen as the particularly sensitive nature of such an approach to recruitment. The diplomatic costs of discovery were deemed so great that CIA officials long ago made the decision to shy away from attempting to recruit many citizens from Western Europe, Japan, and countries such as Israel and South Korea, two key allies.

But according to senior officials at Langley, that is starting to change. In November 1990, the CIA decided to merge the Foreign Resources Division with the National Collection Division. The merger promises to yield more resources, not only in terms of manpower but also in terms of financial inducements. Some believe that the division will be given greater latitude in the recruitment of foreign nationals, particularly "friendlies." One senior official expects the recruitment to take place largely among businessmen, students, and other visitors from Western Europe and the Pacific Rim.

The supersecret National Security Agency has also taken several steps to reorient its electronic eavesdropping capabilities so that it may better focus its efforts in the post–Cold War era. In December 1991, the NSA began a major reorganization intended to meet American security needs minus a Soviet threat. The NSA's Group A, which focused on Eastern Europe and the Soviet Union, was abolished. Its personnel and its massive electronic intelligence systems—including listening posts, satellites, and ships—were added to another group, to bolster the collection of intelligence on all of Europe, including Eastern Europe and traditional U.S. allies in Western Europe.

The NSA's Group B, which had been limited to spying exclusively on Asian Communist countries (the People's Republic of China, North Korea, and Vietnam), had its mission broadened. Henceforth, Group B would focus less on those countries and more on all of Asia, including allies and trading partners such as Japan, South Korea, Taiwan, and Singapore. Whereas the stated goal of the NSA's shift was to keep the organization abreast of international issues such as nuclear proliferation, international drug trafficking, and criminal activities, there can be little doubt that the NSA's ability to monitor the commercial and scientific communications in allied countries has been enhanced.

There are also changes afoot in U.S. counterintelligence policy, in light of increased spying among friendly, economically competitive countries. "Counterintelligence is very important," says Cord Meyer. "In this case it's not an easy target to deal with." Meyer points out that when the premier espionage threat was posed by the Soviet Union and its proxies, "you could track their movement and see where they went." Tracking friendlies is much more difficult. Japanese, French, and German visitors to the United States are quite common, unlike those from the Soviet Union during the Cold War. Given the new counterintelligence challenge, the approach will have to change. "It comes down to the fact that high-tech companies are the main target," he says. "We need to make an effort to track the movements of foreign nationals around these companies, waiting for approaches to come to us."

Senior officials of the FBI (which has prime responsibility for tracking foreign espionage in the United States) are already changing their language when it comes to discussing the threat of foreign espionage. No longer do they speak about countering "hostile intelligence services," but instead they refer to the more general "foreign intelligence threat." "The country can be a close ally but still an intelligence threat," says a senior FBI official. Says Raymond Wannall, "There's an old saying in counterintelligence circles, 'There are no friendly intelligence services, only friendly countries with intelligence services.'"

As discussed in Chapter 1, the new counterintelligence policy for meeting the threat from economic espionage carried out by foreign competitors has also appeared in the form of a new broad counterintelligence policy. For years, the FBI had based its counterintelligence priorities on the Country Criteria List, which named specific countries that posed intelligence threats. U.S. counterintelligence officials had determined which countries to include on the list according to whether a country had an active intelligence service and whether a country was deemed as "hostile." During most of the Cold War, the Country Criteria List included the Soviet Union, its satellites, China, Cuba, North Korea, Vietnam, and various other countries, such as Libya and Iran.

In a speech delivered in October 1991 before a private business organization, Harry Brandon, FBI deputy assistant director for intelligence, announced that the Country Criteria List was being replaced by a National Security Threat List, which outlines new areas for FBI counterintelligence investigations. Brandon described what he saw as a "significant" change in the espionage threat facing the United States. He spoke repeatedly of "nontraditional threats" from friendly nations: "A number of these nontraditional intelligence adversaries currently conduct intelligence operations against the U.S. directly against U.S. firms, which go far beyond their national defense needs," he told the audience of businessmen. "This represents an intelligence threat to U.S. national security." According to Brandon, this reality forced the change in policy. Once limited almost exclusively to thwarting "hostile" nations' spies who seek U.S. defense and political secrets, the FBI would now go after any agents—from any country, friend or foe—engaged in clandestine operations in specific areas. "We consider this a strategic approach," he said, reflecting the arrival of the post–Cold War era.

The National Security Threat List gives the FBI a new flexibility in dealing with foreign spying. It allows the bureau to go after those who engage in spying in the following areas, deemed "threats to U.S. security":

- Operations to enhance or promote the proliferation of nuclear, chemical, or biological weapons

- The theft of "core technologies" identified by the federal government as essential to U.S. security; these technologies need not be secret.

- The theft or illegal acquisition of U.S. industrial, proprietary, or economic information, beyond the core technologies

- Attempts to acquire foreign affairs information and the protection of U.S. officials from clandestine operations

- Information relating to national defense and the U.S. military

- Terrorist-related activity

According to Brandon, activity in any of these areas by any intelligence service would prompt an FBI response. "Our approach in the nineties is going to be that if we find governmental use of an intelligence service in any of these areas, then we believe, and the Attorney General now believes, that it would be appropriate for the counterintelligence community to become involved," he said.

The new counterintelligence policy means FBI agents will now watch certain industries and areas rather than track intelligence agents. "The idea is to let them come to us rather than chase them around," says a senior FBI official. The sites around certain companies, for example, will be watched by agents for any suspicious activity. In the Cold War era, such an approach by itself was deemed too risky. But it was also easier to monitor the movement of Soviet officials, which made a "let them come to us" approach unnecessary. In the post–Cold War era, there will be little choice. Counterintelligence has become more complicated. Economic competitors are interested in a broad range of technologies. And their intelligence services have a variety of opportunities because of the enormous interaction among the major industrial nations. "The situation is definitely more complicated than in the past," says Cord Meyer.

But just how far the FBI will go remains in doubt, absent a hostile intelligence threat from a power such as the Soviet Union. Friendly spying does not evoke immediate concerns about "national security," as Soviet

Cold War espionage did. The announcement in January 1992 that the FBI was shifting three hundred counterintelligence agents (approximately 25 percent of the total number) to fight street gangs in urban centers across America may be a sign of a lack of appreciation for the importance of countering economic spying. This attitude was demonstrated perfectly by the comments of Wayne Gilbert, assistant director of the FBI's intelligence division, when questioned about the problem. "If it's just a question of an American company getting beat out by another company, I don't think we'd launch a major intelligence investigation. When a foreign company actually puts its agents in a company for a long period of time *in a way that directly affects national security,* that's when we'll act."

Russell Bowen, an MIT-trained scientist with more than thirty years' experience in intelligence, including an eleven-year stint at the CIA, doubts that it would make much difference if the FBI were to firmly commit itself to combating friendly economic spying. "We simply don't have enough resources for the problem," he says. "I know how these counterintelligence things work. They concentrate resources to crack one case, hoping to make an example. . . . The trouble is, the chances of getting caught are so low, it won't be much of a deterrent." Ray Cline shares Bowen's skepticism: "We've never been good at counterintelligence. We tend to screw things up. We either go overboard or just give up."

But as the memory of the Cold War begins to fade and interest in economic competition continues to grow, the official government attitude toward friendly spies will probably change. During the Cold War, the United States usually "looked the other way," says Herb Meyer. But that may soon change. With fewer compelling reasons to ensure cooperation among allied intelligence services at all costs, many senior intelligence officials hope the United States will become more vocal when friendly spies are discovered. "During the Cold War, publicizing a case like Pollard was the exception," says a senior FBI official. "During the post–Cold War period, I hope it becomes the rule." Former CIA Director William Colby believes that publicity "to the point of embarrassment" is the best bet for containing economic espionage by friendly countries. Cord Meyer echoes that sentiment. He thinks the United States ought to "protest and protest loudly. We need to shame them into stopping this. Publicity is the best antidote."

But in many ways an American counterintelligence policy—even with changes—is not strong enough. Herb Meyer believes the U.S. government needs to be more aggressive in its attempts to diminish the advantage that economic espionage gives some competitors. He advocates training U.S. business executives traveling overseas in how to look out for, and deal with, espionage. "The kind of security training provided to government officials traveling overseas should be extended, perhaps in modified form, to U.S. executives." The FBI already does some of this. American businesspeople who will be working for U.S. companies overseas can attend FBI briefings. Until recently, these briefings focused mostly on the activities of Soviet agents and the threats posed by international terrorism. But today the FBI warns businesspeople about the threats posed by Western competitors and about the even more subtle and more sophisticated techniques these competitors use, as compared with those of the Soviets. But for Meyer the training should go further and should be made available to more executives. He believes executives need to learn not only about the techniques being used against them but also how to counter them. He also thinks they should "be made aware of the technical devices now commercially available—secure lines for telephones, computers, and faxes"—to defeat attempts at eavesdropping. Far too few executives are participating in the currently formulated FBI program, according to Meyer.

Herb Meyer goes so far as to suggest that the State Department should consider making "secure" facilities at U.S. embassies available to U.S. executives who are overseas negotiating with local executives. U.S. embassies in all foreign countries have secure phones and other communications equipment that uses scrambled signals. American embassies also have "secure rooms," which are assuredly free of electronic bugs.

Whereas William Colby understands the motivation for such a policy, he believes it is unlikely that foreign countries would allow U.S. embassies to provide American businesspeople with such facilities. Colby says foreign governments take very seriously the right to eavesdrop on American businesses. "Almost all the industrial countries do not allow companies or private citizens to use encryption equipment. The fact is that they want to retain the option of eavesdropping when they want to." Are there are countries that allow businesspeople to use such encryption equipment? "Why, yes," says Colby, "the United States."

Noel Matchett has the same reaction. He worked for the NSA for more than twenty years and now consults for American businesses. He says that some clients of his do use an encryption device at their overseas offices. "The trouble is, they can use it only on the condition that they give the keys to the codes to the home government."

Another approach that Meyer suggests is linking the behavior of foreign countries and companies in the intelligence field to trade negotiations and access. "There is no reason on earth why American trade negotiators cannot raise a huge stink over the issue of foreign intelligence services conducting operations against U.S. companies," he says. "New U.S. laws could be enacted to require immediate and massive commercial retaliation against any foreign company that benefits from such activities." The fact is that few companies or allied countries have paid a substantial price for engaging in economic espionage against the United States. Months after it was known to have benefited from spying on IBM and Texas Instruments, France's Compagnie des Machines Bull announced plans to purchase Honeywell Federal Systems, which provided electronics equipment to the CIA and the FBI. After it was caught trying to steal IBM secrets in 1982, Hitachi received a contract to provide the Social Security Administration with computers. Only if the cost of economic espionage increases tremendously is the activity likely to diminish.

One FBI official believes the situation is analogous to the notorious 1987 Toshiba case. The Japanese electronics giant was discovered to have sold to the Soviet Union sophisticated equipment that allows Russian submarines to run more quietly and avoid detection by the U.S. Navy. In response, Congress slapped punitive sanctions on the company. "When there is a cost, their behavior will change. We just need to get their attention," advises Richard Helms.

Regardless of what course the U.S. intelligence community takes, most senior intelligence officials are not optimistic about the future. Perhaps Herb Meyer best sums up this view: "What does not seem likely is any major effort by U.S. intelligence to match foreign practices by collecting and distributing operations intelligence to U.S. companies. Does this mean U.S. companies will remain at a disadvantage vis-à-vis our foreign counterparts, which will themselves continue to receive intelligence assistance directly from their governments? In a word, yes."

Source Notes

Chapter 1   A Matter Between Friends

Michael Alexander, "High-Tech Boom Opens Security Gaps," *Computer World,* April 2, 1990, pp. 1, 119.

Michael Allen, "Security Experts Advise Firms to Avoid Panic, Excess Zeal in Probing Data Leaks," *Wall Street Journal,* September 20, 1991, pp. B1, B8.

Maynard C. Anderson, "Future Threat," *Security Awareness Bulletin* 90, no. 4 (April 1990), pp. 1–5.

Robert Angel, interview with author, January 24, 1992.

William Bader, "The New Global Environment in Defense Industry," *Security Awareness Bulletin* 92, no. 1 (January 1992), pp. 23–25.

August Bequai, "The Industrial Spy: Red Flags and Recourse," *Security Management,* August 1985, pp. 93–94.

Joshua Bolter, quoted in Herb Meyer, "Banker, Broker, Businessman, Spy," *CEO,* October–November 1990.

David Boren, summary of remarks to the National Press Club, Washington, D.C., April 3, 1990.

————, "New World, New C.I.A.," *New York Times,* June 17, 1990, p. 19.

Russell Bowen, interview with author, January 17, 1992.

Harry Brandon, quoted in Bill Gertz, "FBI Expanding Spying to Cover Friendly Nations," *Washington Times,* October 30, 1991.

Herchell Britton, "U.S. Technological Superiority Is Threatened," *Security Management,* November 1981, pp. 15–18.

Duncan Campbell, "The Global Boom in Eavesdropping, *World Press Review,* May 1979, pp. 26–28.

William Carley, "As Cold War Fades, Some Nations' Spies Seek Industrial Secrets," *Wall Street Journal,* June 17, 1991, pp. A1, A5.

Burrus M. Carnahan, "American Competitiveness and Chemical Arms Control: Managing the Approaching Conflict," *Legal Backgrounder* (Washington, D.C.: Washington Legal Foundation), March 16, 1990.

George Carver, "Intelligence and Glasnost," *Foreign Affairs* (Summer 1990), pp. 147–66.

Frank Cary, quoted in Irwin Ross, "Who's Stealing the Company's Secrets?" *Reader's Digest,* February 1983.

Bruce Charnov, "Computer Security," in *Global Corporate Intelligence,* eds., George S. Roukis, Hugh Conway, and Bruce Charnov (New York: Quorum Books, 1990), pp. 151–64.

Leo Cherne, quoted in Herb Meyer, *Real-World Intelligence* (New York: Weidenfeld and Nicholson, 1987).

Ray Cline, interview with author, February 10, 1992.

William Colby, interview with author, January 6, 1992.

Hugo Cornwall, *The Industrial Espionage Handbook* (London: Century Books, 1991).

Robert Courtney, interview with author, July 22, 1991.

Bob Davis, "A Supersecret Agency Finds Selling Secrecy to Others Isn't Easy," *Wall Street Journal,* March 28, 1988, pp. 1, 11.

Howard Ferrill, "OPSEC in the Next Decade," *OPS News,* September 1991, p. 2.

Lynn F. Fischer, "Presenting Believable Arguments," *Security Awareness Bulletin* 90, no. 4 (April 1990), pp. 17–20.

Bill Gertz, "The New Spy: '90s Espionage Turns Economic," *Washington Times,* February 9, 1992, pp. 1, 7.

Philip Gold, "Federal Sleuthing Experts, Private Intelligence Needs," *Insight Magazine,* October 15, 1990, pp. 39–40.

Greg Gwash, "A View from Industrial Security," *Security Awareness Bulletin* 90, no. 4 (April 1990), pp. 14–16.

Peter Heims, "Unethical, but Legal: Industrial Espionage Is Health in the UK (and Europe)," *Security Management,* November 1981, pp. 10–14.

Richard Helms, Remarks before the International Security Systems Symposium, Alexandria, Va., October 28, 1991.

———, interview with author, October 30, 1991.

John Hillkirk, "Trade Secrets: Next Frontier for U.S. Spies," *USA Today,* June 5, 1990, p. A7.

"Hostile Takeovers: How Can a Computer Network Welcome Only Friendly Users?" *Scientific American,* January 1989, pp. 56–57.

Bob Inman, interview with author, February 4, 1992.

"Intelligence Targeting of U.S. Technology," *Security Awareness Bulletin* 92, no. 1 (January 1992), p. 1.

Into Thin Air . . . (Silver Spring, Md.: Information Security, Incorporated, 1990).

Philip Klass, "STU-3 Secure Telephones Offered to U.S. Defense Contractors," *Aviation Week and Space Technology,* February 27, 1989, p. 63.

Gina Kolata, "NSA to Provide Secret Codes," *Science,* October 4, 1985, pp. 45–46.

James Lamont, interview with author, August 6, 1991.

Count Henri de Marenches, *Dans les secrets des princes* (Paris: Editions Stock, 1986).

Pierre Marion, interview with author, March 14, 1992.

Noel Matchett, "Information Security: The Hidden Force Multiplier," *Defense Management Journal* 4 (1986), pp. 23–27.

———, "Industrial Espionage in the Electronic Age," in *Proceedings of the Fifth Annual Symposium and Technical Displays on Physical and Electronic Security* (Philadelphia: Armed Forces Communications and Electronics Association, 1989), pp. A8-1–A8-3.

———, interview with author, May 14, 1991.

Cord Meyer, interview with author, January 8, 1992.

Herb Meyer, interview with author, May 13, 1991.

Kyle Olsen, quoted in Burrus M. Carnahan, "American Competitiveness and Chemical Arms Control: Managing the Approaching Conflict," *Legal Backgrounder* (Washington, D.C.: Washington Legal Foundation), March 16, 1990.

Elizabeth A. Palmer, "Senators Moving to Close Net on New Breed: Hired Spies," *Congressional Quarterly,* July 14, 1990, pp. 2236–38.

Arion N. Pattakos, *Counter-competitor Intelligence: Keeping Your Company Secrets Secret* (Beta Analytics, Incorporated, 1990).

Bill Paul, "Electronic Theft Is Routine and Costs Firms Billions, Security Experts Say," *Wall Street Journal,* October 20, 1989, p. A5.

Hayden Peake, interview with author, October 31, 1991.

Richard Pearson, "Laser Listener," *Radio Electronics,* October 1987, pp. 39–44.

John Quinn, interview with author, December 20, 1991.

Charles Redman, "A Brief Guide to Friendly Spying," *Economist,* December 7, 1985, p. 44.

Oliver Revell, quoted in Michael Wines, "French Said to Spy on U.S. Computer Companies," *New York Times,* November 18, 1990.

Raymond Rocca, interview with author.

Rohm and Haas case, reported in Orr Kelly, "Where There's a Profit, There's a Spy," *U.S. News and World Report,* May 9, 1983, pp. 16–17.

Irwin Ross, "Who's Stealing the Company's Secrets?" *Reader's Digest,* February 1983.

George Roukis, "The Corporate Intelligence Process: Global Perspectives and Approaches," in *Global Corporate Intelligence,* eds., George S. Roukis, Hugh Conway, and Bruce Charnov (New York: Quorum Books, 1990), pp. 3–20.

Joseph Russoniello, quoted in Irwin Ross, "Who's Stealing the Company's Secrets?" *Reader's Digest,* February 1983.

William S. Sessions, "Meeting the Counterintelligence Challenges of the 1990s," *Security Awareness Bulletin* 90, no. 4 (April 1990), pp. 6–9.

———, speech before the New York chapter of the Association of Former Intelligence Officers, New York, October 25, 1990.

———, "Counterintelligence Challenges in a Changing World," *Security Awareness Bulletin* 92, no. 1 (January 1992), pp. 3–5.

Michael B. Smith, interview with author, October 29, 1991.

"Spying for Friends," *Macleans,* December 2, 1985, p. 44.

Tom Squitieri, "New Course May Be Economic Espionage," *USA Today,* April 25, 1991, p. 11A.

Barbara Starr, "Are Data Bases a Threat to National Security?" *BusinessWeek,* December 1, 1986, p. 39.

William O. Studeman, quoted in James Bamford, "Seeking to Retain Its Budget, NSA Wants to Spy (Shhhh!) on Allies," *Los Angeles Times,* July 15, 1990, p. 4.

David B. Tinnin, "A School for Counterspies," *Fortune,* May 14, 1983, p. 107.

Alvin Toffler, *Powershift* (New York: Pocket Books, 1990), pp. 153–62.

Stansfield Turner, "Overhauling the CIA," *USA Today,* September 16, 1991, p. 13A.

———, "Intelligence for a New World Order," *Foreign Affairs* (Fall 1991), pp. 150–66.

———, interview with author, November 11, 1991.

Harlow Unger, "The Spies of Silicon Valley: How Industrial Espionage Is Hurting the Computer Business," *Canadian Business,* December 25, 1980, p. 15.

U.S. Senate, Select Committee on Intelligence, *Intelligence Authorization Act, FY 1992: Report,* May 15, 1991.

315

Michelle Van Cleave, remarks to the Armed Forces Communications and Electronics Association, November 29, 1990.

————, remarks before the National Security Institute, March 12, 1991.

Richard Walker, interview with author, February 18, 1992.

Raymond Wannall, interview with author, November 6, 1991.

Patrick Watson, quoted in Bill Gertz, "KGB Targets U.S. Businessmen, Scientists to Recruit Them as Spies," *Washington Times,* March 14, 1991, p. A4.

William H. Webster, "Intelligence Issues of the New Decade," *Security Awareness Bulletin* 90, no. 4 (April 1990), pp. 10–12.

Michael Wines, "U.S. Urged to Emphasize Economic Strength," *New York Times,* April 4, 1990, p. A5.

Arnold Zais, "*Financial Executive*'s Guide to Blocking Electronic Espionage," *Financial Executive,* September 1981, pp. 44–48.

Chapter 2   Spies Like Us

August Bequai, "The Industrial Spy: Red Flags and Recourse," *Security Management,* August 1985, pp. 93–94.

Celanese Corporation court case (Harold Farrar), judge quoted in "Sends You to Jail," *Economist,* January 12, 1980.

Robert Courtney, interview with author, July 22, 1991.

John Davitt, interview with author, March 6, 1992.

Orrin Hatch, quoted in U.S. Senate, Subcommittee on Technology and the Law, *The Freedom of Information Act,* August 2, 1988.

IBM handbook, from Orr Kelly, "Where There's a Profit, There's a Spy," *U.S. News and World Report,* May 9, 1983, pp. 16–17.

Phillip Knightley, quoted in "The Declining Wages of Espionage," *Fortune,* May 11, 1987.

James Lamont, interview with author, August 16, 1991.

Noel Matchett, interview with author, May 14, 1991.

Herb Meyer, interview with author, May 13, 1991.

Hayden Peake, interview with author, October 31, 1991.

Harlow Unger, "The Spies of Silicon Valley: How Industrial Espionage Is Hurting the Computer Business," *Canadian Business,* December 25, 1980, p. 15.

Michelle Van Cleave, remarks before the National Security Institute, March 12, 1991.

Richard Walker, interview with author, October 18, 1992.

Chapter 3   Big Blue's Crown Jewels

Richard Callahan, quoted in David B. Tinnin, "How IBM Stung Hitachi," *Fortune,* March 7, 1983, pp. 50–55.

———, letter quoted in John D. Halamka, *Espionage in the Silicon Valley* (Berkeley, Calif.: Sybex, 1983).

Susan Dentzer, "Watching Over Silicon Valley," *Newsweek,* March 19, 1984, p. 75.

B. O. Evans, quoted in John D. Halamka, *Espionage in the Silicon Valley* (Berkeley, Calif.: Sybex, 1983).

Alan J. Garretson, in conversation with Michihiro Hirai, quoted in John D. Halamka, *Espionage in the Silicon Valley* (Berkeley, Calif.: Sybex, 1983).

Robin Grossman, "Has Japan's High-Tech Rivalry Gone Too Far?" *BusinessWeek,* July 5, 1982, p. 22.

Zkenji Hayashi, in conversation with Robert Domenico and Maxwell Paley, quoted in "A New Kind of Foreign Espionage," *U.S. News and World Report,* July 5, 1982, p. 66.

———, remarks made at Glenmar Associates, quoted in John D. Halamka, *Espionage in the Silicon Valley* (Berkeley, Calif.: Sybex, 1983).

"IBM, Hitachi Settle Trade Secrets Suit," *Washington Post,* October 7, 1983, pp. D1, D10.

Japanese cabinet member, quoted in Mark Potts, "Computer Court Papers Read Like Spy Novel," *Washington Post,* June 24, 1983, pp. D1, D9.

"Japscam for Computer Spies," *Fortune,* July 26, 1982, p. 7.

Judge overseeing IBM-Hitachi case quoted in Tom Nicholson, "A $300 Million Apology to IBM," *Newsweek,* November 21, 1983, p. 84.

Katsushige Mita, quoted in "Nine Won't Heed U.S. Warrants," *Washington Post,* July 24, 1983.

Maxwell Paley, remarks to Richard Callahan in Tokyo and in telephone conversation with Zkenji Hayashi, quoted in Mark Potts, "Computer Court Papers Read Like Spy Novel," *Washington Post,* June 24, 1983, pp. D1, D9.

Mark Potts, "IBM Charges Two Firms with Stealing Secrets," *Washington Post,* November 26, 1983, pp. C1, C2.

Doug Walgren, quoted in Lloyd Schwartz, "Hint Hitachi Case Bared 'Tip of the Iceberg,' " *Electronic News,* July 18, 1983, p. 16.

Gregory Ward, quoted in John D. Halamka, *Espionage in the Silicon Valley* (Berkeley, Calif.: Sybex, 1983).

William Webster, quoted in "The Real Punishment for Hitachi," *BusinessWeek,* February 21, 1983, pp. 35–36.

Yomiuri Shimbun, quoted in "The Real Punishment for Hitachi," *BusinessWeek,* February 21, 1983, pp. 35–36.

Chapter 4   Stagehands in the Dark

"America Starts Looking over Japan's Shoulder," *BusinessWeek,* February 13, 1984, pp. 136–37.

Jack Anderson, "Japan Pressing for Computer Data from IBM," *Washington Post,* October 14, 1983, p. C27.

Robert Angel, "Prime Ministerial Leadership in Japan: Recent Changes in Personal Style and Administrative Organization," *Pacific Affairs* (Winter 1989), pp. 596–600.

———, interview with author, January 24, 1992.

Stuart Auerbach, "Sting Tapes Stir Anger at Hearings," *Washington Post,* June 28, 1983, pp. D1, D10.

"The Business Intelligence Beehive," *BusinessWeek*, December 14, 1981, p. 52.

Gene Bylinsky, "The Japanese Spies in Silicon Valley," *Fortune*, February 27, 1978, pp. 74–76.

Central Intelligence Agency, *Japan: Foreign Intelligence and Security Services* (Langley, Va.: Central Intelligence Agency, 1987). [Shown to author, April 11, 1991.]

Central Intelligence Agency official, interview with author, September 4, 1991.

Henry Clements, interview with author, September 9, 1991.

Ray Cline, interview with author, February 10, 1992.

William Colby, interview with author, January 6, 1992.

Tracy Dahlby, "Japanese Skeptical of IBM Case," *Washington Post*, June 29, 1982, p. A11.

Richard Deacon, *Kempei Tai: The Japanese Secret Service Then and Now* (Tokyo: Charles Tuttle, 1983).

Susan Dentzer, "Watching Over Silicon Valley," *Newsweek*, March 19, 1984, p. 75.

John Dingell quoted in Lloyd Schwartz, "Hint Hitachi Case Bared 'Tip of the Iceberg,'" *Electronic News*, July 18, 1983.

Joel Dreyfuss, "How Japan Picks America's Brains," *Fortune*, December 21, 1987, pp. 79–89.

Patrice Duggan, "The New Face of Japanese Espionage," *Forbes*, November 12, 1990, p. 96.

Alan K. Engel, "Number One in Competitor Intelligence," *Across the Board*, December 1987, pp. 43–47.

Fairchild Semiconductors security official, interview with author, October 4, 1991.

Clyde Farnsworth, "Washington: The People Who Work for the Japanese," *New York Times*, June 29, 1980, p. F3.

———, "U.S. Tightens Japanese Visas," *New York Times*, October 7, 1980, pp. D1, D17.

Harold Farrar, quoted in "Sends You to Jail," *Economist,* January 12, 1980, pp. 72–73.

Federal Bureau of Investigation counterintelligence official, interview with author, July 17, 1991.

"GAO to Study Japanese Access to U.S. Technology," *Seattle Times,* February 9, 1992, p. E6.

Bill Gertz, "Japanese Intelligence Network Is All Business," *Washington Times,* February 9, 1992.

Robin Grossman, "Has Japan's High-Tech Rivalry Gone Too Far?" *BusinessWeek,* July 5, 1982, p. 22.

Robert G. Harris, "Telecommunications as a Strategic Industry," in *Powereconomics,* eds. Clyde V. Prestowitz, Ronald Morse, and Alan Tonelson (Washington, D.C.: Madison Books, 1991).

Richard Helms, interview with author, October 30, 1991.

"How Japan Will Finance Its Technology Strategy," *BusinessWeek,* December 14, 1981, pp. 50–52.

"How 'Silicon Spies' Get Away with Copying," *BusinessWeek,* April 21, 1980, pp. 181–88.

"Industrial Espionage Case Entangles Japanese Firms," *Wall Street Journal,* July 19, 1991.

Bob Inman, interview with author, February 4, 1992.

"Integrated Circuit Technology Transfer Concerns U.S. Officials," *Aviation Week and Space Technology,* November 10, 1986, p. 31.

"Japanese Multinational Covering the World with Investment," *BusinessWeek,* June 16, 1980, pp. 92–99.

"Japan's Trade Office Plan," *New York Times,* March 1, 1982.

Chalmers Johnson, interview with author, August 12, 1991.

George Keyworth II, *Competitiveness and Telecommunications* (Indianapolis: Hudson Institute, 1990).

Taiyu Kobayashi, quoted in Dan Morgan and Tracy Dahlby, "A Tokyo Giant's View of the War of the Computers," *Washington Post,* January 9, 1983, pp. C1, C3.

Fumio Kodama, "Technological Diversification of Japanese Industry," *Science,* July 18, 1986, pp. 291–96.

Pierre Lacoste, interview with author, March 13, 1992.

James Lamont, interview with author, August 6, 1991.

Count Henri de Marenches, *The Evil Empire* (London: Sedgewick and Jackson, 1988), pp. 41–42.

Pierre Marion, interview with author, March 14, 1992.

Noel Matchett, interview with author, May 14, 1991.

Robyn Shotwell Metcalfe, *The Wizard Wall.*

Herb Meyer, interview with author, May 13, 1991.

"Mitsubishi Electric Diversifying Efforts for Space Advances," *Aviation Week and Space Technology,* August 25, 1986, pp. 81–83.

"A New Kind of Foreign Espionage," *U.S. News and World Report,* July 5, 1982, p. 66.

Tom Nicholson, "The Espionage Boom," *Newsweek,* July 5, 1982, p. 54.

———, "Japan's High-Tech Spies," *Newsweek,* July 5, 1982, pp. 53–56.

National Security Agency official, interview with author, September 17, 1991.

William Norris, "Equalizing U.S.-Japan Technology Flow," *Physics Today,* February 1987, p. 168.

Robert Noyce, quoted in Gene Bylinsky, "The Japanese Spies in Silicon Valley," *Fortune,* February 27, 1978, pp. 74–76.

"On the Way to Securing a World Position? Japan's Intelligence Agencies and Their Activities," *Japan Quarterly* (Fall 1987), pp. 159–62.

Mark Potts, "Computer Court Papers Read Like Spy Novel," *Washington Post,* June 25, 1983, pp. D1, D9.

———, "IBM Charges Two Firms with Stealing Secrets," *Washington Post,* November 26, 1983, pp. C1, C2.

John Quinn, interview with author, December 20, 1991.

George Roukis, "The Corporate Intelligence Process: Global Perspectives and Approaches," in *Global Corporate Intelligence,* eds., George S. Roukis, Hugh Conway, and Bruce Charnov (New York: Quorum Books, 1990), pp. 3–20.

Ruder and Finn spokesman, quoted in Dan Morgan and Tracy Dahlby, "A Tokyo Giant's View of the War of the Computers," *Washington Post,* January 9, 1983, pp. C1, C3.

Rowan Scarborough, "B-2 Contractor Probed for Links to Japanese Firm," *Washington Times,* December 4, 1991.

"School for Spies," *Time,* December 14, 1962.

Michael Sekora, quoted in Philip Gold, "Table Turning Is the Lesson," *Insight Magazine,* September 30, 1991, pp. 36–37.

Michael B. Smith, interview with author, October 29, 1991.

Marjorie Sun, "Strains in U.S.-Japan Exchanges," *Science,* July 31, 1987, pp. 476–78.

Masayuki Taleuchi, quoted in David Lazarus, "New Spies," *Journal* (Tokyo), November 1991.

Andrew Tanzer, "Fujitsu Fumble," *Forbes,* October 6, 1986, p. 96.

Akira Tomioka, "Corporate Intelligence: The Key to the Strategic Success of Japanese Organizations in International Environments," in *Global Corporate Intelligence,* eds., George S. Roukis, Hugh Conway, and Bruce Charnov (New York: Quorum Books, 1990), pp. 211–26.

Stansfield Turner, interview with author, November 11, 1991.

U.S. Congress, Energy and Commerce Committee Subcommittee on Commerce, quoted in Lloyd Schwartz, "Hint Hitachi Case Bared 'Tip of the Iceberg,' " *Electronic News,* July 18, 1983.

Harlow Unger, "The Spies of Silicon Valley: How Industrial Espionage Is Hurting the Computer Business," *Canadian Business,* December 25, 1980, p. 15.

Richard Walker, interview with author, February 18, 1992.

Raymond Wannall, interview with author, November 6, 1991.

Ishiawara Watanabe, interview with author, September 9, 1991.

Bob Woodward, *Veil: The Secret Wars of the CIA* (New York: Pocket Books, 1987), pp. 421–26.

Chapter 5   Les Espions Industriels

Ajoy Bose, "India's Web of Espionage," *Macleans,* February 4, 1985, p. 34.

William Carley, "As Cold War Fades, Some Nations' Spies Seek Industrial Secrets," *Wall Street Journal,* June 17, 1991.

Ray Cline, interview with author, February 10, 1992.

Robert Courtney, interview with author, July 22, 1991.

John Davitt, interview with author, March 6, 1992.

Richard Deacon, *The French Secret Service* (London: Grafton, 1990).

Direction Générale de la Sécurité Extérieure former official, interview with author, November 12, 1991.

Direction Générale de la Sécurité Extérieure, Service 7, two former officials, interviews with author, November 11–12, 1991.

Roger Failgot and Pascal Krop, *La piscine: Les services secrets français, 1944–1984* (Paris: Editions du Seuil, 1985).

"France's Bull Denies Press Report of Spying against U.S. Firms," *Wall Street Journal,* May 18, 1990, p. A8.

Bill Gertz, "French Spooks Scare Firms," *Washington Times,* February 9, 1992.

Richard Helms, interview with author, October 30, 1991.

Fred Hiatt, "Eavesdropping on Allies," *Washington Post,* May 9, 1986, pp. A1, A12.

Pierre Lacoste, interview with author, March 13, 1992.

Jean Lesieur, "Le scandale des espions français," *L'Express,* May 25, 1990.

Paul Lewis, "Paris Spies: Shady Past of Agency," *New York Times,* September 23, 1985, p. A14.

Count Henri de Marenches, *Dans les secrets des princes* (Paris: Editions Stock, 1986).

Pierre Marion, interview with author, March 14, 1992.

"Mitterand Ordering Intelligence Shuffle in Greenpeace Case," *New York Times,* September 20, 1985, pp. A1, A11.

"Paris Intelligence Chief Alleges Plot on Agency," *New York Times,* September 28, 1985.

Jay Peterzell, "When 'Friends' Become Moles," *Time,* May 28, 1990, p. 50.

Larry Reibstein, "Parlez-vous Espionage?" *Newsweek,* September 23, 1991, p. 40.

John Train, "The Law Is the Law," *Forbes,* July 7, 1980, pp. 142–43.

Richard Walker, interview with author, February 18, 1992.

Raymond Wannall, interview with author, November 6, 1991.

Michael Wines, "French Said to Spy on U.S. Computer Companies," *New York Times,* November 18, 1990, p. 4.

Chapter 6   The Mysterious Mr. Spence

Robert Angel, interviews with author, January 24 and March 26, 1992.

Maxine Cheshire, quoted in Phil Gailey, "Have Names, Will Open Right Doors," *New York Times,* January 18, 1982.

Bill Dedman, "Spence Faces Drug, Weapon Charges after Being Found in New York Hotel," *Washington Post,* August 9, 1989, pp. B1, B7.

———, "Lobbyist Spence Subpoenaed by Federal Grand Jury Here," *Washington Post,* August 11, 1989, p. D5.

———, "D.C. Sex Scandal Figure Taped Farewell to Friends," *Washington Post,* November 18, 1989, pp. D1, D5.

———, "Spence Created Fund to Fight Media Accusations," *Washington Post,* January 13, 1990, p. B7.

Phil Gailey, "Have Names, Will Open Right Doors," *New York Times,* January 18, 1982.

Japanese External Trade Organization former senior official, interview with author, January 28, 1992.

"Lobbyist Is Arrested in New York," *New York Times,* August 10, 1989, p. A21.

"Lobbyist Linked to Sex Case Is Found Dead," *New York Times,* November 12, 1989.

Sarah McClendon letter to the Senate Press Gallery, in U.S. Department of Justice, files on Craig Spence, 1979–87.

Policy Study Group, *The Policy Study Group* (Tokyo: Policy Study Group, 1979).

Pierre Rinfret, quoted in "The Shadow World of Craig Spence," *Washington Post,* July 18, 1989, pp. D1, D9.

U.S. Department of Justice, files on Craig Spence, 1979–87.

Martin Weil, "Craig Spence, Figure in D.C. Sex Case, Found Dead in Boston," *Washington Post,* November 12, 1989, p. A12.

Chapter 7   Monica and Her Sisters

Robert Ball, "Ostpolitik: The Era of Negotiation in Europe," *Fortune,* December 1970, pp. 68–113.

"Bavarian Ministry Official Langemann Arrested," Hamburg DPA, March 18, 1982; *Foreign Broadcast Information Service Daily Report,* March 19, 1982, p. J2.

"Bavarian Official Accused of Revealing Secrets," Hamburg DPA, March 3, 1982; *Foreign Broadcast Information Service Daily Report,* March 4, 1982, p. C2.

David Binder, "Strain in U.S.-Bonn Relations Reported," *New York Times,* December 20, 1970, pp. 1, 15.

———"Brandt to Stress U.S.-Market Tie in Nixon Talks," *New York Times,* June 9, 1971, p. 10.

"Bonn Legislator Assails U.S. Companies' Bids to Buy German Firms," *Wall Street Journal,* April 6, 1966.

Willy Brandt quoted in "Willy Brandt's Inheritance: A Survey of Germany," *Economist,* January 10, 1970, pp. ix–xliv.

"Brandt-Nixon Talks," *New York Times,* April 14, 1971.

Bundesnachrichtendienst documents, 1969–71. [Shown to author October 24, 1991.]

Bundesnachrichtendienst former official, interview with author, January 14, 1992.

Bundesnachrichtendienst, Division I former official, interview with author, January 14, 1992.

Central Intelligence Agency former Bonn station chief, interview with author, February 9, 1992.

Ray Cline, interview with author, February 10, 1992.

"Excerpts from Interview with Brandt," *New York Times,* April 4, 1970.

Federal Bureau of Investigation counterintelligence official, interview with author, March 14, 1992.

Federal Bureau of Investigation former official, interview with author, March 1, 1992.

Lawrence Fellows, "Brandt Assures Party on Policy," *New York Times,* May 14, 1970.

Kurt Georg Kiesinger, quoted in David Binder, "Kiesinger to Talk to U.S. as an Equal," *New York Times,* August 12, 1967.

"Langemann Denies Contact with Konkret Magazine," Hamburg DPA, March 4, 1982; *Foreign Broadcast Information Service Daily Report,* March 5, 1982, p. J3.

Wayne Madsen, "Data Privacy: Legislation and Intelligence Agency Threats," in *Computer Security and Information Integrity* (Amsterdam: North Holland, 1991).

Pierre Marion, interview with author, March 31, 1991.

National Security Agency former official, interview with author, November 16, 1991.

"Operation Eva: Ein BND-agent Enthullt Geheimdienst-Skandale," *Konkret,* March 1982, pp. C1–C16.

Hayden Peake, interview with author, October 31, 1992.

Jeffrey Richelson, *Foreign Intelligence Organizations* (Cambridge, Mass.: Ballinger, 1988), pp. 127–49.

Robert Semple, "Nixon and Brandt End Talks in Florida," *New York Times,* December 30, 1971.

Philip Shabecoff, "Leaks in Wiretaps Charged in Bonn," *New York Times,* January 23, 1968.

Tad Szulc, "NATO Commitment Clarified by U.S.," *New York Times,* April 12, 1970, p. 2.

————, "Brandt Exhorts the U.S. Not to Reduce Its Troop Strength in Europe," *New York Times,* April 10, 1971, pp. 1, 8.

John Vinocur, "Bonn Investigates Security Official," *New York Times,* March 3, 1982.

Gerd Wilcke, "German Cartels Back, but in Defensive Role," *New York Times,* May 4, 1969.

Karl Winterstein, memo to Bundesnachrichtendienst, 1969.

Chapter 8   The Liaison

This chapter is largely based on interviews with three company officials, November 6 and 13, 1991.

Bundesnachrichtendienst, Division I, former official, interview with author, July 29, 1991.

Chapter 9   The Diamonds

Harold Bovenkerk, quoted in Lawrence Ingrassia, "How Secret GE Recipe for Making Diamonds May Have Been Stolen," *Wall Street Journal,* February 28, 1990, pp. A1, A8.

Roger Burns quoted in Lawrence Ingrassia, "How Secret GE Recipe for Making Diamonds May Have Been Stolen," *Wall Street Journal,* February 28, 1990, pp. A1, A8.

Central Intelligence Agency official, interview with author, November 11, 1991.

Ray Cline, interview with author, February 10, 1992.

William Crowe, quoted in Lawrence Ingrassia, "How Secret GE Recipe for Making Diamonds May Have Been Stolen," *Wall Street Journal,* February 28, 1990, pp. A1, A8.

Federal Bureau of Investigation official, interview with author, November 2, 1991.

Lowry Manson, quoted in Lawrence Ingrassia, "How Secret GE Recipe for Making Diamonds May Have Been Stolen," *Wall Street Journal,* February 28, 1990, pp. A1, A8.

Chien Ming Sung, quoted in Lawrence Ingrassia, "How Secret GE Recipe for Making Diamonds May Have Been Stolen," *Wall Street Journal,* February 28, 1990, pp. A1, A8.

Chapter 10　The Laughing Bird

Scott Armstrong, "Ex-director Informs on KCIA Action," *Washington Post,* June 6, 1977, pp. A1, A3.

———, "Information from Habib Led to Probe of Korean Influence, *Washington Post,* June 17, 1977, p. A4.

"Assassination in Seoul," *Time,* November 5, 1979, pp. 44–46.

Charles Babcock, "Hill Unit Subpoenas Ex-congressmen," *Washington Post,* May 26, 1977, pp. A1, A21.

———, "McFall's Ties to South Korean Test Ethics Committee," *Washington Post,* June 1, 1977, p. A3.

———, "South Korean Effort to Influence U.S. Policy Described," *Washington Post,* June 23, 1977, pp. A1, A8.

———, "Former Employees of Park Give Details to Congress," *Washington Post,* August 6, 1977, pp. A1, A8.

———, "Hancho Kim Indicted in Korea Probe," *Washington Post,* September 28, 1977, pp. A1, A8.

———, "Effort to Question Tongsun Park Fails," *Washington Post,* October 21, 1977, p. A16.

———, "Korea Panel Wants to Talk to Ex-envoy," *Washington Post,* November 5, 1977.

————, "Personal Diary of Tongsun Park Is Held by Court," *Washington Post,* November 28, 1977, pp. A1, A9.

————, "President Park Said to Direct Lobbying," *Washington Post,* March 15, 1978, pp. A1, A27.

————, "CIA: Seoul Gave $400,000 to Democrats in '68," *Washington Post,* March 22, 1978, pp. A1, A12.

————, "Tip O'Neill Denies Park Relationship," *Washington Post,* April 5, 1978, p. A2.

————, "KCIA Chief Put $250,000 into Two Bank Accounts," *Washington Post,* June 4, 1978.

William Chapman, "Many South Koreans Defend Tongsun Park," *Washington Post,* September 22, 1977, p. A21.

————, "Relaxed at Home, Tongsun Park Says He Has No Regrets," *Washington Post,* January 20, 1978, p. A19.

Maxine Cheshire, "Tongsun Park and the Korean CIA," *Washington Post,* August 28, 1977, pp. A1, A14.

————, "Korean-American Named as Conduit for KCIA Funds," *Washington Post,* March 1, 1978, pp. A1, A11.

"Chun: A Shadowy Strongman," *Time,* May 26, 1980, p. 32.

Ray Cline, interview with author, February 10, 1992.

William Colby, interview with author, January 6, 1992.

"Envoy: Scandal Perils Seoul Ties," *Washington Post,* December 13, 1977.

Federal Bureau of Investigation, report on Suzi Park Thomson quoted in Charles Babcock, "Albert Was Warned that Aide Was on South Korean Payroll," *Wall Street Journal,* December 7, 1977, pp. A1, A4.

Robert Jackson, "Funneled $300,000 to Embassy Aide, South Korean Testifies," *Washington Post,* December 21, 1977.

Haynes Johnson, "An Old Tradition: Getting It in Cash," *Washington Post,* October 23, 1977, p. A14.

Korean Central Intelligence Agency former case officer, interview with author, September 3, 1991.

Korean Central Intelligence Agency former operative, interview with author, August 30, 1991.

Korean Central Intelligence Agency, Sixth Bureau former official, interview with author, September 7, 1991.

"Korean Ex-agent Said Threatened," *Washington Post,* July 4, 1977.

William Lynch, "Governor Edwards Denies Gift from Park," *Washington Post,* January 26, 1977.

Phil McCombs, "Park's Club, as a Magnet for Might, Drew Attention," *Washington Post,* September 7, 1977.

———, "Tongsun Park's Club: How the Korean Built His Georgetown Base," *Washington Post,* October 16, 1977, pp. C1, C5.

"Making the Korean Connections," *Washington Post,* October 23, 1977, p. C6.

Russell Mardon, "The State and Industrial Transformation in the ROK," *Journal of Social, Political and Economic Studies* (Winter 1990), pp. 457–82.

Dan Morgan and Scott Armstrong, "Ex-aide Testifies Edwards Given Cash by Park," *Washington Post,* January 25, 1977, pp. A1, A8.

Park Chung Hee, quoted in "A Second Japan?" *Forbes,* May 1, 1978, pp. 55–57.

"Park Adds More Names, a Few Surprises to List," *Washington Post,* January 15, 1978.

"Park Reportedly Gave Passman $100,000 in Cash," *Washington Post,* November 3, 1977.

Norman Pearistine, "How South Korea Surprised the World," *Forbes,* April 30, 1979, pp. 53–61.

Huin Bok Po, interview with author, September 1, 1990.

John Quinn, interview with author, December 20, 1991.

T. R. Reid, "House Members Listed in Tongsun Park's Little Black Books," *Washington Post,* July 17, 1977, pp. A1, A12.

———, "Senate Unit Wants Early CIA Warning about Alien Agents," *Washington Post,* October 11, 1977.

———, "Ex-Korean Envoy Linked to Payments," *Washington Post,* October 20, 1977, pp. A1, A7.

———, "House Korean Inquiry Told of Coded Operations," *Washington Post,* October 21, 1977, pp. A1, A16.

———, "Korea Led Scheme, Probers Assert," *Washington Post,* October 22, 1977, pp. A1, A10.

———, "U.S. Keeps Door Open to Tongsun Park," *Washington Post,* October 26, 1977, p. A13.

———, "Derwinski Faces Questioning on Leak to Seoul," *Washington Post,* October 29, 1977, pp. A1, A6.

———, "FBI Quizzes Ex-rep. Morgan on Korea," *Washington Post,* November 16, 1977.

———, "Korea Probers Pressing to See Passman Papers," *Washington Post,* December 3, 1977.

———, "South Korean CIA Said to 'Control' Park," *Washington Post,* March 17, 1978.

Bill Richards, "Probers Study Korean's Plea in Smuggling," *Washington Post,* June 30, 1978.

——— and Charles Babcock, "Park to Testify at U.S. Criminal Trials," *Washington Post,* December 30, 1977, pp. A1, A6.

Timothy Robinson, "Ex-Korean Agent Tells Court of Payment in Alleged Scheme," *Washington Post,* March 21, 1978.

Mike Smith, interview with author, October 29, 1991.

"Trial Is Delayed for Hancho Kim in Korea Influence-Buying Case," *Washington Post,* December 28, 1977, p. A12.

U.S. indictment of Tongsun Park, quoted in T. R. Reid, "Korea Influence 'Plan' Bared by House Panel," *Washington Post,* November 30, 1977, pp. A1, A6.

Richard Walker, interview with author, February 18, 1992.

Chapter 11   Mr. X and Mr. Y

Jack Anderson, "The Super-spy behind the Pollard Case," *Washington Post,* January 13, 1986, p. C13.

Scott Armstrong, "Israelis Have Spied on U.S., Secret Papers Show," *Washington Post,* February 1, 1982, pp. A1, A18.

Charles Babcock, "U.S. an Intelligence Target of the Israelis, Officials Say," *Washington Post,* June 5, 1986, pp. A1, A38.

———, "Israel Uses Special Relationship to Get Secrets," *Washington Post,* June 15, 1986, pp. A1, A14.

———, "U.S. Barred Shipment to Israel," *Washington Post,* July 11, 1986.

———, "Firm Says Israel Tried to Steal Technical Secrets," *Washington Post,* August 20, 1986, p. A12.

Richard Berke, "Illinois Company Charges Israel Tried to Gain Technology Secrets," *New York Times,* August 19, 1986, p. A8.

Barbara Bradley, "U.S. Defense Consultants Benefit Foreign Contractors," *Christian Science Monitor,* August 30, 1988, p. 5.

Geraldine Brooks, "Arms Dealers in Israel Operate Quite Openly on the Fringe of Law," *Wall Street Journal,* May 9, 1990, pp. A1, A10.

Brian Carter quoted in Charles Babcock, "Computer Expert Used Firm to Feed Israel Technology," *Washington Post,* October 31, 1986, pp. A1, A24.

Central Intelligence Agency, *Israel: Foreign Intelligence and Security Services* (Langley, Va.: Central Intelligence Agency, 1979).

Central Intelligence Agency former deputy director of counterintelligence, interview with author.

John Davitt, interview with author, March 6, 1992.

Stephen Engelberg, "Spy Met an Israeli through Investor," *New York Times,* July 4, 1986, p. A4.

Federal Bureau of Investigation counterintelligence official, interview with author, November 2, 1991.

Federal Bureau of Investigation former deputy director of counterintelligence, interview with author, November 3, 1991.

John J. Fialka, "U.S. Widening Probe of Alleged Spying by Israel," *Wall Street Journal,* June 5, 1986, p. 36.

Stephen Franklin, "Israeli Firms Feel Pinch As Arms Buyers Cut Back," *Chicago Tribune*, March 12, 1990, pp. A1, A2.

Thomas Friedman, "Peres Sees Effort to U.S. Spy Inquiry to Mar Israeli Ties," *New York Times*, June 9, 1986, pp. A1, A15.

Bernard Gwertzman, "Justice and State Departments at Odds in Assessments on Israeli Spying," *New York Times*, June 10, 1986, pp. A1, A23.

———, "White House Sides with State Department on Israeli Spying Issue," *New York Times*, June 11, 1986, p. A22.

Robert Howe, "Paisley Guilty in Fraud Case," *Washington Post*, June 15, 1991, pp. A1, A7.

"How Much Spying between Friends?" *New York Times*, June 12, 1986, p. A18.

Kenneth Israel quoted in Edward Pound and David Rogers, "An Israeli Contract with a U.S. Company Leads to Espionage," *Wall Street Journal*, January 17, 1992, pp. A1, A5.

"Israel Calls Report of CIA Findings 'Ridiculous,' " *Washington Post*, February 2, 1982, p. A5.

"Israel Considers Slowdown in Lavi Program," *Aviation Week and Space Technology*, February 10, 1986, p. 32.

"Israel Using Atar Tooling Data to Prolong Mirage Usefulness," *Aviation Week and Space Technology*, October 6, 1969, p. 20.

"Israeli Aide Faces Dismissal," *New York Times*, August 27, 1986.

Hesh Kestin, "A $640 Hammer Is a Bargain," *Forbes*, June 30, 1986, pp. 46–50.

Lawrence Korb quoted in Jeff Gerth, "Untangling One Consultant's Web of Industry and Pentagon Contracts," *New York Times*, June 17, 1988, p. D16.

James Lamont, interview with author, August 16, 1991.

"Lavi or Not Lavi?" *Economist*, January 10, 1987, p. 29.

Neil A. Lewis, "Guilty Plea Made in Pentagon Case," *New York Times*, June 15, 1991, pp. A1, A36.

Mildred R. McGerick, quoted in Michael Wines, "Arms Inquiry Adds Two Israeli Concerns," *New York Times*, July 11, 1988.

"Man in Israel Spy Case Is Chosen for New Post," *New York Times,* January 9, 1986, p. A8.

Ruth Marcus, "Pentagon Offices Searched," *Washington Post,* June 15, 1988, pp. A1, A20.

———, "FBI Tapped Phones in Pentagon Probe," *Washington Post,* June 16, 1988, pp. A1, A18.

———, "250 Pentagon Subpoenas Served," *Washington Post,* June 17, 1988, pp. A1, A10.

John D. Morrocco, "Mazlat Develops VTOL RPV to Retain Position in U.S. Military Market," *Aviation Week and Space Technology,* June 20, 1988, pp. 99–100.

———, "Ill Wind Probe Shifts to Corporate Officials Following Paisley's Guilty Plea," *Aviation Week and Space Technology,* June 24, 1991, pp. 27–30.

Caryle Murphy and Michael Isikoff, "Paisley's Pentagon Acts Checked," *Washington Post,* July 9, 1988, pp. A1, A8.

Andy Pasztor, "Prosecutors Close in on Unisys, Other Contractors as Arms-Procurement Inquiry Gains Momentum," *Wall Street Journal,* January 8, 1990, p. A14.

——— and Edward Pound, "U.S. Studies If Defense-Scandal Figures Helped Unisys Get Navy Cruiser Work," *Wall Street Journal,* June 28, 1988.

"Pentagon Purchasing Inquiry Examines Paisley's Actions While a Navy Official," *Wall Street Journal,* June 20, 1988, p. A3.

Edward Pound and David Rogers, "U.S. firms Are Linked to an Israeli General at Heart of a Scandal," *Wall Street Journal,* January 20, 1992, pp. A1, A4.

Dan Raviv and Yossi Melman, *Every Spy a Prince: The Complete History of Israel's Intelligence Community* (Boston: Houghton Mifflin, 1990), pp. 343–420.

Charlotte Saikowski, "Alleged Smuggling Latest in Series of U.S.-Israel Incidents," *Christian Science Monitor,* July 10, 1986, pp. 1, 10.

Philip Shenon, "U.S. Aides Say Pollard Is Giving Justice Department Further Information," *New York Times,* June 6, 1986, pp. A1, B5.

———, "U.S. Reported to Pursue Indictment of Israeli Colonel in Spy Case," *New York Times,* June 19, 1986, p. A7.

Sandra Sugawara, "McDonnell Douglas Drops Consultant Paisley," *Washington Post,* July 16, 1988, p. A9.

Richard Walker, interview with author, February 18, 1992.

"Warrants Indicate Consultants Passed Insider Data to Firms," *Aviation Week and Space Technology,* June 27, 1988, p. 19.

John Whyte quoted in Edward Pound and David Rogers, "An Israeli Contract with a U.S. Company Leads to Espionage," *Wall Street Journal,* January 17, 1992, pp. A1, A5.

George C. Wilson, "Lehman Ally Emerges as Key Figure," *Washington Post,* June 16, 1988, pp. A1, A17.

Greg Wilson, "Consultant Paisley's Method: Big Risks for Big Gains," *Washington Post,* June 28, 1988, pp. A1, A5.

Michael Wines, "U.S. Contractor Cites Two Officials in a Guilty Plea," *New York Times,* December 9, 1989, pp. A1, A37.

Bob Woodward and Walter Pincus, "U.S. Hunts American 'Mr. X' in Pollard Espionage for Israeli," *Washington Post,* February 19, 1988, pp. A1, A6.

Chapter 12   007 Joins the Firm

Stuart Auerbach, "Fujitsu Hiring from State Spurs Debate on Lobbying," *Washington Post,* January 18, 1990, p. C1.

Tim Brown, "U.S. Companies Are Hit Hard in Escalating War," *Seattle Times,* December 8, 1991, pp. E1, E2.

Francis Bullock, quoted in William Carley, "How the FBI Snared Two Scientists Selling Drug Company Secrets," *Wall Street Journal,* September 5, 1991, pp. A1, A6.

Central Intelligence Agency former director, interview with author, November 15, 1991.

Bruce Charnov, "Computer Security," in *Global Corporate Intelligence,* eds., George S. Roukis, Hugh Conway, and Bruce Charnov (New York: Quorum Books, 1990), pp. 151–64.

William Colby, interview with author, January 6, 1992.

Peter Cooney, "Former du Pont Employees Charged with Extortion Try," *Washington Post,* February 28, 1989.

Hugo Cornwall, *The Industrial Espionage Handbook* (London: Century, 1991).

Robert Courtney, interview with author, July 22, 1991.

Claude Deutsch, "007 It's Not. But Intelligence Is In," *New York Times,* December 23, 1990, p. 24.

Brian Dumaine, "Corporate Spies Snoop to Conquer," *Fortune,* November 7, 1988, pp. 68–69.

E. I. du Pont de Nemours security official, interview with author, March 9, 1992.

Miranda Ewell, "Corporate Spies Try to Upgrade Image," *Washington Post,* May 13, 1990, p. H9.

"Fear of Spies Cuts Short Industry Tour," *Science,* January 25, 1980, pp. 388–89.

Edwin Finn, Jr., "That's the $60 Billion Question," *Forbes,* November 17, 1986, pp. 40–41.

"Free Information for Sale," *Economist,* April 7, 1979, p. 86.

General Electric official, interview with author, March 4, 1992.

Bill Gertz, "Model FBI Sting Operation Catches Trade-Secret Spy," *Washington Times,* February 9, 1992.

"Good for Business," *Economist,* July 19, 1980, p. 27.

Richard Greene, "Never Mind R&D, How about T&G?" *Forbes,* September 24, 1984, p. 142.

Ronald Grover, "That's Sam Spade Leafing through the Ledgers," *BusinessWeek,* May 29, 1989, pp. 95–96.

Richard A. Guida, "The Costs of Free Information," *Public Interest* (Fall 1989), pp. 87–95.

Richard Helms, interview with author, October 30, 1991.

R. D. Henderson, "The Future of Ex–Eastern Bloc Intelligence Personnel," *Studies in Intelligence,* Summer 1991.

Jan Herring, quoted in "U.S. Tutors High-Tech Competitors," *Insight Magazine,* January 28, 1991, pp. 40–41.

"How Silicon Spies Get Away with Copying," *BusinessWeek,* April 21, 1980, pp. 181–88.

"How to Protect Corporate Secrets," *Dun's Review,* August 1977, pp. 49–50.

"Information Thieves Are Now Corporate Enemy Number 1," *BusinessWeek,* May 5, 1986, pp. 120–24.

Bob Inman, interview with author, February 4, 1992.

Jeffrey Kovach, "Competitive Intelligence," *Industry Week,* November 12, 1984, pp. 50–53.

James Lamont, "As Red Menace Cools, Spies Go Corporate," *Wall Street Journal,* April 22, 1991.

Fred Lebolt, "Safeguarding Secrets," *World Press Review,* October 1982, p. 50.

Charles Lewis, *America's Frontline Trade Officials* (Washington, D.C.: Center for Public Integrity, 1990).

Kevin McManus, "Double Edge," *Forbes,* May 21, 1984, pp. 29–31.

Gary Marx, "The New Surveillance," *Technology Review,* May–June 1985, pp. 43–48.

Noel Matchett, interview with author, May 14, 1991.

Bernard Mayles–Mario Miscio dialogues, quoted in part in William Carley, "How the FBI Snared Two Scientists Selling Drug Company Secrets," *Wall Street Journal,* September 5, 1991, pp. A1, A6.

Herb Meyer, interview with author, May 13, 1991.

Richard Morais, "Sam Spade Goes Corporate," *Forbes,* February 25, 1985, pp. 126–27.

"New Ways to Battle Corporate Spooks," *Fortune,* November 7, 1988, p. 72.

Claude Olney, "The Secret World of the Industrial Spy," *Business and Society Review* (Spring 1980), pp. 28–33.

James O'Reilly, quoted in Tom Mauro, "When the Government Gives Away Companies' Trade Secrets," *Nation's Business,* November 1983, pp. 62–64.

Arion Pattakos, *Counter-competitor Intelligence: Keeping Your Company Secrets Secret* (BAS Services, 1991).

John Pearson, "The Patent Pirates Are Finally Walking the Plank," *BusinessWeek,* February 17, 1992, pp. 125–27.

"Perspectives," *Newsweek,* January 20, 1992, p. 13.

Private detective, interview with author, February 12, 1992.

John Quinn, interview with author, December 20, 1991.

Robert Redmond, "Defense-Related and Microcomputer Security," in *Global Corporate Intelligence,* eds., George S. Roukis, Hugh Conway, and Bruce Charnov (New York: Quorum Books, 1990), pp. 165–75.

Irwin Ross, "Who's Stealing the Company's Secrets?" *Reader's Digest,* February 1983, pp. 35–42.

George Roukis, "The Corporate Intelligence Process: Global Perspectives and Approaches," in *Global Corporate Intelligence,* eds., George S. Roukis, Hugh Conway, and Bruce Charnov (New York: Quorum Books, 1990), pp. 3–20.

Michael C. Sekora quoted in Eduardo Lachica, "Businesses Try to Get Smart with Ex-spies," *Wall Street Journal,* August 8, 1991.

Tom Slocum, quoted in Tom Mauro, "When the Government Gives Away Companies' Trade Secrets," *Nation's Business,* November 1983, pp. 62–64.

Jeffrey Smith, "Corporate Spying Prompts New Look at Trade Secrecy," *Science,* January 15, 1978, pp. 409–10.

Marcelle M. Soviero, "Lord of the Spies," *Popular Science,* November 1990, p. 43.

Doug Stewart, "Spy Tech," *Discover,* March 1988, pp. 58–65.

"Study: More Firms Gather Intelligence," *Washington Post,* October 14, 1990.

Alexander Taylor, "Protecting Corporate Secrets," *Time,* September 19, 1983, p. 70.

"Textiles: Any Buyer for U.S. Lobbyists' Services," *Dawn,* May 14, 1990.

"Throwing the Book at Industrial Spies," *BusinessWeek,* October 4, 1982, pp. 84–85.

Martin Tolchin, "Ex-State Department Officer Takes Fujitsu Job," *New York Times,* January 17, 1990, p. D5.

Dody Tsiantar, "George Smily Joins the Firm," *Newsweek,* May 2, 1988, pp. 46–47.

Elizabeth Tucker, "Corporate Gumshoes Spy on Competitors," *Washington Post,* March 30, 1990, pp. F1, F2.

U.S. Senate, Committee on the Judiciary, *Hearings before the Subcommittee on Technology and the Law: "The Freedom of Information Act,"* August 2, 1988.

Raymond Wannall, interview with author, February 18, 1992.

David Whipple, quoted in Eduardo Lachica, "Businesses Try to Get Smart with Ex-spies," *Wall Street Journal,* August 8, 1991.

Chapter 13   Reaching for the Stars

Steven J. Bosseler, affidavit, U.S. District Court, *U.S. v. Ronald Hoffman,* June 15, 1990, pp. 1–54.

Federal Bureau of Investigation counterintelligence official, interview with author, March 10, 1992.

Ronald Joshua Hoffman, quoted in Steven J. Bosseler, affidavit, U.S. District Court, *U.S. v. Ronald Hoffman,* June 15, 1990, pp. 1–54.

Science Applications International Corporation official, interview with author, March 10, 1992.

Chapter 14   Socrates and Snowflakes

Robert Angel, interview with author, January 24, 1992.

James Bamford, "Seeking to Retain Its Budget, NSA Wants to Spy (Shhhh!) on Allies," *Los Angeles Times,* July 15, 1990, p. 4.

Jonas Bernstein, "Spy Agency May Have to Come in from Cold," *Insight Magazine,* October 14, 1991, pp. 19–21.

David Boren, quoted in George Lardner, Jr., "Boren Urges Intelligence Upgrades," *Washington Post,* April 4, 1990, p. A7.

———, quoted in U.S. Senate, Select Committee on Intelligence, *Intelligence Authorization Act, FY 1991: Report,* September 19, 1990.

Amy Borrus, "Should the CIA Start Spying for Corporate America?" *BusinessWeek,* October 14, 1991, pp. 96–100.

Russell Bowen, interview with author, January 17, 1992.

Harry Brandon, quoted in Bill Gertz, "Ethics, Economics Fuel Debate over Roles in Spying," *Washington Times,* February 9, 1992.

George Bush, quoted in Brian Duffy and Jim Impoco, "The New Spy Wars," *U.S. News and World Report,* June 3, 1991, pp. 23–32.

George Carver, "Intelligence and Glasnost," *Foreign Affairs* (Summer 1990), pp. 147–66.

Central Intelligence Agency counterintelligence official, interview with author, April 11, 1991.

Central Intelligence Agency former deputy director of operations, interview with author, November 4, 1991.

Leo Cherne, "U.S. Intelligence Requirements for the Late 1980s," *Vital Speeches of the Day,* April 1, 1986, pp. 370–73.

Ray Cline, interview with author, February 10, 1992.

William Colby, interview with author, January 6, 1992.

Robert Gates, quoted in Richard Lacayo, "Crisis in Spooksville," *Time,* September 23, 1991, pp. 16–19.

Bill Gertz, "Technology Opens New Doors for Foreign, Corporate Spying," *Washington Times,* October 20, 1989, p. A12.

———, "FBI Expanding Spying to Cover Friendly Nations," *Washington Times,* October 30, 1991.

———, "Electronic Spying Reoriented at NSA," *Washington Times,* January 27, 1992, p. A4.

Wayne Gilbert, quoted in Bill Gertz, "Ethics, Economics Fuel Debate over Roles in Spying," *Washington Times,* February 9, 1992. [Emphasis added by author.]

Richard Helms, interview with author, October 30, 1991.

"Industrial Espionage?" *Wall Street Journal,* July 6, 1990, p. 1.

"Intelligence Targeting of U.S. Technology," *Security Awareness Bulletin* 92, no. 1 (January 1992), p. 1.

Richard Kerr, quoted in "I Don't See Us Getting into Industrial Espionage," *U.S. News and World Report,* June 3, 1991, p. 30.

James Lamont, interview with author, August 6, 1991.

George Lardner, Jr., "As the Ads Say, CIA Is Looking for a Few Good Economists," *Washington Post,* December 27, 1990, p. A15.

————, "Expert Says Soviets Are Still Spying on U.S.; Warsaw Pact Isn't," *Washington Post,* October 30, 1991, p. A6.

Mark Mansfield, quoted in Brian Duffy and Jim Impoco, "The New Spy Wars," *U.S.News and World Report,* June 3, 1991, pp. 23–32.

Pierre Marion, interview with author, March 14, 1992.

Noel Matchett, interview with author, May 14, 1991.

Cord Meyer, interview with author, January 8, 1992.

Herb Meyer, "Banker, Broker, Businessman, Spy," *CEO,* October–November 1990, pp. 42–47.

————, interview with author, May 13, 1991.

William E. Odom, interview with author, October 31, 1991.

President's Foreign Intelligence Advisory Board staff member, interview with author, October 22, 1991.

John Quinn, interview with author, December 20, 1991.

Herb Romerstein, interview with author, December 19, 1991.

Gerald Seib, "CIA Moves Swiftly toward Basic Change As U.S. Intelligence Mission Is Restudied," *Wall Street Journal,* November 25, 1991, p. A7.

William S. Sessions, "Counterintelligence Challenges in a Changing World," *Security Awareness Bulletin* 92, no. 1 (January 1992), pp. 3–5.

Michael B. Smith, interview with author, October 29, 1991.

Stansfield Turner, "Intelligence for a New World Order, *Foreign Affairs* (Fall 1991), pp. 150–66.

————, interview with author, November 11, 1991.

U.S. Senate, Select Committee on Intelligence, *Intelligence Authorization Act, FY 1991: Report,* September 19, 1990.

————, Select Committee on Intelligence, *Intelligence Authorization Act, FY 1991: Report,* May 15, 1991.

Michelle Van Cleave, remarks before the National Security Institute, March 12, 1991.

Richard Walker, interview with author, February 18, 1992.

Raymond Wannall, interview with author, November 6, 1991.

William Webster, "Intelligence Issues of the New Decade," *Security Awareness Bulletin* 90, no. 4 (April 1990), pp. 10–12.